BLOODY APRIL

BLOODY APRIL

Slaughter in the Skies over Arras, 1917

Peter Hart

WEIDENFELD & NICOLSON

First published in Great Britain in 2005
by Weidenfeld & Nicolson

1 3 5 7 9 10 8 6 4 2

A CIP catalogue record for this book is available from the British Library.

ISBN 0-297-84621-3

Typography by Gwyn Lewis

Printed in Great Britain by Clays Ltd, St Ives plc

Weidenfeld & Nicolson
The Orion Publishing Group Ltd
Orion House, 5 Upper Saint Martin's Lane, London, WC2H 9EA

www.orionbooks.co.uk

Dedicated to my favourites:
Polly, Lily and Ruby

CONTENTS

MAP LIST

PREFACE

The myth of 'Bloody April' is very powerful. As often told the story is deceptively simple: brave young British pilots of the Royal Flying Corps (RFC), with just a few hours training, were sent up daily to face the 'Red Baron' and his ruthless gang of merciless German aces – the dreaded 'Flying Circus'. Outnumbered, lacking even basic flying skills, outgunned and flying totally obsolescent aircraft, the young boys of the RFC went to their deaths due to the blind stupidity and intransigence of their commanders. They died, like the men on the ground, as sacrifices to the doctrine of the offensive at any cost. There is certainly no doubt about the severity of the casualties suffered by the RFC in April 1917. In that month alone the British lost 275 aircraft shot down, suffering 421 casualties of which 207 died. It took just 92 hours of flying time for every tragic death incurred. And indeed the worst carnage was amongst the new pilots – many of whom lasted just a day or two once they actually started flying missions over the front.

This legend of Bloody April is a vital component of the 'sentimental' view of the Great War. The common theme it shares with other popular war myths is that of innocence destroyed in futile attacks carried out for no logical reason against an impregnable foe. Crucially the protagonists have to be seen as victims: of war, of society and, of course, the malign fates that eventually overwhelmed them. Yet the pilots and observers of the RFC flying over Arras were *not* helpless victims cast there by some casual whim of cruel fate. They were there as the eyes of the supreme British weapon of battle in the Great War – the artillery.

The shape of every aerial battle was driven and dominated almost entirely by what was happening to the troops on the ground. That was why the missions were flown, lives risked and casualties accepted. On the

Western Front, no British offensive could have had any real chance of success without fully harnessing the awesome destructive power of the Royal Artillery. It was the guns that blasted away the German barbed wire and trenches, seeking out their headquarters and the fulcrum of their communications; the guns that destroyed or subdued the German batteries; the guns that provided the creeping barrages that 'chaperoned' the infantry across the open wastes of No Man's Land; and the guns that provided an almost impenetrable wall of bursting shells in front of captured positions to thwart any attempted German counter-attack. It may seem strange to start a book on the air war with a paean to the powers of the Royal Artillery – but the RFC existed primarily to serve those guns by aerial photography and artillery observation.

Modern aerial historians know they have to look to the ground to understand the motivation for what was happening in the skies; but in turn military historians also have to recognise the enormous contribution made by the RFC, which optimised the awesome power of the artillery despite vigorous and brilliantly sustained opposition by the German Air Force. I hope this book will be a small part in the process of recognising the sacrifices the RFC incurred in making an outstanding contribution towards winning the war where in the end it always had to be won, on and above the Western Front.

The real story behind Bloody April then is one of selfless heroism for a 'greater' cause. The pilots of the RFC showed a willingness to fly obsolescent aircraft over the lines, knowing the risks that they were taking, in order to carry out their duty to the much larger numbers of men at risk on the ground. And there is another set of German heroes who need our proper recognition. Manfred von Richthofen and his men were genuine heroes fighting and risking everything in the cause of their country. They may have had better aircraft, but they were badly outnumbered and, as the technological tide turned against them later in the war, they too were almost all doomed to die over the next two years. The trivialisation of the story of Bloody April as some pointless, murderous farce does not do justice to the men of either side in the tragic conflict in the skies above Arras. Both sides fought against the odds and both sides knew exactly what they were doing – and why.

I have tried to let the men tell their own stories. Ordinary people soon became very special indeed in the highly pressurised air war over Arras, and their powers of courage and endurance can be inspiring. There is a raw immediacy to their voices as recorded at the time in diaries and letters or retrospectively in memoirs and tape recordings that I could never hope to match. Their hopes, fears and the unbearable tensions of aerial combat ring out in almost every sentence written. These are the echoes of the past amplified for us to hear across the gulf of the intervening years. However, the original quotations have occasionally, where necessary, been lightly edited for overall readability. Punctuation and spellings have been largely standardised, material has occasionally been reordered and irrelevant material has been omitted, usually without any indication in the text. Changes in the actual words used in the original sources, however, have been avoided wherever possible.

CHAPTER ONE

THE REASON WHY

One thing was certain. By the beginning of 1917 the Allies were confident that they had managed to hit the German Army hard and were at last poised to win the war. Their first attempts in the original swirling war of movement of 1914 had stagnated into the frustrating lines of trenches that meandered across France and Belgium from Switzerland to the North Sea. Initially, the French and British were brashly confident that they would smash through the German lines. In the event, their generals spent 1915 trying, for the most part without real success, to master the complex new language of modern industrial war. The trenches, the barbed wire, the machine guns, the huge destructive potential of massed artillery and the incredible numbers of mobilised men all combined to pose new and intractable problems. Finally, in 1916, the industrial might and manpower of the Allies were properly harnessed to the task in hand. The Russians and Italians would launch coordinated offensives, but the pièce de résistance was to be a huge combined Franco-British effort on the Western Front intended to smash through the German line in the Somme sector. Unfortunately, the Germans declined to lie back and simply await their fate, but took the initiative themselves.

The Battle of Verdun launched on 21 February 1916 was a concept born of the twisted logic of total war. The point of assault had been carefully chosen by the German Chief of General Staff, General Erich von Falkenhayn, who knew that the fortress town of Verdun had a huge symbolic significance for the French. For political and military reasons they simply could not afford to allow the Germans to seize it. Falkenhayn wanted to bleed the French Army dry by sucking it into a battle situation where the army would be at a severe military disadvantage. Unfortunately for this cold theoretical approach, though the German Army

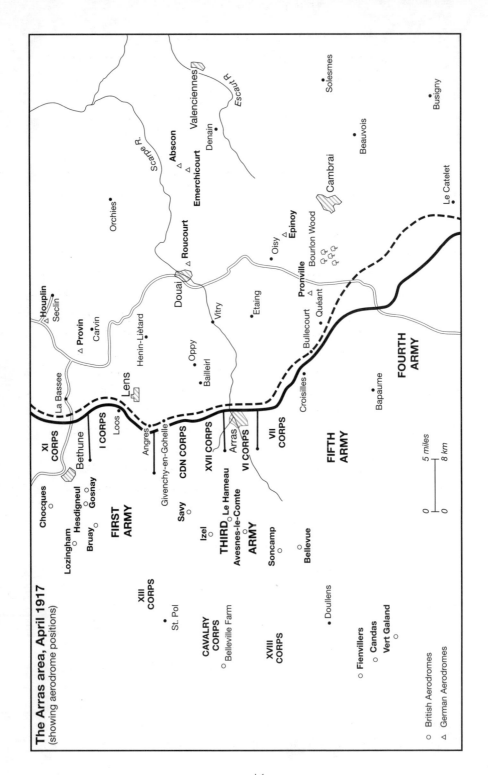

The Arras area, April 1917
(showing aerodrome positions)

Solesmes

Busigny

Valenciennes

Beauvois

Abscon

Denain

Emerchicourt

Cambrai

Le Catelet

Orchies

Roucourt

Epinoy

Bourlon Wood

Oisy

Pronville

Scade R.

Escaut R.

Houplin

Seclin

Douai

Vitry

Etaing

Queant

Provin

Carvin

Henin-Liétard

Oppy

Bullecourt

Bailleirl

La Bassee

Lens

Loos

Angres

Croisilles

Bapaume

Chocques

XI CORPS

Bethune

Givenchy-en-Gohelle

I CORPS

CDN CORPS

XVII CORPS

Arras

VI CORPS

VII CORPS

FOURTH ARMY

FIFTH ARMY

Lozingham

Hesdigneul

Gosnay

Bruay

Savy

Izel

Le Hameau

THIRD

Avesnes-le-Comte

Soncamp

Bellevue

FIRST ARMY

ARMY

St. Pol

XIII CORPS

CAVALRY CORPS

Belleville Farm

XVIII CORPS

Doullens

Fienvillers

Candas

Vert Galand

0   5 miles
0   8 km

○ British Aerodromes
△ German Aerodromes

16

undoubtedly succeeded in placing an almost insupportable pressure and burden of suffering on the French, the local German generals found themselves unable to maintain the necessary detachment. As the year wore on, they were increasingly drawn into a genuine fight to the finish in circumstances that were no longer to their advantage. The Germans, too, had been sucked into the voracious maw of Verdun.

The original Allied plans for a summer offensive in the Somme area were changed as it became obvious that the British would have to take more of a leading role. It was hoped that the vigour of a British assault would relieve the German pressure on Verdun. In retrospect, it is obvious that the British were not really ready to go 'over the top' on 1 July 1916. Their artillery bombardment may have been impressive to watch, but the length and depth of the front attacked meant that the actual number of shells falling on any given area of ground was nowhere near the concentration required to destroy the barbed wire and defences. Furthermore, modern artillery tactics were still in their infancy and there was no sophistication in bombardment techniques. Crudely timed 'lifts' meant that shells ceased falling on the German front-line trenches at the very moment that the British infantry began their advance across No Man's Land. The use of true 'creeping' barrages, lines of bursting shells advancing just in front of the attacking troops, was then only at the experimental stage of development. There was also no real idea of using defensive curtains of fire to break up and destroy German counter-attacks. Indeed most of the British gunners simply did not have the skills or training to carry out such complex fire plans with the requisite degree of speed and accuracy.

As to the infantry tactics, they were so simple that they hardly justified such a designation. The soldiers who went 'over the top' were mostly the inexperienced volunteers of 'Kitchener's Army' and it was generally considered that their best chance of retaining their cohesion in crossing No Man's Land under fire was to advance in long waves at a steady walking pace. Overall, the assault was an utter disaster and resulted in nearly 60,000 casualties on the first day. The offensive carried on regardless; it had to, this was no isolated battle but *the* major Allied offensive of 1916 and a key component of their overall grand strategy. The British took over the bulk of the responsibility on the Somme front and continued through the summer to fight a vicious battle of attrition in an effort to wear out the Germans, inching slowly forward to gain positions of advantage, prior to another huge effort to achieve a final breakthrough launched on 15 September 1916.

This period was dreadful for those involved, the levels of suffering were beyond words, but the hard lessons of war were at last being learnt. It had become obvious that sheer élan could not breach lines of barbed wire, covered by machine guns and massed artillery batteries. In particular the British use of artillery became increasingly scientific. There were more accurate methods of identifying and ranging on targets, new barrage techniques were conceived, tested and refined, and, all the while, more and more batteries of guns, particularly heavy guns, arrived to add their weight to the bombardments. Infantry tactics also improved as the tragic lessons of the first day were slowly taken on board. In particular, it had finally dawned that the artillery were the true masters of the battlefield. The infantry could achieve little unless the gunners behind them had already won the preliminary artillery duel, razed the barbed wire to the ground, smashed the German trenches and dugouts, and assisted them forward under creeping barrages of ever-increasing complexity. True, the infantry had then to occupy the ground, but the guns remained their main shield against counter-attack. There was even a new weapon, the tank, which offered a different scenario for battles of the future.

When so much was new, it was difficult for the generals to pinpoint the exact effects of changes in tactics and the complex methodology of deploying weapons in different combinations. Consequently it is not surprising that there were many mistakes that with the benefit of hindsight look stupid. The losses were painful, but the Germans too were suffering horrendous casualties. The millions of shells that drenched their front lines and rear areas killed and maimed thousands of soldiers; their stubborn tactics of launching immediate counter-attacks in an effort to regain every inch of ground lost meant that they too were constantly exposed to fire while crossing No Man's Land. The German Army was being put through the mangle.

Throughout the Somme offensive the amount of resistance put up by the Germans was closely analysed, prisoners were interviewed and captured letters studied closely for signs of any weakening of collective resolve. These intelligence sources seemed to indicate that the Germans were clearly wobbling under the extreme pressure:

There is deterioration in the morale of the German Army in this battle, although people at home will not recognise it. Surrenders are more ready than they were at the beginning. Though far from being demoralised as an army, the Germans are not nearly so formidable a fighting machine as they were at the beginning of the battle. Our New Army has shown itself to be as good as the German Army. The battle is over and we shall not know the actual effect it has had on the Germans for many a long day, but it has certainly done all, and more, than we hoped for when we began. It stopped the Verdun attack. It collected a great weight of the German Army opposite us, and then broke it. It prevented the Germans hammering Russia, and it has undoubtedly worn down the German resistance to a great extent.[1]

Brigadier-General John Charteris, Intelligence Officer, General Headquarters, BEF

Brigadier Charteris generally took an optimistic approach to his sources, but, in fairness, the Germans were themselves conscious of the grievous damage they had suffered in the attritional fighting on the Somme. A new German command team of Field Marshal Paul von Hindenburg and General Erich von Ludendorff replaced Falkenhayn in the summer of 1916. As they assessed the overall situation on the Western Front they were deeply worried:

On the Somme the enemy's powerful artillery, assisted by excellent aeroplane observation and fed with enormous supplies of ammunition, had kept down our own fire and destroyed our artillery. The defence of our infantry had become so flabby that the massed attacks of the enemy always succeeded. Not only did our *morale* suffer, but in addition to fearful wastage in killed and wounded, we lost a large number of prisoners and much material.[2]

General Erich von Ludendorff, General Staff, German Headquarters

On the Home Front, too, Germany was suffering the crippling effects of a true global war under a tight naval blockade. By the end of 1916 all the essentials of life were severely rationed as bread, potatoes, dairy products and meat all but disappeared from shops and restaurants. German civilians had to negotiate a complicated ration-card system before they could get their hands on what adulterated and poor-quality food remained on offer. Clothes were also rationed and the ordinary German family faced a bleak outlook as the war moved into its fourth year.

The original Allied plans for 1917 were conceived by the French Commander-in-Chief, General Joseph Joffre, who had established a reasonable working relationship with General Sir Douglas Haig commanding the British Expeditionary Force. Joffre envisaged pressing hard on the Western Front during the winter, at least so far as weather permitted, in order to keep up the pressure on the Germans. They would then look to thrust hard in coordinated British and French offensives on either side of the Somme battlefield in the spring of 1917. The British were to attack the German salient exposed between the Ancre and the Scarpe rivers after first capturing the heights of Vimy Ridge. The French were to attack first to the south between the Somme and the Oise rivers, and then their major effort would be along the River Aisne. In addition the British proposed to follow up this spring offensive with a summer offensive in Flanders. Joffre's proposals had been agreed at the Chantilly Conference of 15 November 1916. The Germans were more than a little perturbed at the prospect of just such renewed Allied offensives:

> GHQ had to bear in mind that the enemy's great superiority in men and material would be even more painfully felt in 1917 than in 1916. They had to face the danger that 'Somme fighting' would soon break out at various points on our fronts, and that even our troops would not be able to withstand such attacks indefinitely, especially if the enemy gave us no time for rest and for the accumulation of material.[3]
> General Erich von Ludendorff, General Staff, German Headquarters

The Germans did not just lie back and ponder their fate; they took radical action and slowly began to recast their overall defensive tactics to take account of the increasing sophistication and weight of British assaults. Instead of a static system of front lines, which would be defended to the death and endlessly contested through incessant counter-attacks, they introduced the idea of an elastic defence system. The emphasis switched to strong points and concrete pillboxes across a deep battle zone with masses of barbed wire defences covered by the interlinked fields of fire of their machine-guns. The front-line troops were henceforth permitted to retreat when a position became indefensible rather than be overrun and die *in situ*. Meanwhile the counter-attack divisions were lurking in the rear areas, held back, only to strike if the British appeared to be likely to break out of the front-line zone – when, of course, the British attacking troops would be at their weakest state having advanced beyond the range of their field artillery.

The Battle of the Somme was suspended by Haig on 18 November 1916, but few soldiers on the ground would have immediately marked its passing. A battle does not just switch off at the whim of one side or the other. Although some of the exhausted divisions were withdrawn for rest and training, there were plenty left to ensure that the two sides still scratched and spat at each other across No Man's Land – the guns still roared. Haig had ordered a policy of continuous harassment of the Germans on the Somme front, but in the event the grim winter weather and atrocious ground conditions forestalled any real offensive operations until mid-January of 1917. The resumption of the attacks was the responsibility of the Fifth Army under the command of General Sir Hubert Gough, a former cavalry general who had already impressed as a 'thruster' at the relatively early age of 47. Slowly but relatively surely, the Fifth Army edged their way up the Ancre Valley: trench by trench, shell hole by shell hole. Capturing key observation points, the army used them to dominate and overcome the next German strong point using all the tactical expertise gained at such cost in 1916.

After more than two years as the French commander-in-chief, Joffre seemed like a permanent fixture, but before the dawn of the New Year he was replaced, in effect finally paying the penalty for the devastating casualties suffered by the French Army, year by year, since 1914. Despite all these sacrifices the German Army was still firmly entrenched deep inside France and, as the pervading war weariness took its toll, new solutions and new saviours were called for. Joffre was displaced by General Robert Nivelle, who had risen swiftly to prominence as a result of his success in the later stages of the Battle of Verdun, most notably in an attack launched on 24 October 1916. Nivelle was primarily an artillery general who considered that he had a 'new method' of scientifically con-centrating the guns in such a manner that he could positively guarantee success. After a devastating opening bombardment, a creeping barrage would range deep behind the German front line, thereby allowing the infantry to penetrate right through the whole defensive system, even to the extent of overrunning the German artillery lines. This was a return to a concept of real breakthrough, of smashing the enduring spectre of trench warfare. It was not surprising that the French politicians, deeply aware of the extent of war weariness amongst their people, were interested

– more than interested – in what the charismatic General Nivelle could offer.

On his accession as commander-in-chief, Nivelle immediately discarded Joffre's plans and sought to prove the potency of his new tactics by planning a gigantic offensive to seize the Chemin des Dames on the River Aisne in April 1917. Every available French gun would be concentrated together to provide a devastating bombardment under the cover of which two massed armies would smash their way forward by sheer brute force, with a third army standing ready to immediately exploit the anticipated breach. The breakthrough to outright victory was confidently predicted within a couple of days. The British were almost dumbfounded to find that the French were willing to take up the cudgels in this quixotic manner. Previously Joffre had applied near ceaseless pressure on Haig for the British to pick up their fair share of the fighting on the Western Front, but now Nivelle was cheerfully volunteering to bear the main burden. True, Nivelle required the British to take over a substantial extra sector of the French line, from the Somme to the Oise, in order to release the troops and guns needed to carry out his offensive. He also still required Haig to launch a major diversionary offensive between the Scarpe and the Ancre rivers – the operation that would become the Battle of Arras. Nevertheless, this left Britain very much the junior partner in the main Allied offensive planned for 1917. Haig was naturally wary of agreeing a large increase in the British front, but the principles of the plans were finally accepted in January 1917 at a conference in London at which Nivelle presented his ideas to Haig, Field Marshal General Sir William Robertson the Chief of the Imperial General Staff, and various members of the British government.

Nivelle was an attractive personality: soldierly, eloquent and with the natural confidence to sell his ideas to the British politicians. In this he stood in sharp contrast to that dour Scot, Sir Douglas Haig. Taciturn, if not inarticulate, almost incapable of publicly demonstrating whatever passions burned within, he was the converse to the vehement Nivelle. Although Haig had recently been promoted from general to field marshal, he regrettably did not command the full confidence of the new British Prime Minister, David Lloyd George, who had himself replaced Herbert Asquith in December 1916. As war leaders, Lloyd George and Haig had only one thing in common – a belief that the total mobilisation of the country was necessary if they were ever to win the war.

Haig himself had long favoured an offensive in Flanders. His reasons were clear. Firstly, he wanted to overrun the German occupied Belgian coast to clear out the nests of U-boats that were arousing serious concern within the Admiralty. Secondly, the Germans would have no choice but to stand and fight. Withdrawal was not an option when their strategically important railway junctions lay just 5 miles behind the front line. Haig was certain that the Germans had been left teetering on the edge by the hammer blows of the Somme. He wanted them to have to stand and suffer the battering, in the hope that this time they would finally fall apart. Thirdly, the British tactical situation at Ypres in the heart of Flanders was simply dreadful. Surrounded on three sides and overlooked from low ridges, every day they were suffering an unacceptable number of casualties just to hold on to the cramped salient. The symbolic status of Ypres after the heroic defensive battles of 1914 and 1915 meant the British could not in all con-science retire; but of course they still had the option of an advance to secure far better defensive positions. In 1916, Haig had been drawn by the French into the Somme offensive, but he still harboured plans for a major Flanders offensive in 1917.

Lloyd George very much approved of Nivelle's plan. Here was an ally that offered a guaranteed method of breaking the deadlock on the Western Front without the pain and sacrifice of manpower associated with the horrors of the Somme or some ghastly Flanders bloodbath. Lloyd George himself favoured an attack through Salonika or Italy; he sought a soft underbelly to evade fighting the Germans directly. In a sense, Nivelle was offering another easy option for the British Empire. True, the offensive would be on the Western Front, but the French were willing to bear the brunt of the 'butcher's bill'. Although Haig had some doubts as to the fea-sibility of Nivelle's plans, he, too, had no objection to the French flinging themselves forward. After all, it meant that the main Allied effort in 1917 would be made on the Western Front.

WHATEVER the overall strategic situation in 1917, there was now a new dimension to consider in the conduct and art of war. Aircraft were a rela-tively new weapon, but they had already taken their place at the very forefront of tactical considerations. Flying was a new phenomenon: Orville and Wilbur Wright had first flown an aircraft on 17 December 1903, the nascent RFC was only founded in 1912 and just sixty-three assorted aircraft in four squadrons had accompanied the British Expeditionary Force (BEF) into action in August 1914. In retrospect it is amazing how quickly the RFC matured under the overwhelming imperatives forced on it by the Great War. The original function of the RFC had been one of visual reconnaissance, in essence an adjunct to the cavalry. A pilot and an observer with his notebook had been the norm. Simple messages recording German movements were either dropped in message bags or personally handed to the Headquarters staff. But as the continuous trench lines developed reconnaissance missions took on an ever-greater importance. Aircraft became the only method of finding out what was going on behind the German front line.

In an effort to maximise the information brought back from each reconnaissance mission experimental cameras were taken up in the aircraft. Although early photographs were usually blurred, where military requirements led, technology soon slavishly followed. The humble notebook was abandoned in favour of the increasingly pin-sharp glass plate photographs, which recorded details that would have eluded even the most sharp-eyed of observers in flight. The bulky cameras were clamped to the outside of the cockpit and resulted in a photographic 'map' of everything directly below the aircraft. Prior to any offensive, 'oblique' photographs taken at an angle were also highly prized by the infantry officers for the detail they could give of the hidden ground across which they would soon be advancing. Unfortunately, to be effective such photographs had to be taken from a dangerously low level just a few hundred feet above the trenches. By 1917 thousands of photographs were being taken. Once the aircraft was safely down on the ground the plates had to be developed and duplicated quickly if the photographs were to be of any real value:

> With the crude equipment then in use dry prints were produced thirty-five minutes after the aircraft had landed. The photographic hut was divided into four main compartments. The first of these was for developing plates, the second for exposing and developing of prints, the third for the drying of prints, and the fourth for plotting and the making of mosaics. Plates after fixing and washing were immersed in methylated spirit, and, whilst still scarcely dry, were placed in enlargers and prints taken. The prints were treated in a like manner, and passed in dishes of methylated spirits into the drying room. Here they were separately held over a flame and 'burnt' until dry. Two prints were taken from each negative, and as these reached the plotting room they

were marked with the date, height, and map references and these figures were then copied on to the negative itself. The Branch Intelligence Officer was responsible for choosing the negatives from which prints for distribution to the various Headquarters were to be made.[4]

Second Lieutenant George Banting, 34 Squadron, RFC

Using the developed plates, the art of photographic interpretation was quickly born: German gun batteries were found to be visible even when camouflaged, machine-gun posts stood revealed; dugout entrances, footpaths, headquarters and changes in trench systems – all were immediately obvious to the experts. The ubiquitous BE2cs, the mainstay of the army cooperation squadrons of the RFC, painstakingly photographed every square inch of the opposing German lines.

However, photographs were not the end of the RFC contribution. Once the technological problems of getting a wireless transmitter and aerial aloft in an aircraft had been overcome, it was only natural to use them for artillery observation. Fertile minds soon solved the conundrum of one-way communication and, with the introduction of the clock code, an aircraft could provide the corrections that would range shells directly onto targets completely invisible from the guns or their forward observation posts on the ground:

The method of communication between the aircraft and battery was by means of a Sterling spark transmitter, with a trailing aerial of about 150 feet used by the observer or the pilot to send messages in Morse code to the battery. A series of code letters were used denoting: 'Are you ready to fire?', 'Fire!' Always of course prefixed by the code number of the battery with whom we wished to communicate. The battery replied by placing wide strips of white cloth on a dark background in single code letters acknowledging the message received from the aircraft. These letters could be seen quite easily, as for this type of operation we normally flew at an altitude of 2,000–5,000 feet. The actual position of the enemy battery was marked on a photograph and from the centre three concentric circles were drawn denoting 'X' = 25 yards, 'Y' = 50 yards, 'Z' = 100 yards; also giving north, south, east and west positions. All was now ready to commence the shoot. The observer then sent a message to the battery asking, 'Are you ready?' If in the affirmative, the observer sent by code the letter 'G' for the first gun to be fired, the pilot having manoeuvred the aircraft into such a position so that the observer could see both the flash of the gun as it fired and the burst of the shell. Watching closely, the observer would note the actual position where the shell had burst and advise the battery accordingly. For instance, if the shell burst at 'ZN' it indicated that the burst had taken place 100 yards north of the enemy battery position. Our battery would then adjust their sights accordingly and the same procedure continued with each of the four howitzers until all guns were ranged correctly onto the enemy target, when the observer gave the signal 'GG' when all guns fired as quickly as they could be loaded.[5]

Second Lieutenant Francis Penny, 12 Squadron, RFC

The clock code may seem relatively simple, but its implications were far-reaching. Once the Royal Artillery had swallowed its pride and got used to taking fire orders from observers not under its direct control, the potential of air observation was obvious. Unseen indirect targets could be carefully registered by batteries, which could then hold themselves in readiness to open up a devastating fire as and when required. In particular, hostile German batteries, once identified, could be systematically targeted and eliminated as threats.

The Germans certainly clearly recognised the importance of aerial army cooperation work and placed it at the heart of their considerations in deploying their aircraft:

The main object of fighting in the air is to enable our photo registration and photo reconnaissance to be carried out and at the same time to prevent that of the enemy. All other tasks, such as bombing raids, machine-gun attacks and even distant reconnaissance in trench warfare must be secondary to this main objective. So long as the execution of the main task is not ensured all available forces must be employed for this purpose.[6]

General Otto von Below, Headquarters, Sixth Army, German Imperial Army

The traditional German skills in lens manufacture gave them some advantage in the quality of the cameras used and consequently in the clarity of the photographs taken. In the previous year the German Air Force had reorganised its aerial reconnaissance so that long-range recon-naissance for the Headquarters staff was the responsibility of the Flieger Abteilungen. Their aircraft were far superior in performance, in both speed and altitude ceiling, to any of the British army cooperation machines. The local reconnaissance and direct artillery cooperation required by the infantry were supplied by the Flieger Abteilungen (A). They, too, were better equipped than their British counterparts. Both the British and Germans supplemented their aircraft with kite balloons, whose observers, directly connected by telephone, were ranging the artillery. They could stay aloft all day and severely restrict any movement by the opposing side within their range of vision by calling up immediate artillery intervention.

It soon became obvious that no army could allow enemy aircraft free access above its lines for the purpose of photographic reconnaissance and artillery observation. Soon machine-guns were being taken aloft and by 1915 both sides had developed their first scout aircraft designed to shoot down reconnaissance aircraft. Of course, before they could do that efficiently the scout pilots first had to clear the skies of opposing scouts. Thus a battle for control of the skies developed and began to escalate in proportion to the importance of the prizes to be gained from unfettered observation. Unfortunately, the scout pilots' role soon became so wreathed with glamour that then, and ever since, this allure has deflected attention from the real role of the RFC.

In late 1915 the Germans gained the upper hand through the clear superiority of their Fokker E III monoplane scouts. This simple monoplane of limited performance had one great asset – a forward-firing machine gun that used an interrupter gear to allow it to pour bullets straight ahead without hitting the whirling propeller. Two young but inspirational Fokker pilots, Leutnants Max Immelmann and Oswald Boelcke, set about honing the skills that would come to form the basics of aerial scout tactics. Intuitively utilising the diving ability and forward-firing strength of the Fokker, they sought to dive from out of the glare of the sun, seeking surprise, only opening fire from close range and always looking for an easy kill with the minimum of risk to themselves. It was important not to give a chance to their opponents; to kill without being seen by the victim was the ideal. One pass, then they would zoom away, before considering a second attack if it was necessary. As they mastered their new trade so their score of victories began to mount.

By 1916 the RFC army cooperation squadrons were charged with a series of onerous interlinked tasks: the provision of a comprehensive service of photographic reconnaissance and artillery observation; flying contact patrols during attacks; and carrying out bombing raids to disrupt communications and harass the Germans in their rest billets. All this had to be achieved whilst at the same time beating back the German Air Force and thereby depriving the German Army of the same aerial facilities. In the face of the still potent Fokker threat, truly Herculean efforts were demanded of the RFC and their BE2cs in the months leading up to the Battle of the Somme which began on 1 July 1916. When the BE2cs were ordered in their thousands early in the war, no one had conceived of the necessity for anything other than a stable observation 'platform'. Now faced with the agile Fokkers they struggled for survival:

> The BE2c was totally unsuited to the job of course, it had the observer in front and the pilot behind, whereas with any sense, it should have been the pilot in front and the observer behind, but it wasn't! So the observer sat in a cockpit, with four struts very close each side of him, wires to brace him well in, and in front, none behind. And a little seat he could just get in to. And really he could do nothing at all except keep a look out. When it got at all hot and you were liable to be attacked from the tail as much as anywhere else, he simply had to get up on his seat, kneel on his seat, which was a jolly cold, drafty business at 8,000 feet even in the summer.[7]

> Lieutenant Cecil Lewis, 3 Squadron, RFC

The Battle of the Somme was the first great test for the developing theories of aerial warfare then in the process of being formulated by Major General Hugh Trenchard. After commanding First Wing, RFC during the Battle of Neuve Chapelle in March 1915, Trenchard acceded to the command of the RFC on the Western Front in August 1915, and had already established a close working relationship with Haig. This perhaps was not surprising, for the two men had much in common. Both were less fluent in speech than on paper, both were utterly committed to the ultimate goal of victory, and both proved themselves willing to sacrifice lives where they considered it necessary for the greater good of their country. Trenchard was intelligent, able to grasp complex concepts without necessarily being able to explain them and he relied a good deal on his aide-de-camp, the celebrated author, Captain Maurice Baring, to render his thoughts comprehensible to a wider audience.

Trenchard ordered his men to keep on flying over the line despite the 'Fokker scourge', his only compromise being that formations of aircraft were sent out on missions formerly carried out by lone aircraft. In formation the aircraft could band together to defend each other and find security in numbers. Nevertheless, underpinning everything was the principle that losses must be accepted to get the results required. The gamble worked and covered the cracks until the arrival of a new generation of British aircraft – the FE2b, the DH2, the Nieuport Scout and the Sopwith 1½ Strutter – which allowed the RFC to seize complete control of the skies above the Somme battlefield just at the time when it most mattered, between June and September of 1916. Trenchard, with the assistance of Baring, committed to paper a simple exposition of his relentlessly offensive aerial strategy:

> Owing to the unlimited space in the air, the difficulty one machine has in seeing another, the accidents of wind and cloud, it is impossible for aeroplanes, however skilful and vigilant their pilots, however powerful their engines, however mobile their machines and however numerous their formations, to prevent hostile aircraft from crossing the line if they have the initiative and determination to do so. The aeroplane is not a defence against the aeroplane. But the opinion of those most competent to judge is that the aeroplane, as a weapon of attack, cannot be too highly estimated. On the British front, during the operations which began with the Battle of the Somme, we know that although the enemy has concentrated the greater part of his available forces in the air on this front, the work actually accomplished by their aeroplanes stands, compared with the work done by us, in the proportion of about 4 to 100.[8]
>
> Major General Hugh Trenchard, Headquarters, RFC

It was a simple but effective concept of relentless offensive patrols penetrating deep behind the German lines, designed to beat back German aircraft to keep them as far as possible from the vital front-line areas. Trenchard accepted with equanimity the consequences of an occasional German scout breaking through to prey on the British artillery cooperation machines working above the trenches.

In July and August 1916, the RFC achieved an almost total domination of the skies above the lines and deep into the rear areas behind the German front. The German infantry grew incensed as they were constantly exposed from above, while their own aircraft were conspicuous only by their absence. One German soldier billeted in a village far behind the lines expressed his disgust at the situation:

> Now just a word about our own aeroplanes. Really, one must be almost too ashamed to write about them; it is simply scandalous. They fly up

to this village, but no further, whereas the English are always flying over our lines, directing artillery shoots, whereby getting all their shells, even those of heavy calibre, right into our trenches. Our artillery can only shoot by the map as they have no observation. I wonder if they have any idea where the enemy's line is, or even ever hit it.[9]

Anon soldier, 24th Infantry Division, Imperial German Army

In mid-September, the Germans finally hit back. Their new single-seater scout aircraft, the Albatros DI, marked the advent of the next generation of scout aircraft. Powered by the 160 hp Mercedes engine up to speeds that approached 110 mph, they were armed with twin Spandau machine guns capable of firing 1,600 rounds per minute. These aircraft completely outclassed any of the available British scouts, most of which were armed with only a single Lewis gun capable of firing just 47 rounds before the pilot had to attend to the tricky task of changing the ammunition drum in mid-combat. The German Air Force was thoroughly reorganised and the new scouts were concentrated into 'hunting' squadrons known as Jagdstaffeln or more popularly 'Jasta'. Of these the most immediately influential was to be Jasta 2, commanded by the redoubtable Hauptmann Oswald Boelcke. Boelcke had been thinking deeply about his experiences as a scout pilot and sought to pass on his accumulated knowledge to the young acolytes whom he had personally selected to join his squadron.

One of these *ingénues* was Leutnant Manfred von Richthofen. Born on 2 May 1892, the son of an aristocratic Prussian family, he grew up imbued with a taste for the thrills and trappings of hunting of all kinds. He started his military service as an officer cadet at 11 years old and progressed through a lengthy and strict training before being commissioned into the cavalry in 1912. He served on both the Eastern and Western Fronts in 1914, but the onset of trench warfare restricted the prospects for any further real excitement in the cavalry, and in May 1915 he sought and was granted a transfer into the German Air Service. At first he was an observer, but he was inspired to learn to fly by a chance meeting with Boelcke, desperate to become a scout pilot and prove himself in the greatest of all manhunts.

Richthofen soon attracted attention to himself as a competent and aggressive pilot and joined Jasta 2 at Bertincourt on 1 September 1916. He proved an able pupil and scored his first acknowledged victory on 17 September when he shot down the FE2b flown by Second Lieutenant Lionel Morris and Captain Tom Rees, who thereby earned themselves the kind of immortality they would doubtless have forgone if given the chance. A macabre ritual was triggered when Richthofen was presented with a small victory cup to commemorate his achievement. The young aristocrat was not short of money and he obviously liked the idea, for thereafter he commissioned a silversmith to strike similar silver cups to mark each of his subsequent aerial triumphs.

Trenchard had highly attuned antennae that swiftly detected the early signs of a German aerial renaissance. Just a few days later he wrote to the Director of Air Organisation, Lieutenant-Colonel Sefton Brancker back in London:

> We are fighting a very big battle and fighting in the air is becoming
> intense. The fighting will increase, I regret to say, and not decrease, and
> it is only a question of our keeping it up longer than the Hun. If we
> cannot do that, then we are beaten; if we do it, then we win. I must warn
> you now that in the next ten days, if we get fine weather, I anticipate
> a very heavy casualty list. There are many more German machines
> than there were, fast and much better pilots which have appeared on
> our front.[10]
>
> Major-General Hugh Trenchard, Headquarters, RFC

There is no doubt that Trenchard was seriously worried and successfully sought the backing of Haig in campaigning for the earliest possible delivery of a new generation of British aircraft able to contest the technical superiority established by the Germans:

> The enemy has made extraordinary efforts to increase the number,
> and develop the speed and power, of his fighting machines. He has
> unfortunately succeeded in doing so and it is necessary to realise clearly,
> and at once, that we shall undoubtedly lose our superiority in the air
> if I am not provided at an early date with improved means of retaining
> it. The result of the advent of the enemy's improved machines has
> been a marked increase in the casualties suffered by the Royal Flying
> Corps, and though I do not anticipate losing our present predominance
> in the air for the next three or four months, the situation after that
> threatens to be very serious unless adequate steps to deal with it are
> taken at once.[11]
>
> General Sir Douglas Haig, Headquarters, BEF

Back at home, Brancker was trying his best but found he was competing with every other department of government in a ceaseless battle for resources:

> Unless British aviation can carry more weight in the eyes of the Government than it does at present, we must be prepared to face a very ugly situation at the beginning of next spring.[12]
>
> Lieutenant-Colonel Sefton Brancker, Director of Air Organisation

OVER the next two months, Hauptmann Oswald Boelcke proved a truly great mentor to his young pilots, leading from the front to achieve some forty victories on his own account. Inspired by his example many of them began to score regular victories as they discovered that the British had nothing to compare to the sheer power of the Albatros DI or the newly developed Albatros DIIs, which were also beginning to be delivered to the Jasta. The death of Boelcke following an accidental mid-air collision with his great friend Leutnant Erwin Böhme on 28 October 1916, was a tragedy for the German Air Service:

> Now everything is so empty for us. Only gradually are we beginning to realise what a void Boelcke leaves behind, that without him the soul of the whole squadron is lacking. In every relation he was our unparalleled leader and master. He had a compelling influence upon everyone who had anything to do with him, even his superiors, simply through his personality, the simplicity of his character. With us, we would follow him anywhere. We never had the feeling that something could go awry if he was there among us and almost everything that we tried succeeded. In these one and a half months we had shot down over sixty enemy aircraft without a loss. The superiority of the English was dwindling day by day. Now we must otherwise see to it that his triumphant spirit in the squadron does not perish.[13]
>
> Leutnant Erwin Böhme, Jasta 2, German Army Air Force

Yet in one sense the work of their young master – Boelcke was just 25 years old when he died – was done. Jasta 2 had learnt well and Richthofen, who had already shot down six aircraft, would soon take on his mantle.

The Albatros scouts exacted an increasingly painful toll as the Somme offensive dragged on into the late autumn. Other new German single-seater scouts arriving on the scene in late 1916 were the Halberstadt DII, and the Roland DII, which were perfectly good scout aircraft, but they were overshadowed by the dramatic success of the Albatros designs. Yet, although the casualties rose sharply, the RFC still managed to deliver the services that Trenchard and Haig required. One of the great lessons of aerial warfare had been learnt. Supremacy in the air meant the ability to keep army photographic reconnaissance and artillery observation aircraft above the front and the question of casualties incurred in doing so was almost immaterial. When the battle finally petered out in November there was a general acceptance that, whatever the disappointments suffered in the bitter ground fighting, the RFC had more than discharged their duties in the skies above. They had been tested, in good times and bad, without failing the artillery and hence the infantry that depended on them for their lives. The Battle of the Somme marked the moment when the RFC finally came of age.[*]

In many ways Trenchard proved the ideal subordinate to Haig. He never tried to evade his responsibilities either to his superiors or to the men under his command. Although he had the moral courage to order his pilots up whatever the odds, he also regularly toured the squadrons to ensure his men knew that he stood with them in the battle that raged. At no stage in the Somme battles had he showed any signs of 'going native'; of beginning to adopt the priorities and aims of the RFC rather than the parent body of the army that had not yet weaned them. When the RFC was outclassed by the swinging pendulum of aircraft design, he had the good sense not to blame Haig – he knew that if faults existed they lay with the fledgling aeronautics industry back in Britain. Haig appreciated his efforts and after the Somme took the time to summarise the varied achievements and services offered by the RFC in his official despatches:

> The admirable work of this Corps has been a very satisfactory feature of the battle. Under the conditions of modern war the duties of the Air Service are many and varied. They include the regulation and control of artillery fire by indicating targets and observing and reporting the results of rounds; the taking of photographs of enemy trenches, strong points, battery positions, and of the effect of bombardments; and the observation of the movements of the enemy behind his lines. The

[*] For more on the aerial campaign on the Somme see my previous book, *Somme Success: The RFC and the Battle of the Somme, 1916* (Barnsley: Pen & Sword, 1999).

greatest skill and daring has been shown in the performance of all these duties, as well as in bombing expeditions. Our Air Service has also cooperated with our infantry in their assaults, signalling the position of our attacking troops and turning machine guns on to the enemy infantry and even on to his batteries in action.[14]

General Sir Douglas Haig, Headquarters, BEF

Nevertheless, a shadow still lay across the whole of the RFC. Haig had agreed at Nivelle's behest that the Battle of Arras would start in early April 1917. But there was no way on earth that a new generation of British aircraft would be delivered in sufficient numbers to counter the Albatros menace in the few months that remained. Somehow or other the RFC must continue to carry out its manifold duties in evermore obsolescent aircraft – whatever the human cost. Yet even with this prospect before them, with the German scouts increasingly running rampant, the morale of the RFC endured as they enjoyed simple Christmas festivities in the traditional style:

Spent the day quietly, until the evening; 7 p.m. saw the commencement of 'some' dinner, to which eleven of us sat down. Nothing was left of a 21 lb turkey, plum pudding flaming with brandy (for which occasion the lights were put out), a dozen of champagne and heaps of other little dainties. A highly successful dinner for which we have to thank Madam (the landlady) who did the cooking. We then went round to the men's concert, found them making awful fools of themselves, disgustingly drunk. It was an excellent concert. An exceedingly drunk 'poilu', who came in from no one knows where, caused great amusement by trying to embrace and kiss all the officers, one of whom more inebriated than the remainder of this flight, embraced the 'Frenchie' on the stage; we retired at 11.30 p.m., to let the men go as they liked.[15]

Second Lieutenant William Lidsey, 16 Squadron, RFC

For many of the pilots and observers it would be their last Christmas. By Easter a new sacrifice would be required in the cause of their country at Arras.

CHAPTER TWO

WINTER'S FREEZING

Aerial offensive was not merely rivalry between the opposing air services. It was a definite attempt to obtain aerial observation. As it is now, it is the Hun who doesn't move about near the line by daylight, and who has to submit to having his railheads, stores and billets bombed at our pleasure. And if he fires his guns by day he knows perfectly well their position will be disclosed to the waiting airmen who at once direct counter-fire and photograph them too.[1]

Captain Bernard Rice, 8 Squadron, RFC

War was not a new phenomenon to Arras. The town was of Roman origin and its people had generally been obliged to endure 'interesting times' for most of its existence. A crude history of Europe can be discerned from a study of those who have assaulted, captured and defended Arras over the centuries. It was finally claimed by the French in 1659. After the prolonged social experiment of the French Revolution and the harsh justice meted out by 'Madame Guillotine' in front of the Hôtel de Ville, the town had been threatened but not captured by the German advance of the Franco-Prussian War in 1870. Finally, the Great War brought the most prolonged and destructive trial of them all to the population of 26,080. In September 1914 the Germans had briefly occupied Arras, but soon fell back to establish their trench lines just 3 miles from the outskirts. Once again Arras was under siege and it became a front-line city in the Western Front that stretched from Switzerland to the sea.

There was no respite from the German shells that slowly pounded the once beautiful streets into ruins. It has been estimated that of the 4,521 houses in central Arras only 292 were undamaged. Most of the proud heritage of civic buildings had been blasted almost beyond repair: the

Grande Place, the Petite Place, the Hôtel de Ville and the Belfry Tower, the Palais St Vaast Abbey, the Place de La Gare, the Chapelle des Ursulines, St John's Hospital, the various churches, the schools – all were laid to waste. In 1915, the French had fought a number of battles attacking the ridges lying to the north of Arras in an attempt to relieve the stranglehold the Germans had on the city. The Notre Dame de Lorrette Spur had eventually been captured, but only after the most sanguinary fighting imaginable; Vimy Ridge remained in the hands of the Germans.

The new Battle of Arras in 1917 was intended to act as a diversion to the main French attack to be launched on the Aisne, but it was still a major operation of war with its own clearly defined objectives. The right of the First Army, commanded by General Sir Henry Horne, was to capture Vimy Ridge that lay just 3 miles to the north-east of Arras. This was no small undertaking but if successful would offer a superb observation platform over the whole of the Douai plain. Meanwhile the Third Army commanded by General Sir Edmund Allenby was to take the high ground surrounding the village of Monchy-le-Preux, thereby turning the German lines and allowing a rapid exploitation south towards Croisilles and Bullecourt.

Artillery was at the very centre of Allenby and Horne's plans for the Battle of Arras. The thousands upon thousands of new recruits who had joined the Royal Artillery in 1914 and 1915 had by this time been bedded down into their units and had thoroughly mastered their various specialist trades. Gunnery itself had become an increasingly exact science. The necessity for exact calibration of the guns, the importance of allowing for different meteorological conditions, the ability to organise complex barrages, not just for a battery or an artillery brigade, but for massive concentrations of guns – all these had been thoroughly worked out. The role for each calibre of gun had been clearly defined and laid out within the context of the all-encompassing barrage. Direct observation was supplemented by aerial observation, flash spotting and sound ranging to fix the location of every German gun, ready to 'neutralise' them when the moment came. The efficiency of wire cutting had been improved by the gradual introduction of the 106 fuse, which burst instantaneously on the slightest contact with anything it touched before the shell could bury itself deep in the mud. Ever-increasing numbers of heavy guns were ranged on specific targets so that their destruction could be virtually guaranteed. The creeping barrages were now commonplace and increasing in sophistication and complexity, some even incorporating new smoke shells to try to blind the enemy as the infantry attacked. It was a world away from the long, but ineffective, barrage that had preceded the hopeless attack on the Somme on 1 July 1916.

Throughout the early months of 1917 the preparations inexorably built up to a crescendo in the Arras area. Logistics were all-important and all forms of communications were steadily improved: the veins of war to smoothly transport munitions, stores and men to the front. The whole infra-structure of the area was upgraded: new roads, new railway sidings, railheads and light railways – the rear areas teemed with purposeful activity. Under-neath Vimy Ridge the underground war waged by the sappers of the Royal Engineers proceeded apace, as they sought to establish an underground front line stretching ever forward until it lay directly beneath the Germans. Meanwhile, the network of underground passages and workings that had already existed beneath peacetime Arras was massively expanded to house and protect the thousands of infantry who would need shelter before the storm commenced. Above all the guns had to be moved into the line. This was no easy matter. The term 'heavy artillery' was no misnomer and their transport across the rear areas of muddy battlefields represented a major undertaking. The seemingly infinite number of shells required for any chance of a successful assault had to be painstakingly built up in vast ammu-nition dumps. The RFC was an integral part of this build-up. Its photo-graphs and artillery observation were the key to the detailed planning process but above all to securing the efficient use of the massed guns. Failure was not an option, and RFC casualties were deemed an irrelevance in comparison to the thousands of lives that would be risked in a ground offensive.

AS the New Year dawned with all its fresh and pressing challenges, there was a very definite feeling in the RFC that the old order had changed. The reorganisation of the German Air Service had resulted in the establish-ment of no less than twenty-five Jasta. In contrast the RFC had only eight single-seater scout squadrons, of which only two were armed with machines that could conceivably challenge the Albatros on a head-to-head basis with any realistic hope of success. Despite the RFC's best efforts it was slowly becoming apparent that the focal point of conflict in the air had moved from the German rear areas to hover right above the opposing front lines:

By January 1917, the aerial superiority which we had gained during the earlier phases of the Somme battle had sensibly waned. Nothing alarming had happened, the process had been gradual, almost insidious. Our morale was just as high, we appeared to push just as vigorously over the lines, and yet there was a different feeling in the air. Frank surprise at seeing a Hun over our lines had changed imperceptibly into annoyance.[2]

Lieutenant Roderick Hill, 60 Squadron, RFC

Pilots could not help but notice that formations of Albatros were carrying out more and more regular patrols in a concerted effort to sweep the skies of the British army cooperation machines. Inevitably, as casualties crept up, there was a call for close escorts from the scouts which were still tied to their offensive patrols over the German lines. It was a complicated game of bluff and counter-bluff as each side sought to impose their will over the battlefield skies. If scouts were diverted to a defensive role, then perforce they would not be available for offensive operations, and, as the pressure they exerted waned, so the initiative would pass even further to the Germans. This was the conundrum that had to be resolved by Trenchard before the spring of 1917. It would test even his hardened resolve.

Trenchard knew that army cooperation squadrons needed a better aircraft than the long serving, but hopelessly obsolete, BE2 series. The first BE2c dated back to June 1914 and after three long years of war had only been supplanted by its kith and kin variants: the BE2d, BE2e and BE2g, which shared all its generic faults and offered no real improvement in performance. The intended replacement was the more powerful RE8, inevitably known as the 'Harry Tate' after the music hall performer, which unfortunately seemed to be jinxed right from the start. Design work had begun early in 1916 and the first prototype emerged as early as July 1916. But then a shortage of raw materials and myriad other problems seemed to dog the progress of the aircraft from drawing board to the front. As a result, it was only in November 1916 that 52 Squadron arrived on the Western Front equipped with RE8s. But their pilots seemed to be incapable of dealing with the RE8's flying characteristics. After a painful rash of accidents the RE8s were somewhat embarrassingly withdrawn to be replaced once again with the BE2e.

It is difficult now to determine the cause of these accidents as many of the pilots were sadly inexperienced, but the slightly eccentric appearance of the RE8s, with their long upper wing extensions in sharp contrast to their foreshortened lower wings, failed to inspire pilots' confidence. There were also teething problems with the design of the tail-fin that had to be solved before its flying characteristics could be improved. To make things worse, as the petrol tank was immediately behind the engine, when they crashed any spilt petrol was very likely to catch fire when it came in contact with the hot engine. Soon the RE8 was rumoured to be a jinxed aircraft prone to fatal crashes. Such rumours beset almost every new aircraft introduced on the Western Front. All were routinely traduced as 'spinning coffins' with some flaw that would doom the unsuspecting pilot who flew in anything but the most cautious manner. Yet the RE8, although not as stable as the variants of BE2s, was to prove a perfectly steady and safe aircraft. If anything, like its predecessors, it was far too stable for the hurly-burly of combat and overall it lacked the manoeuvrability needed when the Albatros came too close for comfort.

The first squadron to be effectively equipped with RE8s was 21 Squadron in February 1917. From this point the BE2c and its variants were gradually withdrawn from front-line service during the next few months. As for the RE8 it remained a controversial aircraft throughout the rest of the war. Its additional speed of up to 105 mph was welcome, as was its forward-firing Vickers machine gun and rear cockpit for the observer, with a handy Lewis gun to protect the tail. But the delays of almost a year before it was delivered in numbers meant that by the time it was in action the RE8 was already outdated and its performance suffered in comparison with more recently designed aircraft. Unfortunately, as the designated replacement for the BE2, the RE8 had been ordered in bulk. Thousands were in the process of being built by contractors across the length and breadth of Britain. It was the new army cooperation aircraft and – whatever its flaws – the RE8 was still far better than its predecessor.

Trenchard was also aware that he desperately needed to increase both the number and quality of his scout aircraft. In the interim, he simply had to make do with what he had. Prominent amongst these was the DH2 single-seater 'pusher'* scout that had triumphed in the Somme skies of 1916, but was seriously outclassed by the new Albatros scouts. With a top

*A pusher was an aircraft where the engine and propeller were behind the pilot 'pushing' them along as opposed to the 'tractor' aircraft where they were in front.

speed of just 93 mph and armed with only a single forward-firing Lewis gun, their growing impotency was symbolised on 20 December 1916, when six DH2s of 29 Squadron led by Captain Gerald Knight, an acknowledged ace credited with eight victories, met Richthofen and four other Albatros scouts over Monchy-au-Bois. Knight's considerable skills were irrelevant when faced with the equally accomplished Richthofen flying an immeasurably superior aircraft. Knight was sent spinning down to his death in Adinfer Wood and the rest of his flight were badly shot about. The DH2 was finished as a serious weapon of war. The FE8, another single-seater pusher aircraft that shared most of the characteristics of the DH2, was equally outdated.

One other British scout available was the Sopwith Pup produced by the Sopwith Aviation Company. These aircraft had been supplied to the Royal Naval Air Service (RNAS) Squadrons from the summer of 1916. With the RFC in dire straits the RNAS had sent 8 (Naval) Squadron RNAS, which was partially equipped with the Sopwith Pups, to assist on the Western Front in November 1916. The Pups made an immediate good impression. A simple, well-balanced aircraft, they were a delight to fly – nimble, with a fast turning circle and no bad habits. The problem was that they were badly underpowered; their small 80 hp rotary engine could only generate a maximum speed of just under 100 mph at altitudes above 10,000 feet. Their single Vickers gun armament also left them outgunned by the Albatros. Unfortunately, by the time the RFC squadrons could be equipped with them it was already becoming apparent that, although this lovely aircraft was capable of competing with the Albatros, it would always do so at a slight, but significant disadvantage.

The French had also helped fill the breach by supplying two fine single-seater scouts, the Nieuport 17 and the Spad VII. The Nieuport was well respected as an agile streamlined aircraft capable of reasonable speeds, but it, too, was slightly under-armed, with a single Vickers machine gun and an optional single Lewis gun on the top wing. The Spad VII was less manoeuvrable than the Nieuport 17, but its robust construction and relatively high speed, combined with a forward-firing synchronised Vickers machine gun, soon made it a popular machine. However, none of these aircraft, for all their virtues, could compete with the combination of speed and powerful performance at all altitudes that the Albatros boasted. Nor could they match the impressive firepower generated by twin-synchronised belt driven Spandaus. Most of all there were simply not enough of them available to throw into battle when and where it mattered.

Another Sopwith scout that was at last trickling out in early 1917 was the Sopwith Triplane. This, as the name suggests, had three layered short-span wings that promised and delivered incredible 'lift', great manoeuvrability and a superior field of vision to that found in the usual biplane layout. Blessed with a 110 hp Clerget engine they could reach up to 115 mph and were fitted with one or occasionally two centrally mounted Vickers machine guns. It is conceivable that this aircraft represents the single greatest missed British opportunity of the aerial war, for the design was passed by the Sopwith experimental department as early as May 1916. Yet the revolutionary triplane nature of this excellent scout seems to have blinded the British to the very real 'treasure' they had uncovered. When the usual difficulties haunted its production, the expedient decision was taken to supply them only to the RNAS, in return for which the RFC received in exchange all the Spad VIIs originally intended for the RNAS. In consequence the RFC never flew the Sopwith Triplane in action and the original high production orders somehow withered away. Now it was at last ready to fly into action with the RNAS, but there were simply never enough of them on the Western Front to bring the success that the aircraft deserved. If anything the Germans were more impressed and indeed the legendary Fokker Triplane would be largely based on the template of the Sopwith Triplane.

There was a potent new generation of British aircraft waiting in the wings. The Royal Aircraft Factory at Farnborough was producing the Scout Experimental Mark 5 (SE5), while the British and Colonial Aeroplane Company had built the two-seater Bristol Fighter. Captain Geoffrey de Havilland of the prosaically named Aircraft Manufacturing Company had designed the DH4 two-seater bomber, which looked likely to give a superb performance combining speed, a high altitude ceiling and rugged endurance. The other scout on the drawing board and only finally approved for production in December 1916, was the single-seater chunky little biplane – the Sopwith Camel. This was a more powerful version of the Sopwith Pup and promised higher speed, equal manoeuvrability and twin Vickers machine guns. Unfortunately, there was no hope of them reaching the Western Front before the summer of 1917. Whatever was going to happen at Arras would happen without the Sopwith Camel.

Endemic production problems meant there were chronic delays before sufficient numbers of any of these new aircraft could be secured to equip new and existing scout squadrons. It was against this background that in mid-January the newly promoted Deputy Director of Military Aeronautics Colonel Sefton Brancker revealed that an industrial dispute had once more delayed the expected arrival of the much-needed Bristol Fighter. As might be expected Trenchard was absolutely livid with rage:

> You are asking me to fight the battle this year with the same machines as I fought it last year. We shall be hopelessly outclassed, and something must be done. I am not panicking, but the Hun is getting more aggressive. I warned you fairly as far back as last September, and the Chief also warned you in November. And I warned the Air Board personally on 12 December. All I can say is that there will be an outcry from all the pilots out here if we do not have at least these few squadrons of fast machines, and what I have asked for is absolutely necessary.[3]
>
> Major-General Hugh Trenchard, Headquarters, RFC

It could take a year or even longer to get a new aircraft from the drawing board to active service. Technical problems with new engines were the main stumbling block. Experimental engines could be temperamental beasts, with unforeseen faults tending to emerge only in the later stages of the testing process, while the logistical exercise of securing a stream of production models built to sufficiently high standards was fraught with problems. Magnetos had been imported mainly from Germany before the war and although their manufacture was now underway the numbers produced could not keep up with the voracious demand. There was considerable cooperation with the French but it was entirely natural that their needs came first. As the new engines took so long to develop and manufacture, there was then the problem of judging and balancing the production of aircraft with the engines that would be available at the time. Aircraft sometimes flattered to deceive. What seemed a great performance during testing could be obsolete a year later as the boundaries of progress expanded ever onwards and upwards. Once an aircraft type had been ordered and built in bulk, however, there was really no choice – the pilots had to fly them into action.

Poor Brancker found himself in a truly invidious position. He alone could not shift the priorities of the government; he could not avoid the technical problems that plagued the design and manufacture of new engines and aircraft; he could not stop the labour problems that held up production. Driven almost to despair he tried to volunteer for a return to active service, but his offer was abruptly refused. His organisational skills and drive far outweighed any fighting potential he may have possessed at the front. Trenchard hastened to try and reassure him of his support:

> Keep going on and don't be depressed. You are, I was going to say, my only hope and do not forget that your work influences work out here as a whole more than anything else I can think of.[4]
>
> Major-General Hugh Trenchard, Headquarters, RFC

Despite the inevitable tensions in their relationship, Trenchard knew full well that he needed an ally at home in the battle to secure the manufacture of sufficient modern aircraft.

TRENCHARD'S problems were typified by the continued RFC reliance on the FE2b two-seater pusher as a multi-purpose aircraft. One of the series of aircraft that had seized the initiative from the Fokkers in the late spring of 1916, it had a top speed of just over 90 mph. In the absence of any effective replacement these workhorses were still ploughing on the Western Front. Used mainly in a daylight reconnaissance role, or on bombing missions, although on occasion still carrying out offensive patrols, these trusty old pushers continued to perform valuable work. Yet their inferior speed, manoeuvrability, ceiling and dismal firepower meant that they were totally outclassed if ever caught on their own by one of the latest German scouts. Yet some of the old virtues that had made the FE2b so formidable in 1916 still endured. With the solid engine providing a useful measure of protection for the pilot's back, the FE2b was relatively difficult to shoot down for the more inexperienced German pilots and they retained the capacity to bite back hard when flying in a tight defensive formation:

> When leading an offensive patrol of five FE2bs over Riencourt, we saw two Sopwith Scouts engaged by two Hostile Aircraft (HA) and the Sopwiths seemed to be getting the worst of it. We went in underneath them and fired at the HA until they withdrew. Later on we saw three HA (new type) climbing across our front about 300 yards distant and still about 500 feet below. We led the formation directly at the HA in an

endeavour to drive HA down. They however kept on climbing rapidly and when about 150 yards distant turned directly towards us and, still climbing slightly, opened fire on us. We tried to pass over the top of the first HA, but, failing to do this, we passed about 20 feet under. The fight then became general, the HA being reinforced by six or eight more machines. They kept diving at us from both front and rear. By keeping close together the FE2bs protected each other very well and the HA finally drew off.[5]

Captain Carleton Clements, 22 Squadron, RFC

Flying round and round in circles, with each observer protecting the blind spot of the aircraft in front, and between them sending up a veritable hail of bullets, they presented a formidable collective defensive power. But the pilots had only their disciplined tactics to hold onto – it was vital that each pilot held his nerve and his place in the formation. If the formation cracked, the constituent aircraft were often doomed to destruction. The observers had to ignore the buffeting as they stood in the swaying nacelle cockpit, randomly swinging from side to side, totally exposed and struggling to maintain their precarious balance with nothing to hold onto but their guns:

The pilot was behind the observer in front of the engine and the observer was in the front nacelle or cockpit. In that cockpit I had three clips for the gun mounting to be assembled in. One for nose firing down, one firing to the right and one firing to the left. If you wanted to use the left gun the mounting used to be pulled out of its clip and it was swiveled round onto the left-hand clip. When you fired you had to put your knee against the mounting otherwise it would blow out with the explosion. In the rear you had one gun firing over the top plane on a movable mounting, a plunger arrangement where you just pressed the plunger underneath and the gun used to go as high as possible to fire over the back plane. In the cockpit you had spare drums and it was one of your duties to make certain that when you were firing the Lewis gun to see that you carry out all the necessary things for safe flying. For instance if you changed a drum you had to get hold of the drum on the gun, hold it very tight, take it off the gun, bend down and lay it very carefully in its compartment as an empty drum. We also had on the Lewis gun an ejector bag where the empty cartridge cases fell into. On one occasion my clip on my cartridge case gave way and all the rounds were whisked through the propeller in the wind stream. The observer's job was to in the main keep his eye on enemy aircraft and if necessary to ask the pilot to move the plane into position if they spotted an enemy plane to make sure that he could get into a position to fire at it.[6]

Sergeant Harold Taylor, 25 Squadron, RFC

Any mistake and the cartridges or drums could whip back in the slipstream, endangering the pilot; indeed a loose drum could easily smash the propeller and cause a catastrophic engine failure. In their open front cockpit the crew were completely unprotected from the bitter lash of the wind. And the same westerly winds also proved an additional threat when at last, mission accomplished, they tried to fly back to safety:

The prevailing wind was against us when returning from any flight over the lines and when it was strong, as it often was, our ground speed was much reduced thereby presenting us as 'sitting birds' for the anti-aircraft guns. When landing back at the aerodrome I have known the wind speed to be greater than my landing speed, so that I had to use my engine to get down after finding that my aeroplane was flying backwards relative to the ground.[7]

Second Lieutenant Geoffrey Hopkins, 22 Squadron, RFC

The implications of a reduction in speed from slow to extra slow was particularly serious if pilots were flying at a low altitude. It was open season for FE2bs as they crawled over the German lines:

I was doing end-on photography with Brassington; rather a sticky job at 900 feet above our front line. The Hun threw everything at you at that height: rifles, machine guns, field guns, 'flaming onions' – the lot. My petrol tank was plugged, no time to go over to the gravity tank, so I flopped down in a shell hole, just behind our lines, but fortunately out of sight of the Germans. I was lucky not to damage the camera, as it was said that we had only two or three of that type available. The photographs proved to be quite useful.[8]

Second Lieutenant T. H. Gladstone, 22 Squadron, RFC

All this was bad enough in summer, but in the depths of the winter of 1916–17, they would have needed a whole new lexicon to encapsulate the degree of suffering caused by the biting cold. Most did not try and just suffered as stoically as they could manage:

My feet and hands were frozen, and in spite of my face being well greased with Vaseline, my nose was frozen. On these flights, if any German machine had left its aerodrome to attack me, I could not have fired my guns. When eventually we landed home, all feeling had left my feet and hands and to bring the circulation back was a very painful procedure. I drank very hot milk and rum.[9]

Sergeant Harold Taylor, 25 Squadron, RFC

Once the aircraft were back at the airfield, it was the ground crew's turn to suffer as the freezing cold turned even routine maintenance tasks into tortuous rituals:

Our engines were water-cooled and, as there was no such thing as anti-freeze, radiators had to be drained after every flight. In the very cold spells, engines were very difficult to start, especially as prop swinging was a distinctly hazardous business when standing on frozen, slippery ground. At times the only way to get engines to start was to fill the radiators with water as near boiling point as possible. Water had to be heated by burning quantities of petrol in a small trench over which tins or canisters of water were hung. The unfortunate mechanics had a very rough time clambering up to fill the radiators with scalding water.[10]

Second Lieutenant Geoffrey Hopkins, 22 Squadron, RFC

Whatever the grinding physical discomforts, whatever the threat from the marauding Albatros or the lurking 'Archie', the work still went on. How could it not? In just a few weeks the British and Canadian infantry would be walking across the strip of No Man's Land between the two front lines. The machine guns would spit and chatter; worst of all, any German artillery batteries that had not been spotted and destroyed would fire a withering deluge of shells to sweep away the assaulting troops. The photographs taken from the FE2bs and BE2s were desperately needed to expose the hidden secrets of the German defences – to lay them naked before their enemy's shells:

The weather was at this time very cold with very bright frosty days, which kept both the squadron and the Photographic Section particularly busy. An average number of 2,000 photographs daily were being turned out by the section during this period, all from plates exposed by 22 Squadron, and on one occasion during the hours of 3 p.m. and

4 a.m. the next morning nearly 2,500 prints were made by this section of nine men, which was at that time something of a record, especially as the water for washing the prints had to be obtained from melting solid blocks of ice.[11]

Lieutenant B. F. Crane, Photographic Section, 14 Wing, RFC

ON the other side of the trench lines the situation was far more promising for the German Air Force. Its scout aircraft were outstanding and superior to anything the British could put up against them. The Germans also had in Leutnant Manfred von Richthofen one of the finest aerial leaders of the whole war; the man whose brilliant achievements would come to symbolise the slaughter of Bloody April. Richthofen was a man approaching the awesome peak of his powers as a scout leader and ace, in recognition of which he had been awarded the much coveted *Pour le Mérite* decoration, popularly known as the Blue Max. He was then posted in late January 1917 to take command of Jasta 11, based at La Brayelles on the western outskirts of Douai. Ever forthright in his views, he was not particularly pleased at the prospect of starting from scratch with a new Jasta which at that time had not had any success. Such a lack of results was no means unusual and illustrates how at this stage in the air war leadership was a vital ingredient in the success of the German scout formations. The Jasta was a small unit: normally twelve aircraft and fourteen pilots, with on average seven aircraft ready to fly on a given day. Without strong guidance they often seemed ineffective, not pressing their advantage and thereby allowing the numerical strength of the RFC to dominate the aerial battlefields. Despite the superiority of the German aircraft, most of their pilots were still sadly inexperienced and needed to be shown the way.

Yet there was great potential in Jasta 11 – amongst the young pilots were Leutnants Kurt Wolff and Karl Allmenröder who both were to become acclaimed aces over the next few months. They could not have been assigned a better teacher and leader, for Richthofen was clearly imbued with the spirit of Boelcke and his *dicta*. Richthofen was also flying the potent new Albatros DIII for the first time. This new Albatros had a yet more powerful Mercedes engine, and also incorporated into its basic design the 'vee strut' sesquiplane wing layout copied from the French Nieuport 17 scouts. This smaller lower wing was intended to improve the pilot's downward view. In a supreme gesture of confidence, Richthofen decided to adopt an all-red paint scheme, deliberately to mark himself out in the air and thereby strike fear into his enemies. It was the beginning of the enduring legend of the Red Baron.

It did not take long before Richthofen began to show his new Jasta the way forward. On 23 January he led the attack against a patrol of some six FE8s from 40 Squadron supporting a photographic reconnaissance mission. The FE8s were similar in general configuration to the DH2, single-seater pushers with a single forward-firing Lewis gun and a top speed of about 90 mph. In the mêlée that followed, Richthofen swooped down on Lieutenant John Hay. This was no helpless victim, for although the FE8 was outclassed, it could still be dangerous in capable and determined hands. As if to prove the point, that very morning Hay had shot down an Albatros C type two-seater. Now though, it was his turn to die:

> Together with seven of my aircraft, I attacked an enemy squadron west of Lens. The aircraft I had singled out caught fire after I had discharged 150 shots into it from a distance of 50 metres. The aircraft fell burning. The occupant of the aircraft fell out of it at a height of 500 metres. Immediately after it crashed on the ground, I could see a heavy black smoke cloud rising. The aircraft burned for some time with frequent flares of flame.[12]
>
> Leutnant Manfred von Richthofen, Jasta 11, German Army Air Force

Witnesses claimed that in his last desperate moments, Hay deliberately flung himself out of the aircraft to hasten his end. Once an aircraft caught fire, the inflammable confection of doped fabric, fuel and wood burned all too quickly. It was an agonising death and, unsurprisingly, some brave spirits decided that a leap into clean oblivion was preferable to the agonies of a blazing cockpit.*

The next day Richthofen struck again. On 24 January, seven FE2bs, two of them equipped with the all-important cameras, took off on a mission to take a series of mosaic photographs of the Vimy Ridge. Captain Oscar Greig, accompanied by his observer, Lieutenant John MacLennan, piloted one of the FE2bs charged with taking the photographs:

> When we got near the lines I asked 'Mac' whether our escort were in

---

* Parachutes were simply too bulky to be a practical proposition in the cramped cockpits of the time.

position. He shook his head, so I fired a green Very light as the signal to close up. After some little time he nodded to me and I took course for our photo area.[13]

Captain Oscar Greig, 25 Squadron, RFC

The escort took station behind and above them as they flew over Vimy Ridge. Once they had started their run, Greig and MacLennan were completely preoccupied in trying to achieve the tight mosaic structure required to make a success of the photographs. This was by no means an easy procedure:

This entails great accuracy in the actual exposures, a stopwatch being used so as to entail a correct overlap of each exposure. It is further necessary to keep at an exact altitude and to fly in a direct line, otherwise results obtained are unsatisfactory. Thus the taking of photographs fully employs the attention of both pilot and observer.[14]

Lieutenant John MacLennan, 25 Squadron, RFC

This dedication to the accuracy of their work was highly commendable, but lamentably rare in the view of some of the officers charged with collating and interpreting the photographs on the ground. One such was Lieutenant Thomas Hughes of 53 Squadron, an old RFC hand who over the war years had brought his cynical approach to a splendid peak of misanthropy:

Photographs were taken and a few of them happened to fall on points actually wanted, but it is a slow inefficient process, rather like the shooting of our 'Archies', depending more on plastering the ground with photographs than on deliberate aim – except with a really good observer. [15]

Lieutenant Thomas Hughes, 53 Squadron, RFC

On this occasion, to their credit, Greig and MacLennan were both entirely caught up in their task and consequently paid precious little attention to what was going on around them. They relied entirely on their escort to protect them from predators:

I was standing up on the rudder bar, looking from the map to the ground, getting the machine in exactly the right position and keeping it on an even keel, the camera being a fixed one. The observer was looking through the camera sights and just beginning to take the exposure. There had been a complete absence of anti-aircraft shells, but I thought this was because they were waiting for us to get further from our lines.[16]

Captain Oscar Greig, 25 Squadron, RFC

The problem of judging the appropriate distance between an escort and the naturally pre-occupied photographic machine was always tricky. Too far and the escort would be too late to intervene before the damage was done. Too close and they would have no chance to manoeuvre to interpose themselves between an attacking aircraft and the intended victim. In this case there is little doubt that the escorting FE2bs had allowed themselves to drift too far away. At this moment of maximum advantage Richthofen adroitly seized the chance to surprise his intended victims:

I heard a machine gun and saw several bullet holes appear in the left wing. I turned to the right in a steep bank, nearly upsetting my observer, hoping to get the enemy in front of me and also to get back to my escort, but on completion of half a circle, the enemy fired another burst from the right side, putting the engine out of action and hitting me in the right ankle, knocking that foot off the rudder bar.[17]

Captain Oscar Greig, 25 Squadron, RFC

The shock of that ruthless attack must have been tremendous. The first few shattering moments left little room for doubt as to the eventual result of the contest:

I was actually taking photographs when a burst of machine-gun fire from behind notified the attack. I looked round and perceived a red enemy machine diving away. In the first attack he shot through both oil and petrol tanks and splintered the propeller; Captain Greig was also shot through both legs.[18]

Lieutenant John MacLennan, 25 Squadron, RFC

The escort was too far away to intervene effectively. Indeed the escort pilots were probably more concerned with cutting their losses by protecting themselves and the second FE2b reconnaissance machine from a simultaneous attack by other members of Jasta 11. By this time, Richthofen had learnt through experience that the FE2b was all but defenceless to an attack launched from below and behind. He was expert in exploiting such weaknesses to his own advantage, as Captain Greig became only too aware:

I continued in circles, endeavouring to get a sight of the enemy, but he succeeded in keeping below and behind me. I saw several tracer bullets pass through the instrument board between me and my observer. The firing stopped and we made for the lines but at this turn the observer pointed behind the machine, indicating another attack. A second later a small scarlet biplane passed over us and went away to the right.[19]

Captain Oscar Greig, 25 Squadron, RFC

With the engine useless and Richthofen on their tail, it seemed that death was not so much casually beckoning as screaming loudly in their ears:

The machine could only glide and the manoeuvrability was greatly impaired through lack of any engine power. Von Richthofen attacked all the way down till the machine was but a few hundred feet from the ground. He attacked each time from below and behind, in which position we were unable to return fire. Only once did he get in front when we managed to get off two bursts from the front gun, but at longish range and without result.[20]

Lieutenant John MacLennan, 25 Squadron, RFC

In the circumstances all they could hope for was to get back down to earth with their lives intact and destroy what remained of their aircraft:

Tried everything to get the engine going but it only spluttered fitfully. There was nothing for it but to land, between Vimy and Fresnoy, gliding through a batch of about a dozen field telephone wires, breaking them with the machine and rolling through some more before the machine stopped.[21]

Captain Oscar Greig, 25 Squadron, RFC

MacLennan helped the wounded Greig out of his cockpit and then used his flare torch to set fire to their machine. Ironically, they managed a substantially better landing than their conqueror. For although their one brief burst of return fire had no impact, the inherent weakness that lurked in the sesquiplane wing structure of the new Albatros DIII, caused it to crack and forced Richthofen to make an emergency landing close to his recent victims. He came down to earth with rather a bump and had the additional embarrassment of overturning his Albatros:

The two Englishmen who were not a little surprised at my collapse, greeted me like sportsmen. They could not understand why I had landed so clumsily. They were the first two Englishmen whom I had brought down alive. Consequently it gave me particular pleasure to talk to them. I asked them whether they had previously seen my machine in the air, and one of them replied, 'Oh, yes, I know your machine very well. We call it *Le Petit Rouge*.[22]

Leutnant Manfred von Richthofen, Jasta 11, German Air Service

Richthofen was no fool and invariably took every action possible to reduce the horrendous dangers to which he was exposed on a daily basis. It is therefore no surprise to find that after this close escape for a while he switched to flying the Halberstadt DII Scout. The wing weakness in the Albatros DIII had by that time been linked with several accidents and it was generally withdrawn for modification and much-needed strengthening. In copying the wing structure of the Nieuport Scouts, the Germans had also incorporated its frailty into the Albatros design.

IN a further expression of their increasing confidence and aerial strength, the Germans began to bomb the British airfields on a far more regular basis. Thus it was that at 0300 on 11 January 1917, 16 Squadron based at Bruay had an unscheduled visit from German bombers:

Mr Hun sent 'umpteen' machines over to bomb our aerodrome, he made a very successful show of it, dropped fourteen bombs on the aerodrome. One fell in C Flight hangar, set it on fire and burnt five machines to cinders. There were only five casualties, including Sergeant Drew (a pilot) who was hit by a piece of one of our own bombs – which was attached to one of the machines on fire – whilst he was on the top of the adjoining hangar, preventing sparks from setting that alight too. When he was hit he was blown off the top of the hangar onto the ground – about a 20 foot fall. Within an hour of when the Huns bombed us, we went over and had set fire to one of their hangars at Douai aerodrome. I lay in my bed the whole time and heard the bombs bursting about 50 yards from the house. Did not think it was so near as the aerodrome or should have got up. As it was I missed no end of fun.[23]

Second Lieutenant William Lidsey, 16 Squadron, RFC

The newly arrived 43 Squadron missed none of the fun and games on the night of 21 January when the Germans launched a punishing raid on the Treizennes airfield. They shared the airfield with the FE8 pusher scouts of 40 Squadron, under the command of the pre-war aviator and toast of the London stage, Major Robert Lorraine:

One night all the alarms all over the camp started ringing simultaneously. Fire had broken out in one of his [Lorraine's] sheds which housed four FEs. His fire picket and our fire picket doubled to the spot, but there was nothing to be done except to form a semi-circle around the blazing hangar and let the fire burn itself out. The petrol tanks had gone up, the doped wings were burning furiously, the dried wood of the hangar likewise, while machine gun ammunition went off with continuous pops. Adjoining the hangar was a lean-to shed which held various mechanics' tools. One little sergeant thought that he was being of help by going into the lean-to, which was not yet in flames, and starting to throw out spanners, vices, screwdrivers and other implements. Hardly had he started this somewhat futile task when with a bound Robert Lorraine entered within the ring, darted in front of the assembled squadrons, through the glare and into the shed. Seizing the little sergeant by the coat collar he pulled him away and hurled him towards the fire picket. 'Away! If this is anybody's place it is mine!' He shouted in a voice of ringing tones which carried right across the aerodrome, and then, in order to show, and quite rightly so, that the destruction of the four burning machines was not irreparable, and that he, as the one responsible, could divert his mind to other matters more mundane, he strode to the middle of the arena and there, in the full glare of the light, performed a perfectly natural function in front of the admiring eyes of the assembled officers and mechanics.[24]

Lieutenant Harold Balfour, 43 Squadron, RFC

If the new boys' morale had not been shattered by the sight of a senior officer publicly urinating in such farcical circumstances, there was far worse to come. 43 Squadron was equipped with Sopwith 1½ Strutters, a two-seater biplane typically powered by a 110 hp Clerget. It had a synchronised Vickers gun at the disposal of the pilot and a Lewis gun for the observer behind. As a multi-purpose aircraft it had enjoyed a brief heyday during 1916, but by the standards of 1917 it was slow and under-powered, without the agility necessary to pose a real threat to the single-seaters that so often swarmed around it.

Feeling their way into the air war, 43 Squadron started slowly, trying to introduce their novices with the minimal possible risk. One of the few with active service experience amongst their ranks was Lieutenant Alan Dore, who had already done one tour of duty on the Western Front with 13 Squadron:

> Our first piece of work. Scott leading, myself deputy and one other. Patrol from Estaires to Mour-les-Mines. We rise to 10,000 feet. In spite of Vaseline smeared liberally over my face, the icy blast cuts like a knife. Just before patrol is due home I see a Hun biplane travelling at right angles to us and some 500 feet above. Signal to observer to fire, but gun jams. Swing round, leave formation and attack with front gun, which also stops after firing a few shots. Rejoin formation. In air for two and a half hours.[25]
>
> Lieutenant Alan Dore, 43 Squadron, RFC

After a rash of aerial accidents, their commanding officer, Major Sholto Douglas, was determined to demonstrate to his inexperienced pilots that the Sopwith 1½ Strutter was perfectly capable of withstanding the stresses of aerial combat if it was handled with due skill and attention:

> I took up one of our aircraft to demonstrate to my pilots just what could be done with it. In the back seat I had as a passenger Tom Purdey, my Adjutant, and thinking that thirteen might be the right number, psychologically, for such a display, I performed thirteen consecutive loops. Everything about my demonstration went off very well until I landed, and then I found that I had not warned Purdey about what I was going to do, and that he had not been strapped in. Throughout the whole of the thirteen loops he had been hanging on to the fixtures in the interior of the cockpit, and grim death had been staring him in the face. He could all too easily have fallen out, and I was very angry with myself for such thoughtlessness on my part, although Purdey, after his first fright, took it all in good spirit. My pilots, I need hardly say, were delighted with what they thought was an enormous joke.[26]
>
> Major Sholto Douglas, 43 Squadron, RFC

However, the real combat weaknesses of the Sopwith 1½ Strutter could not be laughed off. When caught flying on their own by the powerful German scouts they were sickeningly vulnerable as, although they had two guns, the layout of the aircraft made it difficult to coordinate their use in action:

> While the pilot was weaving the plane around in order to use his fixed gun, the poor gunner in the rear had little chance of taking effective aim from an unpredictably swerving platform largely obstructed by a swinging and bobbing tail. So only one gun or the other could be effective at the same time, and what we had was two independent gunners, back to back, neither of whom knew what the other was trying to do, and each of whom wondered what was going on when he heard a burst of fire from the other end of the plane. That situation might have been improved by some workable system of communication between pilot and gunner, whose cockpits were a yard or more apart with a tank in between.[27]
>
> Lieutenant Frank Courtney, 45 Squadron, RFC

Once again, the only answer was to come together to achieve a far greater united strength in the face of the common enemy. For outclassed aircraft, strong well-drilled formations were their only chance of survival:

> After some weeks we learnt the best tactics: as soon as ever we saw a gathering crowd of Huns above us we would go round and round in a circle, the whole formation of us, each one chasing the tail of the machine in front, until we formed a perfect revolving wheel. The wheel would then edge slowly towards the lines and woe betide any German who tried to come down on top of that circle. He would get the con-centrated fire of six observers' guns, and, brave fighters as they were, no German could face that with impunity.[28]
>
> Lieutenant Harold Balfour, 43 Squadron, RFC

Naturally the Germans observed the development of British defensive formation tactics with considerable interest:

> When flying in large squads, the English aircraft keep close together in order to be able to come to one another's assistance at any given moment. When attacked, they maintain even closer formations. If an English aircraft which has fallen behind is attacked, the first planes

of the enemy formation make left and right turns and hurry to its assistance. After the rest of the formation has passed them, they close up the rear as the last planes.[29]

Leutnant Manfred von Richthofen, Jasta 11, German Air Service

The method of attack the German pilots developed in such circumstances was simple but effective. Their aim was to split one aircraft away from the safety of the huddle and then to take their kill in relative safety:

Woe betide any one of our people who got out of the circle. I saw this happen twice. On one occasion the wings were shot off a machine in my flight, and one of my best young pilots, a South African named Rymer, and his observer were pitched out into space as the machine disintegrated. I watched Rymer's bright leather coat as his body fell downwards to earth. I could follow it for thousands of feet. The other occasion I think the pilot must have suffered from engine trouble and have been forced to leave the circle. His petrol tank must have been punctured and the aeroplane soaked with petrol, when an incendiary bullet struck it, for, one moment it was gliding away from the wheel and the next it was a mass of flame from wing-tip to wing tip.[30]

Lieutenant Harold Balfour, 43 Squadron, RFC

When smaller numbers were caught, they could not put up the necessary combined firepower to fend off the Germans. In such circumstances disaster could strike very quickly indeed:

An unfortunate day. A patrol of three cut up by eight Halberstadts this morning. Captain Rutter lands with most of his wires shot through and the dead body of his observer, Lieutenant Docking, in the back seat. Lieutenant Rock we hear comes to ground near Merville shot through the back, his observer with a bullet through his hand. Lieutenant Edelston is hit by 'Archie' and his rudder controls shot away. He crashes to earth but saves himself.[31]

Lieutenant Alan Dore, 43 Squadron, RFC

The constant trickle of casualties gradually undermined the confidence of all but the most foolhardy. These were young men, many not out of their teens. Although initially they may not have known the meaning of the word fear, they pretty soon had a fair grasp of exactly what it entailed:

Every night there would be brought to me a sealed envelope containing orders from Wing Headquarters, for our operations for the next day. Tough though some of those orders were, the fact that they came from Wilfred Freeman meant that I was able to accept them with confidence. They would usually arrive when we were about halfway through dinner, and I would read them out and then give instructions about how they were to be executed.[32]

Major Sholto Douglas, 43 Squadron, RFC

His pilots watched their commanding officer in the certain knowledge that the envelope's contents could quite literally seal their fate next day:

Douglas would open the envelope, read the squadron's operation orders from the wing, then detail out to us our jobs for the next day. Somehow food lost its attraction and spirits sank for an appreciable time after we knew the contents of that envelope.[33]

Lieutenant Harold Balfour, 43 Squadron, RFC

Nevertheless, the Sopwith 1½ Strutters were not always helpless victims and Leutnant Erwin Böhme of Jasta Boelcke had good reason to remember an unlucky encounter with one Sopwith as he tried to score his thirteenth accredited victory:

I am writing to you in bed. My left hand is of no use in holding the sheet of paper still. The bed from which I am writing is in a field hospital in Cambrai. I find myself to be in a field hospital because of a malevolent Englishman, who by all rights should no longer be alive, who treacherously shot me in the left arm. It was a two-seater Sopwith which I had already put out of action and who was headed downward. For that reason, I spared him in a burst of sportsmanlike grace – that's what I get for my *noblesse*! Don't fear for my life, not even for my arm! The bones and nerves are undamaged. The round sits in my arm. The thing at times hurts very much. I am only angry about having to leave my squadron in the lurch just now when the spring hunt has begun.[34]

Leutnant Erwin Böhme, Jasta Boelcke, German Army Air Force

To add insult to the undoubted injury caused by his unknown assailants, Böhme had obviously entirely misjudged the amount of damage he had caused prior to his downfall. From the records it appears that the English crew must have escaped relatively unscathed, for there were no casualties reported amongst the Sopwith 1½ Strutters that day!

Even more vulnerable than the Sopwith 1½ Strutters were the venerable army cooperation machines. For the most part these were variants of the hopelessly obsolete BE2s: still far too many BE2cs, but also the BE2es, BE2gs and BE2hs. Outclassed by the Fokker in 1915, an additional small amount of extra engine power still left the BE2 variants death-traps in the face of the Albatros onslaught two years later. Yet the work they did had not diminished in importance. They may have been slow and unmanoeu-vrable, with a negligible ability to defend themselves, but so long as their cameras and wireless transmitters worked they were still deadly and func-tional weapons of war. Every day that weather permitted the artillery observation aircraft plied their trade up and down above the front lines, guiding shells to the points of maximum damage and inconvenience for the Germans below:

> Shoot on two trench junctions with 154 Siege Battery (9.2-in Howitzers). Shoot went very well from observer's point of view, but the guns shot badly and did not hit either of the targets. Shells from these guns take quite a long time to reach their objective. It was quite easy to watch the flash of the gun and then turn round to the target and wait for the shell to arrive. We could see the targets quite well without crossing the line. A 'straffed' village looks very peculiar from the air when there is snow on the ground; Hebuterne reminded me of a model village made in chocolate that had been nibbled by mice. Everything was wonderfully clear at 3,500 feet and one could see that every house had been smashed in by shell fire. The stump of the church spire still stands and looks like a badly damaged pencil point. The cold was simply fierce; after the first hour I felt as if I was dying from the feet up to the waist. After a bit I got used to it and it didn't worry me, but I found I could hardly walk when I got out of the machine. The new jerkin from home kept the top half of my body fairly warm.[35]
>
> Second Lieutenant Charles Smart, 5 Squadron, RFC

A kind of inner serenity and calm was essential on artillery observation missions. There were so many niggling problems that threatened to overwhelm the patience of the most observant of saints:

> There are dozens of pitfalls: badly sighted ground strips, a battery who won't fire when given the word 'Go', slowness in working out the right

correction, stupidity, slackness, bloody jealous mindedness and wireless failures, which may be on the ground or in the air. Then there is the pilot who is always in the wrong position. He never sees a burst, perhaps it is not entirely his fault – the bursts may be 1,000 yards out and fall amongst other shells. Then enemy aircraft appear and chase the observation plane. Failing that the Hun may sit up above waiting for our battery to fire, so that he can pinpoint the position. If our gunners have seen him, they are not going to fire. There are lots of difficulties.[36]

Captain Eric Routh, 16 Squadron, RFC

Yet with patience and skill all the problems could be overcome, and for every flight that failed there were more taking off. Training in the air and on the ground was given a high priority. Gradually the technology was improved to allow ever more aircraft crew to operate their wirelesses on a cramped front. A 'clapper' break gave the wireless set a six-tone range so that from the artillery battery it was easier to identify which aircraft was signalling to them. It was soon found possible to put up artillery observation aircraft at a rate of four for every 1,000 yards of front without their signals jamming each other into a cacophonous inaudibility. A programme of properly training as many observers as possible was begun with the intention of improving their Morse-code skills. Wireless operators were also attached in pairs to each of the gun batteries. Vocal communication was not possible in 1917 and in the crowded skies speed of transmission was all important:

Observers were worked up to 'buzz' at sixteen words per minute. This led to their working at about twelve words per minute in the air; their messages took a shorter time to send with the result that chances of jamming were reduced, and they were able to observe an appreciably larger number of rounds during one flight. We came to the conclusion that it was uneconomical of time to observe for more than one battery at a time. On the whole, an observer took much the same length of time to observe for two batteries in series as to observe for them concurrently; the former method, however, left each battery in turn free for other work.[37]

Major Paul Maltby, 16 Squadron, RFC

Signals between the aircraft and the gun batteries were continuously monitored by central wireless stations established near the front line so that any problems that developed could be rapidly detected and corrected.

Using the superheavy 12-in railway artillery they could even reach deep behind the German lines. The railheads at which troops first arrived at the front, the roads up which they had to march, the ordinary soldiers' billets, the *estaminets* where they tried to relax – they were all liable to disruptive long-range shell fire:

> I had great sport shelling one of their railheads at long range. It was a pretty dangerous shoot by reason of it being so far back but I did it in the evening and got off scot free. There were three engines in the yards when I plopped the first big one in. They were preparing to pull a lot of stuff out to take it back somewhere. However the drivers apparently got wind up, and scuttled for it down the line. I almost got the last one. It *was* exciting. I tried to hit the points in front of him, but he was too quick and got away. After that I let her rip into the goods yard, and when I left they were popping salvoes in smashing things right and left.[38]
>
> Captain Bernard Rice, 8 Squadron, RFC

Day after day their work went on, the danger seemingly never-ending, coming from a variety of deadly sources. Even the British shells flying through the sky could send shivers down their spines as they were buffeted about in the air by the shock waves of near misses to their aircraft.

> Our guns were shooting like steam and we got some wonderful bumps from our own shells when we were hanging over Puiseaux. Should like to know how far these shells are away when you can feel the bump. I think some of the gunners must fire on purpose when they see a machine somewhere in the line of flight of the shell just for the fun of seeing the plane rock up and down – wish I could catch one doing it![39]
>
> Second Lieutenant Charles Smart, 5 Squadron, RFC

The German anti-aircraft fire that many affected to despise could also be extremely dangerous to the corps aircraft. The nature of the pilots' and observers' task meant that they were often flying low and usually in straight, easily predictable lines. This made them relatively easy targets for 'Archie', as the anti-aircraft guns were facetiously known in the RFC messes:

> Fagan and Hopkins came up and told me that Mac had been hit by 'Archie'. Hopkins was up with him and he was hit over Miraumont. He wirelessed down, 'Doctor, hit' but the aerodrome did not get his

message. Counter-batteries got it however and telephoned to us and Ward was waiting with a medical orderly and tender as soon as he landed. They got him out of the machine with difficulty and found three large holes in his stomach and thigh. He was immediately sent to the casualty clearing station and was at once operated on. We have just telephoned (9.30 p.m.) to find out how he is, and he is still under the anaesthetic, so we must wait till tomorrow for news. The doctors however did not give us very much hope. Poor old Mac.[40]

Lieutenant Francis Cave, 4 Squadron, RFC

Captain John McMillan was one casualty amongst many, but he must have been a popular man, for the mess of 4 Squadron was soon hanging on every breath of news from the hospital:

Hopkins went with the CO to see Mac. He says he is fairly cheerful; but that the Doctor does not give a very good report.[41]

Lieutenant Francis Cave, 4 Squadron, RFC

As the wounded man lay in his bed, his worried comrades dropped in one by one to see him. Whatever the bold face that McMillan could rustle up, it was plain to his friends that he was all but doomed:

I went to see Mac. We were only allowed to see him for about five minutes. Poor fellow, he looks very bad, his eyes being all blurred, evidently in great pain. However he was trying to be fairly cheerful and talked about going home. Poor fellow, I'm afraid he *is* going Home as the doctor says he has no hope for him. I do hope he manages to pull through.[42]

Lieutenant Francis Cave, 4 Squadron, RFC

Next day came the news they had been expecting:

As soon as I came into breakfast, Hopkins told me that poor old Mac died this morning. R.I.P. I think it is the worst news we have had since Bunny was killed. We are all fearfully upset and the mess is merely gloomy and nothing else. Poor old Mac was the last man we could spare.[43]

Lieutenant Francis Cave, 4 Squadron, RFC

Another pilot, Second Lieutenant Charles Smart, also had an unpleasant encounter with the German 'Archie' when he went up with his observer

Lieutenant Miller. As they got to the front lines they found themselves literally surrounded by a cloud of bursting shells and whirring shrapnel fragments:

> The Germans knew what we were up for and simply squirted 'Archie' at us, we couldn't get away from it. They started in on us when we were a good mile over our side of the lines and kept it up the whole time we were in view. One shell went off just under my seat and lifted the whole machine up in the air. I felt sure we were hit but the machine seemed alright; after landing about two hours later I found we had been hit and it is a wonder that shell didn't end my career. A large piece had hit the fuselage about 3 feet behind the small of my back and broke one of the longerons. The machine might quite easily have broken in two. To cap everything, the engine conked out when we were right over the lines, fortunately I managed to glide back and land safely in a field about 3 miles from the aerodrome. I had to stick by the machine for four solid hours till help came with the result that I got my lunch at 5.30 p.m. with nothing in between from breakfast at 8 a.m.[44]
>
> Second Lieutenant Charles Smart, 5 Squadron, RFC

On this occasion Smart had been lucky. When he went out to reclaim the BE2e a couple of days later he found that Nature, in the form of the handiwork of a stolid French farmer, had intervened to complicate what he had imagined would be a simple task:

> Went out by tender and on arriving at the field found that the farmer had covered same with heaps of manure all set out neatly in straight lines. This was rather annoying as the only way to take off was down a more or less highly scented avenue between the heaps. The idea struck me that if I swerved in taking off and hit one of the heaps I should hardly land in a bed of roses. Anyhow we got the engine running and I taxied the machine round into position, opened the throttle and the ungainly waddle changed into the tiptoe rush which a plane always makes before it takes off and up we went climbing rapidly in the heavily laden air. Soon we were in fresh clear atmosphere and landed safely in the aerodrome without further adventure.[45]
>
> Second Lieutenant Charles Smart, 5 Squadron, RFC

Whatever the danger posed by 'Archie', the main threat to the army cooperation BE2 aircraft was undoubtedly the predatory German scouts.

Their prime function was to blind the British 'eyes in the sky' and it was not difficult for them to locate their prey. Once they had evaded or broken through the forward British offensive patrols then there were the observation aircraft, as regular as clockwork, above the trenches. The Germans were fighting a serious defensive war. There was no room for knight errantry; the object was to kill as quickly as possible with the minimum possible risk.

> As the artillery machines were to be found singly on both sides of the line, the duty of the German fighting pilot was made easy. The most usual tactics adopted were to attack a two-seater with a formation of about five Halberstadts. Each machine would dive in succession on the two-seater, and open fire at close range. After a dive, machines would turn right- or left-handed and climb, ready to repeat the attack if necessary, or to rendezvous and continue the patrol. On the other hand many of our machines were shot down by single single-seaters. In these cases, the two-seater was either attacked from over the tail or from under the tail. The Scarpe Valley provided the enemy with an excellent background, if flying low, along which to attack. I saw several German machines approach the line in this way, and owing to their colour, they were extremely difficult to see. Thus were they able to arrive unnoticed under the artillery machines, and to climb to the attack.[46]
>
> Lieutenant Donald Stevenson, 12 Squadron, RFC

The BE2s simply had to find some feasible way of defending themselves. Given the forest of wires and struts that surrounded the observer in his forward cockpit, it was essential that he be ready for action at a moment's notice. This meant that more of the observation work had to be carried out by the pilot:

> Observers had to abandon their former role as observers altogether, and had to concentrate their attention on keeping a lookout against surprise from attack. It was difficult trying to maintain the morale of the squadron, and to get the work done, but thanks to the example which the older hands set, both were kept up. The majority of the casualties occurred amongst pilots newly out from England, and were the result of inexperience combined with inferior aircraft. Once past a certain point pilots rarely became casualties.[47]
>
> Major Paul Maltby, 16 Squadron, RFC

The pilots and observers lucky enough to survive their first few clashes with German scouts put their experiences to work to try to maximise their slim chance of continued survival:

> The first precaution we took was to see that the observer knelt on his seat, facing the pilot, and ready to bring the rear Lewis gun into action. It soon became apparent that those who, when attacked, dived steeply away from the aggressor, became casualties. For this reason, the following tactics were adopted: If far over the line: fly towards the line, doing gentle turns to right and left, and at the same time altering the height – switchbackwise. If near the line: fly towards the line, diving and doing gentle turns to the right and left. Both these methods had the advantage of keeping the best field of fire towards the enemy – rear field – whilst it made it difficult for the enemy to use his sights and to follow. If suddenly attacked: should the attack have come as a complete surprise, we thought that to do nothing, or to slightly dive, was to court disaster. For this reason, when a tracer bullet passed the machine, or guns were heard at close range, one of the following movements were made – a 'flat turn' or a 'stall'. Both these movements were sufficient to spoil the shooting of the single-seater, whilst giving one time to see it, and to make up one's mind.[48]
>
> Lieutenant Donald Stevenson, 12 Squadron, RFC

Sometimes no amount of experience could prevent a gut-wrenching surprise. On one occasion Second Lieutenant Wilfred Cox, acting as observer to Lieutenant W. Buckingham, discovered that nothing was necessarily as it seemed in the dangerous skies:

> We were caught napping by a German pilot who was flying one of No. 32 Squadron's DH2s which had been captured the day before. Fortunately his gun must have failed after a short burst, but one of the bullets must have knocked out the screws holding my floor boards in, because when jumping for the back gun the floor gave way and I dropped through as far as my waist, losing the Lewis drums, spare joystick and record of observations.[49]
>
> Second Lieutenant Wilfred Cox, 15 Squadron, RFC

Not surprisingly, there were many who objected to the constant sacrifice that they were being called on to make for the general good:

Wynne Eaton tried in the evening to get an escort for tomorrow from 11th Wing but was told, 'We can't give you a close escort, we can only give you "protection".' When pressed as to what this would mean, it appeared that they would just go on their ordinary patrols this side of the lines and if they saw the BE2e being attacked, would go to it, by which time of course the BE2e would almost certainly be destroyed. This is a good example of the use of army squadrons who simply patrol the lines and are useless for any cooperation with corps squadrons, which brings one back once again to the vital necessity of having at least a scout per flight in corps squadrons as No. 1 used to have last summer. Army squadrons would probably be needed as well, and would be very necessary in a battle, but if one scout squadron was split up amongst the corps squadrons, it would be ten times as valuable.[50]

Lieutenant Thomas Hughes, 53 Squadron, RFC

As is so often the case with cynics who claim to discern the obvious that their foolish commanders strangely cannot see, Hughes was failing to understand the bigger picture. As the casualties mounted Trenchard was walking a narrow line between responding to the cries of his slaughtered reconnaissance crews and maintaining the vitally important offensive deep into the German territory. Once he had surrendered to the siren cries for defence he would inexorably lose all control of the airspace above the battlefields as the German scouts simply pushed further and further forward.

Eventually a compromise was adopted and close escorts of two scouts per artillery observation aircraft were provided, but only in sectors where consistent and excessive losses had been incurred. These dedicated escorts were backed up by general line patrols of up to seven aircraft, while offensive patrols continued to try to intercept and destroy the German predators before they could get anywhere near their prey. It was now apparent that scout aircraft also had to act in formation, flying under the control of a patrol leader at all times. Not only was this vital when the British were flying aircraft inferior to the German scouts, but it greatly added to the impact of an attack when the enemy were surprised and brought into action in circumstances that were unfavourable to them.

One failure of the RFC during January and February of 1917 was that the German construction of the Siegfried Stellung far to the rear of their existing lines was for a long time not adequately reported or photographically reconnoitred. As they gradually became aware of its existence it became known to the British as the Hindenburg Line. The new German fortifications were built to the specifications of Colonel Friedrich von Lossberg and were intended as a safe refuge should the Allied offensive in 1917 force the Germans to fall back. Rather than a single defensive line it was a fortified band that tried to put into action all the Germans had learnt of defensive warfare during the Allied offensives of 1916. A forward zone about 600 yards deep had the garrison concentrated in strong points and machine-gun pillboxes, behind intimidating belts of barbed wire up to 50 feet wide intended to slow the progress of any attack. A second zone of the defence system envisioned a series of pillboxes and fortresses with criss-crossing fields of fire, which would further break up the cohesion of an attack. This would render attacking troops vulnerable to swift retribution from counter-attack troops who would emerge from specially built dugouts deep underground. Other counter-attack divisions were to be held in readiness to move up to any threatened sectors. The cunning use of reverse slopes meant that ground observation would be severely impeded. By any standards it was a massive scheme that dwarfed all previous defensive lines.

The Germans had begun this work in the autumn of 1916, but its piecemeal construction, the prevailing nuisance of winter weather conditions and the more pressing priorities of reconnoitring and photographing other new German lines that lay closer to the current front meant that the enormous significance of the emerging Hindenburg Line was not initially grasped by the British command. Yet eventually it became clear that something big was going on. The Germans could not hide new entrenchments on such a vast scale from the unblinking gaze of the aerial cameras. Bit by bit sections of the new line were photographed and charted by the RFC:

> Our 22 Squadron was ordered to undertake a photographic reconnaissance of the enemy's new defence line. This recce was considered in those days something of an event, as the reported line was about 20 miles behind our present front line. This recce was led by Captain Clements and the squadron commander (Major Learmount) also flew in the formation, the escort being provided by Sopwith Pups of 54 Squadron. Despite the somewhat unfavourable weather conditions very successful photographs were obtained of portions of the line. A second recce was undertaken later under better conditions. On this

occasion the photographs obtained formed practically a complete mosaic of the Hindenburg Line from Havrincourt to St Quentin and were extremely valuable as they showed that the enemy was working hard on a very strong system of defence, with numerous concrete emplacements and with wiring which consisted of three separate lines, each many yards wide along the whole front, and in places large triangles of wire forming a chain were thrown out in front of the other lines of wiring. These made excellent stereoscopic photographs.[51]

Lieutenant B. F. Crane, Photographic Section, 14 Wing, RFC

As the British High Command puzzled as to the meaning of the Hindenburg Line and simultaneously concentrated their minds on the imminent offensives, they were about to be made aware in no uncertain terms of the views of their political masters. Lloyd George may have been unable, for cogent political reasons, to sack Haig, but he could yet bind him to the authority of another.

Lloyd George had become a convert to the Messianic vision that Nivelle projected with such clarity and force. On 26 February 1917 he therefore convened the joint Anglo-French Conference at Calais with the intention of securing agreement by hook or by crook to unambiguously subordinate Haig under the direction and control of Nivelle. Liaising with the French politicians and generals, whilst maintaining a cool detachment from Haig and Robertson, Lloyd George stage-managed the production of a French paper that had the temerity to suggest that the French commander-in-chief should be in full command of Haig and the British Expeditionary Force. Only mundane matters connected with personnel and discipline would be left to Haig and his General Headquarters Staff. A furious row inevitably resulted, as Haig and Robertson rounded on Lloyd George. In the event a complete breakdown in relations between the senior British officers and their democratic leader was only averted by a compromise dreamt up by the wily Secretary to the War Cabinet, Maurice Hankey. It was agreed that the disputed subordination was only for the duration of the Nivelle offensive and that Haig was granted the right of appeal to the British government if he considered that the overall safety of the BEF was at stake.

The British High Command remained absolutely furious at what they considered to be nothing less than a premeditated stab in the back. Their diaries and written accounts seethe with barely suppressed hatred and a blistering contempt for Lloyd George and his ideas of war:

It is all utterly wrong and unnecessary. If the French do get a great success and end the war in their next big attack, which is very unlikely, not much harm will have been done. They will claim all the credit for the whole war, as well as for this attack, but that does not matter. If the big French attack is indecisive in its result, then inevitably, as the war goes on, our army will become the biggest on the Western Front (unless Lloyd George sends everybody off on side-shows), and there is bound to be interminable friction. If the French attack fails altogether, we shall have the whole weight of the German Army on the top of us, and the position will be even more difficult. If Joffre were still in command of the French and they were putting the British Army under him there might be some justification for it, for he has all the experience of the war behind him, but Nivelle is new to the game, with far less experience of actual fighting than Douglas Haig, and, according to what we are hearing from French officers, he does not seem to have the confidence even of his own generals.[52]

Brigadier-General John Charteris, Intelligence Officer, General Headquarters, BEF

In the event, neither the newly supreme Nivelle or the still fuming Haig, would see their plans come to fruition as originally conceived. The Germans proved regrettably uncooperative in refusing to hold on to tactically weak positions. In late February, they began the first of a series of withdrawals from the battle-scarred Somme sector towards the sanctuary of the new Hindenburg Line. This process would accelerate dramatically in mid-March. As an act of defensive generalship it had considerable merits. The German front was shortened at a stroke by 25 miles freeing up to fourteen divisions for rest, training and as a general reserve to be directed as required. How would the Allies respond?

CHAPTER THREE

MARCH SQUALLS

As you see from the papers we have been advancing. The papers appear
to think it is a great victory. It is in a way, but it is not as if we were
pushing them back. They are merely retiring to a very strong line some
distance in the rear. Personally I think it is a very bad thing for us. The
gain of territory is insignificant while the difficulty of attacking the
new line will be very much greater.[1]

Lieutenant Leslie Horridge, 4 Squadron, RFC

The onset of the staged German retirement from the exposed salient of
the Somme battlefields was indeed not good news for the Allies. Their
gain in ground was as nothing compared to the unfortunate tactical implications and the manifold challenges that they would have to overcome in
planning their spring offensives. While the generals scratched their heads
and sought to find out exactly what was going on they sent out ever more
reconnaissance aircraft to try and track the German retirement. Thus, as
a direct result of the confusion on the ground, the scale of aerial fighting
was ratcheted up until it reached an almost unbearable level of tension.
Both sides were frantic to conceal their own movements and plans on the
ground; desperate to discover their enemy's intentions; more than willing
to make sacrifices to achieve their objectives. The British had the numbers
of aircraft backed by the sheer guts and fortitude it would take to succeed,
but the Germans had the superior quality aircraft and an equal determination to extract a heavy price for every contact patrol, every photograph
taken, every artillery target registered.

Some of the adventures suffered by various RFC personnel on just
one 'ordinary' day – 4 March – give a dramatic indication of the nature
of their work and the many trials and tribulations they had to undergo on

an almost hourly basis when they were in the air. That day Lieutenant Charles Smart, accompanied by his observer Lieutenant Cotton, took off on yet another photographic reconnaissance. They were in trouble almost immediately:

'Archie' was simply fierce and started in long before we reached our own front line, they hammered away at us the whole time we were on the job. Just as I got to the far end of our area which was about 6 miles over, there was a terrific 'Crump' and one seemed to burst about 3 feet away from my left ear. Several things happened at once: the machine was lifted bodily about 20 feet into the air, a shower of wood splinters flew into my face, streams of petrol squirted all over me up to the waist and a cupboard fixed in the pilot's seat above my feet fell down onto my left foot and partially jammed the rudder. It was quite evident that we were hit. I was frightened to death, but managed to turn off both petrol tanks, switch off the engine and pull out the wireless plug. 'Archie' was still bursting around us. I heaved the machine round and pushed the nose down so that we were doing about 110 miles per hour towards our own lines expecting every moment that the whole show would catch on fire, for petrol was pouring out of the back tank and I was having a sort of bath in the stuff. Fortunately we were up a good height (about 8,500 feet) so we cleared No Man's Land at about 2,000 feet with the 'Archie' pops getting fainter and fainter as we left them behind. Once over the lines I had a good look round at the machine and saw that the most serious damage was a large hole in the rear petrol tank, so I decided to come down low and try to start the engine again on the front tank. I dropped down to about 1,000 feet, turned on the front tank and after some difficulty got the engine started again, all the time in fear and trembling in case the machine should catch fire. I managed to get home and felt much relieved when I dropped the machine in the aerodrome. The wings and tail were pretty well peppered and the machine will be out of commission for several days. The piece of 'Archie' that hit the tank went in about two feet in front of my shirt and about six inches behind the observer's back, quite near enough for both of us. It was the observer's second trip in the air and he didn't realise that anything had happened to the machine at all, it seemed a bit unfair that I should have had all this excitement to myself. The photographs came out very well and showed a lot of new work in the shape of trenches, gun emplacements etc.[2]

Second Lieutenant Charles Smart, 5 Squadron, RFC

A few days later Smart went home on a well-earned leave – he must surely have needed it! Further along the front another far more experienced observer found that 4 March was not to be one of his better days. First, William Lidsey was put through the full gamut of tortured emotions by a sadly inexpert pilot:

Left the ground at 12.45 p.m. with Lieutenant Morris, had a most awful take-off in a strong wind, very nearly crashed, this sent him practically off his head, so that he nearly lost control of the machine. Had three tries to get back to the aerodrome before landing. On landing he fell forward over the controls practically in a faint. During the flight, which lasted thirty minutes, he stalled the machine three times and side-slipped twice. I do not want another such experience, it was decidedly unpleasant. Left the ground again at 2.20 with Captain Neale, returned ten minutes later owing to engine trouble. Left the ground again at 3.20 p.m. with Captain Neale on photography. When over Bailleul – about 3 miles behind the Hun lines – we were attacked by two Huns, one being the man with a machine painted red, who has done us so much damage. I opened fire with my gun first and they cleared off. During the two hours that we were up, we saw nine other Huns, but did not fight any of them. Exposed four plates all of which were underexposed.[3]

Second Lieutenant William Lidsey, 16 Squadron, RFC

It is difficult on the basis of such misadventures to decide whether Lidsey was extremely fortunate to survive such a string of potential disasters, or wretchedly unlucky to have suffered so much torment in a just a few hours. Meanwhile, 4 March saw yet another sequence of calamities for the Sopwith 1½ Strutters of the benighted 43 Squadron:

Rather an unfortunate day. First formation ran into eleven Halberstadts. Scott's machine landed at Hasdigneul riddled with bullets both occupants untouched. Wood and his observer missing, shot down.[4]

Lieutenant Alan Dore, 43 Squadron, RFC

Richthofen had been grounded that morning by a minor mechanical defect, so it was Leutnant Karl-Emil Schäfer who was leading the flight of Jasta 11 that encountered 43 Squadron on their photographic reconnaissance mission:

> We had scarcely arrived at the front when a British formation appeared, flying low near Loos. We attacked from over Lens; at the same time three Germans from the Boelcke Staffel attacked them. My first opponent eluded me in a steep dive. Before I could follow him I saw Allmenröder being pressed hard by two Englishmen and I gave him some breathing room. As I did, a 'Vickers' single-seater got in behind me.* I made a half loop and went into a spin; two comrades who saw it thought I had been shot down, as did the 'Vickers' pilot, who then left me alone. I squeezed out of that scrape in such a way that I had a measured look at things and then very calmly went after a Sopwith two-seater. After I fired 100 shots it began to burn, then sideslipped down, fell end over end and fluttered earthwards in a burning heap, whereupon I could not help letting out a loud 'Hurrah'![5]
>
> Leutnant Karl-Emil Schäfer, Jasta 11, German Army Air Force

As Schäfer celebrated his victory, the men of 43 Squadron mourned the loss of Second Lieutenant P. L. Wood and his observer Second Lieutenant A. H. Fenton. However, another Sopwith pilot, the veteran Captain Jack Scott, already crippled by leg injuries, had had a miraculous escape:

> He limped out of his machine with it riddled from end to end. How he, with his bulk, escaped the bullets which had even smashed the instrument board and gun sights in front of him is a wonder which I have never solved, either in his case or in other similar cases where it seems as if a Divine Providence had allowed the bullets of the enemy to go everywhere except just in that small space which held the pilot's body.[6]
>
> Lieutenant Harold Balfour, 43 Squadron, RFC

A few days later Scott was posted to what was to be a distinguished career as the commanding officer of 60 Squadron who were flying the Nieuport 17s that at least gave them a fighting chance against the Albatros. But Jasta 11 had not finished yet with 43 Squadron on 4 March, for in the afternoon Richthofen was back aloft and eager for prey:

* The Germans referred to the FE2bs and FE2ds as 'Vickers' due to their generic resemblance as 'pushers' to the Vickers Fighter of 1915.

I take 2 p.m. to 4 p.m. patrol as Balfour has to return to aerodrome with engine trouble. We cross with four Sopwiths and three FE8s. Over Lens, where clouds are thick, my observer signals to me to turn round. I do so just in time to see what I thought to be an FE8, but afterwards proved to be one of our Sopwiths going down like a mad thing. Over and over sideways he fell, the sun glinting on his planes at each revolution until he disappeared like a crazy bird into the clouds. Green is missing as I write. He has gone for certain.[7]

Lieutenant Alan Dore, 43 Squadron, RFC

The missing officers were Second Lieutenant Herbert Green and his observer Second Lieutenant Alexander Reid. They had become separated from the safety of their tight formation when Richthofen and his men pounced:

Accompanied by five of my planes, I attacked an enemy squadron above Acheville. The Sopwith I had singled out flew for quite a while in my fire. After my four-hundredth shot, the aircraft lost a wing whilst trying to do a sudden turn. It plunged downward. It is not worth while to have the aircraft taken back, as parts of it are scattered all over Acheville and the surrounding country.[8]

Leutnant Manfred von Richthofen, Jasta 11, German Army Air Force

It was Richthofen's twenty-second victory. Both Green and Reid were killed.

It was not only the RFC that suffered on 4 March. The inexperienced naval pilots of 3 Squadron, RNAS, who had recently been sent to relieve the pressure on the severely overstretched RFC, suffered their first casualties during an offensive patrol probing deep behind the German lines:

We were returning from Cambrai on completion of the patrol when we saw two two-seater enemy aircraft about 3,000 feet below us. On a signal from the Flight Commander we dived, in formation, to attack. The enemy aircraft dived too but we succeeded in shooting one down. We were climbing to reform for the next attack when twelve enemy aircraft scouts dived into us coming down sun. We were caught entirely unprepared and in the ensuing fight lost three aircraft. After this we never forgot the axiom, 'Beware of the Hun in the Sun'.[9]

Sub Lieutenant Philip Wigglesworth, 3 (Naval) Squadron, RNAS

They had been ambushed by the scouts of Jasta 1. Yet there were many achievements for the RFC and RNAS that day to counter-balance the losses. There were 52 targets dealt with by aircraft artillery observation and 1,187 photographs taken.

THE role of the German Air Force was to prevent British army cooperation aircraft from carrying out their duties while as far as possible protecting their own reconnaissance aircraft. Despite their superior aircraft they were badly outnumbered and had little option but to adopt a cautious defensive posture, which allowed them to concentrate their numbers and fight only in circumstances that they considered to their advantage. However, it was impossible to completely remove the risks from the mad game of aerial warfare as in a dogfight bullets were sprayed liberally in all directions. Unaimed random shots could be as deadly as the most calculated point-blank burst. Thus it was that on 6 March* Richthofen found himself faced with a little more than he had bargained for when he attacked yet another patrol of Sopwith 1½ Strutters led by the redoubtable Lieutenant Alan Dore of 43 Squadron. On this occasion they were escorted by FE8s from 40 Squadron:

> More excitement. Left with six Sopwiths and six FE8s for offensive patrol. Next to Captain Balfour. Dodged a good deal to avoid 'Archie'. Second time over saw eight Hun scouts streaking to cut us off from home 5 miles away.[10]
>
> Lieutenant Alan Dore, 43 Squadron, RFC

Numbers are always a movable feast in these accounts of aerial dogfights – Richthofen himself claimed he had only four of his comrades accompanying him:

> I was flying with the squadron and noticed an opponent who was also flying in a squadron. It happened above the German artillery position in the neighbourhood of Lens. I had to fly quite a distance to get there. It tickles one's nerves to fly towards the enemy, especially when one can see him from a long distance and when several

---

* This date is a matter of some dispute. Several historians have favoured 9 March as the date on which Richthofen was first shot down. I am, however, persuaded by the case made by Norman Franks, Hal Giblin & Nigel McCrery in *Under the Guns of the Red Baron* (London: Caxton, 2000).

minutes must elapse before one can start fighting. I imagine that at such a moment my face turns a little pale.[11]

Leutnant Manfred von Richthofen, Jasta 11, German Army Air Force

As they approached it was obvious to Richthofen that although the Germans had far superior aircraft, they were once again clearly outnumbered:

The English flew about like midges. It is not easy to disperse a swarm of machines which fly together in good order, it is impossible for a single machine. It is extremely difficult for several aeroplanes, particularly if the difference in number is as great as it was in this case. However, one feels such a superiority over the enemy that one does not doubt for a moment of success. The aggressive spirit, the offensive, is the chief thing everywhere in war, and the air is no exception. However, the enemy had the same idea. I noticed that at once. As soon as they noticed us they turned round and attacked us. Now we five had to look sharp.[12]

Leutnant Manfred von Richthofen, Jasta 11, German Army Air Force

Soon the German scouts were in action with the various formations of Sopwith 1½ Strutters and FE8s and a wild dogfight filled the skies:

In a matter of seconds we were in a general mêlée of which I can only remember vague incidents as in a vivid dream. Dived at one wicked looking scout with a red fuselage. Gun jammed after a few shots. Again at another. Gun again stopped. Have confused recollections of seeing machines diving absolutely vertically, others stalling and spinning. The whole formation revolving and intermingling, scattering, converging like swallows on the wing.[13]

Lieutenant Alan Dore, 43 Squadron, RFC

Accounts of dogfights often resemble some kind of surreal dream sequence. Time randomly slowed down and accelerated in utter confusion and total chaos. It is not surprising that little coherent sense can be made of the various reports that survive:

A Hun scout with a red tail passed over my head travelling like lightening in the opposite direction and starting a half loop turn on to my tail. Not for you, dear lad, I thought and pulled my machine up almost on to its back then kicking over rudder. I fell over sideways and almost instantly was falling vertically and spinning as I went for, I suppose, 2,000 feet. I pulled out and found I had shaken off the Hun into which my observer had poured some shots before my manoeuvre precipitated him into the bottom of the machine.[14]

Lieutenant Alan Dore, 43 Squadron, RFC

Richthofen, as was his wont, held himself ready to pounce on any isolated British aircraft; looking to administer the *coup de grâce* with his customary efficiency:

I watched whether one of the fellows would hurriedly take leave of his colleagues. One of them was stupid enough to depart alone. I could reach him and I said to myself, 'That man is lost!' Shouting aloud, I went after him. I came up to him, or at least was very near him. He started shooting prematurely, which showed that he was nervous. So I said to myself, 'Go on shooting. You won't hit me!' At the moment, I think, I laughed out loud. But I soon got a lesson. When I had come to a distance of about 300 feet, I got ready for firing, aimed and gave a few trial shots. In my mind's eye I saw my enemy dropping. My former excitement was gone. In such a position one thinks quite calmly and collectedly and weighs the probabilities of hitting and of being hit. Altogether the fight itself is the least exciting part of the business as a rule. He who gets excited in fighting is sure to make mistakes. He will never get his enemy down. Besides calmness is, after all, a matter of habit. At any rate, in this case, I did not make a mistake. I approached my man up to within 50 yards. I fired some well-aimed shots and thought that I was bound to be successful. That was my idea. But suddenly I heard a tremendous bang when I had scarcely fired ten cartridges, and presently again something hit my machine. It became clear to me that I had been hit, or rather my machine. At the same time I noticed a fearful stench of petrol, and I observed that the motor was running slack. The Englishman noticed it too, for he started shooting with redoubled energy, while I had to stop.[15]

Leutnant Manfred von Richthofen, Jasta 11, German Army Air Force

As the spray of petrol enveloped him, Richthofen had the experience to know that he was in dreadful danger. After all had he not seen the same tell-tale symptoms of imminent immolation in so many of his hapless victims over the past six months? He reacted instantly:

Instinctively I switched off the engine. When one's petrol tank has been holed and when the infernal liquid is squirting around one's legs, the danger of fire is very great. One had in front of one an engine of more than 150 hp which is red hot. If a single drop of petrol should fall on it the whole machine would be in flames. I left in the air a thin white cloud. I knew its meaning from my enemies. Its appearance is the first sign of a coming explosion. I was at an altitude of 9,000 feet, and had to travel a long distance to get down. I have no idea with what rapidity I went downwards. At any rate the speed was so great that I could not put my head out of the machine without being pressed back by the rush of air.[16]

Leutnant Manfred von Richthofen, Jasta 11, German Army Air Force

With tremendous skill, Richthofen managed to flatten out and made a successful controlled landing near Henin-Lietard. This direct experience of the perils of over-confidence became just one more lesson to add to the educational process that would make him the most complete fighting ace of the First World War.

But who had shot him down? In the circumstances this is somewhat difficult to determine. How to track a single stream of bullets amongst so many criss-crossing the skies? In the event both Lieutenant E. L. Benbow and Captain Robert Gregory of 40 Squadron put in victory claims following the dogfight. Both may have had some justification, since another German aircraft from Jasta 11 had also been shot down by the FE8s – the Albatros of Leutnant Hans Lübbert. His aircraft was riddled with bullets, but he survived with only glancing wounds to the chest, thereby to rejoice for just a little longer in his squadron nickname of the 'bullet-catcher'. As Benbow mentioned in his report that his victim went down in flames this could perhaps be taken as an over-optimistic reference to Richthofen's exit wreathed in a cloud of petrol fumes. Whoever it was, they had almost killed the greatest German ace, but as Richthofen was to prove time and time again: a miss is as good as a mile. As for the British, they had performed well. When the Sopwith 1½ Strutters gathered on their own side of the lines they realised that they had only lost one of their number, which in the circumstances was a good result. The victim was the Sopwith flown by Lieutenant S. J. Pepler and Captain T. D. Stuart, which had been shot down in flames by Leutnant Karl-Emil Schäfer of Jasta 11.

The proliferation of references to red aircraft in these accounts had a simple explanation. The other pilots of Jasta 11 were well aware of the risks inherent in Richthofen's decision to fly the all-red Albatros DIII that instantly marked him out to his enemies. Inspired by their leader they decided to join him in trailing their metaphorical coats across the Arras skies. Amongst them was Manfred's younger brother Leutnant Lothar von Richthofen, who had joined the squadron in early March. Born on 27 September 1894, Lothar was two years younger than his brother. He had followed in his brother's footsteps: joining first the cavalry, then becoming first an observer and then a pilot. Although lacking the cool calculation and underpinning caution of his older brother, he proved to be a brilliant pilot although frequently aggressive to the point of foolhardiness in combat. Once he started to score victories in late March he would score at a rate that matched his illustrious brother:

> We had proven ourselves worthy of the red colour by our many aerial victories. The red colour signified a certain insolence. It attracted attention. Consequently, one really had to perform. Proudly we finally looked at our red birds. My brother's crate was glaring red. Each of the rest of us had some additional markings in other colours. As we could not see one another's faces in the sky, we chose these colours as recognition signals. Schäfer, for example, had his elevator, rudder and most of the back part of the fuselage black; Allmenröder used white, Wolff used green and I had yellow. Each one of us was different. In the air and from the ground, as well as from the enemy's view, we all looked to be red, as only small other parts were painted in another colour.[17]
>
> Leutnant Lothar von Richthofen, Jasta 11, German Army Air Force

The end result was a huge expansion in Richthofen's apparent presence over the front, as many RFC pilots naturally considered that every red German aircraft they encountered was flown by the original '*le diable rouge*'.

THROUGHOUT the early months of 1917 the RFC and the RNAS steadily increased the amount of aerial bombing that they undertook. The main targets were German communications – especially the railway junctions and bridges that were particularly prone to effective disruption by bombs. German airfields were also a popular target and it had long been recognised on both sides that the effect on morale of bombing exhausted infantry battalions resting in billeting areas far outweighed the actual physical damage and casualties caused. Many of the British aircraft were still limited in the bomb payload that they could realistically hope to get up off the runway and the method employed in bomb aiming combined naïve optimism with a kind of Heath Robinson science. Racks underneath the aircraft held the bombs, which were dropped by means of simply yanking on a wire that released the clip. The bomb sights were both difficult to use and grossly inaccurate, any allowance for wind speed and consequent drift had to be made by the oldest means of all – guesswork.

The bombs themselves were of three basic types. The 112-lb bomb was the 'heavy' bomb used for attacks on railways and other such significant targets. A lighter bomb intended for more general use was the 20-lb Cooper bomb. It was used against road convoys, troop concentrations and of course German airfields. Many squadrons not actually on the Arras front launched these raids flying diagonally across to their targets throughout the whole campaign. The FE2ds of 22 Squadron based on the Somme front were frequently sucked into the action, carrying out bombing raids on the German lines of communications:

> Bombing raids were usually done from 6,000 feet, an uncomfortable height at which 'Archie' was particularly accurate and where the bombers were very vulnerable to attack from above. It was an altitude which made it easy for enemy aircraft to take off from their aerodromes and climb above us before we got back to our own lines. Those bombing raids were really pretty futile and could do only very little, easily repairable damage. Each FE carried six 20-lb bombs and even a direct hit on a railway line or crossroads did so little damage that it could be repaired at once. Apparently the bombing had some effect because our raids were more and more strongly opposed as time went on. We began to lose aircraft and suffer casualties, as did the Pups of 54 Squadron which escorted us.[18]
>
> Second Lieutenant Geoffrey Hopkins, 22 Squadron, RFC

Many of the aircraft had no bomb aimer at all and there were considerable doubts as to whether anything of real importance was being achieved in the bombing raids, whether impromptu or organised:

> All aircraft, on whatever task they were employed, carried two 20-lb bombs which were dropped on some target in rear of the enemy's

trenches which was selected by Corps Headquarters. This, I think, was a very good thing and should have caused the enemy some discomfort even if it did little damage, but the organised bomb raids by corps reconnaissance squadrons were, I think, a mistake. The daylight raids were particularly unpopular. A few aircraft from each of the squadrons in the Wing were ordered to rendezvous over one of the aerodromes at a certain height and a leader was appointed. There was no particular formation but when the leader was satisfied that all had collected, the cluster was led to the target. Having dropped the bombs there was generally a '*sauve qui peut*'. We had no training and no bomb sights and in a BE, far over the enemy's lines one felt utterly defenceless, particularly since the passenger was usually left behind so as to get better performance, and we had a feeling, probably incorrect, that the raids were ordered because the RFC authorities thought we were not fully employed, and not in order to achieve any particular result.[19]

Lieutenant J. L. Vachell, 15 Squadron, RFC

Although night raids brought the cloak of darkness to the vulnerable bombers they also exposed the bombing crews to a whole new set of problems as all the normal dangers of operational flying were magnified. With no night-flying aids they often got lost even if assisted by the light of the moon:

I did a bit of night bombing last night. It was a bright moonlit night with snow on the ground. The place was about 20 miles away. I lost my way soon after crossing the lines and went on in the hopes of recognising someplace from the map. There was a strong wind blowing and I soon got some way over and passed over a line of trenches which I knew were past the place I had to drop my bombs on, but which was not marked on my map. There was another machine up from some other squadron at the time and I could see him using his machine gun by the tracer bullets. The Huns put up a few 'flaming onions', but as they were going away from me I did not take much notice. When I got over these trenches I turned back and after about a quarter of an hour I picked up a place near the lines which I knew. I had been up about forty-five minutes then. I turned back again and tried to follow the right road to the place, when I saw a train underneath me. So I stopped and I looked and I listened. The 'special place' and trains were the only places we were supposed to bomb, and at below 2,000 feet. I was then at 3,000 feet and by the time I got down to 1,800 feet the train had got into a village and shut off steam. I was just gloating over how happy the people underneath must be, for they would have heard me coming down and I was looking for the exact place, when I heard the popping of a machine gun. It made me feel uncomfortable so I cleared off. By this time I was getting fed up, so I hotted up a village with my machine gun (tracers make a lovely show at night) and buzzed off against the wind back home. Very soon they started giving me some of the 'flaming onions'. These are about twenty flares joined together with wire. I don't know quite how they are fired but I think it is a shell in front. The first two or three went high and in front of me. Then they got my height but they all went past my tail. They don't seem to go very fast and it was great fun watching the wretched things coming up.[20]

Lieutenant Leslie Horridge, 4 Squadron, RFC

IN the dangerous days of March 1917, many pilots prayed silently for 'dud' weather that would give them a precious day of safety, a chance to recuperate. But bad weather was a mixed blessing, as in all but the very worst conditions the army cooperation corps pilots were bound to try their very best to achieve something. Every wasted day was a bonus to the Germans in that it would inevitably materially reduce the effect of the all-important British artillery bombardment at Arras:

Today appears to be a lovely day, but there is a sheet of cloud at about 4,000 feet which makes any photographic or reconnaissance work impossible. I started off as spare man with C Flight reconnaissance at about a quarter to seven. Halfway to the lines one of their men fell out, so I took his place. About five or ten minutes after, as the clouds were seen to be getting worse, the leader fired a coloured light meaning, 'expedition abandoned' so we all came home again.[21]

Second Lieutenant Horace Bawden, 45 Squadron, RFC

However, such a cancellation was only temporary. The necessity for the photographs did not diminish; all that happened was that the whole affair became ever more urgent, more fraught. So it was that later the same morning Bawden and the others had to try again:

We had to make another attempt at the job that was washed out earlier.
This time we only got about half a mile from the aerodrome before all the
machines fell out, bar myself and the leader, with various forms of engine
trouble. So that was no good. Then it was lunchtime. Then we had another
go at 2.20 p.m., and this time all went well except that one machine couldn't
get off, so of course I (the reserve) had to carry on with the others. It was
too bad for photos, but we did a reconnaissance – 1 hour 40 minutes,
about three quarters of an hour over the line only. Did not see a Hun, and
did not get a single 'Archie'. But then we flew at 12,500 feet for a great
part of the time and as it was misty 'Archie' probably could hardly see us.[22]

Second Lieutenant Horace Bawden, 45 Squadron, RFC

This still represented a failure because the real job would still have to be
done – all the risks would have to be run again until the right number of
photographs could be taken at the appropriate height, in conditions of
clear visibility, with the correct print exposure of the exact locations required
by the staff officers. The pressure spread right through the RFC. Flying
inadequate machines operating at the limits of their mechanical capabil-
ity, pilots and observers were stretched to *their* physical and mental limits.
There were bound to be occasions when the underlying strain became
evident. On the morning of 11 March, Second Lieutenants Hopkins and
Fawcett of 22 Squadron were driven to the end of their tether by the
mechanical unreliability of their aging FE2b:

My engine 'revs' started to fall when I was on my way to the lines in
a flight formation. As my engine was by no means giving full power,
I turned back and went home. Nothing specifically wrong with the
engine could be found when we ran it up in the hangar, where it gave
full 'revs'. As a result, I was hauled up before the CO and accused of
going home 'unnecessarily'. This I hotly denied as it was quite untrue.[23]

Second Lieutenant Geoffrey Hopkins, 22 Squadron, RFC

Some pilots undoubtedly used the excuse of engine problems to evade
flying on particularly ticklish missions, but Hopkins was not that kind of
a man. He had faced a real quandary: he could have toughed it out and
hope the engine behaved itself and thereby risked their lives gratuitously,
or as he did, play safe and risk hurtful accusations of cowardice. There
was nothing worse for a conscientious pilot than an engine with an
intermittent fault:

We were never very happy with our engines, some of which were very unreliable and lost 'revs' for no apparent reason. Some pilots were more nervous about this than others, the point being that if one's engine failed to operate on full power, or stopped, when one was some distance over the lines, there was very little hope of getting home again against the prevailing wind. Apart from this, an aircraft falling behind the formation because of a faulty engine was liable to be shot down when unprotected by the rest of the flight. There had been more than one case of a pilot leaving the formation before it reached the lines and returning to the aerodrome with alleged engine trouble which could not be substantiated when the engine was run up again on the ground. Such a case proved nothing, as the fault, dirt in the carburettor, for example, might rectify itself.[24]

Second Lieutenant Geoffrey Hopkins, 22 Squadron, RFC

On this occasion his commanding officer was bleakly unsympathetic and had obviously made his mind up that they were swinging the lead. As a result Hopkins and Fawcett were ordered up to do an offensive patrol later the same morning. They were to be accompanied by a relatively inexperienced pilot, Second Lieutenant Leslie Beal and his observer, Air Mechanic A. G. Davin. Their mission was to patrol along the front lines, but they were ordered not to cross onto the German side. Hopkins was still livid at having his courage publicly disparaged and he was in the mood to take risks, to prove that he was not afraid:

I told Beal to stay close to me whatever happened and so we set off – flying up and down our lines at about 6,000 feet. It was a cloudy afternoon and at times we were flying not very far below a bank of fairly thick clouds. Beal was behind me rather than alongside when, suddenly, five HA dived on us out of the clouds, from the rear. I immediately did a split-arse turn to face the Huns and fired a red Very light to warn Beal, and also draw the attention of any of our own aircraft which might possibly be close by. Beal did not turn and therefore got separated from me. As I completed my turn, Fawcett started firing his gun but the HA which were firing at us at once zoomed away, out of range, before coming round again for another dive at us. I then turned towards Beal who had got below me and off to one side. He had an HA right on his tail, firing at him at close range. Fawcett's gun jammed and he disappeared from my sight, crouched down in the nacelle, trying to rectify the stoppage. I dived towards the HA which was shooting up Beal – smoke was coming from the FE and I was afraid he was on fire – and let off about half a drum at the German; whereupon the HA left Beal and dived off to one side, away from me. More or less simultaneously, one or more of the other HA got on my tail and started firing at me. I was frightened and took very violent evasive action, heaving my FE all over the place and losing height rapidly, with bullets cracking around but not hitting anything vital. Suddenly the firing ceased and the HA disappeared into the clouds. Beal's gunner, Davin, had been severely wounded in the thigh, while Beal's engine and controls had been badly shot about, leaving him with very little control, though his elevator continued partly to function. I followed him down until I saw him crash land behind our lines, and then I returned to the aerodrome. I landed rather groggily as my FE had also been shot about. Some of the bracing wires had been broken and the tail was only just about holding together.[25]

Second Lieutenant Geoffrey Hopkins, 22 Squadron, RFC

In the cold light of day Hopkins knew that he had been irresponsible in flying quite so close to the bank of cloud that had concealed the approach of the German scouts, but he had been determined to act offensively after having his commitment and courage so bluntly questioned that morning. Unfortunately the two FE2bs could hardly have run into a more dangerous opponent, for the aircraft that riddled Second Lieutenant Leslie Beal's FE2b was flown by the redoubtable Leutnant Werner Voss of Jasta Boelcke. If ever there was a natural ace it was Voss. Born of a wealthy industrial family in Krefeld on 13 April 1897, Voss was a supremely talented pilot who seemed to have the ability to extract every last jot of performance from any aircraft, coupled with an almost supernatural 'situational awareness'. He was able to sum up a complex, ever-changing dogfight in the blink of an eye, where a normal man would see nothing but a blur of paternless movement. His sheer exuberant ability had already been rewarded with a string of victories in which Beal and Davin's FE2b counted as his fourteenth success since he had joined the Jasta in November 1916:

The Squadron sent out a rescue party which brought Beal and his FE (7685) back to the aerodrome the next morning. The aircraft was extremely badly shot up and had dozens of bullet holes through the prop, wings etc. – but as the Hun who did the damage had been shooting from directly behind and on the same level, the engine had protected Beal. He had bullet holes through the side of his boots, coat sleeves etc. If he was wounded, the wounds must have been superficial as, though he was badly shocked, he had no bandages on.[26]

Second Lieutenant Geoffrey Hopkins, 22 Squadron, RFC

It wasn't Beal and Davin's week: just a few days earlier they had been shot down on the British side of the lines in very similar circumstances by another German ace, Leutnant Renatus Theiller of Jasta 5. The redoubtable Beal carried on flying only to be shot up for a third time a month later during a photographic reconnaissance on 26 April. This time Beal was seriously wounded. It is difficult to decide whether he was jinxed or lucky in his brief career at the front: ill-starred to be shot down three times, or fortunate to escape with his life fighting opponents who had downed so many of his comrades.

THE German retreat to the Hindenburg Line was a difficult operation conducted with great dexterity. After a preliminary retirement on a smaller scale in late February, they began to fall back in earnest on 14 March. The retreat stretched from the British Third Army front in the north near Arras, all along the Fifth and Fourth Army fronts on the Somme, and right into the French sector in the south, where the retreat was carried out in the very area meant to be the focal point of Nivelle's offensive. The area of the retreat was immense in comparison to the usual gains of ground made during the course of an offensive. Some hundreds of square miles were given up during the course of this radical strategic withdrawal.

The British and French troops soon found that they were advancing into a veritable wasteland, where the Germans had systematically destroyed everything of any possible use. Some 600 French villages were razed to the ground in this manner, their entire infrastructures ruined:

The villages we passed through as we marched to the front line had the appearance of lunatic asylums let loose. Whole companies were pushing walls down or sitting on the roofs of the houses throwing down the slates. Trees were felled, window frames broken, and smoke and

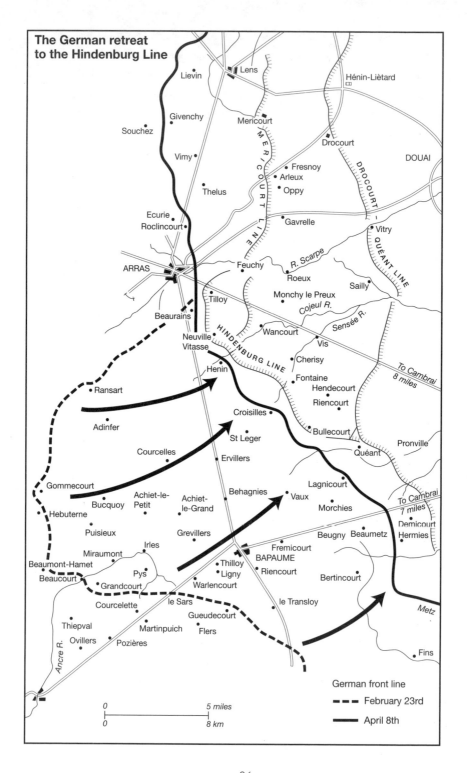

The German retreat to the Hindenburg Line

Lievin
Lens
Hénin-Liètard
Givenchy
Mericourt
Souchez
Drocourt
DOUAI
Vimy
Fresnoy
Arleux
Thelus
Oppy
MERICOURT LINE
Ecurie
Gavrelle
Roclincourt
Vitry
DROCOURT -
ARRAS
R. Scarpe
Feuchy
QUÉANT LINE
Roeux
Sailly
Tilloy
Monchy le Preux
Beaurains
Cojeul R.
Neuville
Wancourt
Sensée R.
Vitasse
Vis
HINDENBURG LINE
To Cambrai
Henin
Cherisy
8 miles
Ransart
Fontaine
Hendecourt
Croisilles
Riencourt
Adinfer
St Leger
Courcelles
Ervillers
Bullecourt
Pronville
Quéant
Gommecourt
Lagnicourt
Behagnies
Vaux
To Cambrai
Achiet-le-
Achiet-
Morchies
7 miles
Bucquoy
Petit
le-Grand
Hebuterne
Demicourt
Puisieux
Grevillers
Beugny
Beaumetz
Hermies
Irles
Miraumont
Fremicourt
Beaumont-Hamet
Pys
Thilloy
BAPAUME
Beaucourt
Ligny
Riencourt
Bertincourt
Grandcourt
Warlencourt
Courcelette
le Sars
le Transloy
Metz
Gueudecourt
Thiepval
Martinpuich
Flers
Ovillers
Pozières
Fins
Ancre R.

German front line
February 23rd
April 8th

0   5 miles
0   8 km

clouds of dust rose from heap after heap of rubbish. In short, an orgy of destruction was going on. The men were chasing round with incredible zeal, arrayed in the abandoned wardrobes of the population, in women's dresses and with top hats on their heads. With positive genius they singled out the main beams of the houses and, tying ropes around them, tugged with all their might, shouting out in time with their pulls, till the whole house collapsed. Others swung hammers and smashed whatever came in their way, from flowerpots on the window ledges to the glasswork of conservatories.[27]

Leutnant Ernst Jünger, 73 Hanoverian Fusilier Regiment

Roads, drains, sewers and water supplies were all left devastated. In the ruins of Péronne they even left a noticeboard that said, 'Don't be angry; just marvel!' The Germans fell back in carefully planned stages, covered by well-sited machine-gun posts that brought death to many unwary patrols. Any Allied pursuit was hampered by the need to guard against the ever-present risk of a sudden German counter-attack seeking to catch them unawares as they moved across razed ground:

Now that we were entering again on a phase of open warfare, although it was only for a short distance and a brief period, it was not my intention to allow the army to move forward in one weak, straggling line without adequate artillery support and supplies: a sudden counter-attack might easily have overwhelmed such a formation. The advance was to be carried out by each corps under cover of properly organised advanced guards, the rest of the corps following in their wake. A cavalry brigade was also ordered forward by the 16 March, to reconnoitre in front of the corps advanced guards.[28]

General Hubert Gough, Headquarters, Fifth Army

The British troops carefully pushed forward and captured Bapaume on 17 March. For all their bitter experience of trench warfare, most of the British troops were untested in the kind of open manoeuvring that pre-war regular soldiers would have had instilled into them as a matter of course. Since the hard-fought battles of 1914 there were very few regulars left in the British Army. At the sharp end for once were small cavalry patrols. After a war spent fretting on the sidelines the cavalry finally felt they had found a real role as they cautiously felt their way forward across the wastelands:

We rode in the shape of a diamond, one man in the front, two on each side and one behind. The officer in charge would be in the middle. It covered the ground and gave us the best lookout. We were approaching a village and right in the middle of the road was a lovely German dress helmet, all shiny black with metal facings. Just the thing to pick up for a souvenir. But we had been warned that things like that would be booby-trapped – so I gave it a wide berth! As I got near the village, everything was quiet and ghostly sort of atmosphere with all the devastation. Then I heard an intermittent sort of moaning sound. It rather worried me a little bit because it sounded as if somebody was in pain. As I got nearer it got louder and louder and eventually I found that it was an old door hanging on a rusty top hinge and the little breeze was causing it to sway. There were no buildings standing.[29]

Trooper John Fell, C Squadron, 1st Surrey Yeomanry

The squadron were all on edge, their nerves jangling with false alarms and extremely conscious that at any moment they could be ripped apart by a stream of bullets:

We went on to this village and it started snowing like blazes. We went off down to the right-hand side and the others went on the left-hand side. We got into the village at the bottom, close by a little stream. The place was full of bricks, walls knocked down so we were dismounted and the colonel and I we were going to walk up through the village. Suddenly a machine gun blasted out and the odd bullet came round our way. We decided to get out. We went out galloping over a long ploughed field. I was crouched down in the saddle, when my horse suddenly went down – he might have put his foot down or he might have had a bullet in the heel or anywhere. My rifle didn't slip off it stuck in the holder. My bloody horse turned off to the left, sort of going to Germany to get his lunch! Bill Cole waited a long time to try and get me on board, but I couldn't mount his horse, I said to Bill, 'Bugger off!' I got down in this lane, ran along it a decent way and then cut across, the way they went, a big long ploughed field. Halfway across they started firing at me. I was right in the open so I 'died'; threw myself down and 'died' facing the enemy so to speak. Then I got up again and chased off.[30]

Trooper Robert Cook, C Squadron, 1st Surrey Yeomanry

As the cavalry patrols felt their way forward they were greatly assisted by contact and reconnaissance patrols undertaken as often as was physically possible by the RFC. It was their duty to identify precisely how far the British cavalry had got, whilst at the same time locating any visible German strong points that might threaten their progress in the near future:

> The Germans had left machine-gun nests behind in the ruined villages and in addition to the physical obstacles these had a serious delaying effect upon our advance. The squadron was given the task of locating these machine-gun nests and it proved very difficult. Villages invariably appeared deserted but by shutting off the engine and circling down over them it was often possible to draw fire. Though we had no casualties the German fire was accurate enough to make the aircraft require a good deal of patching after each flight, but we managed to give Corps Headquarters a very fair idea of the progress of the enemy's withdrawal, and I think by dropping messages prevented the cavalry from running into a great number of traps.[31]
>
> Lieutenant J. L. Vachell, 15 Squadron, RFC

The brief return to the chaos and confusions of open warfare provided the occasional opportunity for the British as well as the retreating Germans. Lieutenant Leslie Horridge found he had a brief chance of easy prey when he saw about one hundred troops in column caught in the act of evacuating a village. Unfortunately, before he could open fire he had to know for certain who they were:

> The only way to tell who people are is to let them shoot at you. I went over these people at a few hundred feet, but as I did not hear them fire I did not take any more notice of them. I watched them standing there for about an hour and then saw some horsemen on another road leading out of the village. I was certain they were ours as I had not heard of any Hun cavalry. I throttled down, went right down and flew over them at about 300 feet. Then they started to fire at me with their rifles. I was never so startled in my life. I thought it was a Hun above me and cleared off. It was not till a few minutes after that I realised the shots were from the ground. If I had only known I could have had the whole lot stiff with my machine guns as well as the infantry who by this time had gone off to the next village.[32]
>
> Lieutenant Leslie Horridge, 4 Squadron, RFC

Often it was extraordinarily difficult to identify exactly who was moving about beneath them in the midst of such a fluid situation. The British cavalry and infantry patrols were wary of revealing their positions to the Germans and, of course, the Germans concealed themselves as best they could from the British aircraft:

> The only way to find this out was to fly over the place and see if they fired at us. We flew towards Croisilles at about 1,000 feet and they started hammering away at us with 'Archie' long before we got there, this of course was not sufficient evidence of occupation so we followed a zig-zag course until we got right over the village where we heard the rat-tat of machine guns. This was good enough and proved that the village was being held. We returned to Ervillers and dropped a note giving full information and also stating the positions of several of our cavalry patrols which we had noted. After we had dropped the message I noticed a suspicious looking machine which was about a thousand feet above us, so I shook the stick and pointed it out to Hendry, at the same time turning our machine west. The machine proved to be a Hun and he got above and behind us in the approved fashion, we at once cleared decks for action. Hendry took off his gloves and goggles and manned his gun. The Hun got right above us and then put his nose down and I thought to myself, 'Now for it!' Hendry looked like a monkey clinging to the back of his gun. Just when it looked like business and I was expecting to get the MC for being frightened to death, the Hun wavered, pulled his nose up and streaked for home before he got within shooting distance. Some of these Huns are poor chaps, there he was half as fast again as ours and miles away from our 'Archie' guns – and yet he dare not tackle us. If he had any guts we might have shared the fate of those four other machines of ours which lay in crumpled heaps beneath us. Hendry is a good chap and I like flying with him. He was worth watching with his steady Scotch eyes glued to the sights of his gun when the Huns started to dive on us. I think he was a bit disappointed when the Hun turned away, I am afraid I can't say that I was.[33]

Second Lieutenant Charles Smart, 5 Squadron, RFC

While the British pilots were distracted by events on the ground, the German scouts were out looking for prey, determined to veil the details of the retreat. The RFC losses continued to rise and in these circumstances no one could remain unaware of the gradual but steady culling of the crews of the army cooperation corps aircraft. Certainly it was uppermost in the mind of Lieutenant Leslie Horridge in one of his letters home:

> Do you realise I have been out here nearly ten months now. It does not seem so long to me. Have you noticed the number of RFC casualties lately? I wonder if Walter still thinks the RFC a cushy job? Lots of people used to say it was a cushy job but they did not transfer all the same.[34]
>
> Lieutenant Leslie Horridge, 4 Squadron, RFC

In his next letter home, Leslie Horridge recorded the loss of another three aircraft from his flight. Meanwhile, Captain Bernard Rice of 8 Squadron had just got back from a much needed spot of leave and he too noticed the pace was quickening:

> Losses have been a bit stiff since I came back. I've attended one double funeral and skipped another – cheery isn't it? However most of these things can be accounted for by inexperience; but the old Hun *has* been trying hard to keep things private his side while he moves back. He sends a small packet of his scouts over to down one of us and hops back before the patrols can come up. I am hoping to bag one of the Huns one day. What would you like as a souvenir of him? Isn't this Hun withdrawal astounding? What do they mean by it? Most people seem to think it is a dodge to put off our offensive.[35]
>
> Captain Bernard Rice, 8 Squadron, RFC

One fierce aerial engagement of this fraught period occurred when nine FE2bs of 25 Squadron, accompanied by eight Sopwith 1½ Strutters of 43 Squadron, were sent on a photographic reconnaissance over the Hindenburg Line. Three of the FE2bs were equipped with cameras. This was by no means an adequate escort and to make matters worse they would have to fly dangerously close to the Jasta 11 base at Douai. One of the Sopwiths was flown by Lieutenant Alan Dore, by this time commanding C Flight, accompanied by his observer Sergeant Cubberley:

> Off at 9 o'clock with eight other Sopwiths to meet nine FE2bs at Auchel. We are to photograph Hindenburg Line. Rendezvous at 8,000 feet and when in formation, cross lines at La Bassée. Reach Annoeullin without interference. At Vittory see Huns coming up to us from Douai.

We make large circles whilst photographic machines do their work. Meantime more and more Hun scouts come up and climb right above into the sun. Knew we were for it. 'Archie' tries to split up formation and then the attack begins. Into the maelstrom they began to dart. I endeavour to keep with the others, but the jumble of machines and the risk of colliding separates me. Twice the cracks of my observer's gun warns me that I am being attacked, but always endeavour to keep my nose into the sun so that he approached blindly. They are driven off, hit. Just by me a blazing wreck falls like a huge fireball. One of ours gone, the tangle seems to lessen, the warring aeroplanes melt away and I find myself alone on our side of the lines watching huge fires and whirls of smoke south of Arras. Does this foretell the retreat of the Germans after their long grip of the French line? On landing find that two of our machines are missing and one observer wounded. Altogether seven Huns sent down.[36]

Lieutenant Alan Dore, 43 Squadron, RFC

Sadly for one's confidence in British victory claims, the Germans do not appear to have lost any scouts that day. In the same affray Richthofen had struck with his customary deadliness shooting down the FE2b of Lieutenant Arthur Boultbee and Air Mechanic Frederick King:

During the fight, I managed to force a Vickers two-seater to one side and managed to bring it down after firing 800 shots into it. In my machine-gun fire, the machine lost its openwork fuselage tail. The occupants were both killed.[37]

Leutnant Manfred von Richthofen, Jasta 11, German Army Air Force

On 19 March, although there were snowstorms in the offing, the rapacious Leutnants Werner Voss and Otto Bernert of Jasta 2 were scouring the skies for suitable victims. They encountered two RE8s of 59 Squadron: one, flown by Captain Elred Bowyer-Bower with Lieutenant Eric Elgey as his observer, was engaged in photographic reconnaissance; the other, crewed by Captain C. P. Bertie and Lieutenant F. H. Wilson, was acting as their meagre escort. Voss swiftly shot down Bowyer-Bower's machine to claim his twentieth victory, which made him eligible for the award of the *Pour le Mérite*. Bernert disposed of the escort with equal ease to bring his total to eight. Bowyer-Bower and Elgey's riddled RE8 crashed to earth near Croisilles where the Germans buried them, their shallow graves simply marked with a rough wooden cross cut from the remnants of their shattered aircraft.

As the troops moved forward on the ground they found that the Germans had sowed the ground with a plentiful variety of mines and booby traps of fiendish imagination. The Royal Engineers were called upon to clear newly captured areas and this was to prove a slow and risky business:

> You began to know exactly what the Germans were likely to do. For instance you'd come to a little road bridge. Of course, being Germans, they were very thorough and always did the same thing. You would find that part of the bridge had been dismantled and that the 5.9 shell that had been put in, there was no wiring or anything like that, it was one of these acid traps – so there was nothing to tell you that there was anything there. The acid eating the wire away was in varying strength: one would go off in say 24 hours, one would go off in 12 hours. So you just had to hunt about. They generally put it in more or less the same place, where it would do the most damage. We couldn't catch them all, we missed one or two, especially where they'd simply dug a hole under-neath the road and covered it up again. There were contact mines, generally on the tracks and roads. You had to find them which was difficult. A road would come to a cutting, where an explosion would do the most damage, so you'd be suspicious then. If you could get hold of the detonator that was all right – but sometimes you had to blow them and just take the consequences.[38]
>
> Lieutenant Martin Greener, 175th Tunnelling Company, Royal Engineers

Perhaps the worst traps were the rather ingenious delayed action fuses. A wire held back the striker but was immersed in a weak acid solution, which gradually ate its way through until the striker sprang into action and detonated the charge. With no lead or fuse wire to give away their location they were completely self-contained and would explode to shat-tering effect days after the Germans had departed. The first to go off demolished the Town Hall of Bapaume on 25 March, some eight days after it had been occupied. It was cunningly set to destroy some tempt-ingly well-furnished cellars, which had just been offered as accommoda-tion to a visiting delegation of French dignitaries, with fatal consequences. Smaller scale booby traps were less spectacular, but nonetheless effective in causing small-scale casualties. Mines under dugout steps and trip wires were commonplace, and simple human weaknesses were ruthlessly exploited. Spiked *pickelhaube* helmets or revolvers were left in the abandoned dugouts to tempt unwary souvenir hunters. They would explode with deadly effect if moved.

One of the sappers assigned to these dangerous duties was Captain Thomas Bowyer-Bower, the father of the unfortunate young man killed in his RE8 by Voss just a few days before on 19 March. Bowyer-Bower was aware that his son had been shot down in the area and, having established from his son's commanding officer, Major Robert Egerton, that in this case 'missing' meant almost certainly dead, he had resolved to discover his grave if humanly possible. The odds were against him as the front line was littered with graves both marked and unmarked. However, he eventually located the RE8's remnants and nearby a humble cross roughly marked in pencil: 'Two unknown captains of the Flying Corps'. Bowyer-Bower was made of stern stuff for he ordered his men to exhume the bodies to discover the decaying remains of his beloved son:

> We have found the plane and grave beside it. We have exhumed the
> two bodies and they have been identified as my dear boy and Elgey.
> I have had them placed in coffins and they were buried yesterday in the
> cemetery at Mory. The plane was riddled with bullets from above and
> the side. My boy was shot in the head and neck and evidently killed
> instantly. The bodies had been robbed of everything even to the
> buttons and badges, and the pockets rifled.[39]
>
> Captain Thomas Bowyer-Bower, Royal Engineers

At least the 22-year-old boy would have a known grave; indeed, his son and Elgey lie side by side to this day in Mory Abbey Military Cemetery.

Of course, the advance involved a prodigious amount of work for the British engineers in trying to swiftly repair the destruction caused by the retreating Germans. Roads had to be painstakingly relaid, bridges and culverts restored, light railways installed. Worst of all was the urgent task of getting the guns forward. Guns could be manhandled forward with considerable difficulty, but the logistical problems encountered in moving forward the millions of shells required to feed those guns were enormous. Most of it had to be done by packhorses carrying just eight shells at a time. This problem was to seriously inconvenience the plans and preparations for the Arras offensive in the area to the south of the River Scarpe, where the new Hindenburg Line joined the existing German trench systems.

THERE was a strange incident when a German royal prince found himself embroiled in actual fighting high above the front on 21 March. A promising German scout pilot, Oberleutnant Adolf von Tutschek of Jasta Boelcke, suddenly found that his patrol had been unofficially joined by no less a figure than Prince Freidrich Karl of Prussia.

Today at 1630 hours I took off with a flight from Jasta Boelcke in weather where one could fish in the dullness. The clouds were hanging at 500 to 600 metres when Voss, Wortman and I, in succession, found a hole in the clouds over Cambrai and climbed though the mountainous mists. We found beneath us a sea of clouds once we were through, while above there was the most beautiful of blue skies. Leutnant Voss was up ahead with the leader, and we followed closely behind. As I glanced backward I suddenly spied a strange Albatros to the left, coming towards us. I quickly recognised it as the green Albatros DI of Prince Freidrich Karl of Prussia as he joined us happily waving his hand. Over Arras we went down in steep spirals hoping to head off an artillery spotter, but there were none. So back we flew just under the clouds over the newly captured Siegfried Line positions toward the south. Coming towards us were the red rump of the Richthofen Staffel who were returning from an equally unsuccessful hunt. With short greetings we passed each other.[40]

Oberleutnant Adolf von Tutschek, Jasta Boelcke, German Army Air Force

The Prince was in command of a neighbouring aerial reconnaissance unit but was seeking a transfer to Jasta Boelcke and had in the interim been given an old Albatros DI for a little practice. The machine was green with a striking skull and crossbones design painted on the side. As the patrol proceeded they eventually sighted a flight of DH2s from 32 Squadron, RFC:

Five of us were in the flight, Voss, Prince Karl, Walz, Wintrath and I. It was clear that we shouldn't become involved in a dogfight as the prevailing strong east wind would surely push us westward. Despite that our leader and Voss turned toward a few Vickers lattice-tailed single-seaters, who were also flying just under the clouds at our altitude over Lagnicourt. Leutnant Wintrath and I followed and the dance began. I went after an Englishman, who instantly headed for the clouds just as additional aircraft were coming out of them. The same thing happened to Voss. When I looked back, I noticed the green Albatros of the Prince nearing the ground and spiralling, closely followed by a Vickers who was, in turn, followed by two other enemy aircraft who were protecting him. While Prince Friedrich Karl was in the process of finishing off an Englishman, he was attacked by a second one, who shot up his motor so that his only recourse was an immediate landing.[41]

Oberleutnant Adolf von Tutschek, Jasta Boelcke, German Army Air Force

The Prince had been shot down by the DH2 flown by Lieutenant C. E. M. Pickthorne. As his machine touched down between the lines, which were spread widely at this point, the Prince made a run on foot, making directly for the German lines, only to be picked off by the excellent marksmanship of the Australians occupying their front-line posts a few hundred yards away. They then broke cover, running out into No Man's Land intent on taking souvenirs. The Prince was picked up and carried back to hospital. Here he proved that he was a good sport if not an accomplished scout pilot:

An Intelligence officer, dressed up as a German and who spoke the language perfectly, was put into a bed in hospital next to Prince Friedrich Karl, in the hope that he might elicit something. But Prince Friedrich Karl was not in the least deceived and, entering with zest into the spirit of the great game, gave most circumstantial accounts of the Germans being already on the move from Mulhausen to the Rhine, and other similar fantasies. Both the officer and the Prince enjoyed themselves immensely, each thinking he was getting the best of the game of wits, and, I fancy, neither got the least advantage except that of enjoyment.[42]

Brigadier-General John Charteris, Intelligence Officer, General Headquarters, BEF

Sadly, the Prince died from his wounds a few days later. As ever the rumour-mill soon started to move into overdrive with the usual heady mixture of truth and fabrication:

That Prince of the Huns who landed this side a week or so ago. Just had 'wind up' at the sight of our scouts! He got out and started to run away when an Australian sergeant shot him through the guts! Dammed good job too. There wasn't a hole in his machine.[43]

Lieutenant Eddie Rice, 55 Squadron, RFC

IN mid-March 1917 a controversial figure made his entrance into the Arras skies. Lieutenant William Bishop was born in Canada in 1894, where he enjoyed a lively childhood before being sent to the Royal Military College at Kingston, Ontario in 1912. Here he fell under a cloud when he was caught cheating in the examinations of May 1914. Soon afterwards the timely outbreak of war washed away such disciplinary worries and he was duly commissioned into the cavalry. Disappointed with the lack of action, he applied for a transfer to the RFC and he was accepted as an observer in the autumn of 1915. He served with 21 Squadron on the Western Front in 1916, before his health failed and he returned, first to England and then to Canada on sick leave. After recovery he trained as a pilot in England and was finally posted out to join 60 Squadron at Filescamp Farm airfield on 17 March. Lieutenant Bishop had his first real dogfight on 25 March. His own account left little doubt that he would become a natural scout pilot:

> From the corner of my eye I spied what I believed to be three enemy machines. They were some distance to the east of us, and evidently were on patrol duty to prevent any of our pilots or observers getting too near the rapidly changing German positions. The three strange machines approached us, but our leader continued to fly straight ahead without altering his course in the slightest degree. Soon there was no longer any doubt as to the identity of the three aircraft – they were Huns, with the big, distinguishing black iron crosses on their planes. They evidently were trying to surprise us, and we allowed them to approach, trying all the time to appear as if we had not seen them. Like nearly all other pilots who come face to face with a Hun in the air for the first time, I could hardly realise that these were real, live, hostile machines. Finally, the three enemy machines got behind us, and we slowed down so that they would overtake us all the sooner. When they had approached to about 400 yards, we opened out our engines and turned. One of the other pilots, as well as myself, had never been in a fight before, and we were naturally slower to act than the other two. My first real impression of the engagement was that one of the enemy machines dived down, then suddenly came up again and began to shoot at one of our people from the rear. I had a quick impulse and followed it. I flew straight at the attacking machine from a position where he could not see me and opened fire. My 'tracer' bullets – bullets

that show a spark and a thin little trail of smoke as they speed through the air – began at once to hit the enemy machine. A moment later the Hun turned over on his back and seemed to fall out of control.[44]

Lieutenant William Bishop, 60 Squadron RFC

Bishop was horrified when his engine then flooded with petrol and stopped dead, leaving him with an anxious glide home, just managing to make enough distance to allow him to force land in safety a few hundred feet behind the British front. Witnesses supported his claim for a first victim, although the victim has not yet been successfully identified. A few days later, on 31 March, Bishop and two other pilots were ordered to provide escort cover for a formation of FE2bs of 11 Squadron engaged in a vital photographic reconnaissance. Although he scored a personal success, his description of the action unwittingly underlines the reason why a little friction could sometimes arise between the corps aircraft and the scouts detailed to escort them:

We were assigned to escort and protect six other machines that were going over to get photographs of some German positions about 10 miles behind the front-line trenches. I had my patrol flying about a thousand feet above the photography machines when I saw six enemy single-seater scouts climbing to swoop down upon our photography machines. At the same time there were two other enemy machines coming from above to engage us. Diving towards the photography machines, I managed to frighten off two of the Boches; then, looking back, I saw one of my pilots being attacked by one of the two higher Germans who had made for us. This boy, who is now a prisoner of war, had been a school-mate of mine before the war. Forgetting everything else, I turned back to his assistance. The Hun who was after him did not see me coming. I did not fire until I had approached within 100 yards. Then I let go. The Hun was evidently surprised. He turned and saw me, but it was too late now. I was on his tail – just above and a little behind him – and at 50 yards I fired a second burst of twenty rounds. This time I saw the bullets going home. I rejoined the photography machines, which unfortunately in the meantime had lost one of their number.[45]

Lieutenant William Bishop, 60 Squadron, RFC

Bishop was perhaps lucky that his temporary abandonment – for perfectly understandable motives – of the all-important photographic machines to rescue a fellow scout did not have more serious consequences. He was lucky the five remaining FE2bs returned safely to base with enough photographs to meet with requirements. There were no reported losses for the Germans that day and it is slightly ironic that Bishop may even have been the victim referred to by Oberleutnant Adolf von Tutschek in an equally vehement, but doubtful claim:

> West of Lens at 3,500 metres altitude, I attacked a Nieuport which was close behind an Albatros two-seater. Immediately the Nieuport let up in his pursuit of the Albatros two-seater, who was going down in a steep glide, and attempted to out-climb Leutnant Koenig and I, but I managed to get behind him. After 150 shots, the machine suddenly stood on its nose, tumbled over, and went to the ground almost verti- cally. I observed the impact near the north-west of Loos and saw the debris of the totally wrecked machine laying about as I flew over at 400 metres.[46]
>
> Oberleutnant Adolf von Tutschek, Jasta Boelcke, German Army Air Force

Strangely there are no reported Nieuport losses for 31 March. Although the claimed Nieuport had fallen behind the British lines, Tutschek's claim was supported by witness statements from Leutnant Koenig and the personnel of a nearby German anti-aircraft unit and so was eventually allowed by the German authorities. In similar fashion, Bishop's claim was to count as his second victory. In such confused fighting there was no such thing as certainty and there was a willingness to allow claims when there was no reason to disbelieve the officer concerned.

AS the old front lines of the Somme battlefield fell farther and farther behind the new front lines, many pilots and observers took the chance to pay a visit to the scenes of death and destruction of which they had heard so much during the Battle of the Somme in 1916:

> This afternoon I managed to get a tender and go up to the old lines which the Hun has just vacated. A battlefield is a wonderful but hardly a pretty sight. I went to Gommecourt Park which had once been one of the stately homes of France complete with chateau, gardens etc. The

whole show was now hammered flat and desolation reigned supreme. Our shell fire is truly terrible; the Boche must have had a fairly rough time in these trenches for there was not a piece of flat ground anywhere – nothing but shell holes. We had a show here in July last year which was a failure and our dead lie about in hundreds in No Man's Land, a truly horrible sight. I wonder what the mothers of these poor chaps would feel like if they could see their sons thrown about in heaps like so much garden rubbish. One can see from each man's attitude that he was carrying on his job when killed. Machine gunners lie alongside their Lewis guns, signallers have their flappers by their sides, bombers their bombs slung around their waists. Here and there a superior pair of boots will show where an officer has fallen. One and all, officers and men, have been left to rot and form part of the awful trail of death and desolation which is left by this terrible war.[47]

Second Lieutenant Charles Smart, 5 Squadron, RFC

It was a cold reminder of who they were risking their lives for – and the awful consequences of failure.

CHAPTER FOUR

FLEDGLINGS RISING

The expansion of the RFC to carry out its vastly expanded role since the start of the war was hampered by severe problems in training an adequate supply of pilots and observers. Even replacing the crews lost was a difficult task, yet Field Marshal Haig and Major-General Hugh Trenchard envisaged up to 106 squadrons with ninety-five reserve squadrons being needed before the end of the war. From the original four squadrons in 1914, the RFC strength on the Western Front had grown to twelve squadrons at the time of the Battle of Loos in September 1915, twenty-seven squadrons in time for 1 July 1916 on the Somme and just over forty squadrons in March 1917. The first aeroplane flight had only been in 1903 and it was inevitable that very few people had had any chance to gain flying experience before the war. As almost all the existing pilots had been sent on active service at the outbreak of war there was a crippling shortage of instructors able to train the new generation of pilots. Flying was not an intuitive skill, it was still barely understood, the training aircraft were not mechanically reliable and the slightest mistake in the air could be fatal. Despite the risks, there was no shortage of willing Albatros fodder. The RFC was an attractive option for young men. Flying offered a kind of glamour in sharp contrast to the muddy squalor of the trenches. Some, fascinated by the chance of flying, volunteered straight from school; others were discontented at the length of time their infantry training was taking and sought a quicker route to the front; others found themselves in a backwater from which they wished to escape.

One amongst many, Lieutenant Gilbert Preston, had already had experience of action with the dismounted yeomanry at Gallipoli, where he had lost the sight of his left eye. On emerging from hospital, he then served as a forward observation officer with the Royal Artillery, after which he conceived a desire to join the RFC to pursue what was essentially the same task from the skies above:

> I thought that I had fooled the doctor, because after I had read the reading board with my right eye, he turned me to the window and said, 'Tell me what you see out of the window'. I knew that I would have to come back to reading the eye chart, so I memorised all of the lines on the board. When I finished describing what I had seen out the window, he swung me around, and covered my right eye and said, 'Will you continue reading the eye chart?' I knew what was coming, so I started to 'read' the board. Suddenly he said, 'You're blind in that eye, aren't you?' I said, 'Oh no, not quite'. He told me, 'Uncover your right eye and look again at the chart'. While I had been looking out the window, and unknown to me, he had turned the chart over and the only single letter on that chart was the letter 'E'. I was heartsick as I thought my own chances were non-existent. He then announced, 'Don't take it too much to heart, because I have orders to send you to the Flying Corps – whether you can see or not!' To my disappointment he informed me that I could not qualify as a pilot and that I would go to France as an observer.[1]
>
> Second Lieutenant Gilbert Preston, RFC

The social mix of cadets gradually broadened out as pre-war snobbery succumbed to the pragmatism required in a global conflict. Yet existing class prejudices were still very much in evidence:

> There are some perfectly appalling people here now. Their intonation is terrible and you can pick out hairdressers, Jews who would sell tobacco, the typical shop attendant, the comic-turn man at a very provincial show, and the greasy mechanic type. These are the class of fellows from cadet schools – mostly conscripts and hardly one of them has any pretence at being a gentleman. There are still a very good crowd of observers and we keep to ourselves.[2]
>
> Lieutenant Dudley McKergow, RFC

Whatever their origins the prospective pilots were sent to an Officer Cadet Training School where they were put through a month of traditional military basic training enlivened as ever by drill sessions under grizzled NCOs:

We soon settled down to the task in hand – that of attempting to digest that prodigious volume known as Military Law, which contains every conceivable subject that an officer must know. Correct words of command in drill, practical demonstrations, in that we were expected to take charge of small and large groups. This was not a problem to me having had considerable experience as an NCO in the Australian Imperial Force. For drill and discipline we had Sergeant Major Sunshine, one time champion heavyweight boxer in the British Army, a real martinet and stickler for discipline in every way, even to making sure that on the first bugle call we were promptly out of bed for PT and drilling sessions. Some of our cadets resented this intrusion so early in the morning![3]

Second Lieutenant Francis Penny, RFC

The young pilots and observers soon became aware of the increasing levels of casualties being suffered by the RFC on the Western Front. Rumours were swirling around, but there was plenty of confirmation from the highest level:

Tales are already about concerning the number of friends and relatives of the fellows who have got killed fatally in the RFC and other stories of a nasty nature. Wonder how long it will take for me to get the wind up … Cheery news today in Parliament: 20 per cent of the RFC become casualties in a week and 20.1 per cent are killed in six weeks. We're all doomed.[4]

Second Lieutenant Frederick Ortweiler, RFC

As their training progressed the young cadets went on to the School of Aeronautics based at Oxford University. Here they were kitted out in their new RFC uniforms, which were radically different from the conventional army tunic:

We cadets now wore our new RFC uniforms – maternity jackets as they were rudely called – and, apart from the Sam Browne belt, we were only distinguishable from officers by a broad white cap-band. The 'double breaster' tunic was just the thing for the cold weather and, as they hooked up at the neck (no collar or tie was worn), were very useful when one was cutting things a bit fine for the morning parade. Apart from our compulsory attendance at lectures and the closing of the college gates at 11 p.m., we were treated like university students and it was up to us whether we did any study or work at all. Most were, like me, so keen to get through, that study was of paramount importance. However, it was great to be living like a normal human being again and more exciting still to think that within a short time I would be a fully-fledged officer.[5]

Second Lieutenant Raymond Brownell, RFC

At the schools in Oxford and Reading cadets were trained in the practical skills associated with flying, including map reading, elementary rigging, wireless signalling using Morse code buzzers, flying instruments, the workings of the engines upon which they would rely for their lives, photographic reconnaissance work, photographic interpretation, contact patrol methods and methods of artillery registration:

The syllabus for this School of Aeronautics appeared to me to be rather frightening. We had to become fully conversant with the technical details of eight types of engines, and other subjects were 'General Flying', 'Aircraft Rigging', 'Theory of Flight', 'Bombs', 'Instruments', 'Morse signalling' and 'Artillery Cooperation'. The two latter subjects caused me no worry as I was already fully conversant with them, but the 'innards' of engines had never interested me and the thought of a stiff examination at the end of the course filled me with dread. We were told the course was to be of two months duration, but towards the end of the third week we were informed that it was to be considerably shortened. So far as I was concerned this meant intensive 'engine' swotting.[6]

Second Lieutenant Raymond Brownell, RFC

A working knowledge of artillery observation was a vital skill for army cooperation pilots and for most of the cadets it was a new experience. One of the training tools was an early 'simulator' providing valuable experience which tried to get them as close to reality as was then possible:

In a large room, laid out on the floor was a model of the Ypres Salient and re-entrant by Messines, made exactly as it would be seen from an aeroplane 8,000–10,000 feet up. With a squared map it was possible to pick out all the various roads etc. and we were given practice in picking out points on the map. Then, by a system of little lights in the model, we were made to imagine that a battery was firing on a target and we were correcting. We would first be shown the target by having it lit up; then a flash would appear as the battery fired and another where the shot fell. Then we would have to send corrections over the buzzer till an 'OK' was registered and the shoot finished.[7]

Second Lieutenant Frederick Ortweiler, RFC

Early on young Ortweiler had the privilege of receiving a lecture from a senior non-commissioned officer on the general standards of behaviour and discipline that would be expected of an officer in the RFC:

There were many tips to pick up. His last remark was his best, 'And if you must go out with a girl who's a little more than she ought to be, for God's sake do it after dark!'[8]

Second Lieutenant Frederick Ortweiler, RFC

Although a few officer cadets still found time for the pleasures of the flesh, most found that their noses were pressed firmly to the grindstone.

Prospective sergeant pilots were also undergoing their training at Reading and amongst them was Sergeant Ernest Cook, a shy young lad with little, if any, experience in the ways of the world. After much heart-searching he plucked up the nerve to speak to a cinema usherette whom he then had the honour to escort innocently home:

She is the only girl I ever walked out with in my life up to the present. Well I met her quite a number of times and took her to theatre and concerts etc. I really believe that girl began to love me because she said I was the first boy she had ever walked with who didn't try to get 'fast' – from which I concluded she hadn't had a good selection. I enjoyed myself very well in her company and I would probably have carried on and become engaged if I had remained at Reading a few months. Fate said otherwise and I never even promised to come back and marry her. I wrote a few times but stopped it as it was no good attaching oneself to a girl on a business which I am now on – it is too mighty risky. If I come through I might go back but something seems to tell me I won't. She was a jolly nice girl but reading between the lines a very devil of a flirt. Well at any rate she wasn't any the worse for knowing me – I hope not any how.[9]

Sergeant Ernest Cook, RFC

In the fashion of a typical public school speech day, with which many of the young officer cadets were already familiar, a senior officer was brought in to pontificate before them. The cadets eyed him with that blank incomprehension that the very young reserve for their supposed elders and betters. What he had to say was not particularly encouraging:

> A General said some very cheerful things. The funny part was that the more he tried to mitigate the outlook he gave us; the worse he made it. At first he suggested that we might get killed. Then, as though that were more cheering, he hazarded the suggestion that a few of us might survive.[10]
>
> Second Lieutenant Frederick Ortweiler, RFC

After they had completed this course the pilots were sent off for practical flying instruction at a preliminary training school. One of the best known of these was located at the Hendon airfield in North London. Before the war Hendon was the home of a dramatic series of aerial flying displays that provided entertainment for huge crowds. It is difficult now to understand the excitement that flying created in those days. It was at the absolute cutting edge of modern science; yet wildly unpredictable and dangerous to boot. Hendon had become the home of several civilian flying schools run by some of the pioneers of British aviation. On the outbreak of war the army rapidly colonised them in the frantic drive to accelerate the stream of pilots to the front.

The first stage in the training process was their first flight in an aircraft. Even in 1917, the techniques of aircraft design had moved on apace and the aircraft used for training were already thoroughly old-fashioned. Although they certainly looked dangerous, in some ways their limited performance provided a kind of safety net:

> The Maurice Farman biplanes, known as the 'Shorthorns' and the 'Longhorns', which even then were regarded as somewhat prehistoric. They were pusher types with piano wire supported wings, out in front of which was a box-like open nacelle with seats in tandem for the pupil and instructor. The 70 hp Renault engine with four-bladed propeller was immediately behind. The Maurice Farman Longhorn differed from the Shorthorn in that the elevators were placed out in front on projecting booms, whereas in the Shorthorn the pilot and passenger were perched right out in front of everything and there was nothing

from which to judge horizontal balance. The elevator and control surfaces were right at the tail end, and the normal flying speed was 55–60 mph. These strange looking aircraft, commonly known as the 'Rumpety', staggered round the sky and were capable of taking an extraordinary amount of punishment.[11]

Second Lieutenant Raymond Brownell, RFC

We cannot now authentically recreate the sense of wonder mingled with very real trepidation at defying the elements that flying then held. Flying in 1917 was an almost unique experience. Hardly anyone had been up aloft in an aeroplane. Now, from the evidence of their own senses, at last they could believe a man could fly. Whether they realised it or not, for many it would be a defining moment for what remained of their lives:

Dressed up in flying coat, gauntlets, goggles and crash helmet and mounted the bus for my first 'flip'. 'Contact!' And after a few spurts of the engine, bounded off over the ground all out, the joystick jerking and the rudder bar swinging. Gradually the jolting became less, and finally ceased, and as the ground rushing beneath began to pass more slowly and included trees, I realised that we were off. Gradually the view included more and more fields and houses and the landscape seemed scarcely to move and just swung about like a slow compass card pivoted on the roaring prop and motor in front. The slipstream and the roar of the motor, before considered a nuisance, now feels like the very lifeblood. The sensation is one of complete comfort and security unless you imagine that the planes might give way, the motor fall out, or the controls break. But speculation shows that such a contingency is unlikely. Height does not trouble at all. The only other consideration is, 'Can I control the machine and right her if she suddenly falls sideways or forwards?' That feeling will no doubt soon come. I felt perfectly at home all the while: I watched and felt the controls and tried to reason out their movements, watched the rev indicator, felt the tension of the flying and landing wires, examined the ground from the point of view of forced landings and was perfectly happy. Then suddenly the nose went steep down, the engine stopped, the horizon rose up in front and we began to glide spirally downwards. The machine banked over steeply and we seemed to be slowly pivoting round on the tip of the inner wing. Gradually the trees rose up to meet us, the ground passed quickly beneath us, the joystick was pulled well back and with a slight jolt we bounded back to the hangars. The whole left me singularly unimpressed. There was a time when I used to get excited merely watching an aviator about to ascend at Hendon – now I feel absolutely unmoved by an actual flight. Right through I was as warm as toast and as happy as a lark. The flight reached 2,500 feet and lasted 28 minutes – it seemed like five minutes.[12]

Second Lieutenant Frederick Ortweiler, RFC

A couple of days later Ortweiler was up again with his instructor. For the first time he actually took control of the aircraft. The training aircraft were equipped with a dual set of controls to allow the pupil to fly the aircraft while still ceding the ultimate power to the instructor in moments of danger or uncertainty:

Took control for a bit, but Allen frequently had to yank the stick about and cut off the engine to tell me my faults, e.g. climbing her too much on the turns, not getting out of banks soon enough, too much rudder etc. After a number of circuits he took control and brought her down again. When we had finished, he told me that I had control of it practically all the time and was doing alright.[13]

Second Lieutenant Frederick Ortweiler, RFC

Ortweiler may well have been fooled by his instructor. Training was still fairly ad hoc and most of the instructors did not themselves fully understand the theory and practice of flying. Their knowledge came from a process of trying something out and, if the results didn't actually kill them, it was added to their repertoire. Many, therefore, had great difficulty in passing on the knowledge they had haphazardly acquired. Without switching off the engine, which in itself was a risky undertaking, there was no chance of talking audibly and non-verbal communication was more usual. They would tap the pupil on the right or left shoulder to indicate a right- or left-hand turn; a light tap on the top of the head meant, 'Put the nose down to descend!' and a tap on the back of the neck meant, 'Pull the control column back and climb!' It was noticed by many pupils that a good clout on the head meant that they had done something really wrong and were liable to be soundly ticked off on landing!

There is no doubt that the instructors were placed under tremendous strain by the requirement to train and pass more and more pilots to service the desperate needs of the army on the Western Front. Some of the instructors found themselves flying up to eight hours of dual instruction in a day. However conscientious they may originally have been, the quality of their teaching inevitably deteriorated and a carelessness born of weariness led to a proliferation of accidents that could probably have been avoided. They simply did not have the time to give instruction tailored to suit the vastly varying temperaments and skills of their pupils. It was no coincidence that many instructors began to refer to their pupils, only half in jest, as 'Huns'; they saw them as the enemy and feared exposure to their ham-fisted flying. Such instructors would take the minimum of chances and often took over the controls for all the dangerous passages of the flight, particularly, of course, on landing. This was much to the detriment of their pupil's learning curve. Many were furious when they at last realised what was happening:

> My instructor is useless. I have just been up with him for fifteen minutes
> and he will not let you have control at all, so I am going to have an
> extremely good try to get changed on to another instructor today.
> I learnt more in twelve minutes with another fellow than I have in an
> hour and three-quarters with my frequent instructor. It's absolutely a
> waste of time.[14]
>
> Lieutenant Dudley McKergow, RFC

The trainee pilots were also under considerable mental stress. Distracted by their own fears and worries, they did not appreciate the problems their instructors faced in attempting to balance the risk to themselves, the risk to their pupils and the ever-increasing pressure to deliver up new pilots for the front. Short cuts had to be taken. A conscientious instructor might legitimately push through a pupil that he felt was a natural pilot. But, shamefully, some instructors abrogated all responsibility and just pushed pupils through as fast as possible, regardless of their ability. There was even a real suspicion that some instructors would rather that a pupil took the risk of killing himself by flying solo before he was ready, than that they should have to endure another dose of their awful flying under dual instruction:

> In just over one week I had been given only nine short instructional
> flights. On my last flight I was handling the controls and was presum-
> ably making the landings. However, I felt that my instructor was

actually putting the machine down himself and on the last landing I decided to find out by taking my hands off the controls altogether. The resultant landing was a poor one and Turner ticked me off properly for being a bloody fool and making a bad landing. I said, 'As a matter of fact you made the landing yourself. I did not have my hands on the controls!' He yelled, 'I suppose you think you could do better yourself?' Rather nettled, I said, 'Yes!' With that he undid his seat belt, jumped out and said, 'Well, take her off yourself!!' That staggered me for a moment, as I realised I had not received more than a bare two hours dual instruction altogether. Not admitting that I was frightened out of my life, however, I decided to have a go at it and attempt my first solo. I took off very carefully and took a long time to climb up to 1,000 feet before daring to make my first turn. Then it took me just on an hour to pluck up enough courage to come down and make my first landing. I bumped rather solidly, but had enough sense to put my engine on and go round again. I repeated this performance twice more and finally decided as it was getting dark that, whatever happened, I would not put my engine on again on coming down the third time. The last landing I made was a very good one and I taxied in quite pleased with myself, though the comments from Lieutenant Turner were anything but complimentary. But I did not mind as I had completed my first solo and had not broken anything, no doubt more by good luck than good management![15]

Second Lieutenant Raymond Brownell, RFC

As if to underline the seriousness of the risks they were taking, Lieutenant Ortweiler saw one of his fellow 'Huns' pile his aircraft into the ground in a spectacular crash in the neighbouring field during his first solo flight:

I imagined him to be in frightful condition, but in a few seconds I saw a figure walking about and found that he had not received a scratch! When he returned he mentioned how his crash helmet had taken the shock – whereupon I, who was just about to go up in a balaclava woollen helmet – snatched his from him and donned it myself.[16]

Second Lieutenant Frederick Ortweiler, RFC

Ortweiler noticed that far too many pupils at Hendon were being pressurised to fly solo before they were ready:

Allen's ruse in getting immature pupils their 'ticket' was evidenced by a very close shave from a crash. The pupil misjudged his landing and was making straight for a hedge when he had the sense to switch on and give up the idea of landing, meanwhile all our hearts stood in our mouths.[17]

Second Lieutenant Frederick Ortweiler, RFC

It is not surprising that there were numerous fatalities amongst pilots under training. The old Maurice Farmans may have been forgiving, they may have absorbed an enormous amount of punishment, but a bad crash still meant serious injury or death. Casualties in training were high and flying was still a very dangerous business. Ortweiler's own first solo flight was not without incident:

Got into the Arzani solo bus and set off on my first solo circuit. Immediately she got off the ground I noticed that the engine was not pulling properly, for I was flying with the joystick well back in my stomach and yet she scarcely rose. After I had got out a little way, I attempted to turn and immediately I began to lose height till I saw myself making straight for a tree. So I put the nose down and gave her a desperate yank back with the result that I just cleared the tree, but nearly stalled in the attempt. Thence floundered across the aerodrome and started a left-hand turn to get back. She again started to lose height so heaved the joystick still further back into my tummy and nearly stalled her. Finally, switched off and sped down to the aerodrome, but having rather misjudged it and making slap for another of the ubiquitous trees, pulled her nose up and switched on and off, a silly thing to do as it did not give me enough flying speed and nearly stalled me. Missed the tree by inches according to the accounts of eyewitnesses and effected a moderate landing. Taxied back to find Allen simply quaking with mixed horror and surprise and almost beside himself with disgust. Mr Warren, the boss, merely put his hand to his heart and sighed. The other instructors and pupils were white with fear and avowed it all the best nerve tonic they had ever had. It was only then that I realised what I had done and during the ensuing half hour the wind sought to gather within me. One pupil drew my attention to the significance of a remark I made just as I went off, 'No flowers, by request!' A remark made in jest almost fulfilled.[18]

Second Lieutenant Frederick Ortweiler, RFC

It seems amazing that after such a close shave Ortweiler should be sent back up to try again. But time for reflection would almost certainly have broken his nerve. Far better to get straight back into the air and face the demons before they had a chance to consolidate their grip on his consciousness:

> After half an hour, during which the engine was repaired, went up for another solo circuit and did alright. So went up for my 'ticket'. Did figures of eight until a white flag was waved and then did one more, went well outside the aerodrome, turned round, nosed down cut off and made an OK landing right by the mark. Without stopping, taxied back and took off again, repeating the evolution and at the end of another five figure eights, came in and made an 'A1' landing. Then up and did a circuit and volplanned down from 550 feet. Did well, but landed with rather a bump. While I still had the engine ticking over young Warren and Allen ran up and congratulated me, and then when I taxied up to the hangars, I was greeted by the other instructors. A great day.[19]
>
> Second Lieutenant Frederick Ortweiler, RFC

The 'ticket' was the basic Flying Certificate test administered by the Royal Aero Club and it meant Ortweiler was a registered qualified pilot. The pilots selected for the corps machines were then sent for training on the new RE8s. Here their problems multiplied. The RE8s were not fitted with dual controls and the training process became almost farcical. They were taken for a brief flight in the rear cockpit from where they could look over the instructor's shoulder to see the various controls, instruments and gauges. This was far from an ideal form of instruction and the numerous accidents fuelled the belief that the RE8 was difficult to fly. The pilots who showed the most promise were assigned to scouts. Many were entranced by rumours of a marvellous new aircraft – this was the Sopwith Camel – that would surely sweep the Germans once and for all from the skies. For once the rumours were true, but sadly the news was irrelevant to most of them who simply ran out of time before the rumour matured into solid fact:

> Someone brought the news, 'Sopwith has produced a machine with a 130 hp engine! It'll do 130 mph level and climbs 10,000 feet in six minutes! It has *two* guns shooting through the prop!' The Camel rumour created a sensation. Everyone delayed graduation until the 'miracle' was attainable and they could go out on a machine which

would assure them a name to be spoken of with Ball, Lanoe Hawker, Immelmann and Boelcke. For some of us the Camel was still far away and with the air throbbing with the news of the arrival 'at any moment' of 'seven brand new Camels' we miserably made our way overseas, on the poor old Sopwith 1½ Strutter.[20]

Lieutenant Stanton Waltho, RFC

Whether assigned to scouts or army cooperation aircraft, the grim reality was that the newly qualified pilots had nowhere near enough time to practise flying the type of aircraft they would be flying over France. Stunting was frowned upon, with the inevitable result that the very manoeuvres that were essential to escape sudden danger were still totally foreign to new pilots when they were posted on active service. They had a lot to learn and they would have to learn it quickly.

Yet there was hope for the future: the RFC was about to have its whole training programme overhauled and invigorated under the influence of the radical ideas of Major Robert Smith-Barry, who had been given a free rein in developing a new approach to teaching combat flying on his appointment to command 1 (Reserve) Squadron at Gosport in December 1916. Smith-Barry used his personal combat flying experience to come up with a brand new training system that sought to equip the new pilot with everything that they needed to know:

The words 'Danger' and 'Nerves' must not form part of the instructor's vocabulary. Nothing that a pupil may do in the air is dangerous, if he knows what he is doing and what the result will be. Almost all accidents are caused by ignorance, and if, instead of telling a pupil that a manoeuvre is dangerous, he is taught how to do it, his instinct of self-preservation will do the rest.[21]

Second Lieutenant Keith Jopp, RFC

This process started with the basic flying training using the relatively high-powered Avro 504 series of aircraft. The trainee pilot would be in the front seat and the instructor behind, each with a complete set of controls and a speaking tube between them to allow proper communication. A large part of Smith-Barry's training philosophy was the necessity to teach every pilot not how to *avoid* dangerous situations such as 'spinning' but how to get out of them with assurance, and to build up the self-confidence they would need to throw their aircraft about the sky if they were *in extremis*:

One morning I was told that the Commanding Officer wanted to take me up again. This rather shook me because one seldom had any dual control after you'd once gone solo. The CO was Major Smith-Barry and I suppose he treated me as one of his early guinea pigs just to try out his new ideas. I enjoyed the few minutes I had with him enormously. He showed me above anything else how to get out of a spin which up to that time most of us regarded as fatal. Smith-Barry was undoubtedly a genius. The confidence that I could always get out of a spin saved my life on at least one occasion.[22]

Second Lieutenant Reginald Fuljames, RFC

In time, Smith-Barry would revolutionise the training of British pilots. But, like the Sopwith Camels, it would be too late for the pilots who would have to face Richthofen and his men over Arras in April 1917. For most of them the reality was just a mad rush and a fatal lack of practical flying experience in the type of aircraft they would have to fly in action:

Holy smoke! What a pickle. In London now destined for overseas squadron unknown. A chap woke me this morning and said I was wanted at the sheds to fly. New instructor told me to do four hours continuous flying and I would be sent to London in the afternoon. Wind up. Had breakfast – did two hours – washed – did two more. Went to Swindon by car, to London by train.[23]

Sergeant Ernest Cook, RFC

One more innocent was on his way to the Western Front.

CHAPTER FIVE

BLOODY APRIL

No one can say that he has the supremacy of the air because we continue
to work on despite our casualties and the Boche never do any work.[1]

Captain Eric Routh, 16 Squadron, RFC

All the work, all the suffering undergone by the men of the Royal Flying
Corps, had been in preparation for the Battle of Arras. The assault
was originally planned to start on 8 April, but had to be postponed by 24
hours at the request of General Robert Nivelle – and thus the designated
first day of the Battle of Arras became Easter Monday – 9 April 1917. By
the start of the month the artillery concentration was almost complete. In
all 2,817 British guns and howitzers had been painfully amassed, massive
shell stockpiles built up, and targets and fire programmes patiently defined.
The British were faced by 1,014 German guns and howitzers.

On the Third Army front, south of the River Scarpe, there had been
some disagreement between Field Marshal Sir Douglas Haig and General
Sir Edmund Allenby over the length of the preliminary bombardment.
Allenby and his artillery specialists originally planned a short, but intensive,
48-hour bombardment which Haig strongly resisted, demanding a longer
bombardment. Whilst the new 106 fuse fitted to shells had proved effective
in clearing German barbed wire, the fuses were simply not available in
anything like the quantities needed to allow the kind of short, sharp bombardment followed by surprise, as desired by Allenby. That lay in the near
future but was not yet feasible in April 1917. As might be expected, Haig
had his way and the barrage was duly extended to four days.

The scale of the bombardment can be judged in comparison with the
much-vaunted barrage that had preceded the Battle of the Somme. There,
in eight days, some 52,000 tons of ammunition had been fired; at Arras

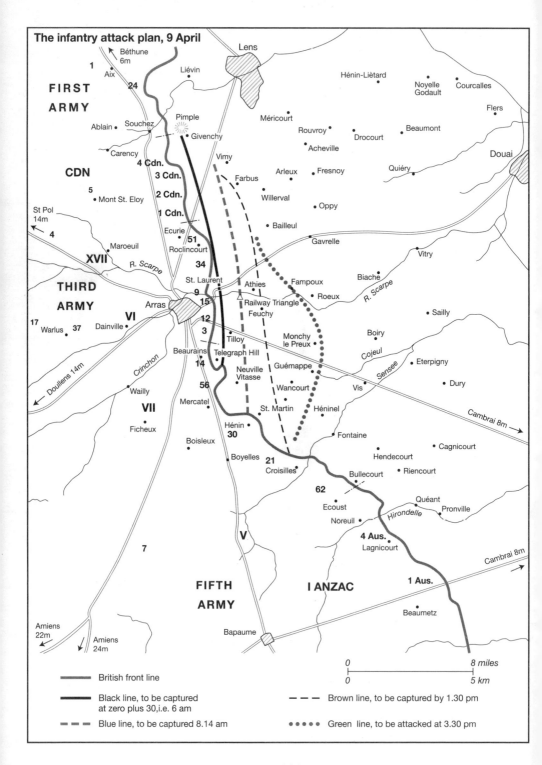

The infantry attack plan, 9 April

FIRST ARMY

Béthune 6m
Aix
1
24
Liévin
Lens

CDN

Ablain
Souchez
Pimple
Givenchy
Méricourt
Rouvroy
Acheville
Drocourt
Beaumont
Hénin-Liétard
Noyelle Godault
Courcalles
Flers
Douai

Carency
4 Cdn.
3 Cdn.
2 Cdn.
1 Cdn.
Vimy
Farbus
Willerval
Arleux
Fresnoy
Oppy
Bailleul
Quiéry

St Pol 14m
4
5
Mont St. Eloy

XVII
Maroeuil
Ecurie
51
Roclincourt
34
R. Scarpe
St. Laurent
9
Gavrelle
Biache
Vitry

THIRD ARMY

Arras
VI
15
12
3
Athies
Railway Triangle
Feuchy
Fampoux
Roeux
R. Scarpe
Sailly

17
Warlus
37
Dainville
Tilloy
Beaurains
14
Telegraph Hill
Neuville Vitasse
56
Monchy le Preux
Guémappe
Wancourt
Boiry
Cojeul
Sensee
Vis
Eterpigny
Dury

Doullens 14m
Crinchon
Wailly
VII
Ficheux
Mercatel
Hénin
30
St. Martin
Héninel
Fontaine
Hendecourt
Cagnicourt
Riencourt

Boisleux
Boyelles
Croisilles
21
Bullecourt
Quéant
Pronville

62
Ecoust
Noreuil
Hirondelle

V
4 Aus.
Lagnicourt
Cambrai 8m

FIFTH ARMY

7
I ANZAC
1 Aus.
Beaumetz

Amiens 22m
Amiens 24m
Bapaume
Cambrai 8m

0   8 miles
0   5 km

— British front line

— Black line, to be captured at zero plus 30, i.e. 6 am

– – – Blue line, to be captured 8.14 am

– – – Brown line, to be captured by 1.30 pm

••••• Green line, to be attacked at 3.30 pm

88,000 tons were to be expended on a shorter front in half the time. Furthermore, problems in shell manufacture, which meant a distressingly high proportion of shells on the Somme failed to go off, had been largely resolved by 1917. The German positions were plastered by a whirlwind of exploding shells. The artillery plans drawn up before the battle showed that many of the lessons of the Somme had been learnt. In particular, counter-battery fire was no longer an afterthought to be tackled as and when desired; it had a fundamental importance. Specific batteries were designated to do nothing other than relentless counter-battery work in an effort to destroy every identified German battery with the combined assistance of the forward observation posts, RFC army cooperation crews, kite balloon observers, flash spotters and sound rangers. Each had their role to play if the German batteries were to be silenced, and as the days passed by they were collectively successful in knocking out battery after battery, gun after gun:

> The counter-battery organisation was extremely well run and very complex. You had a counter-battery officer at Corps who kept very complete records and maps which were circulated regularly. Every gun position seen firing was entered on the map and it was given a number so that an aeroplane seeing it fire could send down the signal 'GNF' which meant 'Gun now firing number so and so'. The counter-battery staff would know at once that battery was in action and they would get someone on to it. The majority of the 4.5 howitzers were gas shelling. On the actual night before the attack we fired more than 500 rounds per gun of gas shell at German batteries. And we were by no means the only battery doing this.[2]
>
> Lieutenant Kenneth Page, 130 Bty, 40th Brigade, Royal Artillery

At the heart of the British plan were great rolling barrages to be launched in support of the infantry attack at Zero Hour. Typically, a standing barrage by the 4.5-in and 6-in howitzers would fall on the German support trench, while the great mass of 18-pounders that made up the bulk of the field artillery would lay down the shrieking wall of shells – 50 per cent high explosive and 50 per cent shrapnel – to precede the infantry across No Man's Land, intended to wash them safely over the German front line. Meanwhile, the long-range guns and howitzers would be sweeping across the German rear areas, seeking out concentrations of troops and possible counter-attack formations. Once the German front line was taken, the barrages would roll forward again, while half the field artillery moved forward to allow them to continue their support as the troops moved beyond the range of their original positions.

The tanks were another method of tearing through the German barbed wire, but here, as with the aircraft, production problems at home had thwarted the generals at the front. The new Mark IV tanks had not yet arrived at the front and the older Mark I and IIs were unreliable, far too slow, vulnerable to German shell fire, and by no means bulletproof. In the end only sixty were available to be thrown into the assault. As any kind of mass tank attack was thus impossible, the meagre number of tanks available were targeted on specific German strong points such as the notorious Telegraph Hill or Railway Triangle. Another innovation scheduled to make its debut at Arras was several batteries of Livens projectors, designed to throw large canisters of gas right into the German front lines with an effective range of about 1,200 yards. This would allow massive concentrations of gas to thoroughly douse German troops before they had a chance to don their gas masks.

In the final days before the attack the infantry were moved forward, many concealed from view and out of harm's way in cellars and interconnected tunnels, which by then ran like a maze beneath the streets of Arras. There they remained, ready to debouch from these places of safety and assume their allotted role in the attack. Naturally, the soldiers may have been nervous but everything possible was being done to ease their passage into the German trenches.

The advance was to be in carefully controlled stages, corresponding for the most part with the main German trench lines. North of the River Scarpe, there was no doubt as to the main objective. The brooding heights of the Vimy Ridge, which provided a superb vantage point of the whole of the Flanders plain, had defied countless attacks over the last two years. This time they meant to succeed. South of the Scarpe, the main objective was the hill of Monchy-le-Preux, which dominated the eastern approaches to Arras. The assault divisions were allotted specific objectives and when these were achieved the reserve divisions would leapfrog them and take the attack to the next line of objectives. The plans were ambitious for they went as far as ordering the capture of the German Third Line lying across the River Scarpe. Success on this scale would enable them to turn the flank of the Hindenburg Line and would leave the Germans with only the partially completed Drocourt–Quéant Switch Line to fall back on some six miles further ahead. The German retreat in March had left the right flank of Allenby's Third Army directly facing the undiluted strength of a section of the Hindenburg Line. As the neighbouring Fifth Army of General Sir Hubert Gough was still toiling across the wastelands left in the Germans wake they would find it almost impossible to launch any meaningful coordinated thrust as had originally been envisaged.

As plans were hammered out, a mountain of detail accumulated. It was the role of the much derided staff officers to make sense of all detail; a role further complicated by the almost farcical inarticulacy of two of the main protagonists:

> No attack we have yet made, not even the Somme, has been as fully and as carefully prepared as this one. General Allenby, who is commanding the main attack for the first time in a big battle, has any amount of determination and 'go'. Allenby shares one peculiarity with Haig, he cannot explain verbally, with any lucidity at all, what his plans are. In a conference between the two of them it is rather amusing. Douglas Haig hardly ever finishes a sentence, and Allenby's sentences, although finished, do not really convey exactly what he means. Yet they understand one another perfectly; but as each of their particular Staffs only understands their immediate superior a good detail of explanation of details has to be gone into afterwards and cleared up.[3]
>
> Brigadier-General John Charteris, Intelligence Officer, General Headquarters, BEF

This process was not helped by Allenby's explosive and hair-trigger temper. The generals were not 'donkeys', but such easily caricatured personal traits made matters much simpler for their subsequent critics when they sought to paint them as idiots.

Meanwhile, the infantry went through a detailed programme of training exercises behind the lines to prepare them, as far as was humanly possible, for the tribulations that lay ahead of them:

> In an area well behind the lines, a large model of the Ridge, showing every phase of the German defence positions as gleaned from aerial photographs was laid out. In turns, our battalions were taken back to this model, where, on a simulated pattern, they were shown exactly what they had to do and where they had to go on the day of the

assault. The troops were told of the massive artillery support behind them and of the great mines which would be blown at Zero.[4]

Private Magnus McIntyre Hood, 24th Battalion, (Victoria Rifles) 5th Brigade, 2nd Canadian Division

This time there were to be no mistakes.

GATHERING STORM

ON the ground the battle had not yet begun; in the air the bitter struggle for control of the Arras skies reached a dreadful false peak as March faded away. Its hard-fought nature can be judged by the fact that the British losses in the air that month alone were equal to *all* of those lost during 1915. The Fokker scourge truly paled into insignificance compared to the deadly threat posed by the Albatros.

The total British strength amassed along the front of the British First and Third Armies was some twenty-five Squadrons. In support of First Army was I Brigade RFC, comprising the First (Corps) Wing (2, 5, 10 and 16 Squadrons all equipped with BE2 variants) and the Tenth (Army) Wing (25 Squadron: FE2bs and FE2ds; 40 Squadron: Nieuport Scouts; 43 Squadron: Sopwith 1½ Strutters; and 8 (Naval) Squadron RNAS: Sopwith Triplanes). The neighbouring Third Army was supported by III Brigade RFC, comprising the Twelfth (Corps) Wing (8, 12, and 13 Squadrons all equipped with BE2 variants; and 59 Squadron: RE8s) and the Thirteenth (Army) Wing (29, 60 and 6 (Naval) Squadrons: Nieuport Scouts; 11 Squadron: FE2bs; and 48 Squadron: Bristol Fighters). There was also the ultimate RFC reserve of the Ninth (Headquarters) Wing (19 Squadron: Spad VIIs; 27 Squadron: Martinsyde Scouts; 35 Squadron: Armstrong Whitworth FK8s; 55 Squadron: DH4s; 56 Squadron: SE5s; 57 Squadron: FE2ds; 66 Squadron: Sopwith Pups; and 70 Squadron: Sopwith 1½ Strutters). Finally there was the night bombing force of 100 Squadron using FE2bs.

In all approximately 365 serviceable aircraft in twenty-five squadrons could be deployed, of which 120 were single-seater scouts. To oppose this, the Germans had just 195 army cooperation and scout aircraft. Between Lille and Péronne – on the wider front – the British First, Third, Fifth and Fourth Armies faced the German Sixth and First Armies. In all the British had 41 squadrons and 754 aircraft, of which 385 were single-seater aircraft. The Germans had 264 aircraft, of which 114 were single-seater aircraft. It should be borne in mind that the main German air concentration of some 480 aircraft, including about 240 scouts, was directed against the French because they were fully aware of the imminent Nivelle offensive on the Aisne.

The crushing British advantage in overall numbers of aircraft was an illusion that would only deceive the foolish. Just as the *Dreadnought* had rendered any number of lesser pre-dreadnoughts irrelevant in any equation of comparative strengths at sea so too the technological superiority of the German Albatros was such that it ruled the skies. A new generation of British aircraft was at last ready to be unleashed, but numbers were still limited. Trenchard decided to hold these new aircraft back until the offensive had actually begun, to try and maximise their impact at the time when it most mattered. In such circumstances only courage could make use of numerical supremacy – the supreme courage to take to the skies knowing that many must die so that a few could succeed. After all, the infantry so far below would die in immeasurably greater numbers if the guns of the Royal Artillery were not properly harnessed to their destructive task. In these circumstances, forceful leadership was essential and Trenchard was not the kind of man to evade his responsibilities. His policy of sustained aerial offensive faced its most crucial test, but he remained grimly determined that the RFC would not be found wanting:

> Trenchard often came to visit us at Treizennes, particularly during the period of our heaviest casualties. Although it was partly as a result of his aggressive policy in the air that we were having those shocking losses, it must not be thought that he was unaware of, or indifferent to what was happening to us. Trenchard was very deeply concerned about that, but it did not change his opinion about what should be done; and that some of us should come to feel that he was wrong in some of his ideas is another matter altogether. The effect that Trenchard's visits had on the morale of those in the squadrons was almost magical. He was a tall man of a commanding presence which was coupled with a personality that was extraordinarily inspiring.[5]
>
> Major Sholto Douglas, 43 Squadron, RFC

Trenchard saw the larger picture; he knew that certain missions simply *had* to be successfully accomplished. If one attempt should fail then another effort must be launched immediately regardless of the inevitable casualties.

This was not stupidity or bravado; it was just a grim military necessity.

Ironically, Trenchard himself was laid up at the crucial moment with an attack of German measles, an unfortunately named disease that caused much innocent hilarity around the RFC messes at the great man's expense. As a result, for the first few days of April, he was confined to his sick bed. There he fumed at his temporary impotence as the men under his command risked everything to get the reams of photographs that the desperate staff officers were clamouring for:

> Prior to the Vimy Ridge attack we had only the old 'P' type and hand operated cameras for oblique and vertical photography. Photographs with the former were most popular with the Canadian Corps just before the attack, as they gave such an excellent perspective view of the hilly ground over which the attack was due to pass. Mosaics with the latter were somewhat difficult to ensure. The hand operated camera often left serious gaps. In addition the area behind the Vimy Ridge was a re-entrant into the enemy lines, caused by the Lens salient, whilst the ridge itself was particularly carefully 'marked' by enemy fighters. The consequence was that photographic reconnaissances seldom were able to complete their work without being attacked several times. We found that formations of three or five, working at hours when our offensive patrols were due to be in the area, were the best method of ensuring success. We used to keep in touch with the Army Wing in order to find out suitable hours. It was useless to send any but our most experienced pilots in these formations, as they were the only ones capable of holding together under the conditions in which they had to work.[6]
>
> Major Paul Maltby, 16 Squadron, RFC

Artillery observation duties were unceasing. For the crews the weather was just one more enemy to be overcome. Unfortunately, 1 April 1917 marked the beginning of a noticeably raw month; any promise of spring was held firmly in check by the full gamut of winter weather. By this time Second Lieutenant Charles Smart had been temporarily transferred to 16 Squadron but there was to be no easy introduction into his new unit. Straight away he was in action above Vimy Ridge:

> Tried to do shoot with 5th Canadian Siege on hostile battery No. 1313. My first attempt at a shoot and of course the weather was dud. I found the ground strips alright and also the target; fired three shots then the

clouds came down, stopped the battery firing and hung about for forty-five minutes to see if weather would clear. Instead of clearing a violent hail storm came on and the clouds must have dropped almost to the ground so I at once cleared off home and was jolly glad to find the aerodrome. A hailstorm is a rotten thing to be up in, I could hardly see the ground from 400 feet and the hail stung like fury. It was amusing to watch the hailstones bounce off my nose onto the windscreen.[7]

Second Lieutenant Charles Smart, 16 Squadron, RFC

The weather was so bad that a British kite balloon was struck by lightning and one of the ground crew was killed. All the British could hope for during the next few days was that these harsh weather conditions, although dangerous and inconvenient in the extreme, would at least keep the Germans on the ground or blind those that got aloft.

At first light on 2 April, the weather seemed to have relented and the early birds once more took to the air. Amongst them were Second Lieutenant Charles Smart with his observer, Lieutenant A. M. Harvey in their BE2e:

Early job, left the ground at 6.45 a.m. to do a shoot with 69th Siege Battery on hostile battery No. B13. Took over an hour to put ground strips out at the battery, discovered later that they had only just come into position and did not put their wireless mast up till 8 a.m.. This wasted the best part of the weather for it began to go dud. I managed to observe twenty-four shots for them and we did quite well, though no 'OKs' were registered. It is fine to sit up in the air and have four great big 9.2-in howitzers under your command, you just press the button and a few seconds later a small puff of smoke appears somewhere round the target, just like magic.[8]

Second Lieutenant Charles Smart, 16 Squadron, RFC

However, the weather soon deteriorated again into a nasty combination of rain mixed with frequent lashings of snow and hail, all driven by a gale-force wind that headed straight towards the German lines. Pilots flying later in the day found progress was almost impossible:

Snow, hail and 60 mph wind – some flying attempted and several machines crashed by wind when trying to take off. Quite a number of Huns up over the lines – not long ago they rarely were seen in bad weather.[9]

Captain Ewart Garland, 16 Squadron, RFC

One such intrepid German was Oberleutnant Adolf von Tutschek, the scout pilot who had accompanied Prince Freidrich Karl of Prussia on his last flight. Tutschek was an ambitious pilot who was exceedingly keen to match the exploits of his heroes:

> I planned to shoot down an Englishman but before I could make up my mind which one to take on after a collision with the 'Tommies', they either escaped or were sent down for repairs by the fire of Voss or Bernert. That situation caused me to fret terribly, as I was 'too late' with regularity. And so, because everything was always being snapped up before my nose, I took off by myself while the others were peacefully sleeping. The front was quickly reached, and I climbed to 4,500 metres and waited for something to show up. There was serenity and peace everywhere. Below me the newly constructed Siegfried Line positions with its wire obstacles appeared from up here as a dark veil against the white snow, while 500 metres above me was a layer of clouds. I searched and searched for an English machine beneath me, and I became so occupied with my searching that it was only after a sudden rattle above me that I looked up and saw five Nieuports diving down on me. 'Too many of them!' I thought, so I stand my crate on its nose and tear out.[10]

> Oberleutnant Adolf von Tutschek, Jasta Boelcke, German Army Air Force

The aircraft he had encountered were Nieuport Scouts from 60 Squadron:

> The Nieuports are close behind me but I am faster and I had a head start. I'm several kilometres behind our lines and observe with satisfaction how four of my pursuers veer off while the fifth bravely follows. I throttle my motor and let the enemy catch up. Now I have him close enough and I turn and head toward him at top speed. 'Tommy' accepts the challenge and we roar around each other. Neither of us is able to get the other in his sights – not even for seconds – but I am constantly above him and we are gradually losing altitude. My partner gives up and flies homeward – that is he banks, loops, slides as he tumbles westward. His flying is excellent as I never get the opportunity to shoot as I am experiencing a jammed loading chamber in one machine gun. In the meantime another German single-seater has arrived and is idly watching our contest, but I am unable to recognise him. Again 'Tommy' tumbles off and I can't catch up with him. My competitor is already

behind the fellow and after a few shots the Englishman tilts forward with flames shooting from his machine. The wings break away and the fuselage hits the ground near Quéant. Furiously I stare at the victor – it is Bernert again – and he has the nerve to wink at me cheerfully![11]

Oberleutnant Adolf von Tutschek, Jasta Boelcke, German Army Air Force

Lieutenant V. F. Williams was the pilot shot down by the competitive Oberleutnant Otto Bernert who was also from Jasta Boelcke. The bespectacled and inoffensive looking Bernert was born the son of a local politician in Ratibor, Upper Silesia on 6 March 1893. Before the war he had served in the infantry and was commissioned into the 173rd Infantry Regiment in 1914. He was unlucky to receive multiple wounds including one from a bayonet, which severely damaged his main nerves. Unable to continue in the infantry he had transferred as an observer to the German Air Force before qualifying as a pilot and beginning a remarkable career as a scout pilot.

In the late morning of 2 April, Lieutenant Alan Dore, commanding C Flight of 43 Squadron, was charged once again with the responsibility of photographing the section of the Hindenburg Line that lay to the east of Vimy Ridge. The importance and urgency of such a mission was all too obvious to both sides just a few days before the British offensive:

Set out at ten o'clock with formation of six machines. Clouds above and below us. At 5,000 feet we saw some Huns. Presently I noticed what appeared to be Nieuports following us, and a moment later I heard my observer let off his gun. I shouted to him to stop but his gun continued. He was right. A few minutes later I saw the red belly and fish tail of an Albatros Scout diving on to one of our Sopwiths which disappeared under control into the clouds.[12]

Lieutenant Alan Dore, 43 Squadron, RFC

Dore had undoubtedly been fooled by the similarity between the Albatros DIII and the Nieuports with which they shared many design features. The Sopwith 1½ Strutter attacked by the Albatros was piloted by Lieutenant Peter Warren, accompanied for the first time by Sergeant Reuel Dunn as his observer. Their opponent proved to be Richthofen himself:

I was flying at the end of the 'V', in the last position, which made me the highest. Richthofen dove down out of the sun and took Dunn by surprise. The first notice I had of the attack was when I heard Dunn from his seat behind me shout something at me, and at the same time a spray of bullets went over my shoulder from behind and splintered the dashboard almost in front of my face. I kicked over the rudder and dived instantly, and just got a glance at the red machine passing under me to the rear.[13]

Lieutenant Peter Warren, 43 Squadron, RFC

With his machine already riddled with bullets, Warren took emergency action, which, although it provided a temporary relief, meant that he was inevitably separated from the rest of his formation. In the circumstances he had little choice:

I looked back over my shoulder, and Dunn was not in sight. I did not know whether he had been thrown out of the plane in my quick dive or was lying dead at the bottom of his cockpit. I realised that he was out of action however, and that I was quite defenceless from the rear. I endeavoured to get my forward machine gun on the red plane, but Richthofen was too wise a pilot, and his machine was too speedy for mine. He zoomed up again and was on my tail in less than half a minute. Another burst of lead came over my shoulder, and the glass faces of the instruments on the dashboard popped up in my face. I dived again, but he followed my every move. I had lost several thousand feet, but still below me was a layer of clouds. I dove for it, hoping to pull up in it and shake him off.[14]

Lieutenant Peter Warren, 43 Squadron, RFC

But the solid-looking mass of clouds below him proved to be just a thin layer, useless for any kind of effective concealment. And, sure enough, Richthofen was not the kind of man to be thrown off so easily. He stuck to Warren as a dog to a particularly juicy bone:

I found that the red Albatros with those two sputtering machine guns had come through with me. Another burst of lead from behind and the bullets spattered on the breech of my own machine gun, cutting the cartridge belt. At the same time, my engine stopped and I knew that the fuel tanks had been hit. There were more clouds below me. I dove for them and tried to pull up in them as soon as I reached them. No luck! My elevators didn't answer the stick. The control wires had been shot away. There was nothing to do but go down and hope to keep out of a spin as best as I could. I side-slipped and then went into a dive which fast became a spiral. I don't know how I got out of it. I was busy with the useless controls all the time, and going down at a frightful speed, but the red machine seemed to be able to keep itself poised just above and behind me all the time, and its machine guns were working every minute. I found later that bullets had gone through both of my sleeves and both of my boot legs, but in all of the firing, not one of them touched me. I managed to flatten out somehow in the landing and piled up with an awful crash. As I hit the ground, the red machine swooped over me, but I don't remember him firing on me when I was on the ground.[15]

Lieutenant Peter Warren, 43 Squadron, RFC

There was a chilling implacability about the nature of Richthofen's pursuit and some controversy over the final stages:

The enemy plane tried to escape and hide in the clouds after I had holed its benzene tank. Below the clouds I immediately attacked him again, thereby forcing him to land 300 metres east of Givenchy. But as yet my adversary would not surrender and even as his machine was on the ground, he kept shooting at me, thereby hitting my machine very severely at an altitude of 5 metres. I once more attacked him, while on the ground, and killed one of the occupants.[16]

Oberleutnant Manfred von Richthofen, Jasta 11, German Army Air Force

This account, taken from Richthofen's combat report, does not tally well with the account of the action left by Warren, who, as we have seen, claims that he was helpless after his observer had been badly wounded during Richthofen's first pass. Warren further insisted that neither he nor Dunn fired at Richthofen from the ground. Indeed, he was too busy trying to drag his unconscious and mortally wounded observer out of the rear cockpit to think of anything else. Richthofen may well have been confused by bursts of machine-gun fire emanating from another of the Sopwith 1½ Strutters. The rest of the Sopwiths got back safely, but, sadly, the vital photographs proved to be useless. The whole mission would have to be repeated next day. Failure was not, would not, *could not* be acceptable.

On 3 April there was more terrible flying weather. Every delay just made the photographic reconnaissances even more urgent as the clock ticked down towards Zero Hour. As the army cooperation machines took to the air, so, of course, did their German predators. As soon as it was physically possible, Captain Ewart Garland, accompanied by his observer, Lieutenant Baerlein, in a BE2e, went up to see what could be accomplished:

> High wind and snow in morning. Cleared after lunch. Took Baerlein for photos of Givenchy and area – very cloudy. When at 6,000 feet a LVG attacked us, but we drove him off. Later three Albatros Scouts came at us. Baerlein's gun jammed and the Albatros dived at us again and again, firing incendiary bullets, as well as ordinary. I side-slipped and stunted and dived towards the ground between attacks by the Huns. My escape from the truly desperate situation, owing to the one and only gun jamming, was due not so much to violent aerobatics as to a suicidal manoeuvre I employed in the last resort. I literally hurled my machine at each attacking enemy fighter in the hope that they would avoid collision and certain death, thus enabling me to further my escape while they swerved away – it also shortened the time each attacker had of firing his guns at us. Dire ills need dire remedies. At last five FEs rescued us. Our machine gun did not fire a single shot. Landed OK at aerodrome and found forty holes in machine, but camera undamaged. The photos are OK and being rushed to Canadian Headquarters by motorcycle.[17]
>
> Captain Ewart Garland, 16 Squadron, RFC

The FE2ds may have rescued Garland on this occasion, but time and time again, they themselves proved excruciatingly vulnerable to the German Albatros scouts. Second Lieutenants Donald Macdonald and Jack O'Beirne of 25 Squadron had already completed one flight that day, when the call for volunteers took them aloft again. Moral blackmail and a less than subtle appeal to their natural pride in their squadron was all it required for them to risk death once again:

> Major Cherry asked us to go and obtain photographs of Vimy Ridge. These photographs were particularly required by Headquarters and many were the attempts that had been made to get them by other squadron commanders and squadrons. We all naturally volunteered – there were three machines, and off we went with cameras, etc. We were supposed to be met by an escort at the lines, but we were disappointed in not finding one over them when we arrived. However, we were not to be

daunted by this, chose our moment and over we went. Every one of us, as far as I have found out, succeeded in getting the required photographs, about sixty plates each, and then our group leader gave us the order to close in as a preliminary to returning home. All this took about twenty-eight minutes, and, luckily enough, we had not so far been spotted.[18]

Lieutenant Donald Macdonald, 25 Squadron, RFC

After completing their run of photographs, they sighted three German scouts rising from below and rashly accepted the implicit challenge. In this, for all their undoubted courage, they showed a reprehensible failure to realise the true importance of the pictures that they had risked so much to obtain. Suddenly, the three German aircraft multiplied into a swarm of aggressive scouts buzzing around them from all sides:

There were from a dozen to sixteen almost on top of our tails then! We had then a very one-sided scrap, of course keeping ourselves in a small circle and endeavouring to keep them outside, but they were too many for us. When it got hot for any one of them, he dropped out and another couple had a go at us. Jack was firing over my top plane (to the rear) when suddenly a close burst from behind hit him right in the head and he dropped down in his seat. The machine tossed and dropped its height! It was but a matter of a few minutes before some of them got my engine while I was endeavouring to steer and shoot at the same time, and I was forced down to the ground just outside Lens on the south-east side. The Hun followed me right down to the ground, firing all the time, till he almost shot away every control I had. I made for a good-looking field, but, as luck would have it, beneath the long grass were barbed wire entanglements and with all my instruments shot away, I landed at a faster pace than I should have done and caught in the wire, going head over heels. Fortunately the machine went right over the top of me when I was thrown out. I was picked up unconscious.[19]

Lieutenant Donald Macdonald, 25 Squadron, RFC

It was the ubiquitous Richthofen that had shot them down, flying this time alongside his younger brother Lothar von Richthofen. Strangely, his account makes no mention of the horde of German scouts that Macdonald claimed had attacked them. Such contradictions in accounts are now irresolvable, coloured as they frequently are by a mixture of special pleading, patriotic pride and the confusion of combat:

Together with Leutnant Schäfer and Leutnant Lothar von Richthofen I attacked three enemy planes. The plane I myself attacked was forced to land near Liévin. After a short fight, the motor began to smoke and the observer ceased shooting. I followed the adversary to the ground.[20]

Oberleutnant Manfred von Richthofen, Jasta 11, German Army Air Force

Leutnant Schäfer's victims were Lieutenants Dodson and Richards. Whatever the details for the fight, one thing was certain – the vital photographs had been lost and the mission would have to be flown again.

A little later that day, another FE2d, piloted by Lieutenant Godfrey Hopkins accompanied by Aircraftman H. Friend acting as observer, found themselves in extreme difficulties:

I was one of the rear aircraft in a flight formation when a Hun dived on me and started shooting at very long range. Just as my observer stood up to open fire at the Hun over the top plane, there was a loud thud or clank under my seat. A bullet had penetrated the main petrol tank, on which I was sitting, and made a large ragged hole in it (as I discovered later). The result was that air pressure in the tank immediately dropped, my engine ran out of petrol and stopped. This might perhaps have been avoided if I had had the wit and time to switch over to my reserve gravity supply tank. However, one is perhaps liable to forget to do the right thing when one is being shot at and there was a very strong smell of petrol as it spurted out over my feet. When my engine stopped, we were somewhere just about above the Hindenburg Line, but the situation on the ground was so muddled and uncertain that nobody knew just which part of the area was held by evacuating enemy troops and which by ours. It was thus advisable to glide back as far as possible towards our own side of the lines. This I did. My observer took the guns off their mountings and stored them in the bottom of the nacelle, as we prepared for a crash landing. The whole locality was a mass of shell holes, old trenches, barbed wire and so on; so I was lucky to be able to land without crashing or turning the aircraft over. We landed with a bit of a bump with the wheels either side of a shell hole, and came to rest tilted up on one wing but otherwise undamaged. The place appeared to be deserted when we landed, but very shortly several khaki clad figures appeared and advised us in lurid terms to, 'Get out of that **** plane before the **** Jerries start to shell it!' So we scrambled out and went down a trench for some distance, eventually reaching a dugout where some infantry officers entertained us. By that time it was getting dark and the FE was not, in fact, shelled at all.[21]

Second Lieutenant Geoffrey Hopkins, 22 Squadron, RFC

WEDNESDAY, 4 April marked the beginning of the final awesome stage of the preliminary artillery bombardment. Innumerable shells rained down on the German lines and splattered around their artillery batteries. Shells of all sizes smashed down – clearing barbed wire, smashing trenches, seeking out strong points and dugouts, remorselessly cutting communications and thereby slowly isolating the front-line garrisons from any possible succour. The Vickers machine guns roared in a different toned but deadly harmony, firing on fixed lines, aiming high into the air to bring a hosing stream of bullets down from the heavens on targets such as supply routes or road junctions. Time after time the massed Livens projectors belched out their poisonous cylinders of gas to burst in deadly synchronicity within the German lines. The British were bringing hell on earth to the Germans in preparation for Easter 1917.

The roar of the guns was accompanied by the start of the formal air offensive. Whatever the casualties, the clear intention was to sweep the Germans from the skies to enable the army cooperation corps aircraft the freedom to attend to their multifarious duties. Trenchard had issued his orders to his brigade commanders a few days earlier on 26 March. There was to be no flinching in the face of the Albatros scourge:

The aim of our offensive will therefore be to force the enemy to fight well behind, and not on, the lines. This aim will only be successfully achieved if offensive patrols are pushed well out to the limits of army reconnaissance areas, and the general officer commanding looks to brigadiers to carry out this policy and not to give way to requests for the close protection of corps machines except in special cases when such machines are proceeding on work at an abnormal distance over the lines. The aerial ascendancy which was gained by our pilots and observers on the Somme last year was a direct result of the policy outlined above.[22]

Major-General Hugh Trenchard, Headquarters, RFC

The scouts would swarm over the German lines in an attempt to dominate the battle zone, which was about 20 miles wide and reached back as far as 15 miles from the front lines. Within this zone they would shoot down any German aircraft they encountered, while the airfields and the communications infrastructure were to be bombed. Closer to the lines the German kite balloons would be targeted.

As if to show lofty disdain for human timetables, the vagaries of the weather once again intervened and restricted the planned aerial operations to the extent that almost nothing of any importance could be achieved. Another day lost – time was running out. It was then less than a week before the British infantry would have to leave the shelter of their trenches and walk into the open wastes of No Man's Land. If the German artillery batteries had not been accurately located, registered and silenced, if the German trenches and strong points had not been pulverised, if the machine-gun posts had not been identified and dealt with, then the British and Canadian infantry were surely doomed. The Germans were certainly confident they could throw back a Canadian assault:

> The Germans knew we were coming because in one of the previous trench raids we had captured a German officer. He was very arrogant and told us, sneeringly, that he knew we were going to try to take Vimy Ridge. He said that some of the Canadians may try to reach the top of it, but all of them that got there you'll be able to take back to Canada in a rowing boat.[23]
>
> Private George Hiscox, Princess Patricia's Canadian Light Infantry, 7th Brigade, 3rd Canadian Division

On 5 April, Trenchard finally played one of the trump cards that he had been withholding for the right moment – on this day the Bristol Fighters were thrown into the fray for the first time. Great things were expected of this new two-seater scout aircraft. The pilot had a fixed forward-firing synchronised Vickers machine gun, whilst the rear gunner had a Lewis gun. Its great advantage, over existing two-seaters such as the Sopwith 1½ Strutter, lay in its new Rolls Royce Falcon engine which powered it to a top speed of just over 110 miles per hour at 10,000 feet, with a correspondingly impressive fast rate of climb. The first squadron to be equipped with the Bristol Fighter was the newly arrived 48 Squadron. This in itself was a controversial decision, for many more experienced pilots and observers daily risking their lives in the FE2bs felt that they should have been re-equipped first:

> We had been promised Bristol Fighters, but did not get them until July 1917. We felt very strongly that fitting out new squadrons with such machines was wasteful and that had we been fitted with new machines the results would have been spectacular.[24]
>
> Second Lieutenant Geoffrey Hopkins, 22 Squadron, RFC

The risks of equipping a new squadron with the precious new aircraft were rendered all too obvious when its first patrol led to an utter calamity. Captain William Leefe Robinson VC, who had no previous experience of air fighting on the Western Front, led a first offensive patrol towards Douai. His accelerated promotion had been made on the basis of his courageous achievement in shooting a Zeppelin airship raiding Britain in September 1916. Unfortunately, this milestone feat had no relevance to the tactical maelstrom into which he was thrust as a patrol leader.

The Bristol Fighter pilots were unlucky; the first time over the lines they ran straight into an Albatros formation commanded by Richthofen. In the ensuing dogfight four of the Bristol Fighters were shot down, including the hapless Leefe Robinson. The other two were lucky to escape from the debacle:

> It was foggy and altogether very bad weather when I attacked an enemy squadron while it was flying between Douai and Valenciennes. Up to this point, it had managed to advance without being fired upon. I attacked with four planes of my Staffel. I personally singled out the last machine, which I forced to land near Lewards after a short fight. The occupants burnt their machine. It was a new type of plane, which we had not known before, and it appears to be quick and rather handy, with a powerful motor, V-shaped and 12 cylindered. Its name could not be recognised. The DIII Albatros was, both in speed and ability to climb, undoubtedly superior.[25]
>
> Oberleutnant Manfred von Richthofen, Jasta 11, German Army Air Force

It was Richthofen's thirty-fifth victory and his thirty-sixth followed immediately afterwards when, after a tussle, he forced down another Bristol Fighter on the German side of the lines. The crew once again bravely contrived to burn their aircraft before they were captured. This calamitous aerial battle caused a great amount of consternation and depression within the RFC:

I saw the first flight of No. 48 Squadron Bristols cross the line and go into action. I saw them shot down with the exception of one aircraft. It seemed to me, standing safely on the Arras railway embankment, that they broke formation very quickly and allowed the 'circus' to concentrate on individual Bristol Fighters. The scrap was watched from the ground as much was expected of the new Bristols, and I had to submit to some leg pulling.[26]

Lieutenant John MacDonald, 48 Squadron, RFC attached to 50th Field Artillery Brigade, Royal Artillery

Captain William Leefe Robinson was shot down by Vizefeldwebel S. Festner of Jasta 11. He was captured, but unfortunately was mercilessly targeted for rough treatment throughout his time as a prisoner of war. Released after the Armistice, he was by then in a weak state of health and soon fell victim to the influenza pandemic and died on 28 December 1918.

All in all, the whole affair was bitterly disappointing for the British. It appeared that the Bristol Fighter had failed entirely to live up to expectations. Indeed, flown as a conventional two-seater, relying on the observer to shoot down opponents and sticking to rigid flying formations, it *was* an ineffectual aircraft. There were also the usual unfounded rumours, that accompanied almost every new aircraft, that unspecified structural weaknesses meant that the Bristol Fighter would surely fall apart in the skies if handled too roughly in action. Fortunately, before too long it was realised that, on the contrary, the Bristol Fighter was a sturdy and formidable aircraft that could be flown and thrown about the sky exactly as if it were a single-seater scout. The forward-firing Vickers machine gun was the primary weapon while the rear gunner, with his trusty Lewis gun, could cover the tail *in extremis*.

On the same morning that the Bristol Fighters first went up, 43 Squadron had a horrendously dangerous mission to carry out. Like the halt leading the lame, their Sopwith 1½ Strutters were selected to escort a group of BEs during a bombing raid to take place far behind the German lines:

We are to escort or protect some BEs detailed to bomb the railway junction at Don. I lead. It is a ticklish job. We cross fifteen minutes before the BEs and go 10 miles inland over Hénin Lietard to Annoeullin and Don. Can see nothing of the bombers. We return against wild wind

one after another and see the Hun scouts rise up after us, attracted
by the black puffs of 'Archie'. Near the line there are about fifteen
following. Our formation of five is well closed up and gunners ready.
Just before crossing the line they dive at us. Both my guns are jammed.
I see one get on to my tail, so stall and go down in a spinning nosedive.
The formation becomes broken and we cross the lines separately. When
a mile out, a scout again attacks but I fling him off and return to
aerodrome. Thornton and his observer Blackburn do not return.[27]

Lieutenant Alan Dore, 43 Squadron, RFC

In the afternoon a young pilot, Second Lieutenant Gordon Taylor of
66 Squadron, took off for a solo patrol in his nimble Sopwith Pup. He
was looking for stray German two-seater reconnaissance aircraft, but
sighted about six Albatros aircraft casually strafing the British lines below
him. With the assurance born of youth and inexperience he dived to
intervene:

I decided to break up their party. From 10,000 feet it seemed all too
simple, such confidence did I have in the manoeuvrability of my Pup.
I hauled her over, and pressed her down in a dive for the Huns. The
specks grew quickly into aeroplanes, and the aeroplanes into brilliant
Albatri – unaware, so I believed, of my approach. I selected one, a red
machine with some chequered marks on the fuselage, and started to
turn in behind him as he was soaring round for another dive on the
trenches. I don't think he saw me, for he made no attempt to evade
the attack and I got a good burst into him, and saw him rear up in a
terrific zoom, fall over the top and dive for the near earth. But if he
had not seen me, one of the others had; as I pulled out there was the
sound of machine-gun fire close behind my tail.

My machine swept into a climbing turn before I knew my hand
had moved the controls even. I was aware of a Hun going by, so close
that I instinctively shrank back from the threat of collision. But he
passed, and another was on my tail instead. Again the instant evasion.
I was suddenly conscious of the shark-like creature closing in on me.
I held full throttle and tried to climb away, but it was futile. Whatever
I did the Huns just soared above me. I continued to take evasive
action, using my gun whenever I could make an opportunity. They
had me cold. I couldn't reach them to attack, and couldn't climb

away to escape. The instant I flew straight they would nail me.

There was only one remaining possibility, a move which I had always avoided and from which there was no turning back. I decided to dive right down on the deck, and hare off home below the trees and the church towers. There was only a thousand feet to lose. I shook off a Hun with a sideways loop, ruddered down off the top and dived for the earth. This manoeuvre gave me a few seconds start. I remember the broken earth, with the shell holes, my wheels only a few feet off the ground. A Hun began to overtake me, diving, turning to get me in his sights. I had to watch him, and also avoid flying into the ground. I swerved away as his nose was coming on, and he was forced to pull out to avoid crashing. If I could get through without colliding with some obstruction I'd be all right. A broken village came rushing up and I went skating round the ruined houses, past some splintered trees, and once more down flat against the earth. Then there were fields, green and brown, behind the lines, and a fold in the ground. I poured the Pup down the low valley, almost brushing the grass that flattened itself beneath my wings. A quick look behind. The Huns had gone, the air was clear.[28]

Second Lieutenant Gordon Taylor, 66 Squadron, RFC

Taylor had been lucky to survive. That evening another young and untested pilot, Lieutenant Norman Birks, was flying his Nieuport over the lines for the first time along with a patrol of 29 Squadron:

I was piloting the leading machine about 4 miles behind the enemy lines and we attacked an enemy patrol just below us. I saw Rodgers diving down on my right and I presume the remainder of our flight followed suit. I never learnt the result of this encounter. My petrol tank was hit very early in the engagement, my engine stopped and I was soaked in petrol, making it a much more hazardous position as all guns (enemy and friend alike) were firing tracer bullets of about one in five. I turned for home and my aggressor followed me down, firing continuously, causing me to twist and turn and lose height very rapidly. I saw my instruments in front of me disintegrate, but the only bullet hitting me was in my right buttock – now known as my 'dishonourable wound'! I crash landed on the edge of a shell hole just behind the German front-line trench, and turned turtle. I always like to think that if I had had my bulldog mascot fitted to my new machine, I would have got over to our own lines. Such is superstition. I undid my safety belt and flopped into the mud and water to find there was fairly heavy shelling of the German lines by the British, and apparently all the enemy were safely underground or back in their reserve trenches and no one had seen me land.

When the bombardment eased off somewhat, I crawled into the enemy firing trench and then into a sap leading towards the British lines. These saps were open trenches as used by the British and Germans as night listening posts. My vague idea was to get as close to our own lines as possible and lie 'doggo' until nightfall, when I would have hoped for help and guidance to safety. Having got only a few yards I was knocked down by an explosion on my left (probably a hand grenade) which wounded me severely on my hip. I found myself on my back with my feet pointing towards the German trenches where there were two young German soldiers about eight feet away aiming their rifles at my head.[29]

Lieutenant Norman Birks, 29 Squadron, RFC

Birks was taken prisoner. He had been shot down by Vizefeldwebel K. Menckhoff of Jasta 3.

While the scouts tussled in the clouds, the corps aircraft went about their business, thankful that on that day at least the Albatros had other fish to fry:

Took Baerlein on photos in morning – two others and I had to take the whole Corps area up to 5 miles back of the lines. Three FEs came as escort. I had 54 plates to expose. There were patchy clouds but we managed pretty well – no Huns attacked – time three hours. Went up again at 5.30 to take whole of front line, which I did from 4,000 feet. All our best machines were out today and the Hun did not bother us.[30]

Captain Ewart Garland, 16 Squadron, RFC

The night of 5–6 April saw the beginning of a new lease of life for the struggling FE2bs. It had been decided to establish a new unit specifically to carry out night bombing raids and the FE2b was chosen as the aircraft. In many ways it was ideal: reliable, robust and capable of carrying up to eight 20-lb bombs. The disadvantages so apparent during daylight operations all but evaporated when they were cloaked by darkness. So it was that 100 Squadron came out from England in late March 1917 and set up base at Izel le Hameau on 1 April. Their FE2bs had been equipped with special bomb dropping gear and luminous night flying instruments and they were soon ready for action. Their first night raid, carried out on the night of 5–6 April, was on Richthofen's lair at Douai airfield. Richthofen and his pilots were relaxing in the officers' mess when they were warned by telephone that British bombers were heading in their direction:

> The Englishman was apparently flying at a great altitude. At first he circled around our entire establishment. We began to think that he had given up and was looking for another objective. Suddenly we noticed that he had switched off the engine. So he was coming lower. Wolff said, 'Now the matter is becoming serious.' We had two carbines and began shooting at the Englishman. We could not see him. Still, the noise of our shooting was a sedative to our nerves.[31]
>
> Oberleutnant Manfred von Richthofen, Jasta 11, German Army Air Force

As the FE2bs dropped lower so as to have a better chance of actually hitting their targets, the Germans finally saw what they were up against:

> Suddenly he was taken up by the searchlights. There was shouting all over the flying ground. Our friend was sitting in a 'prehistoric packing case'. We could clearly recognise the type. He was half a mile away from us and was flying straight towards us. He went lower and lower. At last he had come down to an altitude of about 300 feet. Then he started his engine again and came straight towards the spot where we were standing.[32]
>
> Oberleutnant Manfred von Richthofen, Jasta 11, German Army Air Force

The German sense of wonder at this bold use of the obsolescent FE2bs can be easily discerned even in Richthofen's somewhat complacent account. The eighteen FE2bs dropped their bombs – some 128 20-lb bombs and another four 40-lb bombs – targeting the airfield hangars and subsequently claimed a good number of hits, which left four of the hangars on fire. They reported the loss of one FE2b, flown by Second Lieutenant Richards with his observer Air Mechanic Barnes, which failed to return. In contrast Richthofen claimed that the raid had achieved nothing:

The first bomb fell and it was followed by a number of others. Our friend amused us with very pretty fireworks. They could have frightened only a coward. Broadly speaking, I find that bomb-throwing at night has only a moral effect. Those who have funk are strongly affected when bombs are falling at night. The others don't care.[33]

Oberleutnant Manfred von Richthofen, Jasta 11, German Army Air Force

Yet Richthofen's pride was hurt that the FE2bs had been able to drop their bombs from such a low height with relative impunity, especially as he had fancied himself a good shot with the rifle. He resolved to do better next time:

Richthofen is now arranging with his men some friendly target shooting, during the night, since the English will simply not let him sleep in peace. After these nightly extremely low flying aircraft dropped a couple of bombs on his airfield, he had seventeen sets of English machine guns, which he had commandeered from previous victories, installed around the mess. Then the guests waited.[34]

Leutnant Erwin Böhme, Jasta Boelcke, German Army Air Force

On the night of 7–8 April the FE2bs of 100 Squadron returned to the scene of the crime and this time Richthofen was ready for them:

Suddenly an orderly rushed in shouting, 'They are here! They are here!' and disappeared into the next bombproof shelter in his scanty attire. We all rushed to our machine guns. Some of the men who were known to be good shots had also been given a machine gun. All the rest were provided with carbines. The whole squadron was armed to the teeth to give a warm reception to our kindly visitors. The first Englishman arrived, exactly as on the previous evening, at a very great altitude. He then went down to 150 feet and, to our greatest joy, was making for the place where our barracks were. He got into the glare of the searchlight. When he was only 300 yards away someone fired the first shot and all the rest of us joined in. Quick firing from many guns received him. Of course he could not hear the noise of the machine guns. The roar of his engine prevented that. However, he must have seen the flashes of our guns. Therefore I considered it tremendously plucky that our man did not swerve but continued going straight ahead in accordance with his plan. He flew exactly over our heads.[35]

Oberleutnant Manfred von Richthofen, Jasta 11, Imperial German Air Force

Richthofen insisted that the vigour of his response put the British off their bomb aiming and further claimed they shot down three of the FE2bs. In contrast, the 100 Squadron pilots claimed to have dropped some eighty-two 20-lb bombs on the airfield as well as successfully bombing the nearby Douai railway station and sidings. Only one FE2b flown by Second Lieutenant L. Butler and Air Mechanic Robb was reported missing. Whatever the truth of the various claims, it appears that the pilots of 100 Squadron subsequently gave the Douai airfield a wide berth as they concentrated, with some success, on trying to disrupt German rail traffic in the following weeks. They claimed that numerous trains were derailed, stations, engine repair shops and sidings pasted, and targets of opportunity such as MT columns hit hard. Much of this damage would be overstated in the more optimistic reports – much could be swiftly repaired – yet still interdiction bombing was coming of age as a harassing nuisance to the enemy in his efforts to move troops and supplies around far behind the front line.

ON 6 April, the United States of America finally declared war on Germany. The Americans had given up their highly profitable perch on the fence and joined the Allied side, finally pushed over the edge by the German policy of unrestricted submarine warfare. The loss of the Russians to the Allies after the fall of the Tsar was perhaps of more immediate import, for the United States was not then a great military power, but the potential of her manpower, raw materials and manufacturing capacity was so enormous that the Allies had plenty to celebrate.

Yet 6 April was also the day on which all the stress and strain endured by the pilots and observers of 45 Squadron finally boiled over. Although based to the north in the Ypres area, they had been drawn inexorably into the overall air offensive during the accelerating countdown to the Battle of Arras. Over the previous month the squadron had become increasingly concerned that its Sopwith 1½ Strutters were wholly inadequate:

> It wasn't so much the losses themselves that distressed us; we knew very well that the whole RFC was going through a tough time. What perturbed us was that the Staff appeared greatly to overestimate the capabilities of our Sopwiths, and we were losing too many men and planes on ill-considered assignments that we were too feeble to carry out.[36]
> Captain Frank Courtney, 45 Squadron, RFC

Courtney was not alone in his opinions. It seemed obvious to all the pilots that their machines were not up to the difficult missions that they were being assigned:

> Every hostile machine *completely outmanoeuvred* us and were capable of beating us in climbing, turning and speed.[37]
>
> Second Lieutenant Geoffrey Cock, 45 Squadron RFC

In these circumstances it was obvious that on long-range photographic reconnaissance missions they would be particularly vulnerable. Yet this is just what they were regularly called on to perform:

> Since the camera planes were supposed to be part of the fighter formation, the whole patrol was tied down to sets of tracks over the localities specified on the charts. The enemy's higher performance gave us little freedom to attack in any case, but now what little of that freedom we had left disappeared in the need for attending to photographic requirements. All fighting initiative had to be left to the enemy, giving them all the time they needed to climb, mass, and manoeuvre for the most favourable attack conditions, while we plodded along the prescribed tracks waiting for what was coming to us when the enemy was ready. Our fighting objective was no longer to destroy the enemy; it was to try to ensure that at least one of our camera planes got home.[38]
>
> Captain Frank Courtney, 45 Squadron, RFC

Day by day, mission by mission, the drip, drip, drip of casualties accelerated until morale finally began to crack under the strain:

> We became used to losing two out of five planes or three out of eight, and there were occasions when we wondered how any of us got back at all. Often the planes we got back with were not usable any more. We began to run out of replacement planes, and at one time, in a desperate effort to keep the squadron up to strength, Headquarters tried to fill our gaps by calling on the French for some superannuated Nieuport two-seaters – which at least gave us something to laugh at, because the Nieuports had only two and a half hours' fuel and couldn't even keep up with the Sopwiths. It was, however, the extent of our crew losses that became crippling and eventually notorious.[39]
>
> Captain Frank Courtney, 45 Squadron, RFC

In truth Courtney himself was part of the problem. A brash and outspoken Australian, he was not shy of expressing his opinions in public. This posed considerable problems for his long-suffering squadron commander, Major William Read:

> Courtney returned from No. 70. He has come back to me as flight commander of B Flight. He seems to have annoyed 9th Wing and 70 Squadron by talking too much about our losses and giving his views – probably correct ones – on the frailty of the Sopwith two-seaters. I am glad to have him back I think.[40]
>
> Major William Read, 45 Squadron, RFC

Frank Courtney may have been indiscreet but at least he was a competent pilot. Many of the new pilots arriving at the unit had only the bare minimum of experience and simple flying accidents were distressingly frequent. Major Read was not by nature an overly sympathetic man and his young charges must have been terrified when faced by his trenchant criticisms:

> Several crashes today. Macmillan – a new pilot in C Flight – broke three wires in his undercarriage through an atrociously awful landing. Cock then proceeded to stand his machine on his nose in a ditch through overshooting the aerodrome. Harriman in getting off in another machine – he is another new pilot in B Flight – got his tail up so much that the propeller hit the ground and broke off a blade. He let his engine continue running and so completely wrecked the whole fuselage. I have not struck such a rotten batch of pilots as this last crowd. Forbes, Evans, Harriman, Macmillan and Forrest are the absolute edge in rottenness – as pilots. Have applied for Harriman to be sent back for further instruction.[41]
>
> Major William Read, 45 Squadron, RFC

One of these beginners was Second Lieutenant Norman Macmillan, who later blossomed into a first-rate scout pilot – so the potential was clearly there – but for him and several of the others it was all too much, too soon. New pilots, who had taken months to train, often lasted just a few minutes in combat situations. Although there appeared to be a ready-made supply of possible observers trained to use the Lewis gun in the infantry, this obvious solution only generated more problems:

The situation became so chaotic that it was almost funny. As casualties whittled down our normal airman resources, we were reduced to calling for volunteers from line regiments. Soon even those were hard to come by, because rumours about the 'Suicide Club' were filtering down to the infantry, who became sarcastically curious to know why we couldn't supply our own gunners. Almost none of those who did volunteer had ever been up in the air; no qualifications were required of them beyond the ability to load and fire a Lewis gun. Too often those unsung heroes were airsick in the whirlings of a dogfight, or else they used the gun installation as something to hang onto instead of to shoot with. Then again, we occasionally got specimens such as my completely fearless Scottish infantry lieutenant: full of guts and ignorance, highly belligerent and trigger-happy; he itched to shoot at anything, everything, or nothing, regardless of range. In one dogfight in which our Sopwiths received unexpected reinforcements from some FEs from No. 20 Squadron, he opened fire on one of the FEs merely because it looked different, and I had to kick the rudder hard to throw his aim off. The only things I ever knew him to hit for certain were our own tail, rudder and wing tips.[42]

Captain Frank Courtney, 45 Squadron, RFC

As commander of B Flight, Courtney found his frustrations steadily increasing. Every day brought a new cross to bear, a new corpse to bury. He found himself charged with the responsibility of making decisions that would decide the life and death of his men, of his friends:

It was now my dismal duty to pair off the pilots and gunners of my flight for the next day's sorties. We had perhaps three or four of the original gunners left in the squadron, and the eager courage of the newcomers was no substitute for skill and experience. For pilots we were in no better shape; I think I was one of three survivors of the eighteen pilots who had left Boisdinghem, and only a few other pilots had much experience. It would be murder to send out a green pilot with a green gunner. So then what? Should I send out an experienced gunner with a pilot who could hardly fly, or an experienced pilot with a quite useless gunner behind him? There was nothing to do but guess and trust to luck.[43]

Captain Frank Courtney, 45 Squadron, RFC

The stress was also deeply personal. Courtney was all too aware that he was also living on borrowed time. Every mission he survived brought him closer to what seemed an inevitable fate:

> I needed a heavy overdraft on my brimming store of luck. On the various occasions when they shot up my plane or gunner, the Germans seemed to have developed the knack of missing my person completely and never doing quite enough damage to the plane to prevent me reaching at least our side of the lines. But this sort of luck could not go on forever, and, like most of us now, my early eagerness for battle had worn very thin.[44]
>
> Captain Frank Courtney, 45 Squadron, RFC

Such was the situation when Courtney was ordered to lead yet another long range reconnaissance patrol over Lille on 6 April. Earlier a single aircraft had failed in a brave attempt to steal the photographs by stealth at dawn. This meant that the mission had to be repeated and later in the day it was felt that eight aircraft would be needed if they were to have any chance of success. Amongst the Sopwith 1½ Strutters was one flown by Second Lieutenant J. A. Marshall with his observer Second Lieutenant F. G. Truscott, who had conceived of a cunning plan to thwart the malign fates:

> Truscott was Mess President of B Flight and kept the Mess funds in assorted bunches of French currency. One morning a reconnaissance was announced which promised to be sticky (it was) and Truscott was going as observer with Marshall. As we got ready, Truscott made a big show of putting a fat envelope of paper francs into the pocket of his flying coat and informed us: 'This is my special system of self-preservation. You see, when you observe my machine being attacked you will all say, "Look, there go our Mess funds" and you will all rally round to protect me.' I suppose, at the age we were then, the idea of being shot down was always somewhat academic, so nobody took any more notice.[45]
>
> Captain Frank Courtney, 45 Squadron RFC

Inevitably, they once again ran straight into a formation of German scouts:

> The first hostile machine came up on the right of the formation, flew along at the side and slightly in front, firing at about 300 yards range; he then crossed well in front of the formation and I got in a burst of

about seventy rounds from the front gun. Then the other hostile machines came up behind the formation and attacked the rear and middle machines of the formation.[46]

Second Lieutenant Geoffrey Cock, 45 Squadron RFC

If they could maintain their formation all might still be well. The German scouts buzzed round them, seeking an opening:

During the show, Campbell was shot down first. Marshall, with Truscott, was flying a little high to the left and slightly behind me, and another machine was between us. Six or eight Huns were coming up, apparently too far behind to start shooting. We never knew what actually happened, but possibly a long-range fluke shot from the Huns hit Marshall's rigging, for I saw his right wing fold up and, as he twisted round, he crashed into the next machine. Both wrecks, with bits flying in all directions, missed my tail by a few feet and, of course, there was no hope for the four fellows inside. With the inevitable lack of any sense of proportion which goes with such affairs, I thought, 'Goodbye Truscott, but what about our mess money?' And then another dogfight started and there was no time to think of anything else.[47]

Captain Frank Courtney, 45 Squadron RFC

Truscott had gone to his death, but there was to be a bittersweet postscript to the affair when the depressed survivors of 43 Squadron eventually got back home to their airfield:

When Austin, my observer, and I finally walked into the mess hut, a corporal came up to me, with a fat envelope, 'Mr Truscott told me to give you this if he didn't come back this evening'.[48]

Captain Frank Courtney, 45 Squadron RFC

Unfortunately, the clearly shaken and still grieving Courtney then ran straight into his commanding officer, the irascible Major William Read who was, furthermore, accompanied by the distinguished figure of Brigadier-General Tom Webb-Bowen then in command of II Brigade. It is fair to say that Courtney rose to the occasion:

One of the four pilots, full of anguish at the thought of the men who had been lost, in the hearing of the Brigadier General, made the classic remark which caused him to be transferred to the Home

Establishment, 'Some people say that Sopwith two-seaters are bloody fine machines, but I think they're more bloody than fine!'[49]

Second Lieutenant Norman Macmillan, 45 Squadron RFC

This was not how junior officers were expected to address their superiors no matter what the situation. From our perspective and with the benefit of hindsight, we can appreciate that Brigadier Webb-Bowen was caught in an unfortunate situation. After all, what other aircraft could have flown these long-range missions that the army required? The BE2es were even older, slower and worse armed; the FE2bs were already fully engaged in a multiplicity of roles for which they, too, were overstretched. There were just not enough of the new aircraft available. Yet the missions had to be completed. The chain of command stretched from Haig, through Trenchard, to Webb-Bowen, then via Read and ultimately to Courtney and his fellow pilots at the sharp end. None of them could evade their responsibilities. This is not to say that Courtney's anguish was not real, or any less justified, it was just that there really was no alternative to the use of the Sopwith 1½ Strutters. No senior commander could allow such insubordination to pass unpunished and it must have been obvious that Courtney would not have responded terribly well to a lecture on the primary role of the RFC in delivering for the infantry. Webb-Bowen therefore had little option but to send Courtney home a few days later:

> Stories of my departure from No. 45 went the rounds for a long time afterward, with gleefully lurid versions of what I was supposed to have done or said to our Brigadier-General. I had already had several clashes with the brigade, usually in efforts to make sense out of some of our missions. One day the Brigadier, who had never himself flown in any serious action, visited the squadron and broadcast some ill-timed comments that implied we were not using our planes to best effect. I replied with some undiluted remarks concerning the brigade's directives. A few days later I was sent home, and I have to admit that I was not inclined to dispute the sentence – if that's what it was.[50]

Captain Frank Courtney, 45 Squadron, RFC

Major William Read was also approaching the end of his tether. He was a brave man but he felt utterly trapped by the situation he found himself in:

The prohibition, at that time, of commanding officers flying nearer the front than 5 miles behind our front lines made him feel his position keenly. He would have loved nothing better than to have led us in person as a real leader. And, as we continued to fly our formations far eastward of the scout patrols, we collected the Albatros scouts like deep-sea birds in the wide sky eastward of our own scouts' beats. The squadron casualty list mounted steadily. Finally our CO said that he would rather return to his regiment than continue to command a squadron which he could not lead. He was taken at his word, and returned to cavalry work down south, a very gallant gentleman, whose only fault was loathing of command to slaughter.[51]

Second Lieutenant Norman Macmillan, 45 Squadron RFC

But 45 Squadron were not alone in their predicament. While their aircraft were indeed of a mid-1916 vintage, the men of 16 Squadron were still flying the BE2cs and BE2es that would have been all too familiar to the pilots of 1914.

Managed to get out of a rotten job today, was down to go and take photos well over the line with an escort of three FE fighters; the Wing phoned up and reduced the area to be taken, so my part of the business was washed out. I went to my Flight Commander, asked for the day off and cleared out of camp before he could change his mind and find me another job – this is the spirit that will win the war. Taking photographs is a poor game, it is highly dangerous and it doesn't give one a chance of telling any fairy tales. It is of no use you coming back and saying – to use a Canadian expression – that you have been 'Away over to hell and gone' unless you can bring back a clear and distinct photo of Hades to prove your statement. The route you have taken is recorded on the photographic plates with the same clearness as the track of a snail is marked upon the wall up which it has climbed. The people in this squadron have fairly 'got wind up' about crossing the lines, not without reason perhaps for a great number of machines have been shot down. It is rather amusing though, we are told we are not to cross the lines without an escort and yet no escort is supplied for no end of jobs that cannot be done without crossing the lines. The position reminds me of a verse I saw somewhere which runs:

Mother, may I go to swim?

Yes, my darling daughter

Hang your clothes on a hickory limb

But don't go near the water![52]

Second Lieutenant Charles Smart, 16 Squadron, RFC

Smart was lucky that day, but Captain Ewart Garland who was once again above the lines, was soon in trouble:

Again took Baerlein on photos – no escort – two other BEs were taking photos of next sector and I saw three Albatros scouts attack first one then the other, quickly shooting down both in flames – one was Whitaker and the other Knight, who was with me yesterday. Both had observers. The FEs did their best to rescue, but were not fast enough. The same three Huns then turned their attention to me, but I kept a close watch on them and made off at full speed over our side of the lines the moment they turned in my direction. They did not attempt to venture our side of the lines and I managed to get all my photos while the Huns patrolled their side of the lines. As soon as they spotted me and turned towards me, I scuttled back over our side. I came back safely with the necessary photos, but felt a bit off seeing those two going down in flames.[53]

Captain Ewart Garland, 16 Squadron, RFC

Yet there was hope for the future. A month earlier 55 Squadron had arrived in France equipped with a startling new aircraft for which great things were confidently predicted – the DH4 designed by Geoffrey de Havilland. It was the first two-seater aircraft specifically designed as a day bomber, able to carry a substantial bomb load and powered by the new Rolls-Royce 250 hp Eagle engine. The end result was a fast, powerful aircraft that was easy to fly, capable of reaching high altitudes, able to defend itself with a forward-firing Vickers machine gun and a further Lewis gun for the observer, with a useful bomb load of up to four 112-lb bombs and a robust construction that enabled it to take considerable punishment if things did go awry.

The DH4 was another of the new generation of aircraft held back by Trenchard specifically to increase its impact during the Arras air offensive and they made their first bombing raid when six of the 55 Squadron DH4s attacked the railway station at Valenciennes on 6 April. Bombing from over 11,000 feet they scored hits on the station buildings, the engine sheds and associated railway sidings. When the inevitable Albatros scouts climbed to intercept them on the long return journey, they found they were simply left behind while still struggling to gain the necessary altitude. These DH4s were long-range aircraft that could look after themselves. Even if they were caught by the German scouts they were manoeuvrable and well armed: they were by no means the sitting ducks that the BE2es had been. This was the first of a series of coordinated bombing raids by the DH4s. The new aircraft was also increasingly used for long-range photographic reconnaissances of the very kind that had so upset Captain Frank Courtney and the men flying the Sopwith 1½ Strutters of 45 Squadron.

At the end of a hard-fought day on 6 April, the RFC could look on what it had achieved with considerable pride. Some 700 photographs had been taken and safely returned for detailed analysis and interpretation, some 123 artillery targets had been engaged using aerial observation and a large number of direct hits had been reported. Meanwhile, the bombing squadrons had been attacking the airfields, railway communications, ammunition dumps and billeting areas of the Germans.

AIRCRAFT were not the only source of artillery observation for the Royal Artillery. There were also the kite balloons, which were of vital importance to the gunners. Hanging from the balloons were observation baskets directly linked to the ground by a telephone line. As such they provided a semi-permanent observation platform in the air and their presence hampered the work of concealed German batteries who found they could not suspend their firing while the balloons were aloft, as they usually did during the relatively brief periods when British reconnaissance aircraft were overhead. However, there was a reverse side to the coin, as the German kite balloons were obviously performing exactly the same function. As the day of the offensive approached it became increasingly vital to put out these unblinking eyes in the skies. On 7 April there were a concerted series of attempts to blind the Germans:

> No. 1 Squadron were sent out to destroy balloons this morning and
> found them protected by about four aeroplanes each, so none were
> brought down. Bevington was lost though none saw what happened to

him – another good man thrown away by the muddleheaded red-tape methods of the authorities. Instead of allowing pilots to snatch an opportunity for bringing down a balloon they forbid attacks on balloons until one day a 'general balloon strafe' is 'ordered' from Brigade, no matter whether it is a suitable opportunity or not, so that the pilot has to do his best to get the balloon under the existing circumstances however adverse. And so, I suppose, our GREAT GENERAL STAFF will continue to muddle away lives until there are no more left to muddle away, or until we, too, have a revolution against our Military Bureaucracy.[54]

Lieutenant Thomas Hughes, 53 Squadron, RFC

Despite what Lieutenant Hughes thought the German kite balloons were always well defended with anti-aircraft batteries and there was never a suitable opportunity that did not entail severe risks for the attacking pilot. The Staff ordered the mass attack on 7 April because they had the solid military imperative in the imminent Zero Hour. Lieutenant Hughes was not in a position to be able to see the bigger picture – his response was essentially personal and thereby clouded by sentiment.

Of course, the Germans attacked the British balloons as well. Lieutenant Devenish witnessed a lone German scout launch a courageous and successful attack on a British balloon nestling just below the clouds at 3,200 feet:

Suddenly we saw two men jump out of a 'sausage' near the side of the road, in parachutes. Near the balloon, 'Archie' (ours) was bursting; going away towards the Hun lines was a Hun scout. The next moment the balloon burst into flames and started coming down. It was an awful sight. For a terrible moment it looked as though it was going to fall on the two parachutists which were slowly descending below it, but it cleared all right and very soon the two observers landed quite all right, and a huge cheer went up from all the men round about.[55]

Lieutenant George Devenish, 35 Squadron, RFC

The balloon observers were Captain G. S. Sansom and Second Lieutenant W. G. Dreschfield. They had been shot down by Leutnant Hans Klein of Jasta 2. High above them was Lieutenant William Bishop in his Nieuport 17, who was coincidentally just in the process of setting out after a German kite balloon:

On my way there I had to pass over one of our own observation
balloons. I don't know what it was that attracted my attention, but,
looking down I saw what appeared to be two men descending in parachutes. A moment later the balloon below me burst into flames. I saw
the enemy machine which had set it on fire, engaged with some of
ours. But as I had definite orders to proceed straight to the lines and
destroy the hostile balloon which had been allotted to me, I was
unable to join in the fighting.[56]

> Lieutenant William Bishop, 60 Squadron, RFC

The contiguous events of Bishop setting off to get his balloon and the
shooting down of a British balloon caused some considerable panic back
at his aerodrome where it was feared there had been some kind of awful
mistake. Bishop flew straight on to his target:

I discovered it and circled around as a preliminary to diving down
upon it. But just then I heard the rattle of machine guns directly
behind me and saw bullet holes appear as if by magic in the wings of
my machine. I pulled back as if to loop, sending the nose of my
machine straight up into the air. As I did so the enemy scout shot by
underneath me. I stood on my tail for a moment or two, then let the
machine drop back, put her nose down, and dived after the Hun,
opening fire straight behind him at very close range. He continued to
dive away with increasing speed, and later was reported to have
crashed just under where the combat had taken place. This victory
I put down entirely to luck. The man flew directly in line with my
gun and it would have been impossible to have missed him.[57]

> Lieutenant William Bishop, 60 Squadron, RFC

Perhaps there is an element of false modesty in Bishop's report – he may
well have missed the vital points – his claim was for an 'Out of Control'
and no corresponding German scout loss has yet been traced:

I proceeded now to dive for the balloon, but having had so much
warning, it had been pulled down to the ground. I would have been
justified in going home when I saw this, for our orders were not to go
under 1,000 feet after the 'sausages'. But I was just a bit peevish with
this particular balloon, and to a certain extent my blood was up. So
I decided to attack the ungainly monster in its 'bed'. I dived straight for

it and when about 500 feet from the ground, opened fire. Nothing happened. So I continued to dive and fire rapid bursts until I was only 50 feet above the bag. Still there were no signs of it catching fire. I then turned my machine gun on the balloon crew, who were working frantically on the ground. They scattered and ran all about the field. Meantime a 'flaming onion' battery was attempting to pelt me with those unsavoury missiles, so I whirled upon them with a burst of twenty rounds or more. One of the onions had flared within a 100 yards of me. This was all very exciting[58]

Lieutenant William Bishop, 60 Squadron, RFC

Bishop's engine faltered, and for a moment he thought he was doomed, before it kicked back in again and he hared off home at low level. Behind him, he found time to see his target balloon at last beginning to burn.

They were now in the final couple of days before the offensive. By this time every minute spent in the air by a reconnaissance and artillery observation aircraft was considered worth its cost in corpses. Yet they were now sharing their airspace with a vast number of flying shells as the intensity of the bombardment ratcheted up:

Line patrol. Clouds very low and snowstorms. Tremendous bombardment of Vimy Ridge in progress. Once I felt the concussion of a big howitzer shell pass so near that the whole aeroplane shuddered as though struck. Later I actually saw a shell come up and pass by me on its way to the Germans. It seems like a swiftly moving ball of black. Chased an enemy Scout; great difficulty in getting back to our lines owing to wind.[59]

Lieutenant Alan Dore, 43 Squadron, RFC

This kind of close encounter in the air was rare, but by no means rare enough for the pilots who experienced such events:

One of the problems was anti-aircraft fire and shells from our own barrages, especially during an attack when we had to carry out contact patrols. I remember once feeling the heat from a 17-in shell – like a blast from hell – which knocked my aircraft sideways, and another time when my machine was actually hit. This shell passed through the fuselage, just behind my legs. I knew nothing about it – no doubt it was one of the many buffets I received on the trip. When I got out after landing, my mechanic said, 'You've been lucky, Sir!' and pointed out a hole in the canvas of the nacelle with charred edges on both sides where a red-hot 3-in shell had passed through a bracing wire intersection without touching.[60]

Second Lieutenant C. Darly-Pine, 16 Squadron, RFC

Second Lieutenant Charles Smart had a different kind of problem that day. His observer completely lost whatever nerve he had ever possessed as they searched over the German lines for their intended target:

Passenger shall be nameless for I never saw a man in such a pitiful state of blue funk in my life. Went up to do a shoot on a hostile battery, weather very dull, high north wind and low clouds. Skated along at about 1,500 feet going through thick mist and rain clouds, bumped around and it took me all my time to keep the beastly thing the right side up. I noticed my observer clinging on to the side of the machine and looking thoroughly scared; as we neared the lines he suddenly jumped up in his seat and shouted something at the top of his voice, of course I couldn't hear him so he sat down again and wrote on a piece of paper, 'You must not cross the lines in these clouds!' I screwed the note up in a ball and chucked it overboard and then as well as I could under my goggles, I raised my eyebrows as much as to say, 'Are you flying this machine or am I?' He understood perfectly for he sat down again and watched the lines very suspiciously.

Just behind our front line I turned and flew up and down for about ten minutes trying to locate my target, the weather was awful and we flew for minutes at a time in thick mist with everything blotted out from view, my passenger meanwhile sitting in a most hopeless state of 'wind up'. At last I managed to spot the target and then turned back to our battery and called them up, they were very smart and got their ground strips out in no time. The weather cleared a bit and the clouds went up to about 200 feet so we got to work. The battery shot well, after the first few shots we got right on the spot and fairly hammered the target. To observe each shot I had to go right over the Hun front line and on each trip he let go at us with machine guns and 'Archie', in addition to this our own guns were shooting hard and we got shell bumps every few seconds. After I had observed twenty-six shots and was over the lines doing the twenty-seventh there was a bang and a ping of a bullet came through the plane and carried away one of the main flying wires. This was rather a serious business for when one wire goes it puts extra strain on the others and they are liable to snap like carrots with the result that the wing comes off. By this time my observer was beyond hope and waved his arms feebly in the direction of home. I sent 'C.I.' to the battery meaning 'going home' and flew back over them – they put out 'V' which meant observe for salvo fire, there was such a general look of disappointment at me chucking the job that I really couldn't leave them, so I turned back to the lines and observed twenty-four salvos for them which were right on the spot and then I came in. My passenger's eyes came right out of his head and flattened against the glasses in his goggles when he saw me turn back to the lines with the broken wire. The CO strafed me first of all for not coming in immediately the wire broke and then complimented me for carrying on, at which I was mightily pleased. I do hope this observer will not be sent up with me again, it won't be his fault if he is for I fairly opened my heart to him after we landed.[61]

Second Lieutenant Charles Smart, 16 Squadron, RFC

On the same day there was to be a dreadful blow to the family of Second Lieutenant Charles Smart. His brother, Lieutenant George Smart, was serving at the front with 60 Squadron and that Saturday afternoon he had the signal misfortune to encounter Richthofen. The Nieuport Scouts were good machines, but the Albatros had the edge when it came to sheer brute power. If things started to go wrong they were difficult to evade:

Together with four of my gentlemen I attacked an enemy squadron of six Nieuport machines south of Arras and behind the enemy lines. The plane I had singled out tried to escape six times by various tricks and manoeuvres. When he was doing this for the seventh time, I managed to hit him, whereupon his engine began to smoke and burn, and the plane itself went down head first, twisting and turning. At first I thought it might be another manoeuvre, but then I saw the plane plunge without catching itself to the ground near Mercatel.[62]

Oberleutnant Manfred von Richthofen, Jasta 11, German Army Air Force

George Smart was dead. Richthofen then attacked another Nieuport in the same patrol, this one piloted by Second Lieutenant Tim Hervey. As unerringly accurate as ever, Richthofen's first burst smashed Hervey's joystick, shattered the instruments and cut his rudder control wires. The Nieuport went into a spin to try and escape:

> Steep turns without rudder did not work very well! On pulling out, there was the Baron right on my tail and still firing; not at all a nice position to find oneself in.[63]
>
> Second Lieutenant Tim Hervey, 60 Squadron, RFC

He spun again and after emerging at just 900 feet scuttled home. Hervey had been extremely lucky to survive his encounter with the great German ace.

By this point, the ground just over the German lines was littered with the burnt out carcasses of assorted BE2es, FE2ds and Sopwith 1½ Strutters. The Germans were having minimal casualties, whatever the extravagant claims being made by the more optimistic British scout pilots. On 7 April, Trenchard was still feeling ill and he therefore used his assistant Captain Maurice Baring as his eyes and ears, sending him out and about to see how his men were reacting to their losses. It was soon apparent that the situation was grave and that the RFC was being tested to destruction by the exigencies of the Battle of Arras:

> The General sent me out by myself to see squadrons. The battle was now upon us. Fighting in the air on a battle scale had begun. We had not got the necessary number of fighting machines. One gap was, fortunately, filled by the French. Du Peuty gave us enough Nieuports to supply a whole squadron. It was evident that we should not get through the battle and do the work of the armies without severe loss.[64]
>
> Captain Maurice Baring, Headquarters, RFC

In such a crisis, help was urgently needed. One obvious source was the Royal Naval Air Service which had previously assisted their comrades in the RFC during the later stages of the Somme. In early April, the No. 8 (Naval) Squadron moved into the Arras sector equipped with their new Sopwith Triplanes. One of their pilots, Flight Lieutenant Robert Little, soon attracted considerable attention:

> At 6.45 p.m. on 7 April 1917, a Sopwith Triplane, working alone, attacked eleven hostile machines, almost all Albatros Scouts, north-east of Arras. He completely outclassed the whole patrol of hostile

machines, diving through them and climbing above them. One Albatros Scout, painted red, which had been particularly noticed by this section, dived on to him and passed him. The Sopwith dived on him and then easily climbed again above the whole patrol, drawing them all the time towards the anti-aircraft guns. As soon as they were in range, the anti-aircraft guns opened fire on the patrol, which turned eastward and the Sopwith returned safely. The officers who witnessed the combat, report that the manoeuvring of the Sopwith Triplane completely outclassed that of the Albatros Scout.[65]

Anon Officer, Anti-Aircraft Group, Royal Artillery, Third Army

Robert Little was a real character, a hero now forgotten to all but a few:

A brilliant lone hand. I feel safe in saying that there have been few better shots, either in the Services or outside, than this man. I have seen him bring down a crow on the wing with a .22 rifle and break bottles thrown into the air while they were still travelling upward; what more deadly foe could be found than such a man, armed with two machine guns firing at the rate of 2,000 rounds per minute? Once Little came within range of an enemy he did not give up until: 1. The enemy was shot down. 2. His own engine failed. Or 3. He ran out of ammunition. He had in human guise the fighting tendencies of a bulldog – he never let go. Small in stature, keen-eyed, with face set grimly, he seemed the epitome of deadliness; sitting aloft with the eyes of a hawk he dealt death with unfailing precision. Seldom did he return to the aerodrome reporting an indecisive combat, for as long as petrol and ammunition held out, Little held on until the enemy's machine either broke up or burst into flames.[66]

Flight Lieutenant Robert Compston, 8 (Naval) Squadron, RNAS

Such men as this were an invaluable addition to Trenchard's meagre and hard-pressed forces as they too joined the battle above Arras.

A further piece of news to cheer the ailing Trenchard was the arrival of 56 Squadron. They were equipped with the SE5 Scout, one more vital piece in the jigsaw of new aircraft that would take the RFC into the final two years of the war. A strongly built single-seater biplane, it was primarily armed with a Vickers machine gun fitted with a Constantinesco inter-rupter gear, but it also carried a Lewis gun mounted on the top wing. The Hispano-Suiza engine could generate 114 mph at 10,000 feet and gave the SE5 an effective ceiling of 17,000 feet. But it was not just the aircraft that made 56 Squadron special. It was, de facto, an elite formation of scout pilots who had been specially selected by their squadron leader, Major Richard Blomfield, because of their proven fighting qualities or great promise demonstrated at the flying training schools.

Amongst them was the redoubtable Captain Albert Ball MC, DSO and Bar, the hero of the entire RFC. Ball had come to prominence in the air battles over the Somme in 1916. Impossibly brave, he had his own method of aerial fighting that no one seemed to be able to emulate. Whatever the odds, he would fly his Nieuport 17 straight into a German formation, split them up and then pounce on the weakest and most isolated. He would dive under his prey, pull back the Lewis gun on his top wing and riddle his victim from below. Then he was quickly away, before anyone else in the now scattered formation had time to react. It was a risky method of fighting and Ball often flew home with his aircraft badly damaged. His luck had held out during the Somme campaign, but by the end he showed clear signs of incipient combat fatigue. Now, after an all too brief period of being fêted on the Home Front, he was ordered to return to the fray.

At first, Ball thought the SE5 to be totally unsuited to his unique method of fighting. The SE5 was an aircraft built for power: the ability to power dive, fire and rapidly zoom away was the key to its performance in action. Ball favoured the manoeuvrability and fast turning of the Nieuport and was not shy of putting his point of view forward:

> They have put me on a **** machine, but I should like to get back to my old machine as soon as possible. Oh, I shall never be able to do my job. I must fly another machine and then I shall get along with the job.[67]
>
> Captain Albert Ball, 56 Squadron, RFC

Ball was not alone in harbouring considerable doubts about the SE5. The aircraft was plagued by minor faults of the kind that simply infuriated pilots. From their perspective they did not understand how aircraft could get so far down the production line without the correction of obvious design flaws:

> Right in front of the pilot's nose was a sort of inverted celluloid coal scuttle. It was supposed to be a windscreen and pointing ahead through the middle of it and anchored to the top of the fuselage was a long black tube, an Aldis telescope sight. Needless to say, the sheets of

celluloid of which this 'greenhouse' was made were difficult to see through and subject to all kinds of distortion. In addition we knew that any small oil leak could mist up the whole thing and make it pretty well impossible to see forward at all. Finally the aluminium frame of the 'greenhouse' had a rough, blunt metal edge within a few inches of our faces. In a crash this would cut us up nicely.[68]

Lieutenant Cecil Lewis, 56 Squadron, RFC

The pilots refused to accept this impractical monstrosity and instead fixed a small adjustable Triplex windscreen that would protect them from the blast of the slipstream without obstructing their forward view. Ball may have been prejudiced against the SE5, but he had the good sense to try his very best to overcome the various teething problems:

Albert Ball finally decided that the SE5 was such a bad aeroplane that it would be quite unsafe to fly it over the lines. He got General Trenchard to let him have a 110 Le Rhone Nieuport again. He and I sat for many hours at night trying to work out how to make the SE5 work. He was a very unusual combination of a fighter pilot with a real interest in aeroplanes. The majority of them didn't have aeroplane knowledge but he definitely had. Between the two of us we finally cooked up the SE5 so that it really worked. [69]

Engineering Officer Lieutenant Hubert Charles, 56 Squadron RFC

Many of Ball's proposed changes proved impractical for general use. They reflected Ball's own idiosyncratic methods of aerial fighting. But as a result of their hard work, many changes were made. Some were trivial, others crucial, but all gradually raised the performance of the machine to a more acceptable level:

From April 7th to the 23rd, we spent much of our time remodelling the SE5. When delivered, it had a sizeable canopy installed on the fuselage to assist one in correcting a jam of the Vickers machine gun. We also had a Lewis machine gun mounted on a clutter on the top wing. The idea of the canopy was to give one a little protection while working on a jam, but it was impractical. When you're in combat and your guns jam, the best thing to do is to get the hell out of there if you want to keep your health! We had a sheet of armour steel, about an inch thick, under the seat in the cockpit. It was supposed to prevent some nasty character from shooting up your behind! There was also a lever that would raise your seat so that it would be easier to get at the Vickers gun. We modified the SE5 by removing the canopy, eliminating the armour plate, and tossing out the seat-raising lever-and mechanism. As a result, we got approximately 7 mph additional speed, which was well worth while. If I'm not mistaken, in those days it did about 110 mph over the ground; this was about 10 mph faster than the V-strutter Albatros – and that's what mattered![70]

Second Lieutenant Reginald Hoidge, 56 Squadron, RFC

The SE5 was soon ready to take its place as the most effective British scout of the war, the dedicated work of a few pilots and mechanics released the great warplane that had been concealed behind a mass of design faults. Ball himself was itching to get back in harness:

Five of my best pals were done in yesterday and I think it is so rotten. We have not got our machines ready yet, but when we do, oh, I do hope we shall let them have it.[71]

Captain Albert Ball, 56 Squadron, RFC

AT last, on Sunday 8 April, Trenchard rose from his sick bed, just in time for the final preparations for the offensive:

The General decided to make a tour of the squadrons, and as there would not be time to visit all those he wished to see by road, he decided to go by air. He still had a touch of bronchitis, and did not seem fit for a journey by air. The doctor said it might either do him good or kill him. However, we went. The General in an RE8 and I in a BE2c. We saw eleven squadrons altogether. The General talked to all the pilots. While we were at Le Hameau Aerodrome, Ball landed there, having followed us from Vert Galant. He wanted the General to let him keep his Nieuport machine instead of the SE5 he was now flying. Afterwards he was very glad to have the SE5. Harvey-Kelly, whom we saw at Vert Galant, said the Germans he met in the air now were like floating meat.[72]

Captain Maurice Baring, Headquarters, RFC

The artillery observation pilots were still doing their best to get a few more precious hours above the lines; a last determined effort to try to guide

British shells into the German batteries who would spell death for the infantry if they were not dealt with by the next day. Second Lieutenant Charles Smart was accompanied into the air by his observer Lieutenant Lytton:

> Shoot with 68th Siege on hostile battery B63. Quite good although we did not actually hit the target. Observed forty-five shots and got all round the parapets but not right in them. Saw no Huns and had quite a quiet time. Tomorrow the infantry go over to take the Vimy Ridge, good luck to them. They have been marching past the aerodrome towards the lines all day, all of them looking very pleased with life and ready for anything. We have got a tough time on tomorrow, if the weather is fine I shall probably do about six hours in the air.[73]
>
> Second Lieutenant Charles Smart, 16 Squadron, RFC

Such artillery observation and reconnaissance missions were carried on all day behind a larger than usual screen of vigorous offensive patrols by the scouts. Yet over the last week ever more BE2c and BE2e wrecks had littered the ground in the front line area. Lieutenant John MacDonald, a wireless officer attached to an artillery brigade of the 9th (Scottish) Division, could bear witness to the scale of the cull inflicted by the Germans on the army cooperation aircraft:

> From my dugout I could count twelve crashed BEs. When an aircraft crashed or was compelled to land, I made a point of getting to it where possible and retrieving the wireless transmitter. On one occasion I found myself forestalled by a South African soldier who was busy with his jack-knife dismantling the transmitter. He assured me he already had three safely hidden away where he hoped to find them after the war. His intention was to become an enthusiastic wireless amateur when he returned to South Africa, and with this object in view he was laying in a stock of aircraft transmitters.[74]
>
> Lieutenant John MacDonald, 48 Squadron, RFC

Unsurprisingly, Richthofen was once again in action, this time catching Lieutenants John Heagerty and Leonard Cantle as they carried out a line patrol in their Sopwith 1½ Strutter:

> The German scouts were higher than we were, and they dived down on us from out of the sun. They seemed to drop from all directions,

pumping lead as they came. Cantle was working the aft Lewis and I heard him let out a good blast at someone in back of us. At the same time, a spray of lead whipped past my head, and several bullets tore through the woodwork beside me. I kicked over the rudder just in time to see the red plane passing below. He swerved at the same time, and round and round we went, each trying to get on the other's tail. With six or ten planes all mixed up and flying around, it took almost all of my attention to avoid collisions, but I managed to rip out several bursts from the forward-firing Vickers. In the spiral fighting, we two-seaters lost height steadily, and the German scouts, climbing quicker, were able to keep just a little above us most of the time. Cantle's gun was rattling away, when suddenly he ceased firing, and at the same time, the pressure on the joystick was released. It was useless. My controls had been shot away. They must have gone in the same burst that killed Cantle. From a glide, we went into a dive. All the way down the red machine, or some machine, kept right in back of me, ripping burst after burst of machine-gun bullets into the plane from the rear. I remember seeing the windshield in front of my face fly away in small pieces, and then the propeller stopped. Our speed was terrific. There was no chance to choose a landing place. I could only hope to get her out of that dive. I recall putting all my weight on one foot on the rudder and seeing one wing tip swing toward the ground, which was coming up at a fearful rate. That was my last recollection. I figured it was all over. I must have fainted; anyhow, I don't remember the crash.[75]

Lieutenant John Heagerty, 43 Squadron, RFC

He woke up badly bashed about and a prisoner of war; the unfortunate Lieutenant Cantle was dead and his body lay alongside the wrecked aircraft until it was buried by the advancing British troops a week later. Richthofen was going from strength to strength in the hunting grounds above Arras and Heagerty was his thirty-eighth victory. A little later Richthofen encountered a BE2g of 16 Squadron flown by Second Lieutenants Keith MacKenzie and Guy Everingham. He took them by surprise as they attempted to take a photographic mosaic of Farbus and shot them down without any ceremony in just a few shots for this thirty-ninth victory. They fell behind the German lines but a few days later the tides of battle washed over their crashed aircraft:

Flight Sergeant Gee and the Sergeant Major buried poor MacKenzie and Everingham. Mack was looking most peaceful and quite normal being shot through the back and arm. But Everingham looked as though the end had not come quite so peaceably. He was not shot but badly broken by the fall some 4,000 or more feet. They were buried close to what was left of the machine; all around were hundreds of dead bodies – our own and Huns.[76]

Captain Eric Routh, 16 Squadron, RFC

They were just another pair of victims for the seemingly unstoppable Richthofen. One former comrade from their shared Jasta Boelcke days, Leutnant Erwin Böhme, now looked on Richthofen with awe:

Amongst us there now prevails – at least among most of the squadrons – a spirit that is quite magnificent. Would Boelcke ever be happy about it! This morning I was with Richthofen, who has now been promoted to Oberleutnant. He had just shot down number 38. It is amazing to what level he has brought his squadron in such a short time. He has nothing but great young men around him who would jump through fire for him. Richthofen himself is full of vigour. Even if on some days he flies five sorties, one does not notice a trace of fatigue in him. What makes me happy is that he is completely free from boasting. He is a distinguished but very down to earth man. To me, he is always particularly cordial. It would be good if they soon made him head of the entire Air Service, he would be, after Boelcke, the best man for it.[77]

Leutnant Erwin Böhme, Jasta Boelcke, German Army Air Force

And, of course, Boelcke was dead. Richthofen had stepped into the great man's shoes and was setting an example that was invigorating the entire German Air Service. A minor comfort for the RFC as they approached the denouement of the bitter aerial campaign was that the almost equally deadly Leutnant Werner Voss was sent home on a well-deserved leave on 8 April. Voss had been awarded the much coveted Blue Max after achieving the then accepted 'benchmark' figure of twenty confirmed victories some two days earlier. Voss would not return to the front until May. But there were plenty of other aggressive and skilful young German scout pilots and Richthofen himself had no intention of going on leave until he had scored fifty victories. April would be a long month for the RFC.

STORM BREAKING

ON the night of 8 April, hordes of British and Canadian infantry moved with grim purpose towards the front line. Once in the trenches they took what shelter they could find to spend the remains of what, for many, were their last few hours:

> A filthier night could scarcely be imagined. Rain, mud – tons of it – cold, the lot. I was just passing a small recess in the trench, dug just below the parapet, just large enough to shelter two men in a sitting position with their legs straight in front of them. This one was so occupied and the sacking curtain was drawn across the front. Two pairs of feet in army boots protruded into the mud outside. As I passed I heard one of the occupants remark to the other, 'You know, Bert, I'd give quids to have me feet in the middle of the old woman's back tonight!' What a story. What courage in face of desolation.[78]
>
> Second Lieutenant Arthur Worman, 6th Battalion, Queens Royal West Surrey Regiment, 37th Brigade, 12th Division

As dawn approached the prospects if anything got worse:

> It was a cold raw morning, with sleet sweeping down the hillside. The soil on the ridge was a chalky white clay, and it became slimy and treacherous under the abominable weather conditions. We were in our jumping off trenches well in advance of Zero Hour. We were well laden with equipment and ammunition, each man carrying additional bandoliers of .303 ammunition, a few had grenades, while Stokes Trench Mortar crews man-handles extra supplies of shells We had iron rations in our haversacks and of this, with our rifles, Lewis guns and other impedimenta made a formidable load to carry on the slippery hillside.[79]
>
> Private Magnus McIntyre Hood, 24th Battalion, (Victoria Rifles) 5th Brigade, 2nd Canadian Division

Crammed into dugouts and tunnels or herded into the 'jumping off' trenches, however crowded, they were nevertheless mostly alone with their thoughts as the long hours slowly passed. A final prayer, a daft joke, a last meal, a cup of tea or tot of rum, the stupid, nervous tick of endlessly checking and rechecking equipment and weapons, yet another last cigarette – few had managed much sleep the night before the attack. Around them

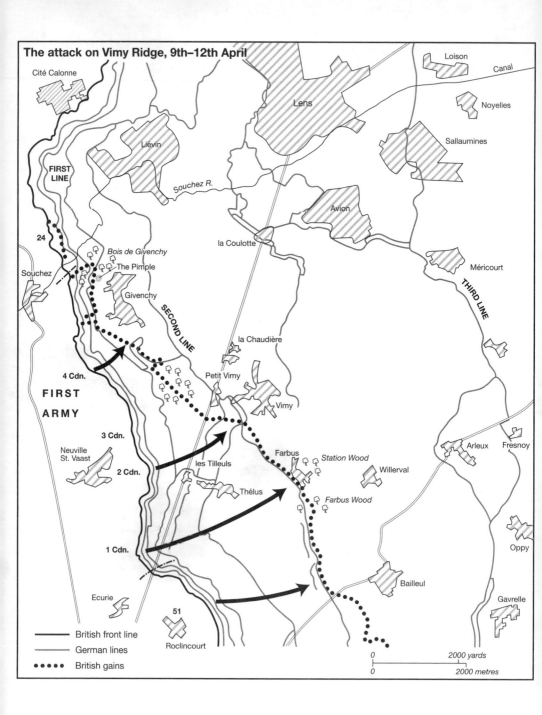

The attack on Vimy Ridge, 9th–12th April

Cité Calonne

Loison

Canal

Lens

Noyelles

Liévin

Sallaumines

FIRST
LINE

Souchez R.

24

Avion

Bois de Givenchy

la Coulotte

Méricourt

The Pimple

Souchez

THIRD LINE

Givenchy

SECOND LINE

la Chaudière

4 Cdn.

Petit Vimy

FIRST
ARMY

Vimy

3 Cdn.

Neuville
St. Vaast

2 Cdn.

les Tilleuls

Farbus

Station Wood

Willerval

Arleux

Fresnoy

Thélus

Farbus Wood

1 Cdn.

Oppy

Ecurie

Bailleul

51

Gavrelle

Roclincourt

British front line

German lines

British gains

0   2000 yards

0   2000 metres

the scatter of freezing showers, flurry of snow and sodden sleet marked the onset of another wintry spell in the middle of that bleak spring.

Finally, at 0530 on Easter Monday, 9 April, after all the preambles, the Battle of Arras began in earnest. The greatest ever concentration of artillery power amassed up to that point in time opened up and tens of thousands of shells brought destruction to the German lines. The barrage was utterly deafening, men could not hear themselves speak and could only cling to the fond hope that each shell that crashed down within the German lines might be the one that destroyed the bullet or shell with their name on it.

On the left the Canadian Corps, under the command of Lieutenant-General Sir Julian Byng, was ready to attempt the impossible and capture Vimy Ridge. Many of the troops had quietly moved into No Man's Land during the night and were ready to lunge forward when at 0530 two huge mines were exploded beneath the German lines. As thousands of shells simultaneously drenched the German positions for just three minutes, the Canadian infantry advanced behind the creeping barrage with the additional protection of being partially concealed by a smoke screen. During the crucial minutes that the troops were exposed in No Man's Land, the German batteries were lashed with a storm of shells to prevent them intervening. The whole idea was to gain a stunning surprise, a veritable *coup de main*. The top of Vimy Ridge was far too small an area to allow any practical expression of the 'defence in depth' policy with the result that German dugouts packed with troops were all within half a mile of the Canadian front line – well within reach of the initial assault:

> All of a sudden the 18-pounders started up their drum fire, it was like 10,000 thunders. Such a wonderful boost to those going on an uncharted trip. After a few moments, there were two excessive explosions. Our miners had mined the enemy front line, and this was the result. Before the stuff had stopped falling, we had to man the lip of the crater that was caused. Going through the wire was not bad, our artillery had busted it up fine. Our objective had been a stump of trees called Nine Elms. Our artillery was going full blast; yet now and then we would have a dud shell explode behind us, but in the main our presence was discovered by the Germans a little too late.[80]

> Private George Alliston, 7th Battalion, 2nd Canadian Brigade, 1st Canadian Division

For the most part the German front-line trenches were overrun before they knew what was happening:

> It seemed as if the whole world had exploded when these mines went up, tearing huge craters and leaving huge gaps in the enemy line. From where we went over the top, it was impossible to know what was going on else-where. We were concerned only with our own small sector. Remembering what had happened in our attacks on the Somme front, we were prepared for violent resistance. There was no rash charge, no dashing forward like a rugby scrum. We climbed out of the jumping off trench, aligned ourselves with each other, and with a steady stride, with our rifles and bayonets at the ready, started towards our objectives. The German front line had just ceased to exist. There were several bodies lying in its ruins, and there was no resistance until we had passed it, making for the second line.[81]
>
> Private Magnus McIntyre Hood, 24th Battalion, (Victoria Rifles) 5th Brigade, 2nd Canadian Division

There were carefully controlled pauses to allow the artillery to move up and a renewed barrage to fall on the next line of German defences, they moved forward again, reaching beyond the ridge and down onto the reserve slopes towards the villages of Vimy and Farbus:

> Then we came under fire from machine guns in pillboxes on the hillside. Still we went forward, losing only a very few men at this stage, until, as if from nowhere, there came a withering burst of fire from hidden machine-guns well ahead of us. We were really into it now. We halted for a short time, to get our breath back and plan for the next move. Then a trench mortar group came along, sighted on the machine-gun post and secured direct hits on it. We again went forward, slowly and deliberately. When we finally reached the point at which we were to halt and allow other units to continue over our heads, we were surprised to find that we had been in action for three hours. It had been hard slogging but we had reached our objective.[82]
>
> Private Magnus McIntyre Hood, 24th Battalion, (Victoria Rifles) 5th Brigade, 2nd Canadian Division

Deeper lying machine-gun posts were at the heart of the German defence system and the well-concealed new concrete pillboxes that housed them were difficult to crack open without achieving multiple hits by heavy shells:

Our artillery did a great job, but it took them some time to silence the machine guns in the pillboxes, which seemed to be the only German guns firing. All our casualties were caused by the machine guns. A sergeant right in front of me got hit by a machine-gun bullet and, as he fell, he nearly knocked me down. He was killed instantly. By his side were two dead Germans, one lying crosswise over the other. My first view of dead Germans and it was pretty gruesome because one of the bodies was headless. I particularly remember one German popping up out of his trench with his hands up, pleading for mercy as I approached, giving him quite a scare with my bayonet. But he had no gun, so I motioned for him to go to the back lines where they were herding the prisoners.[83]

Private J. Gordon MacArthur, 13th Battalion, 3rd Canadian Brigade, 1st Canadian Division

For many of the surviving German infantry, penned below in their deep dugouts, the experience was one of utter confusion and despair:

We were lying on our bunks which were swaying with the concussion of the shells. Suddenly our electric lights went out and we lit candles. Our sergeant ordered us up the stairs, himself going first. Suddenly he yells, 'Tommies!' and fell back dead, tumbling down the steps. We all panicked and ran back into the cave and threw ourselves down with arms over our head, fearing a bomb at any second. Then one of our 'old hands' – he was 22 – came down the steps and told us to abandon our weapons and come up the steps one at a time as the position was hopeless, the English were all over us. I walked up the steps behind a corporal who was very defiant and he spat on the floor when he reached the exit, but this did him no good for he was hit over the head by a huge Tommy who was brandishing a baseball bat. I covered my head with my hands and closed my eyes, expecting the same, but the blow did not come. Perhaps it was because I was so young. Looking at the soldiers, I noticed that they all had their faces blackened. I was prodded in the stomach by one with a bayonet and told to keep my hands on my head.[84]

Private Herman Kraft, 3rd Bavarian Reserve Infantry Regiment, Imperial German Army

Those 'English' soldiers were in fact Canadians. The Germans had been trapped by the speed of the advance, hard on the heels of the creeping barrage. Only on the northern flank sector was there a problem, where the interlinked defence of the Pimple and Hill 145 held up the whole of the 4th Division for most of the day. Nevertheless, it had been a magnificent achievement. In essence the Germans had been blown off Vimy Ridge and the Canadians had had the pluck and drive to take advantage before the Germans had any chance to reorganise their defences. The German counter-attack divisions were marooned some 20 miles from the front line and by nightfall the British grip on the ridge had been firmly consolidated. Together the Royal Artillery and the Canadian Corps had won a great victory.

The Third Army alongside them did even better. On the southern portion of Vimy Ridge, alongside the Canadians, the Scots of the 51st (Highland) Division of Third Army kept up with their neighbours. They initially encountered problems with uncut British wire and German machine guns but soon surmounted them to charge forward, deep into the German defences:

> We traversed many trenches which were very deep, but did not encounter any active German except those wounded and killed. One German was knelt in the trench rocking to and fro with his head in his hands – I do not know whether he was saying his prayers or pegging out. It was a work of art pulling our feet out of the sticky mud to clamber over the men laid in the trenches. By this time we were hopelessly mixed up and in the trench, along with two others and myself of our battalion, were Gordons, Argyles and 6th Seaforths. On the near side of the crest of the hill was a deep trench in which were some splendid dugouts. Into these many of the Germans had crowded so that we had them 'bottled up'. Close beside the point where myself and another had dropped into the trench was one of these dugouts, at the entrance to which was laid a dead German and another was just coming out. He immediately put up his hands in abject fear on seeing our bayonets waiting for him and began talking wildly in his own language which we could not understand. One of our officers came along and after placing us one at each side of the dugout entrance, he endeavoured to make the German go back into the dugout and bring

out his companions. But the Boche was not having any and with a face as white as a sheet appealed to us not to send him back. Our officer thereupon rolled into the dugout a smoke bomb which exploded and filled the place with smoke. Within a few minutes out came three big Germans wearing gas masks and spluttering and fuming. As soon as they came to the top, up went their hands.[85]

Private S. Bradbury, 1/5th Battalion, Seaforth Highlanders, 152nd Brigade, 51st Division

The mopping up of such dugouts could be a brutal business and the Scots could not take any chances with leaving parties of German soldiers behind them, who could re-emerge to shoot them in the back once they had passed on to the next objective. But many took a little too much pleasure in gleefully tormenting the hundreds of German soldiers caught cowering in their deep dugouts:

We got to the German front-line trench. It was smashed to bits but there were several dugout entrances. We dealt with these first. I pulled the pin from a Mills bomb and chucked it down the steps. 'Come out, you fuckers!' There was a crash followed by shouts and screams. Jock Leishman threw another one in for good measure – CRASH! – and another, 'Come out, you bastards!' Up the steps came four Jerries with their hands up. '*Kamarad, kamarad!*' they wailed. 'Never mind the fucking "*kamarad*", lets have you bastards out now!' Prodding them in the bellies with our bayonets, 'Keep those hands up!' we shouted. They were terrified and grovelling. Two of them were youngsters who started to blubber. I suppose they thought we were going to do them in. We got them out by the scruff of their necks and directed them back to our lines, giving them a boot up the arse each, to help them out of the trench.[86]

Private William Hay, 1/9th Battalion, Royal Scots, 154th Brigade, 51st Division

Yet the capture of Vimy Ridge was not the main event of the day. This had been a tactical necessity to protect the left flank of the real assault by the bulk of Third Army, which was directed along both sides of the Scarpe Valley towards Monchy-le-Preux. Carried forward by the naked power of their massed artillery they hammered into the German line. This time, in sharp contrast to the debâcle on 1 July 1916, the British counter-battery arrangements had been successful. The German batteries were for the

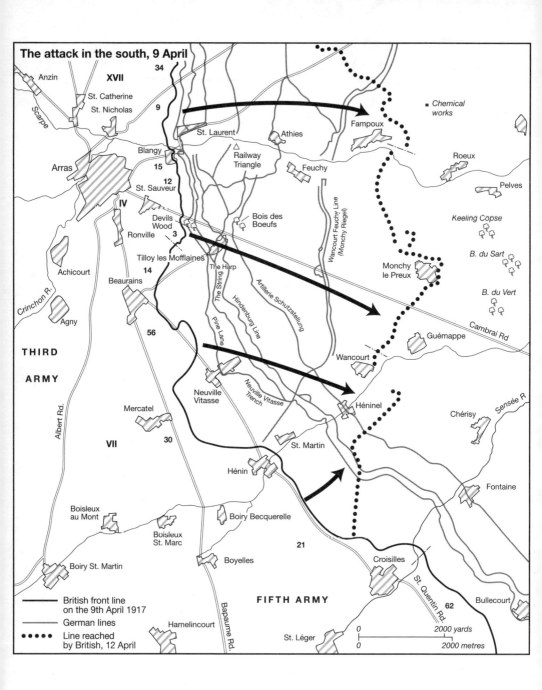

The attack in the south, 9 April

XVII

34

Anzin

St. Catherine
St. Nicholas

9

Scarpe

Blangy

St. Laurent

Athies

Railway Triangle

Fampoux

Chemical works

Roeux

Pelves

Arras

15

12
St. Sauveur

Feuchy

IV

Devils Wood

Ronville

3

Bois des Boeufs

Keeling Copse

B. du Sart

Wancourt Feuchy Line (Monchy Riegel)

Tilloy les Mofflaines

14

The Harp

Monchy le Preux

B. du Vert

Achicourt

Beaurains

The String

Artillerie Schutzstellung

Cambrai Rd

Crinchon R.

Agny

56

Pine Lane

Hindenburg Line

Guémappe

Wancourt

THIRD

Sensée R.

Neuville Vitasse

Neuville Vitasse Trench

Héninel

Chérisy

ARMY

Mercatel

St. Martin

Albert Rd.

VII

30

Hénin

Fontaine

Boisleux au Mont

Boiry Becquerelle

Boisleux St. Marc

Boyelles

21

Croisilles

St. Quentin Rd.

Bullecourt

Boiry St. Martin

Boyles

Bapaume Rd.

FIFTH ARMY

62

───── British front line
on the 9th April 1917

───── German lines

••••• Line reached
by British, 12 April

Hamelincourt

St. Léger

0   2000 yards

0   2000 metres

most part either destroyed or neutralised by enough shells falling around their gun positions to make it impossible for them to man and fire the guns to any military effect:

> There is no doubt whatever that a lot of the early success on that first day was due to the fact that we had really got the German artillery right down. I happened to be the forward observation officer with another officer and we had not the alarming day we expected but an extremely interesting one. We actually got into a tunnel near Arras Station and we emerged in No Man's Land five minutes after Zero Hour. To our great amazement there was practically no German artillery fire whatever. Undoubtedly a great deal of this was due to the intense gas shelling that had gone on the previous nights. In fact 36 hours later when we were advancing ourselves and we saw a convenient German position we found it stank so much of the gas we had fired that it was still unusable.[87]
>
> Lieutenant Kenneth Page, 130 Battery, 40th Brigade, Royal Artillery

Only occasional shells fell amidst the exposed advancing infantry. Any prospective German counter-attacks were destroyed by the overwhelming British barrage before they had a chance to take shape. Under the seemingly endless rain of shells many isolated groups of German soldiers lost their nerve and actively sought the relative peace and security that they hoped captivity would bring. The British assault battalions smashed their way forward, overrunning trench after trench. Yet it was not easy. Not all German resistance had withered away:

> The Hun was trained to fight. This was brought right home to me when I was moving forward with my platoon to our objective. A Hun was lying on the ground just ahead of us, apparently very dead. I had passed him and was amazed that, with such life that he had in him, he twisted himself over and fired an automatic pistol at my batman. He was fortunately too far gone to find his mark and it was his very last effort. But what stamina and what hatred.[88]
>
> Second Lieutenant Arthur Worman, 6th Battalion, Queens Royal West Surrey Regiment, 37th Brigade, 12th Division

Many lives were lost as the infantry attacked the interlocked system of small fortifications that defended Battery Valley, or the imposing embankments that anchored the Railway Triangle fortifications. Personal accounts left by the soldiers give a catalogue of sad losses and poignantly relate how thousands of men were wounded or killed in achieving these successes; the kind of devastating losses that placed the casualties suffered by the RFC firmly in context.

On the right of the attack the troops were faced with the full might of the Hindenburg Line proper, which began just north of Neuville Vitasse. They were assisted by several tanks to crash through the wire and knock out any machine-gun posts that were encountered. The Mark I and II tanks were not the super-weapons of myth and legend. They were mechanically unreliable – their armour was not even proof against ordinary bullets and they had a distressing tendency to ditch in rough ground. Yet when they managed to be in the right place at the right time they proved an important element in the steadily developing all-arms battle. Private Richards was in charge of one of the 6-pounder guns that each 'male' tank carried in its side sponsons:

> There was a terrific bang on the sponson and a piece of metal struck me in the mouth, smashing my two front teeth. Spitting out the blood and bits, I carried on firing the gun. Suddenly bullets came flying into the tank and we all threw ourselves on the deck. They whizzed round like bees for several seconds. Then we hit his main trench. As we went into the parapet we all hung on, and then down came the tank on the other side. What a bang! It almost jarred my head off. Well, I shot straight down the trench and skittled the Jerries who were running like hell.[89]
>
> Private Archie Richards, C Battalion, Heavy Brigade Machine Gun Corps

AS the troops pushed forward on 9 April, the contact patrols and artillery observation aircraft of the RFC were flying above them. Any surviving German batteries were bound to open fire now the moment of decision had come and the corps aircraft would be ready to record their locations and call down immediate retribution:

> My job was to direct the artillery and let them know which enemy batteries were in action. This was done by sending down what was know as a 'Zone Call'; by this signal a certain number of batteries would fire on the target indicated and go on firing till I told them to

stop or they had expended their quota of ammunition. It was grand to see them answering and the Hun getting hell. I managed to send down fourteen calls on active batteries which was great fun. After ten minutes shells could be seen falling all round the located batteries, the gunners are bursting with joy. I should think that our casualties from German artillery must be small as every time a battery opened fire it was immediately 'zone called' and shelled to hell.[90]

Captain Eric Routh, 16 Squadron, RFC

Second Lieutenant Charles Smart was also up early that fateful morning:

Infantry went over at 5.20 a.m. this morning, so was sent up on NF patrol (spotting flashes). Terrific wind blowing and as bumpy as Satan. First passenger soon got fed up with things and passed me a note saying he felt sick and wanted to go home. I passed a note back reminding him that there was a war on and telling him to think of the poor devils down below. He said he couldn't stand it any longer so I brought him in after an hour and thirty-five minutes and he cleared off. I got another observer (Lt Boyle) at once and went up again, this chap was the real thing, he felt very sick in the bumps but did not say anything about it. We had a great time and sent down a number of 'Zone Calls' and had the satisfaction of seeing several active enemy batteries strafed and silenced, thus making things easier for our infantry. Our shell fire today was worth seeing, the enemy lines were simply seething with bursting shells and it looked impossible for anything to live there.[91]

Second Lieutenant Charles Smart, 16 Squadron, RFC

Of course, they were severely hampered in their work by the appalling weather conditions. When they were caught in flurries of snow it was almost impossible to function properly:

The BE2c has a very open cockpit, very draughty, so that the snow came in from all angles, covering the windscreen completely, the alternative was to put my head out to see where I was going. In doing this my goggles became covered in snow; if I took them off snow got in my eyes and they watered so there it was. The only way I could see was to hold my hand in front of my face so that I could see downwards and occasionally slightly forwards.[92]

Captain Eric Routh, 16 Squadron, RFC

The determined efforts of Captain Routh and Second Lieutenant Smart to stay up as long as was humanly possible were very much appreciated by their squadron commander:

> Two of the six aeroplanes due to be up remained throughout their allotted time, in spite of the weather, and were of great assistance in sending calls upon active batteries. They had to fly at a few hundred feet and I believe were the only ones working anywhere. The moral effect of the success of the attack was most marked upon everyone.[93]
>
> Major Paul Maltby, 16 Squadron, RFC

As they fought, some of the artillery observers working in forward observation posts on the ground could see the valiant efforts of the flying men above:

> Saw three planes brought down while I was up observing this morning, two of ours and one Hun. Two of them came tumbling down in flames. One of our observing machines was suddenly attacked by two fast fighters, vainly it circled and dived, trying to get to the ground, suddenly it burst into flames and fell headlong, then righted itself and, blazing fiercely, tried to land, but all at once it crumpled up and smashed to the ground a mass of flames.[94]
>
> Lieutenant John Lyne, 64th Brigade, Royal Field Artillery

As the aircraft flew above the line the usual risk of being smashed to pieces by a passing shell was exacerbated as both sides seemed to be attempting to fill every square inch of the very air with flying shells:

> The risk, however, of flying low down, even though on our side of the lines, was considerable because of the shells from the artillery of both sides. I know of several instances where an aeroplane was flying happily and peacefully one second, and the next, there was nothing to be seen except perhaps a little piece of wood and canvas floating down to earth. With a direct hit by a shell there is complete disintegration of the aircraft, instant obliteration of its crew. Actually, I heard passing me several shells. If one liked to shut one's engine off, one could hear the whistling through the air over and above the roar of the artillery putting up the barrage and counter-barrage.[95]
>
> Lieutenant Harold Balfour, 43 Squadron, RFC

About mid-morning, Lieutenant Alan Dore was ordered up in his Sopwith 1½ Strutter:

> Fortune favours me. I am detailed to do reconnaissance alone. Arrived at lines at 10.30 a.m. to find attack had swelled to diapason. Clouds about 2,000 feet. An amazing sight, giving the impression of enormous industry. All along the Vimy Ridge a white line of bursting shrapnel told me that we had reached the summit. Below the contact patrol and artillery machines swept backwards and forwards – little shuttles. Behind me a string of observation balloons peered weirdly into the smother of smoke and cloud. I climbed above the clouds better to observe. No enemy machines to be seen. Far below, behind Vimy, I locate by flash the position of one or two hostile batteries, firing like tired men. Then suddenly one of our observation balloons breaks loose and passes above us, the observers jumping out by parachute. We immediately try to shoot it down by shelling it, and I put one hundred bullets into the gasbag, but apparently without effect.[96]
>
> Lieutenant Alan Dore, 43 Squadron, RFC

This dramatic incident was a timely reminder of the many risks endured by the observers in the kite balloons in the service of the guns. The escaped observation balloon was an FMI French manufactured Caquot balloon, which was normally kept steady in the air by large stabilising fins. That morning Captain C. M. Down had gone up with Major F. Maude Roxby commanding the No. 2 Balloon Company:

> The weather was about as unpromising as it could be for balloon observation. It was bitterly cold with a strong westerly wind, bringing flurries of sleet every few minutes, which effectively blotted out the landscape while they lasted. However, it was *der Tag*, and we had been brought down to the Canadian Corps especially for this show. Major Roxby and I, therefore, decided to go up to see if it were possible to give any effectual assistance by observation. The FMI was hitched on to the winch with some difficulty owing to the strong wind, and up we went. The wind seemed to get stronger as we ascended, and at about 1,200 feet the Major stopped the winch. The view was very patchy, whole areas being practically invisible owing to cloud, but there were bright patches here and there, and we were soon able to pick up the flashes of some very active hostile batteries,

positions of which we duly pinpointed and phoned down for transmission to the Canadian Counter-Battery Office.[97]

Captain C. M. Down, No. 2 Balloon Company, RFC

The men tried their best but the weather was totally inappropriate for the
unwieldy balloons:

Apart from poor visibility, the balloon was bumping about so badly in
the high wind, that it was almost impossible to use glasses at all. For
possibly twenty minutes the Major and I did our best to pick up and
pass on observations that might be useful, when there was a sudden
rending crack, as the stabilising fin on the starboard side of the
balloon ripped up like tissue paper under pressure of the wind. FMI
began by making a swooping nosedive from 1,200 to about 200 feet.
The Major yelled, 'Hold on!' and I held on. As I told him afterwards,
'I was going to anyway!'

Plunging like a mad thing she swooped up to the limit of her cable
again and then dived again, just as I have seen a kite do on a windy
day. Our winch, which was mounted on a heavy lorry chassis, was
located in a field, screened from enemy observation by a thick wood.
FMI dived on to this wood, where she rolled over so that the balloon
basket, for a short moment, was actually balanced on top of the
balloon! I remember vividly looking over the side of the basket, into
the rigging of which I had wound my arms, and seeing the grey-green
belly of the balloon *below* me with the tops of the trees just below that,
and beyond the winch and a crowd of men with upturned faces. The
wire cable, in great coils, seemed to be lying all over the place.

How many times the balloon dived almost to earth and then
plunged up again like a shying horse, I cannot remember. She rolled
and somersaulted so that the basket seemed to be upside down more
often than not. The fabric ripped still further and the rigging began to
give way. I felt that this sort of thing could not last, but what would
happen I did not try to guess! I merely concentrated on holding on. It
was impossible to do anything, anyway. But something had to go. Eventually it was the cable that went. At the top of one of the balloon's
upward plunges, during which she pulled the winch-lorry, weighing
some 10 tons, half the length of the field, the cable snapped, and away
we went. The blessed relief when, like magic, the balloon stopped her

mad antics, and went sailing away on a perfectly even keel. The only snag was that we were proceeding towards Hunland on the wings of a gale![98]

Captain C. M. Down, No. 2 Balloon Company, RFC

It remained a truly desperate situation. Down was qualified as a 'free' balloon pilot but the prospect of landing on the German side of the lines was not terribly appealing. There was one other option but they would have to be quick:

I had a look over the side to see if the parachutes were still there. We carried three, hanging outside the basket in their cases, looking like huge acorns. One had gone altogether, but luckily the other two were still there, but so wrapped about with rope that it took quite a while to free them. I worked feverishly on one, while Major Roxby freed the other, and we clipped on. I ran my hands very carefully along the rope which led from the waist of my parachute harness to the parachute. The great thing was to avoid getting hung up in one of the many ropes of the basket suspension rigging – a thing that I have seen happen to more than one luckless observer. In a moment I was sitting on the edge of the basket. Then, 'Good luck, Sir!' and I pushed off and dropped feet first into the blue. I remember having an entirely detached feeling at that moment, rather as if I were a mere spectator of what was happening. After what seemed rather a long drop, the chute opened with a tremendous jerk, which caused me to somersault in the air. Almost at the same moment I saw Major Roxby's chute come out of its case and open, and the sight was a very cheering one. Quick as we had been in getting out, the balloon had got up to nearly 5,000 feet before we left her. Swinging like a pendulum in mid-air, as I now was, I cocked an eye at FMI , which was now shooting up very fast, with every anti-aircraft battery on both sides shooting at her. She was sailing along Hunwards with 'Archie' bursting on all sides, apparently without any effect on her buoyancy.[99]

Captain C. M. Down, No. 2 Balloon Company, RFC

In addition, the Sopwith 1½ Strutter flown by Lieutenant Alan Dore had added a burst of machine gun fire, but all to no avail. Surrounded by chaos, Captain Down and Major Roxby floated down to earth:

Major Roxby, who was 6 ft 5 ins tall and broad in proportion, was dropping much faster than I, who was very light. I waved to him vigorously and saw him wave back. I now began to wonder where I should land; my chute was blowing along at a great pace towards the line, and the battle was getting nearer every moment. The noise of the bombardment was terrific, and I felt quite unpleasantly conspicuous, suspended between heaven and earth. As an infantryman I had many times been under fire, but had never occupied such an exposed position in a battle! I imagined large numbers of unpleasant German gentlemen laughing heartily as they lined up their sights on my gently swaying body.[100]

Captain C. M. Down, No. 2 Balloon Company, RFC

Captain Down was lucky for any German soldiers that sighted him from Vimy Ridge were far more concerned with preserving their own lives from the attacks of the Canadians. They certainly had no time to laugh at the misfortunes of others. Down just had to negotiate a landing without killing himself:

As I got nearer to the ground I realised how fast I was travelling. I managed to fish a penknife out of my breeches pocket and opened it, with the fond idea of cutting myself free the moment I hit the ground, but when the bump came the knife flew out of my hand. The trouble was that the chute did not stop for a moment but blew along at a good 20 miles an hour, dragging me, of course, with it. It was exactly like being dragged by a runaway horse. I was quite helpless to stop it, as there was 10–12 feet of rope between me and the rigging of the chute, and I was quite unable to get on my feet. Off I went across country on my tummy, hanging on to the chute rope for dear life. The terrain was mostly shell holes and wire, and I had an unhappy passage. I was just about done when the remains of a hedge loomed up ahead – a hedge practically obliterated by shell fire, but with one blasted tree about 5 feet high sticking up like a lone sentinel – and my chute blew straight on to that tree and stopped! I just had strength to unhook myself before passing out, and the next thing I knew I was in a dugout in the support trench line, receiving first aid. I felt a wreck and looked it. My clothes were literally in ribbons, and I was barefooted, having lost both my flying boots, also helmet, gloves and glasses in my high speed cross-country journey on my tummy. I was badly scratched and bruised black and blue pretty well all over, but, almost miraculously, nothing was broken.[101]

Captain C. M. Down, No. 2 Balloon Company, RFC

Major Roxby was slightly less fortunate as he landed into a roofless house and suffered bad head injuries.

THE men on the ground had continued to do very well. Following in behind the initial attack on 9 April were two more divisions used to leapfrog over the assault divisions and carry the assault forward. Amongst the fresh troops were the regulars of the 2nd Essex Regiment of the 4th Division. At first they found the going relatively easy:

The barrage kept a wonderfully even line, a curtain of continuous fire about a hundred yards ahead of us, creeping forward at a walking pace. The smoke and the fountains of earth helped to conceal our advance a little as well as tending to diminish any fire from snipers, machine guns or any entrenched infantry that might be in front of us. We had gone about 500 yards, when two field guns of German artillery, hidden in a dip across our front, suddenly opened fire point-blank at us. We took them in one concerted rush after they had bowled over a few of our men. A few of the Germans who resisted with small arms were bayoneted; the rest had their hands up to surrender.[102]

Captain Robert Monypenny, 2nd Battalion, Essex Regt, 12th Brigade, 4th Division

On and on they went, overrunning German defensive lines, capturing the village of Arles and pressing on towards the next objective. It was at this point that the troops realised that the generals and their artillery experts had not yet discovered the complete answer to the endless conundrums of trench warfare. The bulk of their guns were the 18-pounders and 4.5-in howitzers of the field artillery, which had a limited range of around 6,500 yards. As the gun positions had to be located at least a couple of thousand yards behind the British lines, this meant that once the infantry had gone forward further than perhaps 2,000 yards, they lost the gunners' support as they moved out of range. True, some batteries had been reserved to move up immediately, and others moved forward across No Man's Land as quickly as was possible. But the end result was still, inevitably, a massive quantitative drop in the amount of artillery support available to the infantry as they moved ever forward to attack new targets. For the same reason the German defence works here had been spared the day by day pulverising from the massed British artillery over the previous weeks and naturally the garrison troops were comparatively fresh compared to the battered front-line troops. In consequence, as the British weakened, the Germans, well ensconced in defensive positions, gained in relative strength:

> Our own artillery had ceased to function, or we were so far ahead as to be useless to us until they had moved forward. Then, within sight of our last objective, the Green Line, we came under really heavy fire. Undaunted, we pressed on, men were dropping faster here and the gaps were filled up from behind. We moved steadily on with casualties continually increasing. When within charging distance we rushed at the barbed wire, which to our dismay we found almost untouched by our artillery and at least 30 yards deep.[103]
>
> Captain Robert Monypenny, 2nd Battalion, Essex Regt, 12th Brigade, 4th Division

Going to ground, Captain Monypenny and his men considered the situation until a small party on their right discovered a gap in the wire and after the most vicious fighting the position was captured. Still they went forward:

> The enemy fire was very heavy now, especially machine-gun fire at long range from Greenland Hill, beyond the Hyderabad Redoubt. Our right flank, after a desperate assault, captured Fampoux, but our centre and left got a heavy mauling and were held up until further reinforcements reached the line and pushed on. The German shelling was now becoming very heavy and in our last dash towards Hyderabad Redoubt, what felt like a thunderbolt struck me in the region of the heart and I went down in an agony of pain.[104]
>
> Captain Robert Monypenny, 2nd Battalion, Essex Regt, 12th Brigade, 4th Division

The redoubt was eventually captured, but the wounded Captain Monypenny was already on his way back to Blighty. He and the men of the 4th Division had spearheaded the unprecedented advance under the trench warfare conditions of the Western Front of some three miles. The Germans were about to run out of completed defensive lines – but had not quite.

The British needed a further fresh surge if they were to isolate or capture the key village of Monchy-le-Preux, and they needed it quickly before the German reserves and counter-attack divisions could move forward to plug the gaps. Tanks were out of the question: there were far too few, they were too slow and they would have struggled to rumble forward the distances required. The only exploitation strike force at the disposal of Allenby was his cavalry. Moved up so often in battles over the last two years, only to be doomed to disappointment, they had been concentrated too far to the rear at Arras. By the time Allenby and his senior commanders had realised their chance, it was gone as the Germans swiftly moved forward their reserves, plugged the gaps and reorganised their defences. Tomorrow would be another day.

TUESDAY, 10 April brought the eagerly awaited news to the RFC of the progress of the offensive. First reports were extremely favourable. The attack had been very successful and the dramatic capture of Vimy Ridge naturally figured prominently in the initial reports:

> We got news that 10,000 prisoners and fifty guns had been captured on the Vimy Ridge. I went to see the artillery squadrons at Bruay, which had done grand work during the fighting. The work of the army had been done in spite of the weather, in spite of our inferiority in machines, and in spite of the casualties.[105]
>
> Captain Maurice Baring, Headquarters, RFC

Haig, Horne and Allenby knew the importance of speed if they were to exploit the fleeting opportunities that had opened up before them. Yet this was easier ordered than done. In the Great War the follow-up of an initially successful offensive was still an intractable military problem. It was far easier for the Germans to move forward their reserve troops from the nearby railheads than to get new British assault divisions across the shell-drenched wilderness their artillery had so painstakingly created. The appalling weather did not help. With impeccable pro-German timing the worst snows of the winter arrived to plague the British efforts. Moving a gun at any time was back-breaking, hard work, but it was almost physically impossible to get the heavy artillery forward in these conditions. The natural fog of war meant that orders to attack were both given and countermanded, the infantry waited for the cavalry, the cavalry were endlessly delayed and ultimately made only a token effort to explore the possibility of taking Monchy-le-Preux. They were swiftly repelled. The German line had been re-established and it would take a properly coordinated offensive to break through.

The snowy weather meant there was inevitably very little flying possible on the morning of 10 April. However, Second Lieutenant Charles Smart and Lieutenant Lytton were once again up in their BE2e. Taking to the air in these conditions was almost suicide. Yet they did not hesitate:

> Early job out of bed at 4.40 a.m. – in the air at 6 p.m. prompt. Doing another NF patrol. Very high wind blowing with odd snowstorms thrown in. Nothing much doing at the lines but I sent down one or two active batteries and pinpointed some fire. Just finished our time at the lines when we ran into a most awful snowstorm, turned west at once and flew for ten minutes at a height of 600 feet absolutely blind, could hardly see my hand before my face. I got most horrible 'wind up' for there is a lot of high ground about here and I was afraid of running into a hill. As soon as I saw the earth I made straight for it and landed safely. Was told by some soldiers that I had just missed a chimney stack almost by inches and I also saw a haystack just in the nick of time to avoid it. Without any doubt my luck was in and I was never more pleased to reach the ground.[106]
>
> Second Lieutenant Charles Smart, 16 Squadron, RFC

Another pilot, Second Lieutenant Albert Fanstone, was less fortunate as a snowstorm lashed his aircraft out of the skies:

> I started out on a dawn patrol with my observer, Musson; my orders being to watch and record troop movements in the enemy trenches. Once airborne, we were suddenly enveloped in the most appalling blizzard I have ever witnessed. We had just reached the lines when the storm, driven by a 60 mph wind, reduced visibility to nil. Flying at a height of 1,200 feet and knowing that the gale was steadily pounding my machine into enemy territory, I realised that our only chance was to get down and I signalled to Musson that we were going to land. We descended carefully as I was, of course, flying blind. When the altimeter eventually recorded nil, and I still could not see the ground, I started to sweat a little. Suddenly, we were relieved to see the rubble of a ruined village, which I think was Adinfer, but there was obviously no chance of landing in that mess.

I climbed for a second or two and tried again. This time open ground appeared through the driving snow, but this turned out to be completely devastated by shell fire. Being unsure of our position now, I decided to chance it and praying above all hope that we were facing into the wind, I went in. I was hoping to 'pancake' as a long run into the shell holes would almost certainly wreck us. As luck would have it we came to rest between the many craters. Scrambling out of the aircraft we leaped at the wings but were too late to prevent the wind from lifting our machine into the air. It rose slowly on its port wing tip then flopped over down again with a hard bump. Using the opportunity we grabbed the wings and successfully lashed the wing skids to the ground. Save for one slightly buckled wing tip, she was still in one piece so we wrenched the machine gun from its mounting and dived into the nearest muddy shell hole. At best we thought ourselves to be in No Man's Land and for the next hour or so we lay, straining our ears for any sound of activity, but the only sound that reached us through that white wall of snow was that of the howling wind.

It was now several hours since we set out from base and suddenly, probably due to the tension we had recently suffered, we were completely overcome with a feeling of hunger we could not ignore. Encouraged by the fact that we heard no indication of fire, we crawled from our shelter and moved slowly forward. Our flying jackets were held open, displaying the khaki of our uniform to any of our troops that might see us; if they turned out to be Germans then we would have closed our 'leathers' in the hope we would be mistaken for German flyers. Eventually we reached the first trenches and to our horror we saw signs everywhere in the German language. Still finding no signs of life, we cautiously crept forward and after a few moments of hesitancy I saw to my delight, trampled in the mud of the trench, a packet of crumpled English cigarettes. Reassured, we moved forward and finally caught sight of a number of troops working on a rough track. It was with extreme relief that we found them to be a group of our lads from the Pioneer Corps who informed us that this very position had been taken from the enemy only a few hours previously. Their officer provided us with a welcome tin of Machonacies and due to my hunger that trench dinner was the most delightful meal I had ever tasted.

Having reinforced ourselves, Musson and I returned to the aircraft where we found that the engine, having been exposed to the damp conditions, refused to start. We were, by now, in such high spirits having come through the recent events unscathed and therefore determined not to let a wet engine stops us from getting back in the air. It was then that we did a foolish thing, but at the time neither of us had any regard for the consequences: a few rags and maps were held together and, holding them under the engine, we set fire to the lot. This seemed to do the trick for a little while later we managed to get the engine going and, with the aircraft headed into a strong wind, were able to take off after only a short run. The incident did not end there, however, for the storm worsened yet again and we were forced to land four times in all. Finally, when daylight was fading, we reached La Bellevue where we refuelled, then telephoned Avesnes. We learned that our aircraft had been reported missing some time ago, and by the time we reached the welcoming fires of No. 12, we had been away for over fourteen hours![107]

Second Lieutenant Albert Fanstone, 12 Squadron, RFC

As the weather picked up a little later in the day, the army cooperation corps machines found themselves busier than ever. Contact patrols were being regularly undertaken by 12, 13 and 16 Squadrons. To be useful they were forced to fly ever lower over the shattered landscape, often under heavy ground fire. Yet the service they were providing was truly life saving to the hard-pressed troops:

On occasions, when the weather conditions necessitated flying at about 300 feet, it was difficult to pinpoint a position, or a flare, during an attack, or a counter-attack. The flare was found to be the most reliable means of identification, its steady light being readily seen through the 'fog of war'. The 'LL' call was used with success on several occasions, as was the 'GF' call. On one occasion the enemy was seen to be massing for a counter-attack east of Monchy. An 'LL' call was used and the concentration disappeared under the 'gun fire' of practically every battery on the front.[108]

Captain Donald Stevenson, 12 Squadron, RFC

Several machines in each squadron were also held in readiness to respond to any urgent request from the infantry:

As well as keeping patrols up all day, we have to stand around in the office for urgent calls such as this one, 'Can a machine range X, Y, Z Batteries on Z41e78 our infantry are being held up here?' or 'Cavalry being badly shelled at Savy please send plane to counteract fire'. I took on one such, tumbled aboard and taxied out to take off with two men steadying main planes, others holding the tail down, and two more holding the aileron flaps from being wrenched off by the gusts. Off we went, and so strong was the wind we were up 500 feet before getting outside the aerodrome! We soon found the point at which our men were being held up, and diving down loosed a bomb on the veritable hornets nest of machine guns from 1,000 feet. Almost before the smoke had cleared our men were in the place, so raking the back traverses with my machine guns I pushed off in search of something else to strafe. This soon turned up in the shape of shrapnel bursts over our splendid infantry fellows below, so we hunted around and soon found the offending battery, my observer locating it and sending it down. The gunners didn't open on it at once, so I climbed to 4,000 feet and swished over, and bombed them, which effectively stopped them laughing in church!

They were a good long way over and I was watching intently to observe the damage I'd done, when 'Rat, tat, tat', behind and over me! My left plane canvas was going rip, rip and large gashes were appearing, so I kicked over the rudder, and stood her on her wingtips straightening her out on a new course. I looked back, and saw a wicked looking little scout spitting fire and coming down on us at a frightful speed. My observer fired like stink while he was manoeuvring to get behind us again. Just as he was about to make another dive on us I turned again and we kept on firing. By the time he was ready to dive again, he was up to 30 yards of us, so I went into a split-arse spiral, which did him altogether, so he made off. Flattening out we sent another shower of bullets after him. Eventually regaining our own lines with sixteen holes in our biplane. Even then they couldn't let us alone but sprinkled us well with shrapnel from field guns.[109]

Captain Bernard Rice, 8 Squadron, RFC

From the heavens they could look down on the tiny figures far below. Rice even saw the rarest of all sights – a cavalry attack:

I saw the cavalry go galloping through – a grand sight. They looked like ants and I am proud to say we were able to silence a battery that was pumping hell into them. Tanks are quite difficult to spot, but we find them by following their trail which looks like the trail left by a snail with the tank at the end of it.[110]

Captain Bernard Rice, 8 Squadron, RFC

When the German guns opened on their targets, the artillery observation aircraft were ideally situated to record their previously concealed location and bring down devastating counter-battery fire. They also had a means of checking the effectiveness of their reconnaissance work:

When we captured Vimy Ridge a Boche gunner who had just come up to the trenches to look for an observation post was also captured, and with him a map showing all their battery positions. Only two batteries in our area had escaped our notice. The sound ranging and photos had every other one accurately.[111]

Captain Eric Routh, 16 Squadron, RFC

This kind of relentless pressure made it almost impossible for the German artillery to operate as they would have wished:

Due to the vigorous counter-battery policy pursued by us, the enemy withdrew his batteries to their extreme range from their SOS lines. His batteries were harassed day and night. He therefore adopted what measures he could. Batteries were kept continually moving from one position to another. Batteries were split, one section being in one position, and the other section occupying a different position some distance away. Before the battle, the enemy had usually built an emplacement first, then placed the guns in, and finally camouflaged it. Now, however, he reversed the procedure. This made it difficult to find the position.[112]

Captain Donald Stevenson, 12 Squadron, RFC

The German aircraft had, however, not been overcome and they took a steady toll of victims from the all-but-helpless observation aircraft. It was a price that had to be paid, but that did not make it any easier. Squadrons tried different solutions: sometimes they worked, sometimes they didn't – indeed, sometimes the methods seemed to be blindly contradictory:

It was difficult to obtain photographs, owing to the continual interference from enemy aircraft – the greatest care had to be taken by the pilot. The study of wind and sun was of importance, as in many cases it enabled the work to be done more quickly. The use of escorts was abandoned early in the battle. In the case of No. 12 Squadron, each machine worked separately, for the following reasons: escorts of fighters were not available; a machine was usually attacked by a patrol of German fighters – it would therefore be increasing the 'bag' for the enemy if both machines were sent together as he still outnumbered two, and more could not be spared; the single machine working independently is not so easily picked up, and can, on the other hand, more easily seize an opportunity.[113]

Captain Donald Stevenson, 12 Squadron, RFC

Yet, in an exact reverse, some squadrons abandoned solo missions for the illusion of collective protection:

The photographic job was an unpleasant one and had to be carried out by specialists who knew the front well. I had three pilots brought down while engaged in photographic duties in quick succession and eventually we had to send up two machines together. This plan worked very well as the rear machine acted as escort.[114]

Major Andre Walser, 52 Squadron, RFC

In reality it probably did not make much difference what the reconnaissance aircraft did. If they were caught by the Albatros aircraft then they were almost certainly in real trouble. The British scouts did what they could to protect the corps aircraft but their main role was to sweep the German scouts and army cooperation aircraft from the skies:

All the time our pilots were being kept hard at it doing offensive patrols and escorts for No. 25 Squadron. We got on extraordinarily well with this squadron, and, although escort work was always difficult and unpopular with the fighter pilots, our fellows had the greatest admiration for the photographic work being carried out by the FEs and it was realised that one of our most important jobs was to see that these machines did their work unmolested.[115]

Squadron Leader Geoffrey Bromet, 8 (Naval) Squadron, RNAS

In the variable weather that prevailed on 10 April, any kind of flying could be lethally dangerous:

> We had had some snow and hailstorms during the forenoon, but in the middle of the afternoon the wind changed and the weather became fine with no indication of further storms. No. 25 Squadron had some urgent photographs to get, and as the job would take them some distance over the lines, we were asked to provide an escort. Arnold, Little, Booker, Cuzner and Crundall went with them, but no sooner had they left than the weather broke again, and we had a succession of heavy snowstorms. We had an anxious time waiting for the machines to return. Eventually, Little and Arnold found the aerodrome, but we heard nothing of the others until after dark when all reported as having landed safely at various aerodromes round about. As it was snowing up to 8,000 feet, and the wind was of gale force at times, they did well to get down without damage.[116]
>
> Squadron Leader Geoffrey Bromet, 8 (Naval) Squadron, RNAS

ON 11 April, the British renewed their offensive. Allenby was determined to keep the initiative and prevent stagnation setting in. In truth they were already too late. The German reserves of infantry and artillery were moving up to the threatened Arras sector. It was now decided that Monchy-le-Preux was the key to any further great success. Its capture would very possibly unhinge the Hindenburg Line stretching away to the south. At 0500 on the bleakest, dark morning imaginable, three divisions struggled through the snow in a desperate attempt to get into Monchy. Bursting forwards with the support of a couple of tanks and even a stray squadron of cavalry, the troops managed to penetrate the fortress village outskirts and desperate street fighting began. House by house, cellar by cellar the British started to slowly clear the village despite the concentrated attentions of the remaining German artillery, who filled the air with exploding high explosive and shrapnel shells.

However, the advance had not been uniform. To the north of Monchy-le-Preux, a strong concentration of Germans in undamaged defence works within the shell of the old Roeux chemical works succeeded in hurling back the attacking infantry. Without a mantle of shells smashing down into them the massed German machine guns had a field day and inflicted severe losses. To the south, a similar fate awaited the troops launched forward behind an inadequate barrage to attack the village of Wancourt. The Germans once again had a firm defensive line that had the strength to resist any ad hoc attempt to breach it.

One late addition to the British plans was a subsidiary attack assigned to the Fifth Army and intended to distract attention and hopefully threaten the flanks and rear of the German defenders facing the main assault at Arras. The Fifth Army had only just followed up the German retreat to take up their new positions facing the Hindenburg Line. There was no time for the usual preparations for an offensive:

> To play our part in assisting the Third Army called for some sacrifices. The main problem was to defeat the German Armies, and the mission of the Fifth Army was merely to assist the Third as far as its limited means would admit. Its position enabled it to threaten the flank and rear of the Germans opposing the Third Army, if sufficient resources could be concentrated to make the threat a real one. Just as the attack of the Third Army was subsidiary to that of the French, so the Fifth Army was to operate in support of the Third. If successful, such an attack might be a great embarrassment to the German defence, and in any case it would draw troops from the front of the Third Army.[117]

> General Sir Hubert Gough, Headquarters, Fifth Army

Gough's army, however, was already stretched and he was hard pressed to scrape together sufficient troops to form a reasonable attacking force. The shortage of troops forced Gough to plan a narrow front offensive and the position selected was Bullecourt where the disadvantage of striking directly against the Hindenburg Line was, he hoped, soon to be ameliorated by the possibility of a link up with the advance of the Third Army. It was a grim undertaking – an attack on such a constricted front meant the attacking troops would be subject to far more fire from the unengaged German troop on the flanks. Gough was fully aware of the risks:

> Not an attractive proposition, certainly, but the object in war is primarily to assist the main plan – to adopt that course which helps most to achieve eventual success. A tactical defeat would be justified if it helped secure the strategical success of the Higher Command.[118]

> General Sir Hubert Gough, Headquarters, Fifth Army

In the event, the Fifth Army assault launched at 0445 on 11 April was a complete disaster. Without any proper artillery barrage or support, they relied on tanks to provide paths through the masses of German barbed wire and the mechanically unreliable tanks let them down. The Australian 4th Division managed to get forward into the village of Bullecourt and then unwisely pressed on towards Riencourt, where they were effectively cut off to be slaughtered en masse.

The British had shot their bolt at Arras. Small-scale attacks would continue to try and straighten the ground or seize key points like the Roeux chemical works. Small scale they may have been but each one brought another raft of casualties. The British were not, and could not be ready for another full-scale assault. Fresh divisions were needed, the artillery needed to get forward and register in the guns. Whatever was going to happen would not happen quickly. In a sense, the overall result of the battle was already decided.

All through 11 April the battle raged on, both on the ground and in the skies above. One ordinary young RFC officer, Captain Bernard Rice, inspired by a visit from Trenchard a few days earlier, wrote home to explain what it was they were trying to achieve. His words show that Trenchard had got through the essence of his policy of continuous aerial offensive to his men and that they understood why they were risking their lives on a more than daily basis. Rice is perhaps a little more optimistic than the situation really justified, but his words have the ring of convinced sincerity that allow us to see just how the corps pilots endured with none of the promise of death or glory offered up to the pick of the scout pilots:

> General Officer Commanding Flying Corps landed here, congratulated us on our excellent work and expressed a wish that we would let you at home know what we are doing. So I am going to let you into some of the work we do. You can tell people about it as much as you like. In the first place there is no reason to be alarmed at our casualties, we are not going under but just emerging out on top again. The Huns have been making a bid for air supremacy, and failed. Just before this 'push' started we let loose 'umpteen' squadrons of new and very powerful machines of the fighter sort, and met his forces in many battles. It has admittedly cost us dear, but we have achieved our object, and the Hun losses must have been terrific.

I have seen some of the people who did the job and they are all hugely elated at the results. Most of these great struggles have taken place miles in Hun land, where our people daily go to seek them out. Can you imagine the moral effect of this? But yet more has been done: all his railway centres, billets, dumps and aerodromes are visited daily and nightly, and tons of bombs loosed off on them. Never do they get a minute's peace. And they can't stop us. All his reserve defences are photographed several times per week, so we know just what he is doing. In a few days time we shall come up against another line of trenches which will check us a bit. This has been the most signal victory I've yet taken part in. We have captured whole batteries of artillery abandoned by their gunners, so hasty was their flight, and thousands of prisoners fell into our hands.

We have been working in close contact with artillery and infantry. The infantry always feel they are being watched over, and indeed a plane goes over first, and bombs the points they are held up at, signals to Headquarters where they have got to, and generally looks after their interests. Another plane watches for Hun gun flashes and immediately on seeing any, signals down position etc., by wireless, to our gunners who proceed at once to silence them, being corrected on to the target the meanwhile by the plane. I've seen 'umpteen' tanks go into action crushing through all obstacles, parties of Huns rushing towards our people with hands held high, and isolated battles in communication trenches. We have frequently swooped down, and cleared a trench with our machine guns. All this of course has cost us some casualties but it is worth the price, and most of them are wounds only.

You start at dawn or a little before, and finish about 8.30. We fly no matter the weather excluding continuous snow and rain. Up to now we have been having storms only, which we can fly round and dodge, and high gales. The latter very often so strong and gusty that only the older hands can weather them, and not turn sea-sick. This sort of work is going on all day long and everybody is sticking it well The Hun does not attempt such work. He goes about in bunches, and a few of his scouts try and catch us napping from time to time, while patrols of our own endeavour to catch him at it and keep us pretty well protected. Don't get anxious about me. I am taking risks of course, everyone is, but I am coming back alright never fear.[119]

Captain Bernard Rice, 8 Squadron, RFC

One notable event that day was a bombing attack made by five BE2cs of 4 Squadron, accompanied by a Sopwith Pup escort from 3 (Naval) Squadron, RNAS and some Spads of 23 Squadron. On the way to their objective some of the pilots of 3 Squadron, RNAS shot down an Albatros two-seater. But trouble really started once they were over their objective at Cambrai when they were suddenly attacked by a veritable swarm of Halberstadt and Albatros scouts:

> When BEs were attacked at Cambrai I attacked HA head on at about 8,000 feet. I saw many tracers go into his engine as we closed on one another, I half looped to one side of him, and then the HA dived with a large trail of blue smoke. I dived after him down to about 4,000 feet and fired about fifty rounds when he went down absolutely out of control. I watched him spinning down to about 1,000 feet, the trail of smoke increasing. I was immediately attacked by three more Albatros which drove me down to about 200 feet. We were firing at one another whenever possible, when at last I got into a good position and I attacked one from above and from the right. I closed on him, turning in behind him and got so close to him that the pilot's head filled the small ring in the Aldis sight. I saw three tracers actually go into the pilot's head; the HA then simply heeled over and spun into the ground. The other two machines cleared off. I saw two other HA spinning down out of control and while fighting saw two other BEs being attacked by HA.
>
> Having lost sight of all the other machines and being so low, I decided to fly home at about that height (200 feet). A company of German cavalry going east along a small road halted and fired on me; also several machine guns opened fire. After flying west for about five minutes I was again attacked by a Halberstadt single-seater and as he closed on me I rocked my machine until he was within 50 yards. I side-looped over him and fired a short burst at him. He seemed to clear off, and then attacked me again; these operations were repeated several times with a slight variation in the way I looped over him, until within about five minutes of crossing the lines (flying against a strong wind), when he was about 150 yards behind me, I looped straight over him and coming out of the loop I dived at him and fired a good long burst. I saw nearly all the tracers go into the pilot's back, just on the edge of

ABOVE Major-General Sir Hugh Trenchard
RIGHT Field Marshal Sir Douglas Haig (Q 3255)
BELOW General Sir Edmund Allenby, standing
in the centre (Q 1667)

ABOVE Officers of 40 Squadron. Left to right: Lieutenant C. W. Cudemore, Lieutenant Edward Mannock and Lieutenant D. H. de Burgh (Q 94936)

BELOW Lieutenant William Bishop (CO 1744)

OPPOSITE PAGE

TOP Officers of No. 40 Squadron (Q 94940)

BOTTOM Captain Mackenzie and Padre Keymer of 40 Squadron, RFC (Q 94943)

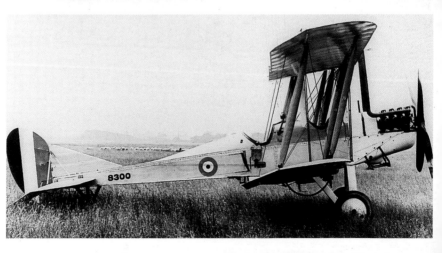

TOP RE8 reconnaissance aircraft (Q 55991)

ABOVE Lieutenant William Bishop leaning against his Nieuport 17 scout (CO 1751)

OPPOSITE PAGE

TOP SE5 scout of 56 Squadron, April 1917
(Courtesy of Alex Revell)

CENTER Sopwith Pup scout (Q 81679)

BOTTOM BE2c reconnaissance aircraft (Q 56847)

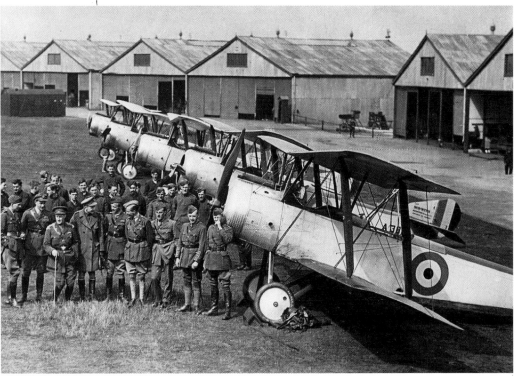

TOP RE8 ready for take-off (Q 3912)

ABOVE Sopwith 1½ Strutters, used for long-range reconnaissance (Q 33840)

OPPOSITE PAGE FE2b: ageing multi-purpose aircraft (Q 69650)

ABOVE Albatros DIIIs of Jasta 11 (Q 50328)

OPPOSITE PAGE

TOP Rittmeister Manfred von Richthofen sitting in the cockpit of his all-red Albatros DIII. His Jagdstaffel 11 comrades are, from left: Karl Allmenröder, Hans Hintsch, Sebastian Festner, Karl-Emil Schäfer, Kurt Wolff, Georg Simon, Otto Brauneck. From left seated: Karl Esser, Konstantin Krefft. Sitting in front: Lothar von Richthofen (Q 42283)

RIGHT Adolf Ritter von Tutschek (HU 64742)

FAR RIGHT Leutnant Werner Voss (HU 64740)

ABOVE AND BELOW Oblique aerial photographs of Bullecourt sector
(Q 57688) and Gavrelle sector (Q 56604)

TOP Observation balloon (Q 27265)

ABOVE Infantry moving forward to the front lines (Q 5117)

TOP New-won ground in the Feuchy sector (Q 5183)

ABOVE Waiting for a breakthrough: the cavalry at Arras (Q 1991)

OPPOSITE PAGE The power of the guns: the 9.2" howitzer under camouflage (Q 6460)

TOP Mark II 'male' tank, driving through the ruins of the suburbs of Arras (Q 6418)
ABOVE Troops in Monchy Le Preux sector, shells bursting in the background (Q 6292)

OPPOSITE PAGE
TOP The view of the German lines from the top of Vimy Ridge (CO 1351)
CENTER German prisoners under escort, Vimy (CO 1155)
BOTTOM Arras town centre (Q 2044)

ABOVE Albert Ball while training at Hendon, 1915 (Q 69593)

TOP Second Lieutenant Edward Mannock (Q 73408)

the cockpit. He immediately dived straight into the ground. I then went over German trenches filled with soldiers, and I was fired at by machine gun, rifles, and small field guns, in or out of range. There was a lot of small artillery firing and many shells bursting in and about the German trenches, somewhere in the vicinity of the Cambrai–Arras road. I saw many small companies of infantry and cavalry of about 10–50 in each going east along small roads. I noticed no convoys or movement of artillery. I landed at the first aerodrome I saw. My machine was badly shot about.[120]

Sub-Lieutenant Joseph Fall, 3 (Naval) Squadron, RNAS

Fall claimed three victories as a result of this frenetic action lasting just five minutes and in May he was awarded the Distinguished Service Cross in recognition of his efforts. His claims cannot now be corroborated and indeed the Germans only claim to have lost one aircraft in any of the fighting that day.

NEXT day, on 12 April, there were once again heavy snow falls that severely hampered aerial activity, and once again Lieutenants Smart and Lytton defied the elements to keep up the good work:

After a completely dud day and no flying, we were all sitting in the mess at 6 p.m. when the CO rushed in and said, 'The Huns are shelling the Pimple' (a small hill we have just taken in the Vimy push) and ordered a machine from each flight up on a NF patrol. As I was first for duty in A Flight I at once ran down to the aerodrome and ordered my machine. It was raining hard and thoroughly miserable, however we had to go, so up we went with the best of luck and made for the lines. I shall never forget the sight when we reached Arras, all the guns on both sides in the district were firing away at full speed. The whole ground, particularly on the enemy's side, was simply reeling with bursting shells, these together with the gun flashes presented a wonderful sight, there seemed to be millions of spots of flame spread all over the countryside and it must have been as near hell as possible for those down below. The air was just stiff with flying shells and we got no end of bumps from them as they passed under and over us. Our C Flight machine was struck by a passing shell, both observer and pilot

being killed. We did quite well in the NF line and sent down the Zone
Call for about ten enemy batteries. It was almost dark when we got
back to the aerodrome and they were firing flares for us; we got down
alright.[121]

Second Lieutenant Charles Smart, 16 Squadron, RFC

AT last, on 13 April, the weather started to improve. The air was soon
alive with aircraft. However, 59 Squadron suffered an utter disaster when
a patrol of six RE8s set out on a photographic reconnaissance of the
Drocourt–Quéant Switch Line. Only two of them had cameras, the other
four were acting as close escorts. They should have had an additional scout
escort, as it was obvious that they would be passing dangerously close to
the Douai lair of Jasta 11. Unfortunately the escort failed to arrive and
Richthofen and five of his scouts did indeed make a most unwelcome
appearance. The combat that ensued, if it could be called that, was per-
functory and all six RE8s were soon shot down. Afterwards, victors and
vanquished met in the Jasta 11 officers' mess:

> One of the Englishmen whom we had shot down and whom we had
> made prisoner was talking to us. Of course he enquired after the 'red
> aeroplane'. It is not unknown even among the troops in the trenches,
> and is called by them '*Le diable rouge*'. In the squadron to which he
> belonged there was a rumour that the red machine was occupied by a
> girl – a kind of Joan of Arc. He was intensely surprised when I assured
> him that the supposed girl was standing in front of him. He did not
> intend to make a joke …[122]
>
> Oberleutnant Manfred von Richthofen, Jasta 11, German Army Air Force

It is to be feared that Richthofen, all conquering in the air, was falling
victim to the verbal crossfire of the practised RFC 'wind-up' merchant!
The anonymous RFC hero doubtless cherished this exchange during the
long dreary months he would endure as a prisoner of war.

Meanwhile, Second Lieutenant Charles Smart had been posted back
from 16 Squadron to rejoin his original unit of 5 Squadron, based at Savy,
which they shared with the Nieuport Scouts of 60 Squadron. He was still
oblivious to the death of his brother, George Smart, killed by Richthofen
a week earlier on 7 April:

Was told this morning that I had been re-transferred to No. 5 Squadron so I had my things packed and flew to Savy with the front seat loaded up with gear like an old taxi cab. Was received with open arms at No. 5 everyone seemed to be very glad to see me back and I was jolly glad to get back! I got the afternoon off and walked over to 60 Squadron where I got an awful shock being told that George was shot down over Arras last Saturday. Poor old chap he hasn't had much of a run. The news has depressed me terribly.[123]

> Second Lieutenant Charles Smart, 5 Squadron, RFC

The RFC was suffering heavy casualties as the inexperienced pilots and observers sent out as replacements would often only last a matter of hours over the front before they fell victim to the practised German aces. Some squadrons were losing almost their entire force within a single week, as illustrated by 48 Squadron who lost ten crews between 5 and 11 April. Squadrons could lose three, four, five or even six aircraft in a single operation, which added up to a third of their effective strength. This was on top of the daily trickle of casualties that threatened to slowly erode the squadrons to impotency. Experience was at a premium and, in the revolving-doors environment of the officers' mess, as one pilot was lost another would arrive within a few hours.

So it was that yet another new pilot had arrived to join 40 Squadron at their Aire airfield on 6 April. Already aged 29, Second Lieutenant Edward Mannock was distinctly older than most of his contemporaries in the mess. An imaginative and highly intelligent man, he found it difficult to ignore the risks that pilots were forced to endure every time they flew their Nieuport Scouts over the German lines. Like many other beginners he also struggled to master the many interrelated disciplines that were needed to become a successful scout pilot. His first flight over the lines on 13 April was as part of an escort to a bombing raid carried out by a group of nine FE2ds:

> I went over the lines for the first time. Escorting FEs. Formation of six machines all together. Heavily 'Archied'. My feelings very funny. A group burst near me – about 100 feet. I did some stunts quite inadvertently. Lost my leader and deputy leader, but led the patrol down south. Returned safely after a very exciting time. Saw a few HA far away but couldn't get near.[124]
>
> Second Lieutenant Edward Mannock, 40 Squadron, RFC

Another new 40 Squadron pilot made his first flight on the same day as Mannock. Lieutenant Herbert Ellis was equally inexperienced but found his fighting career miraculously took off in a blaze of glory when he encountered a stray Albatros C observation aircraft:

> Ellis went over the lines on patrol this morning for the first time and got a Hun! It was quite comical too. He was out with two others and when over the lines got lost in the clouds. He searched around for some time, not knowing at all where he was, and then suddenly a Hun two-seater came out of a cloud and flew at him. Ellis fired promptly and saw the Hun turn over, go down spinning and crash to the ground.[125]
>
> Captain William Bond, 40 Squadron, RFC

Such instantaneous success was extremely unusual and less fortunate pilots were green with envy. Mannock made a characteristically wry comment:

> Ellis pulled his trigger, and managed to kill the pilot. The machine crashed in 'Hunland'. Great rejoicing here over this feat. I wonder which was more surprised, the CO or Ellis at this piece of luck?[126]
>
> Second Lieutenant Edward Mannock, 40 Squadron, RFC

FOR five long days the British had fought their diversionary battle on the Arras front. Yet they had to keep the pressure up for two more days until the main French assault was launched on 16 April. Since the photographic reconnaissance that had cost the RE8s of 59 Squadron so dearly on 13 April had utterly failed, there was nothing for it but to order an immediate repeat performance next day. This time the FE2bs of 11 Squadron were charged with getting the vital photographs. They set off on the morning of 14 April and at least, they had the benefit of an escort of Nieuports of 29 Squadron. Once again the mission could not be completed because the German Albatros scouts intervened, although this time at least only one FE2b and one Nieuport were lost. The fighting became general across the sky and an offensive patrol of five Nieuport Scouts of 60 Squadron led by Captain Alan Binnie was soon sucked into the action. Amongst them was an inexperienced young pilot, Lieutenant William Russell, flying on only his second patrol:

After about one and a half hour's flying, my flight commander suddenly dived. I followed him down, and at about 8,000 feet I perceived two enemy two-seaters to my right. I attacked one of these machines, and then discovered to my horror, that I had lost my engine. After descending about another 1,000 feet, I was attacked by two enemy scouts and I was obliged to make a zig-zag descent to the ground and landed at Bois Bernard. Unfortunately, it can scarcely be termed a combat, as, by the time Richthofen arrived, I had already lost the use of the engine and so, therefore, I had not the honour of 'putting up a show' against him.[127]

Lieutenant William Russell, 60 Squadron, RFC

With his engine spouting petrol and Richthofen sat behind shooting at him all the way down, Russell was extremely fortunate to survive. The patrol leader, Australian Captain Alan Binnie, was soon in an equally dangerous position:

They were engaged with a mob of machines I had noticed previously over Lens. When I overtook the first he was in the middle of a batch of hostile aircraft and one comfortably sitting on his tail, and on this one I was able to give half a drum from 20 yards. He immediately went into a spinning nosedive. I then began to change the drum, at the same time trying to keep any HA from getting on my tail. Had just finished when I got an explosive bullet through the left arm from somewhere underneath. Since I couldn't see the HA, I was now out of action and made for the lines, but fainted at 3,000 to 4,000 feet somewhere over Lens. When I came to I was on a stretcher with my wound bound up, lying beside my machine which was a total wreck and about 500 Huns round me.[128]

Captain Alan Binnie, 60 Squadron, RFC

Binnie's arm had been shattered by a burst of fire from Leutnant Lothar von Richthofen and in the circumstances he, too, was lucky to be alive. His arm was later amputated at the shoulder and he was repatriated in consequence in 1918. Meanwhile, as his aircraft fell to earth, the remnants of his patrol were being dismembered by the lethal scout aces of Jasta 11, as Leutnants Kurt Wolff and Sebastian Festner shot down Second Lieutenants Lewis Chapman and J. H. Cock – both of whom died. Only one Nieuport Scout, flown by Second Lieutenant G. C. Young made it back.

That same morning another patrol, this time from 54 Squadron, found themselves under heavy attack. Once again a young pilot, this time Second Lieutenant Russell Smith, found himself cut off from his comrades:

> We came upon hostile aircraft and drove them down. As my tracer bullets appeared to be hitting the target without causing any apparent damage, unfortunately I stayed in the power dive too long. When I pulled out, I'd lost contact with the flight. I started to regain altitude keeping a sharp lookout all around, especially above me, but there was no one close. I soon spotted three aircraft in 'V' formation, below and behind, coming up from the east to attack. I carried on, watching them and looking for any others. When those below me got closer, I was convinced by their speed and peculiar markings, that they belonged to Richthofen's 'Travelling Circus'. When I estimated that my machine would have come into their gun sights as they climbed, and before they started to fire, I turned quickly and dived on the leader on a collision course firing continuously. The two outside planes fanned outward in climbing turns and the leader soon pushed his nose down and passed under me. I started evasive action and then my engine misfired and I knew I had run out of fuel. Without the engine there was only one defence. I closed the throttle and put the machine into a tight, vertical spin intending to come out of it at a low altitude and land. There was no indication that my attackers were following me down and I didn't see them again. It may be they thought they had finished me.[129]
>
> Second Lieutenant Russell Smith, 54 Squadron, RFC

In such circumstances it was almost impossible to tell whether an aircraft was fatally damaged or merely feigning injury to get away from the pursuing hunters. As height was all-important in aerial fighting, it was often considered pointless to descend alongside a doomed aircraft just for the satisfaction of seeing it splinter into smithereens on crashing. This was, of course, exactly what Russell Smith was relying on:

> When in a small plane, spinning in a tight corkscrew motion, one seems to be in the centre of a huge bowl of which the horizon is the brim and the whole earth, as far as one can see forms the bowl which is turning about a point directly below, at the same speed and in the opposite direction from that in which the plane is spinning, When nearer the ground, I abandoned the spin and glided west taking evasive action

against possible ground fire. When the throttle was opened, the engine started but only for a moment; the tank was empty. I could see trenches but not occupants and thought I was near the front lines but couldn't determine on which side, or if I was in No Man's Land. I was surprised that there were not more shell holes. Right in front of me, the ground appeared level so I touched down as slowly as possible in a tail-down stall landing and was out of the cockpit before the plane had stopped running. The aircraft was intact; it just lacked fuel.[130]

Second Lieutenant Russell Smith, 54 Squadron, RFC

It did not pay to linger too long above the pock-marked surface of No Man's Land. Smith had to go to ground as quickly as possible:

Without a moment's delay I started to run, or scramble as quickly as possible in full flying kit, to the nearest shell hole and was about to jump in when I saw that it was half full of water. Continuing to another hole further from the plane, I found it dry, clean and still warm from the explosion of the shell that had created it. Artillery was ranging on my machine and the ground around me shook continually from the near misses. When the bombardment slackened, there was the noise of a rifle bullet passing over my head. After one or two more bullets, I suspected a sniper was busy.[131]

Second Lieutenant Russell Smith, 54 Squadron, RFC

Now the stress and tension of his awful experience began to catch up with him. As is often the case, it left him plagued by an immediate feeling of exhaustion:

It was still early in the morning and I thought of the long day ahead of me. I don't know if I slept. In fact I don't remember anything more until I regained consciousness in the late afternoon when I found myself kneeling in the bottom of the shell hole with my head and shoulders slowly swaying from side to side. I was still wearing my fleece-lined sheepskin hip flying boots, my heavy wool-lined leather coat and my leather flying helmet. I felt hot and removed the helmet and found it soaked with blood where it had covered my right ear. The bleeding, which had stopped, began again so I jammed the helmet back in place and pressed the fur-lining against the wound before I began to black out again. As the bleeding stopped, I soon was able to see again and noticed a clump of damp clay as large as my head lying beside me and, embedded in it, a metal shell splinter with only a small, sharp, jagged point protruding slightly. Could this chunk of clay and splinter have been hurled from a nearby shell burst and fallen on the side of my head as I lay on my side? I thought so.[132]

Second Lieutenant Russell Smith, 54 Squadron, RFC

This wound and a fitfully spluttering consciousness were additional problems to add to Smith's woes trapped as he was in No Man's Land:

I now had a very pressing problem. Should I wait for darkness to try to get medical aid and risk being too weak from loss of blood; or, should I make a dash for it now while I still had the strength, and risk being shot? I decided to go at once. I crawled up the side of the shell hole and out on top; nothing happened, so I started to run with my head and shoulders as low as possible. Glancing back to the right toward the place I had left the plane, I saw wreckage only; to the left I saw a body in German uniform lying on the parapet of a communication trench (the sniper) and looking straight ahead I saw a 'tin hat' slowly rising above the parapet of a trench some distance in front of me. The 'tin hat' stopped, leaving only enough space below the brim for the wearer to see me. Then two more hats came up, one on either side and stopped. That was a wonderful sight, for they were *not* German helmets. I raised my hands above my head and struggled forward. When I reached the parapet, they were still in the same position and the soldiers reached out and pulled me into the trench. They were men of the Newfoundland Regiment and my arrival in the morning had subjected their battalion to very heavy fire and I'm afraid I was not very popular. They told me that they had shot the sniper. One of them took me back to a first-aid station in the old wine cellar under the ruins of the mansion at Monchy-le-Preux.[133]

Second Lieutenant Russell Smith, 54 Squadron, RFC

Against all the odds, Smith had survived a series of life-threatening experiences.

It is important to remember that not all flying missions ended in failure. The basis of the RFC success was that their sheer numbers allowed them to bear the losses, to keep on going and, most importantly of all, keep getting the results the army wanted. One successful photographic reconnaissance on the morning of 14 April was carried out by 25 Squadron who had the benefit of being escorted by the Sopwith Triplanes of 8 (Naval) Squadron, RNAS. Amongst them was Flight Sub-Lieutenant Edward Crundall:

At 8 a.m. Booker led C Flight on a patrol to escort the FEs of 25 Squadron, RFC, who were on photographic duty. My engine was running badly and I could not keep up with the formation. At about 9 a.m., when a long way on the German side of the lines, I saw two machines flying parallel to the west. I had never seen a type of aeroplane quite like them. They looked somewhat like Nieuports but much bigger. I realised they were probably Huns which C Flight had not seen. I was a bit scared because I was a straggler all on my own and these ominous looking aeroplanes blocked my way to safety. I was at a great disadvantage because my engine was running so badly. I realised I must make a decision. The thought of being taken prisoner terrified me, so I decided to go and have a look and sell my life as dearly as possible if I had to fight.

I climbed as steeply as I could and they immediately did likewise so I became more suspicious than ever. They were about 2 or 3 miles away, so when slightly above them I turned abruptly to the left and approached. At about 100 yards distance I saw they were both two-seaters and almost immediately afterwards the iron cross on the top plane of one of them so I knew for certain they were Huns. At that distance one of the observers on the back seat opened fire on me. This made me furious, I literally saw red and dived on the tail of the nearest firing my gun all the time. I got closer and closer to his tail until I was almost touching it and could see the pilot and observer's heads and every detail of the machine. Suddenly the German machine fell over on one wing and went down in a steep nosedive. I was thrilled and started to relax, but only for a moment, because I was attacked from behind by the other enemy machine.

Again I saw red and was just as furious as on the first occasion, I swung round, got on his tail and opened fire at the same close range. After a long spell of firing, he started to dive and it got steeper and steeper until I realised the Triplane's wings would break off if I increased my own dive. Previously I had thrown caution to the winds because, as I entered each fight, I did not expect to come out of them alive. So I shut off the engine and eased the Triplane out of the dive when I found it was very left wing heavy and I had to fly with the stick fully over to the right.

I had started the first fight at 14,000 feet in the vicinity of Lens and ended the second at 7,000 feet to the east of Douai and the engine had been running at full throttle all the time. When I returned to 'C' Flight I was told my Triplane was almost falling to pieces and quite unsafe to fly in its present condition. The flying wires were stretched and very slack and one of the centre section struts had cracked and bent out of shape. Only one bullet hole had been found which was in the lowest left-hand plane.[134]

Flight Sub-Lieutenant Edward Crundall, 8 (Naval) Squadron, RNAS

It had been a narrow escape. Backed up by corroborative reports from kite balloon observers and one of the pilots from 25 Squadron, Crundall was awarded the two victories. Perhaps more to the point, the FE2bs had managed to complete their mission undisturbed and taken a full set of photographs.

From the tone of many of the British reports it may be imagined that the sky was literally teeming with German scouts. In fact there were usually well under fifty of them in action on any given day along the whole of the Arras front. Thus there was nothing but frustration in store for the Nieuport Scouts of 40 Squadron during their series of offensive patrols on 14 April. On one of the early patrols was another new arrival at the front, Captain William Bond, who was accompanied by Captain Gregory and Lieutenant Herbert Ellis:

I was put on the first offensive patrol and went over with two others. I thoroughly enjoyed it. We started at 6.45 in triangular formation and worked down on our side of the lines, crossed it at 12,000 feet, and worked back north about 8 miles the other side. We saw five Hun machines which kept a long way clear and were 'Archied' nearly all the time. I saw a good deal of the line though I was busy mostly trying to keep my place in the formation. Gregory leads our patrol, and I need not assure you how closely I hang on to his tail. We have tremendous confidence in him. The principal thing I felt was that comical sort of detachment – as if someone else were doing the show and I were

looking on. But I was elated to be so high above the clouds looking
down through the holes on towns and villages 8 or 10 miles behind the
German lines. It was thrilling but not exciting. It was thrilling to be
alone in my machine, depending on myself and good luck. And yet
I could not help being astonished at the absolute absence of emotion –
no anxiety, no fear, no care – except one, to stick close to the patrol
leader. We were out one hour and forty-five minutes and I was told that
I had flown quite well. And so to breakfast.[135]

Captain William Bond, 40 Squadron, RFC

Most of the 40 Squadron patrols aloft that day seemed to be unable
to find trouble, no matter how hard they looked. Lieutenant Edward
Mannock was also flying with a patrol led by Captain F. E. Brown. They too
were unable to bring, or tempt, the various German aircraft they sighted
into action:

Another offensive patrol this morning with Brown leading. Kept
formation grandly. Brown tried to lose me but failed. Observed fires in
Lens. Saw two formations of HA very far away. They won't wait.[136]

Second Lieutenant Edward Mannock, 40 Squadron, RFC

Outnumbered as they were, the German scouts were carefully hus-
banded and came together only for a specific purpose. Above all they were
not there for the amusement of British scout formations who were striving
to bring them to action – the German scouts were not obliged to take on the
British aircraft. Outnumbered, the Germans were fighting a defensive
battle and they would only engage in combat when they considered it was
to their advantage. Precious, trained scout pilots could not be thrown away
in useless gestures against the odds.

Many of the British pilots took heart from the recent advance on the
ground. They could see the advances the army had achieved and although
the new German lines and belts of barbed wire were equally obvious, they
felt that at last there were real grounds for hope:

You know I think next autumn will see the final coup if not actually the
end of the war. We are still advancing. There has been a pause while
we cleared a line of heights, I think we got them this morning, in which
case we shall make another rush forward.[137]

Captain Bernard Rice, 8 Squadron, RFC

In reality the situation on the ground was, if anything, fast deteriorating. None of the recent British small-scale attacks had succeeded in achieving their objectives. In truth they were doomed to fail. Made on narrow fronts designed to seize specific tactical objectives, the British fell hapless prey to the concentrated fire of the German artillery and machine guns from both flanks who were not under attack and could pour in a murderous fire. Despite all the efforts of the RFC the infantry casualties were rising fast.

ON 15 April, the weather was for the most part unsuitable for flying, combining blustery conditions with low visibility. Yet some aircraft managed to brave the elements and get aloft, one of which was the RE8 flown by Lieutenants W. Buckingham and Wilfred Cox of 15 Squadron. At first their mission seemed a hopeless wash out:

> The weather was unfit for our shoot, the clouds were at about 1,000
> feet and it was raining heavily. We decided to have a look at the line
> instead, and if the weather cleared to carry on with the shoot. On the
> way we heard heavy rifle fire about 4,000 yards behind the front line
> and saw considerable numbers of our troops in extended order,
> obviously in action. Further inspection revealed that the enemy had
> launched an attack against the Australians who were on our right and
> facing Quéant, and that they had been driven back to the point where
> we heard the rifle fire. We heard afterwards that the initial surprise of
> the German attack was so complete that they were able to destroy a
> battery of 4.5-in howitzers by hand. One brigadier is said to have
> fought in his pyjamas. By the time we had appreciated the situation it
> was about 0600 hours. No other aircraft was up at the time because of
> the weather, and but for the chance suggestion which led to our setting
> out to look at the front line, we too would have been on the ground at
> Courcelles. Under these circumstances it was something of a field day
> for us. There were infantry targets everywhere for, confident that the
> weather was keeping aircraft away, the Germans seemed to make no
> attempt at concealment. We commenced sending Zone Calls and soon
> obtained replies from the artillery. Occasionally there was an opening
> for the machine gun, but most of the time W/T cooperation was the
> more important work. We did silence one machine-gun nest and had

the satisfaction of seeing our infantry overrun it and capture the guns. By 0830 the enemy had been forced back as far as our front line, where he broke and fled back across No Man's Land for the gap which had been cut in their wire during the night. We saw great congestion at these points. It was like a crowd struggling to rush through a narrow door. Our machine guns and field guns were firing into the mass and caused many casualties. Over 200 prisoners had been captured by our troops.[138]

Second Lieutenant Wilfred Cox, 15 Squadron, RFC

Buckingham was, coincidentally, an Australian, so he had been able to have the additional pleasure of materially benefiting his own countrymen in their hour of need. This kind of exploit was the absolute essence of the work of the RFC. The veritable deluge of shells brought down by their Zone Calls had probably killed more Germans than were killed by any of the First World War aces over the whole of their flying careers.

Yet, overall, the 15 April was such a 'dud' day that many pilots, including Alan Dore, took the opportunity to visit the recently captured Vimy Ridge that loomed above the Arras countryside. They were fascinated by a battlefield that they had previously only seen from thousands of feet above:

Wet. So we take a tender to explore the Vimy Ridge. Near Estrées–Cauchy the roads are blocked with traffic – lorries, guns, infantry etc. – and we make a mile an hour progress. Cut off north to Souchez where we leave tender and climb up the famous Ridge. Near our old front line you could hardly put a pin's point between the shell craters. Everything seemed obliterated and mud, mud, everywhere. We struggle across the No Man's Land skirting old mine craters until the old German line was reached. Some devastation and mud. Ground littered with debris and dead or portions of dead. Rifles and equipment, shells and grenades abound. Only the deep German dugouts remain. We look over the crest to Lens. Almost immediately we are shelled, one bursting a few yards away. I take cover in a trench, but realise that I have lost the art of taking shells complacently. All the way back shells burst near us. At last, thankfully, we reach our tender and return.[139]

Lieutenant Alan Dore, 43 Squadron, RFC

The grim reality of the infantry war was a chastening reminder that, whatever the RFC problems and complaints, others were also suffering the horrors of war – and without the benefit of a warm, safe bed at night.

A CHANGE IN THE WIND?

THE next day, 16 April, marked a sea change in the fortunes of the Allies in 1917. It was the day that Nivelle finally launched his postponed offensive, which he had confidently boasted would achieve success within 48 hours and finally drive the Germans from France. At last, at 0600, the French infantry went over the top supported by the fantastic firepower of 5,350 guns all along the Chemin des Dames. Some early successes proved nothing more than a false dawn as the German counter-attacks crashed home. Around 120,000 casualties were suffered in the first two days.

Nivelle's plans had already been compromised by breeches in security but they were also intrinsically faulty. In essence, Nivelle failed to take all the facts into consideration. His successful plan of attack at Verdun had relied on massed artillery over a relatively short frontage encompassing three or four attack divisions. This could not be replicated with the same devastating effect on a front covering up to twenty-five divisions, especially without any degree of tactical surprise. Nivelle had also failed to take into consideration the possibility of a varying quality in the opposition offered. The German divisions that Nivelle had faced in the Verdun sector in late 1916 had been all but denuded of their artillery, such were the voracious demands of the Somme battle to the north. Many had already been battered by their awful experiences on the Somme or at Verdun. They were therefore in no fit state to resist a renewed French offensive at Verdun in 1916. This does not reduce Nivelle's achievement in recapturing much of the ground originally seized by the Germans in the first dramatic phases of the Battle of Verdun; he could after all only fight the forces that the Germans chose to place in front of him. It does, however, mean that he was unwise to draw general principles for the future conduct of offensives from these circumstances.

The British High Command had always been dubious about Nivelle's grander promises, but the die had been cast and it was apparent that in order to give Nivelle the best possible chance the pressure at Arras must be maintained to assist their French Allies. The local attacks would continue while new plans were hastily thrown together for a further large-scale attack along most of the Arras front on 23 April. Nine divisions would attack along a 9-mile front, but this time they would be faced by the fresh troops of an equal, if not superior, number of German divisions. The decision to prolong the British offensive meant that the agony of the RFC would continue well into May.

Over Arras, the corps machines returned once more to their daily duties as the weather briefly improved. Every day saw newly arrived replacement pilots and observers taking their first tentative steps above the lines. This was their time of maximum danger. If they were lucky nothing would happen; experience would swiftly accrue until they, too, were seasoned warriors:

> I went on my first job today. I formed part of an escort for a machine
> that was taking photographs of a special kind. They were taken low
> down, about 1,000 to 2,000 feet, and just our side of the German line.
> We, the escort, kept about 1,000 feet higher, also a sharp lookout for
> Huns. We were too low to be 'Archied', but they fired field guns at us.
> Only one shot came anywhere near, and two small fragments went
> through the planes. We were under fire about twenty minutes, and
> then, the great drama having been filmed, the producers returned.
> During the show my observer fired about half a drum into the Boche
> trenches; we could see the German Army quivering![140]
>
> Second Lieutenant Marcus Kaizer, 18 Squadron, RFC

Although 'Archie' may have been more a nuisance than a major threat, that is not to say it was *always* ineffectual. Anti-aircraft shells could and did occasionally hit their targets, striking like the proverbial bolt from the blue, shattering any complacency in a moment. The BE2c of Lieutenants William Green and Cecil Wilson suffered just such a shattering direct hit over Savy by the K Flak 93 Battery. Lieutenant Green certainly remembered very little about it:

> Our old BE was slow, but we had two Lewis guns, and both of us
> thought we knew how to handle them pretty well, although several
> times we brought the old 'bus' back limping with a peppering of bullet
> holes through the planes and fuselage. I recall leaving the aerodrome
> on the afternoon of 16 April and our job was an artillery patrol. So far
> as I know, we had done rather nicely, although my recollection of details
> is most indistinct. I remember once calling to Wilson and pointing

below to something I thought he should mark on the map, and I have a dim memory of the plane making a sudden plunge, out of which I was able to pull it. But that's all. When I came to myself again, and that only for a minute, I was in bed, and a pretty lass with black hair was holding my hand, and she told me that I had been sound asleep for five weeks.[141]

Lieutenant William Green, 7 Squadron, RFC

Green had a fractured skull and a broken leg but his observer was a mangled corpse crushed beneath the aircraft. The ordeal was only just beginning for Green; nightmares haunted him as he lay in his hospital bed:

Then the hysteria would come on me. Sometimes I would wake up with a jump and the sweat breaking out all over me. I was in a long ward, you see, and it had six windows in the wall opposite me. To me it would seem like a long railway carriage and I always had the feeling that it was moving along at a terrific speed. The conviction would come over me that just up ahead on the track somewhere was a sharp curve in the road and that it would be impossible for our car to get around it. Maybe the first section would get around, maybe the second section might make it, but I was certain that my end of the car would crumple up with an awful crash. I couldn't understand what it was then. I never had any fear of railway trains before, but the fear would paralyse me. I would shriek for the nurse, and the orderlies would run in and hold me down on the bed, although, what with a fracture at the base of the skull and my right leg broken above the knee, I had no chance of getting up.[142]

Lieutenant William Green, 7 Squadron, RFC

ON 17 April a belt of non-stop rain was followed up by four days of low clouds and rain with the inevitable result that almost no flying was possible for the next four days. During a brief break in the cloud on 19 April, Lieutenant Edward Mannock took off to practise his marksmanship while diving down onto a ground target:

The great question of the moment was, 'Would a Nieuport's wings come off if you dived it too steeply?' Rumour had been going round, and I believe it was founded on fact, that there was a bad batch of

Nieuports coming to the RFC whose timber was rotten. We noticed that Mannock was in the habit of diving his machine more steeply than anyone else, and we were anxious, and said so. It was here that I first noticed a characteristic of Mannock, which he afterwards showed on other occasions. He was only too ready to seek and accept advice, but he always liked to prove a thing for himself as well. He continued to dive his machine steeply.[143]

Second Lieutenant de Burgh, 40 Squadron, RFC

As Mannock dived down he was the natural focus of attention for many of the officers and men of his squadron:

Another fellow on target practice was diving vertically at the target from 1,500 feet when his right-hand lower wing came off. He heeled over to the right but managed to get her level with his aileron controls, shut off his engine and glided down slowly and crashed in a ploughed field without being hurt. It was a splendid effort. I saw the whole thing happen.[144]

Captain William Bond, 40 Squadron, RFC

Mannock himself seems to have realised just how lucky he had been to survive the incident:

On the 19th did some gun practice and in one dive from two thousand my right bottom plane broke and fell clean away. Managed to right the machine after desperate efforts with the joystick and landed slowly and safely about half a mile away from aerodrome. Such a thing has never happened before where the pilot has not been killed or injured by the fall.[145]

Second Lieutenant Edward Mannock, 40 Squadron, RFC

As he remarked in a letter home, 'Some pilot!' His sense of humour remained intact but he was not above teasing his faithful rigger:

When his rigger reached the crash, Mannock scared the life out of him by asking him what he meant by it, but seeing the rigger's face drop to 40 below zero, he burst out laughing and cheered him up by showing him the defective strut socket which had broken.[146]

Sergeant W. Bovett, 40 Squadron, RFC

At last, on 20 April, the weather began to clear and there was a return to some limited flying. Contact patrols were sent out to establish touch with the infantry. By then Mannock was suffering the mental after-effects of his fortuitous escape the day before. His nerves were never strong and he found it difficult to conceal his fears when he suffered further engine problems during a routine flight:

> Now I can understand what a tremendous strain to the nervous system active service flying is. However cool a man may be there must always be more or less of a tension on the nerves under such trying conditions. When it is considered that seven out of ten forced landings are practically 'write offs', and 50 per cent are cases where the pilot is injured, one can quite understand the strain of the whole business.[147]
>
> Second Lieutenant Edward Mannock, 40 Squadron RFC

ON 21 April, the RFC tried to resume their aerial offensive in preparation for the next big attack scheduled for the 23 April. There was still a problem with low cloud and mist but some army cooperation corps aircraft attempted to get the photographs that had been denied them during the bad weather. Amongst them were Captain Eric Routh and Second Lieutenant MacKenzie:

> The CO sent for me and said, 'I am sending Second Lieutenants Jock Mitchell and Lieutenant Rogers over to Lens to try and get some vital information. I require a machine from your Flight to go as escort.' God what a thought! A real forlorn hope – one BE2c to escort another – futile of course, but nevertheless, orders is orders, and I thought, 'This is where I meet my end'. Being the flight commander it was only right that I should go myself. We started from Bruay and proceeded via the Ridge. As soon as we crossed the line hell was let loose, we were only about 500 feet up, and had to fly low to get his information. Every gun, machine gun and rifle which could be brought to bear on us was blazing away, black smoke from the guns was all round us, bullets were passing by. Was I frightened? – talk of the cold sweat of fear! It was horrible, added to which I could hardly keep up with Mitchell, he was going flat out. As to being of any use to him, it was out of the question, though the fact that I was following him may have been considered as

moral support and I might draw any attack. He did not waste time over Lens, no sooner was he over than we turned for home, back through the barrage, it was even more intense than on the outward journey, but luck was with us so far and we reached our lines. I heaved a sigh of relief. That was the hottest journey I had ever had in my life, certainly the most terrifying. However, it was over, Mitchell had done his job, so what mattered.

I got out my map and started to make a reconnaissance of the German barbed wire. I had made one or two notes on the map when I happened to look round to see where Mitchell was; what I saw filled me with horror. His machine was on fire and he was halfway to earth, he had jumped out. At this instant I was shot through the hand, why I was not riddled I don't know – the machine was hit in front and behind me. My observer also escaped. My first reaction was to put the aircraft into a right turn and look for my enemy, he was in close attendance, he dived, but believe me a rubber-neck was not in it. I did not let him get a bead on me, but he succeeded in putting a bullet through my engine, camera and petrol tank. I found myself getting nearer and nearer to earth. My observer was doing his best to get bursts in at the Hun but he was not very successful, chiefly I fear, because I kept moving the aeroplane violently round the sky. I was now below the level of the Ridge, the Hun still in attendance and the engine damaged. Blood was streaming from my wound, there was no alternative but to land among the shell holes.

I flattened out and waited for the crash, but no, my luck held and I landed without even tipping up on my nose. Having seen the ground one would have said it was impossible, but we did it. Our troubles were not over, the Hun was determined to get us, he dived firing as he came, his shooting was not too good and I jumped out and got into a shell hole, yelling to my observer at the same time, 'Give the bastard hell!' Which he did from the machine and drove him off. The Machine Gun Corps also fired at him for all they were worth but their shooting was very much behind. He was not the one who had shot down Mitchell, there were two of them. The Hun who got me must have come out of the clouds from in front, and from our side of the line. He effected a complete surprise. The next thing to do was to get my hand bound up and give what information I had got to the gunners. I found a battery a few yards away where I handed over my report, was dressed and given half a tumbler of neat whisky to restore my somewhat shattered nerves. I was sorry for my observer; the experience had been too much for him. His nerve went and I heard that he never flew again. One day like that is sufficient for a life time.[148]

Captain Fric Routh, 16 Squadron, RFC

On 22 April the weather was much better and 11 Squadron made two more desperate attempts to get a decent set of photographs of the Drocourt–Quéant switch line. Harassed to distraction by swooping Albatros scouts, they were repaid for their brave efforts with five shot down and others badly shot up – and they still failed to get the photographs. Another photographic reconnaissance mission was undertaken by Second Lieutenant Albert Fanstone accompanied by Lieutenant B. W. Fryer, an American volunteer who had been a cartoonist with the *New York Sun* newspaper:

We had just completed a batch of plates when I saw in front, and immediately above us, an enemy fighter diving to intercept. I shouted to Fryer who swung around in his cockpit to put the German (an Albatros) in his line of fire. In his eagerness, poor Fryer pulled the gun completely off from its mounting, leaving us entirely at the mercy of the German machine. Fryer had no hope at all in replacing the gun on its mount, as he needed both his hands to keep himself in the aircraft whilst I was taking violent evasive action. I saw a solitary cloud below us, which seemed our only hope and I dived towards it. The Albatros by now had realised we had spotted him and he hurtled after us in a steep dive. Just as he opened up and his bullets punched holes in our fabric, the cloud enveloped us. Here we lingered for a while and when we finally emerged he was too far away to cause us any further concern, so we made a dignified turn for home happily totting up the number of bullet holes in our machine.[149]

Second Lieutenant Albert Fanstone, 12 Squadron, RFC

Meanwhile, Captain William Bond and the other scouts of 40 Squadron were still frustrated by their lack of contact with German scouts:

We crossed the lines at 8,000 feet and climbed steadily, going due east. For nearly half an hour we had the sky to ourselves; then we saw

Mackenzie whip round to the left and dive. Looking down in his direction we saw Huns. Real Huns! Four big, fat ones! Two were painted a vivid red; the others were a nasty mottled yellow and green. But we didn't mind. They could have had puce hair and scarlet eyes, for all we cared. Now, when you're on patrol and the leader dives on a Hun, the other scouts have to search the sky above and behind them for other Huns before following. It is a favourite trick of the Boche to plant a couple of machines below you as bait, and then wait above until you go down. Then they dive on you when your attention is occupied.

Neither Ellis nor I overlooked this, and before we had dived far we saw that this had happened. Five Huns were on our tail! We opened out, and went past Mackenzie. Mackenzie looked round and saw the Huns, and started to climb dead into the sun and forward of the five. They turned off at this, and passed us about 2,000 yards away. We continued to climb and circle, so that we got the sun behind us. Then we began to see Huns in earnest. From every one of the 360 degrees of the compass they came. Still we climbed and circled, waiting for their attack. Gradually they gathered together, until we could count fourteen. Some could outclimb us we could see; but they stayed together, and when we were as high as they, Mackenzie headed straight for them. Immediately they split into parties, left and right; while two dived underneath us. This was the bait trick again, and we refused it. Again we circled back into the sun and awaited their attack. It never came; but all the time the west wind was drifting us further over Hunland.

The finish was a comedy. Mackenzie made a quick left turn, and Ellis, on the inside, tried a vertical bank; but so absorbed was he in watching the rainbow formation in front of us that he turned right over and went down in a spin. I thought, perhaps he had been hit, and looked behind. Three more Huns on our tail! Ellis had gone right down into the clouds. I looked for Mackenzie, and could not see him. I was alone against the whole Hunnish Flying Corps. When I stopped spinning, I was just above the clouds at 7,000 feet. My spin had started at 13,000 feet. I headed carefully for the sun, due west, and home. Then I looked back. The Huns were still there – just a few dots in infinite distance. Sometime later I picked up Ellis, and together we tootled home. Mackenzie landed a few minutes later. Neither Ellis nor

Mackenzie nor I were feeling absolutely full of confidence, nor pleased with life, last night. The idea of Huns jostling in the sky like that was not nice to think of. Ellis and I thought we'd dream of Huns – pink ones and red and green – but we didn't![150]

Captain William Bond, 40 Squadron, RFC

At least the pilots were able to report that their desire for combat had on this occasion been more than adequately catered for by the German Air Force.

ON Monday 23 April, at 0445, nine divisions went over the top between Gavrelle and Croisilles along the Arras front. This was St George's Day, but no sane man would have wanted to share the glory that was to be found in the Second Battle of the Scarpe. The German artillery had adjusted its tactics and lay further back and safely out of range of all but the heaviest British artillery. In their defensive capacity the German gunners did not need to reach deep behind the British lines; all they needed to be able to do was pour shells into troops advancing across No Man's Land. This they did to devastating effect. The tired troops, many of whom had already been through the mill at Arras earlier in the month, faced fresh German divisions in reorganised defences. To the north, the land-locked 'sailors' of the 63rd (Royal Naval) Division had somehow got through the German lines to capture the village of Gavrelle. Amongst them was a young veteran of both Gallipoli and the Somme, Leading Seaman Joe Murray of the Hood Battalion:

We dug some trenches in front, jumping off trenches and overnight we went out to them. In the early morning we were lined up ready for the attack, it was almost daylight. The barrage opened. Asquith came along and we were given instructions before we left. We were not supposed to move until the barrage lifted off the German front line immediately in front of Gavrelle. Any old campaigner knows, that to wait until the barrage moves and then have a couple of hundred yards to walk is just simply murder. But Asquith, instead of waiting until the barrage lifted, he took us forward. We went forward to within about 50 yards when it lifted. His judgement was perfect and we were on top of his line before Jerry knew anything about it. We men who survived that battle owe our survival to Asquith ignoring orders. The ground in front

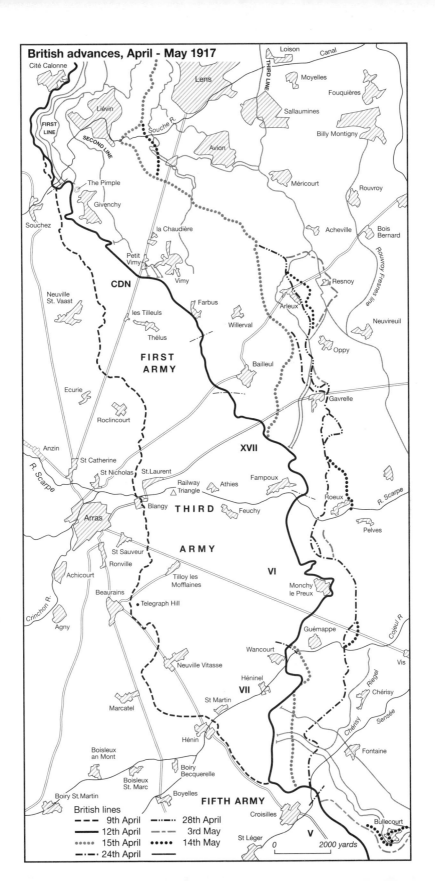

British advances, April - May 1917

Loison
Canal
Cité Calonne
THIRD LINE
Lens
Moyelles
Fouquières
Liévin
Sallaumines
FIRST LINE
Souche R.
Billy Montigny
SECOND LINE
Avion
The Pimple
Méricourt
Givenchy
Rouvroy
Souchez
la Chaudière
Acheville
Bois Bernard
Petit Vimy
Resnoy
Rouvroy Fresnes line
CDN
Vimy
Neuville St. Vaast
Farbus
Arleux
Neuvireuil
les Tilleuls
Willerval
Thélus
Oppy
FIRST ARMY
Bailleul
Ecurie
Gavrelle
Roclincourt
Anzin
XVII
R. Scarpe
St Catherine
St Nicholas
St.Laurent
Railway Triangle
Athies
Fampoux
St Sauveur
Blangy
THIRD
Feuchy
Roeux
R. Scarpe
Arras
Pelves
ARMY
Ronville
VI
Achicourt
Tilloy les Mofflaines
Monchy le Preux
Beaurains
Telegraph Hill
Crinchon R.
Cojeul R.
Agny
Guémappe
Vis
Wancourt
Neuville Vitasse
Héninel
VII
Riegel
St Martin
Chérisy
Marcatel
Sensée
Hénin
Chérisy
Fontaine
Boisleux an Mont
Boiry Becquerelle
Boisleux St. Marc
Boyelles
Boiry St.Martin
FIFTH ARMY
Croisilles
Bullecourt
St Léger
V

British lines

- – – – 9th April
- —— 12th April
- ·········· 15th April
- –·–·– 24th April
- –··–··– 28th April
- – – – 3rd May
- •••••• 14th May

0   2000 yards

of us was not pock-marked with shell holes – it was quite level really – open. Ideal territory for tanks, but we didn't have any! Open is all right because we could go forward more or less in a line whereas on the Somme you were in and out of shell holes, you're all over the place. As we got to the first objective it wasn't so bad, we seemed to be organised. Having captured this trench we had another one to go beyond there about three parts of the way through the village – directly in front of us. When you got in the village it was a different kettle of fish because Jerry was in the cellars.[151]

Leading Seaman Joe Murray, Hood Battalion, 189th Brigade, 63rd (Royal Naval) Division

As the men entered Gavrelle itself they had their first experience of street fighting. The Germans could be hidden anywhere, every corner could be a death-trap and the village was still being lashed by fire from both sides:

It was now quite light and being in the open we were perfect targets. There were bricks flying about, rifle fire, machine-gun fire, there was shelling. You couldn't keep in any sort of formation at all. Sometimes you got underneath a half blown down house; sometimes you went over the top. The wire that was in front was piled up in heaps as it usually is by our artillery bombardment. We had to keep gathering together to get through a particular place. You couldn't climb over 10–15 feet of bricks. All the time we were being fired on. There was no sort of line, no sort of direction, you couldn't see any officers, you couldn't see any men. Sometimes there were three or four; sometimes you were on your own – where has everyone got to – you don't know. You don't like to be alone. We were quite close to the road and I came across an officer lying flat. I tried to undo some barbed wire round what was left of one of his legs, a sub-lieutenant. I turned him over and he had a sort of grin on his face. His face was red – there was red brick dust as well as blood. Of course the smoke, you were spitting all the time, you keep on rubbing your eyes.[152]

Leading Seaman Joe Murray, Hood Battalion, 189th Brigade, 63rd (Royal Naval) Division

The village cellars concealed many small parties of German soldiers engaged in a last, almost suicidal defence. There was rarely any chance for the Germans to surrender:

Sergeant Kloke shouted, 'Tommies are here!' so we took up positions by the shattered windows on the ground floor. Before we got the chance to open fire, a Tommy threw a grenade into the room which bounced along the floorboards. We all threw ourselves down, but Kloke picked up the grenade and threw it back out of the window where it exploded. We began to shoot at the English, but being at ground level we made easy targets. Two of my school chums from Warin were shot through the head. Resistance seemed useless as we were surrounded. Then another grenade was thrown into the room and Kloke picked it up to throw back, but this time he was too late, it exploded in his hand. There was a terrific bang and then whistling in the ears and the next thing I know, I woke up in the street outside the house where I had been dragged. I had many shrapnel wounds from the British bomb.[153]

Fusilier Hans Lutmer, 90th Fusilier Regiment, Imperial German Army

Leading Seaman Murray was with one of the isolated groups feeling its way along the main road towards the Mayor's house in the centre of Gavrelle:

There were four or five of us, not more. There were some in front, there was some to the left, but there wasn't any sign of organised advance. Just before we got to the Mayor's house, I was fooling round trying to get over an old door of a house and as I stood on the damned thing it went over and it went forward. As I slipped, I saw a rifle, from a cellar; I could only see the barrel. I saw it move, instinctively I turned quickly round to the left and fired, I had got a revolver as an NCO Lewis gunner – but I always carried a rifle with me on these occasions as well. I fired but I didn't need the smoke from his rifle to know that I'd been hit. My hand was in my pocket and it went through my wrist. I couldn't get me hand out of my pocket, paralysed. The rifle was swinging and I crawled forward to where the rifle was, three or four feet. The Jerry was firing out of the entrance of a cellar and I'd shot him, blown half his head away. I got in there, I've got him for company – he's dead of course. A shell burst very close – there were doors and window frames flying about, I thought to myself, 'I'm going to be buried here in a moment!' The blood was running down my trouser leg, excruciating pain. I tried to get my rifle off but I couldn't get my hand out of my pocket. I thought I've got to get out of here somehow. The shells were banging all the time, the rifles going, bricks, sulphur, noise.[154]

Leading Seaman Joe Murray, Hood Battalion, 189th Brigade, 63rd (Royal Naval) Division

Murray was eventually helped back to the dressing station by a young German soldier where the men of the Royal Army Medical Corps helped him as they helped so many others.

Stretcher Bearer Private Joseph Yarwood was with an advanced dressing post of the 94th Field Ambulance based in some old concrete German gunpits:

We came to a belt of barbed wire, and there were poor devils lying in this barbed wire, an awful sight. You didn't stop to look around too much there because it wasn't a pleasant place to be. I had the wind up good and proper. Then you would go down to the village about dusk and do what evacuations we could of the wounded at night time. If you got any wounded your idea was to get them back as quickly as possible, the facilities were so crude. You daren't move about in the daylight, if you got too active, he'd drop over a few shells. After you left the village coming back you had to pass over a trench and if you've got a wounded man on a stretcher you were naturally apprehensive in the dark, but there was five German corpses lying there so you took your bearings by the stench of these bodies lying there in the sun and the rain.[155]

Stretcher Bearer Joseph Yarwood, 94th Field Ambulance, Royal Army Medical Corps, 31st Division

Gavrelle had been taken, but the battle was only just beginning. Leading Seaman Thomas Macmillan was back at the Advanced Headquarters of 189th Brigade. The commanding officer was desperate to discover where the new front line had settled:

The enemy had been completely cleared from the village but fresh troops could be seen mustering in all directions for a counter-attack. Almost all telephone lines between Advanced Brigade Headquarters and battalions had been cut by the German artillery fire while the astute Boche had blocked our wireless sets and rendered them useless. Visual signalling was an impossibility on account of gun smoke, so that all communications to and from the scene of the fighting had to pass over the few artillery lines which remained intact, or to be conveyed by runners. As the intervening ground was swept by fire, the brave runners who managed to worm their way through were often delayed so long as to render their orders useless. From Zero Hour the Brigade Major had done everything in his power to ensure smooth working, but the destruction of the signal lines had upset his plans considerably. By 6.30 p.m. it was impossible to determine the exact positions of the battalions, whereupon he ordered a contact aeroplane to fly over the ground and report. The plane flew low and in response to its klaxon horn seven flares were lit. These were plotted with wonderful speed by the observer, and the plane made off at top speed to its station. Within an hour from the plane setting off, the exact location of the flares had been wired to Advanced Brigade Headquarters. The Major plotted the particulars on three copies of a Gavrelle village map and sent them by separate runners to battalion commanders for identification. Commander Bennett identified the three flares on the right, Commander Asquith the two central flares, and Colonel Lewis the two on the left. By connecting the plottings, Major Barnett determined the approximate line held by the brigade and wired the information to Divisional Headquarters, from whence it was sent to the Headquarters of First Army.[156]

Leading Seaman Thomas Macmillan, Headquarters, 189th Brigade, 63rd (Royal Naval) Division

The RFC contact patrol had proved its worth, although the German army cooperation aircraft could be just as useful to the Germans. Both sides were equally desperate to find out the situation in the disputed village:

A hostile aircraft flew over our front and signalled to the German artillery, who concentrated on the village with all the venom they possessed. When the fire cleared the counter-attacking troops came on, but they were caught in the open and decimated by our artillery and machine-gun fire. At dawn on the 24th, our positions were bombarded relentlessly and throughout the day the bombardments were repeated with such frequency that it seemed as if the enemy intended to blast us out of the village. When the fire lifted to our back areas, however, wave after wave of German infantry pressed forward and counter-attack succeeded counter-attack. Our artillery were now functioning as never before. No sooner was each attack launched, than they placed a heavy barrage behind the advancing columns, which crept towards our lines and met a similar protective barrage placed in front of our positions. Through this inferno our men poured rifle and machine-gun fire. In all, seven organised attacks were met in this manner. When at last the guns were stilled and the air was clear again, out in the open fields lay the mangled remains of thousands of our adversaries, while here and there a solitary figure was seen to stagger and fall to rise no more. Gavrelle was ours.[157]

Leading Seaman Thomas Macmillan, Headquarters, 189th Brigade, 63rd (Royal Naval) Division

The accurate reports brought back by the RFC contact aircraft had allowed proper defensive fire plans to be constructed once the massed gun batteries of the Royal Artillery knew exactly where the infantry were situated. No flesh and blood could hope to pass through a full-scale artillery barrage unscathed. Without the protection of the guns, Gavrelle would surely have fallen against the massed German counter-attacks.

Further to the south the infantry of the 51st (Highland) Division hurled themselves forward against the dreaded chemical works at Roeux. Here the fighting raged with an unparalleled intensity. Time after time the British thought they had captured their objective; again and again the Germans counter-attacked under the cover of their artillery bombardments and threw the intruders back in scenes of near-total confusion. All along the line the fighting raged and confusion reigned.

In these circumstances the work of the RFC contact patrols was more vital than ever, but just as difficult to carry out effectively. The attacking British infantry fought shy of lighting the flares meant to indicate their positions to the RFC because they would at the same time attract unwanted attention from the Germans. To make matters worse the RFC had by no means achieved aerial dominance above the battlefield. Although there were swarms of British scouts and corps machines aloft, they could not knock all their German equivalents out of the skies. Frequently the smaller British patrols found themselves overwhelmed by the stronger concentrations of German scouts. Of course, the continued presence of German aircraft above them made the ordinary 'Tommy' even less likely to light a flare that could give away his position. To directly assist the troops, the RE8s of 59 Squadron flew in pairs and made low-level ground attacks against the ceaseless German counter-attacks – this new development presaged a new role for aircraft in the last years of the war.

Monday 23 April also marked the day the first real patrols were undertaken over the lines by 56 Squadron. At last its new SE5 Scouts were considered ready for action. The squadron's leading ace, Captain Albert Ball, had already flown several patrols in his personal Nieuport Scout, which he was permitted to fly on solo patrols due to his unique status as the premier ace in the RFC. Ball had made his first flights back on 14 April and was obviously intent on feeling his way back into the saddle after his six month lay-off:

> I had my first two flights this morning. In the first one the Hun ran off, but in the second I managed to get a few rounds in and made him run. In a few days we shall start real work and then I hope to have tons of sport.[158]
>
> Captain Albert Ball, 56 Squadron, RFC

The introduction of the SE5 marked an important moment in the air war. If the new aircraft failed then the British would be left in severe difficulties for the rest of the year, with only the still delayed Sopwith Camel holding out much hope for the future. But now, as the infantry attacked on the ground, Captain Albert Ball and 56 Squadron at last flung themselves into the fray. Ball was immediately successful:

> Am so fagged tonight, but feel that I must send you a line. We did our first two real jobs today, and I got two Huns – one I crashed, and the other I set on fire. I had six fights altogether. One of the Huns I got with a Nieuport, and one with a SE5. My machines were very badly hit about, and are having new planes tonight. Well, now I am on a job at 5 a.m., so simply must sleep.[159]
>
> Captain Albert Ball, 56 Squadron, RFC

These were the first victories claimed by 56 Squadron. Ball remained an effective scout pilot, but regrettably he had not developed his combat method to adapt to the increasingly crowded and deadly aerial environment that prevailed in the spring of 1917. He still took enormous risks and, as was not unusual, his aircraft suffered considerable damage as a direct consequence:

I had three fights, and managed to bring one down, crashed in a road. This I did with my Nieuport. After coming down I had to have five new planes, for the Hun had got about fifteen shots through my spars. Well, next I went up in my SE5 and had a very poo-poo time – five shots in my right strut, four in the planes, and two just behind my head. This was done by five Albatros Scouts, but I got one of them and set it on fire at 14,000 feet. Poor old chap inside. I should simply hate to be set on fire.[160]

Captain Albert Ball, 56 Squadron, RFC

Amongst the other British scouts flying that day, Captain William Bond of 40 Squadron also found plenty of German aircraft to occupy and amuse him, but this time he was continually thwarted by problems with his machine guns:

At 11.00 a.m. we went over the lines. We crossed at 9,000 feet and almost immediately saw one Hun. We looked for the others, but they were not there. It seemed too easy. When we first saw him we were above him and a long way to his north – all going east. We climbed behind him, and got right round to the east of him and dived. Mackenzie fired first and passed under him, and I then went all out for him. I got him dead in the sights, and when less than 100 yards away I fired. One shot answered, and then the gun stopped. I sheered away and climbed, trying desperately to clear the gun, which had jammed. I cocked it as I thought, and went in again down on his tail. At not more than 50 yards range I fired again – at least I pulled the lever – but nothing happened. Still sighting dead on, I cocked the gun twice more. It was hopelessly jammed. The Hun had turned on me now. I spun in the approved Central Flying School way. When I turned level, Ellis was diving on him, and I saw him going down, turning over slowly until he fell into the clouds. We came home fearfully bucked; but I pulled down my gun – it is mounted over the top plane above my head – and found a hellish jam. I blasphemed and yelled to myself all alone![161]

Captain William Bond, 40 Squadron, RFC

Bond and Ellis took off again for the afternoon patrol and sighted two German reconnaissance aircraft below them when they were about 5 miles over the front lines. The scouts dived down to intercept them:

I went down nearly vertically, sighting on. I fired a burst at 150 yards range and felt sure I had hit the machine near the observer's seat. I passed right underneath him, pulled up quickly, turned, and found myself facing him broadside on. I fired two more bursts. I wondered why the observer did not fire at me, and concluded I had put him out. Then my gun stopped, and at the same moment the Hun turned and got his forward gun on me. I heard and thought I saw about twenty shots come my way and decided it was enough. Out came the spinning trick on once more, and when I came out and looked round, the sky was bare.[162]

Captain William Bond, 40 Squadron, RFC

Such machine-gun jams were extremely frustrating and, of course, damaging to the Allied cause as the German reconnaissance aircraft escaped unscathed.

That day also marked the successful return to action of a future German ace, Leutnant Hermann Göring of Jasta 26, who would certainly tower above his contemporaries in the post-war period, albeit for shameful reasons unrelated to his aerial prowess. Göring was born on 12 January 1893 and had been commissioned into the army in 1912. After a period of service in the infantry on the Vosges front he developed chronic rheumatism, which caused him to seek a transfer to the German Air Service in October 1914. He served for a while as an observer before learning to fly and then flew on reconnaissance and scout missions before being wounded in November 1916. On his recovery he was posted to Jasta 26 who were equipped with the Albatros DIII. During the early evening gloom of 23 April, in company with other Albatros scouts, he sighted the four FE2bs of 18 Squadron engaged in a bombing raid. Göring swiftly claimed his fourth accepted victim:

Aerial fight with British two-seater from a squadron of four English. I set on fire an opponent after a short fight with PH ammunition. Burning crash north-east of Arras. Shortly afterwards two more aerial fights with a two-seater and a single-seater without result.[163]

Leutnant Hermann Göring, Jasta 26, German Army Air Force

The FE2b was flown by Second Lieutenant Edmund Zink accompanied by his observer Second Lieutenant George Bate. Their engine was on fire but the wounded Zink managed to keep on flying for safety while Bate did his

223

best to prevent Göring from applying the final *coup de grâce*. The two British men claimed to have shot down at least one of the Albatros that pursued them, but this has certainly not been substantiated. The FE2b landed relatively safely the British side of the lines, although Second Lieutenant Zink was sent back to England to recuperate. Second Lieutenant Bate survived unharmed despite a bullet scarring through his uniform and leather jacket. His luck was to run out just a few days later on 29 April.

BOTH in the air and on the ground the fighting continued to rage throughout 24 April. The Germans were not disposed to sit back and allow the British to retain their gains and as their reserves moved up to the front the counter-attacks became ever more threatening. In these circumstances the infantry were heavily reliant on the British artillery to keep them back. Lieutenant Reginald Haine had taken up defensive positions in the salient around the newly captured Gavrelle:

> The Germans attacked in mass. It's the only really mass attack I saw in the whole war. We knew several hours before we were actually attacked that they were coming, because by getting this part of the Hindenburg Line we had got observation right down to Douai, which was about 6 miles away. It was the most astounding thing to have observation and the Germans not! We wondered what on earth was happening because we saw all these troops coming up in a column of fours. They were outside the range of our normal artillery, so we got a bit perturbed about this and got on the wire – they said, 'Well it looks like a German attack, but don't worry we've got it all taped!' And it was taped. I've never seen such a fiasco in all my life. They came on in mass on a glorious April afternoon, line after line of them and our gunners just let fly into them. We had practically nothing to do, we merely just mopped up the fellows who got anywhere near moderate rifle range – about 200–300 yards. As far as I am concerned only one German reached our trenches, and he, poor little chap, was completely dazed.[164]
>
> Lieutenant Reginald Haine, 1st Battalion, Honourable Artillery Company, 190th Brigade, 63rd (Royal Naval) Division

Above the artillery the spring skies were full of a bedlam in which experienced crews could only survive by dint of all their accumulated skill, determination and luck in situations where others would surely have been doomed. One such team was Captain Bernard Rice and his observer Second Lieutenant A. C. Heaven, who found themselves perilously close to disaster:

> We got set upon by four Hun scouts, and gave them a good peppering, incidentally getting a bit ourselves. We scraped back to the 'drome with fifty-four holes in the machine which was forthwith 'written off'. We were a bit embarrassed at the number of people below who seemed to have seen us![165]
>
> Captain Bernard Rice, 8 Squadron, RFC

Every close escape the pilots survived increased their experience and gave them the confidence to try out the convoluted manoeuvrings necessary to throw off the nagging fire of their assailants. During a low-level photographic mission, Second Lieutenant Marcus Kaizer came under fire from German field guns:

> The field-gun fire was much more accurate and of much greater intensity – shells bursting all round. It is at moments such as these, when a loud 'WHUF!' comes just under your tail, that you yearn to forsake aviation and take to driving a milk cart or something equally restful. However, by dint of throwing the machine about all over the place, climbing, diving and all sorts of manoeuvres, the bus wasn't touched.[166]
>
> Second Lieutenant Marcus Kaizer, 18 Squadron, RFC

Yet 24 April was the day on which Oberleutnant Otto Bernert of Jasta Boelcke achieved one of the most remarkable feats of the entire air war. He had been awarded the *Pour le Mérite* the previous day, but now on one single patrol he shot down five British aircraft. This was no exaggeration or vain *braggadocio*, for all his victims have been clearly identified beyond reasonable doubt. Bernert's first victim came when with five other pilots from Jasta Boelcke he attacked a dawn reconnaissance mission carried out by nine Sopwith 1½ Strutters of 70 Squadron over the Cambrai region. He swooped on the faltering Sopwith of Lieutenant C. H. Halse and Aircraftman W. Bond and soon succeeded in sending it down in flames. Both the crew were killed.

He then sighted three BE2e aircraft on a bombing mission in the same area. The pilots were flying without observers to allow them to carry a bigger bomb payload, which, of course, left them utterly without any means of defence. They were sitting ducks to the experienced Bernert and in five deadly minutes he accounted for them all: Second Lieutenant F. A. Matthews and Lieutenant C. L. Graves were both killed, but Lieutenant G. E. Hicks survived to become a prisoner of war.

Bernert was still not sated for he then sighted and pursued a stray DH4 of 55 Squadron flown by Lieutenant A. M. N. de Lavison and Aircraft-man K. Oliver which was on a mission to bomb La Briquett. In the form of his life, Bernert was an unstoppable force that day and the DH4 tumbled from the skies to crash land on the British side of the lines with de Lavison wounded and Oliver dead. In under half an hour Bernert had scored an amazing five victories to take him to a total of twenty-four. At that stage in the war no pilot on either side had matched his feat.

The British were desperate to remove the German kite balloons that peered down on all their movements and on 24 April they launched a concerted effort by the Nieuport Scouts of 1 and 60 Squadrons. Amongst the pilots involved on this dangerous mission was Second Lieutenant William Molesworth, who had only just shot down his first aircraft two days before:

> I tackled my first balloon yesterday, and consider it even more difficult
> than going for a Hun; at least, I think one gets a hotter time. We had
> received orders a week ago that all balloons *had* to be driven down or
> destroyed, as they were worrying our infantry and gunners during the
> advance. We had been practising firing the Le Prieur rockets for some
> time – a most weird performance. One dives at a target on the ground,
> and when within about 50 yards of it presses a button on the instru-
> ment board. Immediately there is a most awful hissing noise, which can
> be heard above the roar of the engine, and six huge rockets shoot
> forward from the struts each side towards the target. We did not think
> these were much of a success, owing to the difficulty of hitting
> anything, so decided to use tracer and Buckingham bullets instead.
> These are filled with a compound of phosphorus and leave a long
> trail of smoke behind them.
>   On the morning we were detailed to attack the balloons the
> weather was so dud that none of them were up, although we went

across twice to have a look. We got a pretty hot time from 'Archie', as we had to fly below the clouds, which were about 2,000 feet, and dodge about all over the shop. Next day the weather cleared and we decided to carry out our strafe. We all went off individually to the various balloons which had been allotted us. I personally crossed the trenches at about 10,000 feet, dropping all the time towards my 'sausage', which was 5 or 6 miles away. It was floating in company with another at about 3,000 feet, and reminded me of that little song, 'Two Little Sausages'!

I started a straight dive towards them, and then the fun began. 'Archie' got quite annoyed, following me down to about 5,000 feet, where I was met by two or three strings of flaming onions, luckily too far off to do any damage. Then came thousands of machine-gun bullets from the ground – evidently I was not going to get them without some trouble. I zig-zagged about a bit, still heading for the balloons, and when within 200 yards opened fire. The old Huns in the basket got wind up and jumped out in their parachutes. Not bothering about them, I kept my sight on one of the balloons and saw the tracer going right into it and causing it to smoke. As our armament consists of a Lewis gun, I had to now change drums. This is a pretty ticklish job when you have about ten machine guns loosing off at you, not to mention all the other small trifles! However, I managed to do it without getting more than half a dozen or so bullet-holes in my 'grid'. By this time the second balloon was almost on the floor. I gave it a burst, which I don't think did any damage. The first sausage was in flames, so I buzzed off home without meeting any Huns. On the way back a good shot from 'Archie' exploded very near my tail, and carried away part of the elevator. Don't you think this is the limit for anyone who wants excitement?[167]

Lieutenant William Molesworth, 60 Squadron RFC

Molesworth was credited with shooting down the kite balloon over Boiry-Notre-Dame. Naturally, the Germans were attempting exactly the same missions – on occasion with equal success:

Balloon attacked twice by Taube and destroyed in flames. Observer Lieutenant Sharp (American) suffering from loss of memory. He dropped by parachute and was found unconscious gassed by balloon gas.[168]

Air Mechanic Ray Fletcher, Transport Section, 14 Balloon Company, RFC

As the fighting rose to another crescendo, the RNAS scout pilots were playing an increasingly important role in supporting the hard-pressed RFC. Flight Sub-Lieutenant Jack Malone of 3 (Naval) Squadron caught a German army cooperation aircraft somewhere behind the German lines:

> I was flying with A Flight formation led by Flight Lieutenant Travers above the Cambrai–Bapaume road in the direction of Cambrai. I was unable, owing to a faulty engine, to keep up with the formation and was 2,000 feet below it. Flight Lieutenant Travers and Flight Sub-Lieutenant Casey attacked a DFW two-seater which was flying at about my level. I remained in the sun and dived down with them. Casey turned away after firing at close range. I then closed in but did not attack, still remaining in the sun. At about 4,000 feet Travers turned away after firing at the EA [Enemy Aircraft]. Both he and Casey had gun jams. I was then in a good position to attack and after a burst of fire the rear gunner dropped down into his cockpit but soon came up again and fired at me when I had closed to about 20 yards' range. He then disappeared again into his cockpit. I forced EA to land intact. I then opened my throttle but my engine refused to respond. So, I landed beside the EA and we were shelled by German artillery after helping the German pilot to remove the badly wounded observer from his cockpit. He died within about ten minutes. The German pilot was slightly wounded in the head. He said he did not see me approach to attack out of the sun and he thought he was landing behind his own lines.[169]

> Flight Sub-Lieutenant Jack Malone, 3 (Naval) Squadron, RNAS

The German pilot, who survived to become a prisoner, was Unteroffizier Max Haase and the deceased observer Leutnant Karl Keim.

In another engagement, Lieutenant Robert Little of 8 (Naval) Squadron RNAS, launched a joint attack with Lieutenant I. P. R. Napier of 40 Squadron, flying a Nieuport Scout, on a German Aviatik CII two-seater. The reconnaissance aircraft was successfully shot down for a joint victory but there was to be an amusing postscript to the engagement:

> We had a splendid view of a fight in which the principals were Little in a Sopwith Triplane, a Nieuport from No. 40 Squadron and a two-seater Aviatik. The Hun was sighted over the aerodrome at about 10,000 feet and Little went up after him. A Nieuport appeared about the same time and both British machines got into action with the

enemy at 12,000 feet, between our aerodrome and Bailleul. After scrapping for about twenty minutes, during which time the enemy machine was being forced lower and lower, Little managed to get a shot into the Aviatik's petrol tank and the last we saw of the fight was the Hun diving down over the Bois de Revillion followed at a terrific pace by the Sopwith and the Nieuport. The fight had an amusing finish. Forced down owing to loss of petrol the enemy machine landed without damage in a field at Les Facons. A few seconds later Little followed and, in his haste, made a rough landing and turned upside down. The Nieuport did exactly the same thing, and when Little crawled out of his machine to claim his prisoner, the German pilot saluted smartly and said in English, 'It looks as if I have brought you down, not you me, doesn't it?'[170]

Squadron Leader Geoffrey Bromet, 8 (Naval) Squadron, RNAS

The captured Germans were Leutnants Friedrich Neumuller and Hans Huppertz.

ON 25 April and 26 April, low clouds restricted the scope of aerial operations. By this time the utter failure of the Nivelle offensive was clearly apparent and the French were now in total disarray. After the horror of Verdun in 1916, this new cataclysmic reverse was more than the French troops could bear. As the promised 48-hour offensive extended into a fortnight of fighting with nothing to look forward to but another unending attritional nightmare, the French infantry began to mutiny. The first isolated cases mushroomed, spreading like a viral plague from battalion to battalion. Collectively the French troops made themselves plain: they would man the trenches and defend their country if attacked, but they would not sacrifice themselves on the altar of *l'offence* any more.

Nivelle's position was fatally undermined and the politicians acted swiftly to remove the man who had pulled the wool over their over-optimistic eyes and led them to vainglorious defeat. Haig had no time for any feelings of *schadenfreude* at the fall of his notational superior, or indeed to enjoy the discomfiture of the man who had manoeuvred to put Nivelle there – Prime Minister David Lloyd George. Haig was clear where his duty lay. The exigencies of allied warfare meant that the British Army would have to do everything in its power to assist their staggering ally.

Once again Haig would have to postpone his long cherished Flanders offensive to intensify the effort at Arras in an attempt to buy the French some breathing space.

The consequences of these strategically significant events could be severe for ordinary individuals as the men of the RFC were pressurised into more and more missions to satisfy the insatiable demand for photographs. Second Lieutenant Geoffrey Hopkins of 22 Squadron was 'sweating' on his imminent home leave, when the hand of fate intervened on 26 April:

> That morning I had got my leave voucher from the recording officer and had arranged with the transport officer for a tender to take me to Amiens. Unfortunately, my tender was filled up by a party of B Flight officers, including my observer, Fawcett, going to Amiens just before I was ready to get into it, having been delayed in the Squadron Office, reporting my departure. However, the transport officer said another tender was available and I could go in that. While I was waiting for this tender, I was told that my Flight Commander Captain H. R. Hawkins wanted to see me.[171]
>
> Second Lieutenant Geoffrey Hopkins, 22 Squadron, RFC

It was at this point that Hopkins might have made himself scarce. However, he was still very young and did not react as perhaps an older soldier would in similar circumstances. His flight commander had been asked to help with yet another bombing raid, this time over Bohain. The plans for the raid reflected the gradually increasing sophistication of the British tactics. They had begun to fly in layers – different flights flying at the levels that best suited both operational requirements and the capabilities of the available aircraft – all the while ready to combine their strengths should the German scouts appear. Increasingly it had become the norm to coordinate reconnaissance flights, bombing missions, escort patrols and offensive patrols to allow flights of aircraft to support each other in a given targeted sector. Together they were stronger – or at least that was the theory:

> This particular job was given to C Flight, which proved to be two machines short. It was B Flight's turn to 'fill in'. We kept a roster for this purpose and this showed that the next in line for duty were G. M. Hopkins and his observer J. D. M. Stewart; H. R. Hawkins with G. O.

McEntee as observer. The Acting Flight Commander of C Flight asked me, as B Flight Commander, if I would lead the formation. I replied, 'It is your show, you should lead it'. The formation was to consist of three layers: six artillery BEs with 112-lb bombs under each wing, but no gunner, six FE2bs in the middle layer and six Pups on top.[172]

Captain H. R. Hawkins, 22 Squadron, RFC

As Captain Hawkins had no idea that Hopkins was 'sweating on leave' and as young Hopkins was evidently too tongue-tied in front of authority to tell him, the result was inevitable:

As I was the only B Flight pilot available, I had to go on the raid. I was not particularly upset about this, as I imagined that it would just be another raid, that we would be back for tea, and that I'd get off on leave in the evening. Hawkins did not know, or had forgotten, that I was going on leave and I didn't think of telling him. As my observer, Fawcett, had gone to Amiens, I had to take another observer, Second Lieutenant J. D. M. Stewart, with whom I'd never flown before.[173]

Second Lieutenant Geoffrey Hopkins, 22 Squadron, RFC

The idea of layers of aircraft working together towards a common end was excellent in theory, but when it went wrong the results could be disastrous:

At 5.45 p.m. we duly set off to our rendezvous with the BEs and Pups. On the way, or at least long before reaching our target area, Bohain, some 25 miles over the lines, all four C Flight FEs left the formation and went home, all with engine trouble I presume. I personally only saw two BEs; therefore to the best of my knowledge, the raiding force consisted of only two BEs in the bottom layer, two FEs in the middle layer and six Pups in the top layer. We had previously found that Pups were inclined to continue to climb without their pilots realising this and that, as escorts, they were often too high above us to be of much use if we were attacked.[174]

Second Lieutenant Geoffrey Hopkins, 22 Squadron, RFC

Captain Hawkins was becoming increasingly concerned as one by one the other aircraft dropped out and it became apparent that the mutual support they needed was not going to be forthcoming:

The leader did a very unusual thing by leading the formation from the bottom layer and so reducing the strength of the middle layer. By the time we crossed the lines, the two B Flight machines were the only machines in the middle layer; the Pups were too high to be of value and at that stage I consider that the leader would have been quite justified, and in my opinion should have washed out the patrol.[175]

Captain H. R. Hawkins, 22 Squadron, RFC

Sure enough, the disconnected elements of the mission were left to fight it out on their own as the German scouts of Jasta 5 arrived in force:

As we reached the target area we could see a large number of HA [Hostile Aircraft] climbing up towards us, and they reached us, or got above us, just as we got to the target. There, of the BEs, I saw only one which having dropped its bombs was, very wisely, streaking for home with its nose well down. The six Pups were well above us and behind I counted eleven HA which were about to attack them, so they would obviously have no chance to do anything in the way of protecting our two FEs. Hawkins and I were attacked by seven HA, which dived on us from various directions. We could do little except circle and try to keep together for mutual protection. But, being outnumbered and often having to fight two or more HA at a time, we soon became separated.

During violent manoeuvrings and split-arse turning, an FE soon lost height, particularly as the pilot couldn't concentrate on the niceties of piloting when he was also firing his Lewis gun at a Hun who was shooting at him. So much happened so quickly during that scrap that I will mention only one incident. Stewart was standing up, firing the rear gun at an HA diving on us from the rear, when I heard and then saw another HA diving and firing at us out of the sun at about one o'clock. As I could hear his bullets cracking by uncomfortably close, I snatched the rear gun from Stewart, swivelled it round in the general direction of the new attacker and let off a burst of ten or fifteen rounds, watching my tracers, and that drove him off, at least temporarily. While this was happening, I was turning round as fast as possible to get rid of the Hun on our tail. As I was about halfway round, this Hun suddenly appeared, zooming out of his dive only a few feet above us. He only just missed colliding with us and as he passed I had a second or two to turn my gun on him and rake him with bullets. As his machine had streamers on its struts, I presume he was the formation leader. We did not see him again.

Meanwhile my engine had been hit several times, made odd noises and finally stopped. There was then nothing to do except take evasive action whenever one of the two Huns which were still with us fired at us, and to land as quickly as possible. As we landed in a large field fairly smoothly, the Huns clearly indicated that they would machine gun us if we didn't leave the FE at once, which we did. We scrambled out and moved away some distance and were then surrounded by hostile German soldiery, who appeared to want our personal belongings as souvenirs. However, one of the German pilots had meanwhile landed and he ran over to us. Cursing the soldiers, he knocked down one of the more violent of them with his fist, which calmed the situation. We caught a glimpse of Hawkins' FE about to land, apparently undamaged, though we were too far away to see clearly.[176]

Second Lieutenant Geoffrey Hopkins, 22 Squadron, RFC

Hawkins had fought the same desperate fight, almost without hope, until he too was obliged to land behind German lines:

We managed to drop our bombs and were immediately involved in very heavy fighting. We became separated from Hopkins and later saw him going down, but were too heavily involved ourselves to be able to help him. The Pups were still far too high and I doubt if they even saw we were in trouble. We were losing height from having to throw the machine about. The prevailing wind towards the Hun also made things worse. Then we were hit in the engine, which ran very roughly with marked loss of power. Eventually we were skimming the ground near Estrée and forced to land. A machine gun was turned on us from the air, so we got out of the machine and were quickly surrounded.[177]

Captain H R Hawkins, 22 Squadron, RFC

These victories were claimed by Leutnant Rudolph Nebel and Offizier-stellvertreter Sturm of Jasta 5. Back in the mess of 22 Squadron the mood was pretty bloody. Perhaps the men realised that the FE2bs had not been left unescorted deliberately, but from their perspective, whatever the good intentions the end result was obsolescent aircraft fighting against hopeless odds:

Just another example of the criminal folly of sending FE2bs over the lines unescorted as we are just cats' meat for the Huns.[178]

Lieutenant C. Furlonger, 22 Squadron, RFC

Just over a week later, on 9 May, Lieutenant Furlonger himself was shot down by Leutnant Werner Voss to become a prisoner of war.

MISTAKES are a part of warfare. Lieutenant Harold Balfour, who had survived several traumatic encounters with superior German scouts in his Sopwith 1½ Strutter, found himself shot down on 27 April after a trifling misjudgement led, in a matter of minutes, to a life-threatening situation:

I was interested in the battle below me, watching the shell bursts and the infantry crouching in the remains of their trenches and in the water-filled shell holes and craters. It was only when I had flown some way down the ridge that I realised that at the height of 1,500 feet I was a mile and a half the German side of the front line. The wind had drifted me gradually eastwards while the line of the ridge itself turned rather west, tending to make my straight course one which would take me farther and farther over the enemy side. I swung for home and, putting the nose down, opened the throttle wide.

The wind was against me and almost as I carried out this change of course the infantry machine guns and rifles started at me. I swung the machine about from side to side, flying a zig-zag course and managed to avoid most of the bullets, with only an occasional hole appearing in one or other of the wings. But before I had reached the front lines there was a harsh metallic clang, and the engine and propeller stopped. One of the cylinders must have been shot through and the motor, suffering internal damage, had packed up. There was nothing for it except to glide dead straight, nursing every bit of height that I had left to me, if I wished to reach our sector.

This was one of the most unpleasant moments that I have ever experienced, because on every other occasion when I had been fighting I have had command of my machine, the ability to manoeuvre, and the power to retaliate. Now, my front machine gun pointed only to the British lines. I did not dare to divert from the straight path and could only hope and trust that I should have sufficient height to land somewhere where I should not be made a prisoner or shot down by rifle fire.

As I glided down the last 200–300 feet, I flicked up the safety catch of my belt. We just tipped the ridge, with a few feet to spare, and then stalled the last 20 feet to the ground on the further side of the slope. We touched the edge of a mine crater as we dropped. I was thrown through the centre section struts directly in front of the pilot's seat, a narrow triangle which would certainly have taken a good deal of effort and skill to have wriggled through normally. I was not grazed by either of the struts or the top of the wings, which, on looking back, seems nothing short of a miracle. I was pitched head first on to the mud, where my body lay unconscious on the lip of the crater. My observer was less lucky for he did a long shooting dive forwards through the air from the rear cockpit at the moment of impact.[179]

Lieutenant Harold Balfour, 43 Squadron, RFC

His observer, Second Lieutenant E. H. Jones, was indeed badly injured, but survived. Lieutenant Balfour, although uninjured, had other problems that he had to contend with in the immediate aftermath of the crash. During his first tour of duty on the Western Front with 60 Squadron in 1916 he was approaching nervous breakdown so tormented was he by the stresses of aerial combat. Balfour had bravely overcome these fears and returned, but now his demons made an unwelcome and public reappearance:

The Squadron sent up a party that night to try and salve the wreck, but within a quarter of an hour of the crash the enemy started shelling and what was left was valueless. I was moved back with other wounded cases and can just remember coming to as I was put into a Field Ambulance. I was being very sick and as the ambulance started rattling down the road some of our howitzers let off from one of the battery positions near by. I suppose that this was too much for me, and that, with the crash, my nerves had for the moment gone. I can remember crying to myself with fright and self-pity as these appalling crashes and discharges continued.[180]

Lieutenant Harold Balfour, 43 Squadron, RFC

Stressed beyond reason by his accumulated combat experiences, this final blow shattered him. One of his comrades recorded his departure with a few unsentimental words. Lieutenant Alan Dore knew any of them could be next:

> Balfour, Flight Commander of B Flight, is on the way home having concussion from landing in a shell hole behind Vimy. He is said to be temporarily 'loony'.[181]
>
> Lieutenant Alan Dore, 43 Squadron, RFC

Another man who intermittently had trouble with the effects of nervous tension, yet gained ever greater honour by dint of his total fearlessness in the frenzy of combat, was Captain Albert Ball. He was now truly back in harness. Dogfights between increasing numbers of aircraft from many different units had become more common, but to Albert Ball superior numbers were as a red rag to the proverbial bull. Just the day before, on 26 April, he had a terrible clash with German scouts, totally outnumbered and miles behind their lines:

> I was attacked by twenty last night and had to fire all my ammunition, getting two of them. It was dark when I returned, and everyone thought that I must have been done in, but I had to stop on their side until it was dark, for I could not fight my way through without ammunition. My right plane was hit a few times, and I had to have a new one. I have now got another two Huns making four this time, and my total is thirty-four. Only three more to be got before I am top of England and France again. In order to whack the German man (Boelcke), I'd love to get about ten more. If it's God's will that I should do it, then I will come home; oh, I do so hope it can be managed. Tonight if it clears up I am taking all my Flight out for a real good smack. I am off on my Nieuport then and at 5.30 I come back and do a job on SE5 with my Flight. You see they do one or two jobs each day, and I lead them, but during the remainder of the day I go up in my Nieuport and have a try myself. This is the only way to get them. Just keep at them all day.[182]
>
> Captain Albert Ball, 56 Squadron, RFC

Although he did his duty as a flight leader, Ball's real love remained his solo patrols flying as a lone wolf. The result was that he spent more time in the air than almost anyone:

He preferred to patrol alone rather than to lead his flight on patrol. He wanted always to be in the air. During flying weather he was up and out by five o'clock in the morning and – completely exhausted by his efforts – would be in bed and asleep by six o'clock in the evening.[183]

Recording Officer Lieutenant Thomas Marson, 56 Squadron, RFC

In another letter Ball calculated his kills: 'Total Huns now thirty-five. Two more to beat Frenchman.'[184] In all probability, Ball had not really recovered from the combat fatigue that had forced him back to England in October 1916. Adding up his victories seemed to fill a competitive need deep inside him. He appeared to be obsessed with beating the scores of other aces – in particular, the French ace Capitaine George Guynemer who at that time was credited with thirty-six victories – and doing so became a large part of the motivational force that drove him on to take ever greater risks.

MORE poor weather on 27 April restricted both aerial activity and casualties, but on 28 April the resumption of the ground offensive meant that the corps machines had no choice but to engage in contact patrols and artillery observation. Once again the troops were sent forward all along the line. Once more they met with disaster although some insignificant gains were made. The policy of try, try and try again was not working but the British needed to fight: anything to maintain the pressure at Arras and distract the Germans from the faltering French Army. Their allies needed them to fight on, so they fought on.

Above them Richthofen was once again marauding through the clouds that hung low over the battlefield and he succeeded in ambushing 13 Squadron's Lieutenant R. W. Follitt and Second Lieutenant Frederick Kirkham in their BE2e while they were carrying out an artillery observation mission. Engrossed, they evidently failed to observe his approach until it was far too late:

I was watching the ground for the arrivals of our shells when a burst of machine gun-fire came to my ear directly behind me. I turned quickly and stood up to man the rear gun. I was too late. The red Albatros had continued its dive downward just in back of our tail and was way out of range. He was away in the flash of an eye. I saw two others swing by, so I knew that at least three of them had dived on us from above and behind.

They had taken us quite by surprise. We were quite low – not over 3,000 feet, I believe, and 'Archie' had been giving us some close attention. Our plane dove straight down, so that, standing up as I was in the forward seat, the back of my neck was to the ground and my face to the sky. I pulled back into the seat and looked into the pilot's box. Poor old Follitt had sort of crumpled up and fallen forward on the stick. I couldn't see his face, but I knew that some of that first burst had hit him. His body on the stick sent the plane down in a steep dive. He must have rolled off it, however, because we seemed to straighten out once or twice.

It had only been a comparatively few seconds since that first burst, but here was the red Hun scout back in position again just behind and above my tail. I fired round after round from the gun attached to the upper plane, but, as our machine was out of control, I couldn't aim well. The red plane just hung on my tail and kept firing all the time. We were going down at a frightful rate. There was a dual-control stick in my seat which I might have rigged and pulled her out of the dive, but that would have meant turning my back to the Hun scout's machine gun, and I should have got it the same as Follitt. I figured everything was over but the final fadeout, so I just stuck to the rear gun and fired away at him in the hope I might get him also. Apparently not a chance. I emptied the entire drum without effect. The red scout stuck right there on the tail, and his two machine guns were pumping lead all the time.

I had a number of bullet splashes in my face and hands. The sleeves and shoulders of my flying jacket had several dozen holes through them and then one bullet hit the barrel of the machine gun right under my nose. I remember looking over my shoulder, and the ground didn't seem over 10 feet away. I closed my eyes and said, 'Goodnight!' I had seen it happen before. But luck was with me. The plane hit a clump of small trees in the German big gun positions. I woke up while German gunners were cutting me out of the wreckage. The first thing I heard was Follitt's voice, 'God, we're on fire!' he shouted weakly. I think he must have been unconscious and raving. The tanks had split wide open and petrol was over us and everything, but no fire started, although the wireless key had not been switched off. I was pretty well shaken and sore all over, but aside from cuts and bruises and the bullet splashes on my face, I was all right.[185]

Lieutenant Frederick Kirkham, 13 Squadron, RFC

Richthofen reflected with justifiable pride on the professionalism of his achievement. After all, another artillery observation aircraft had been shot from the sky. The shell fire of the battery they were controlling would be rendered at a stroke unfocused. German concentrations of troops would be less vulnerable to the depredations that a well-timed Zone Call could unleash. And one more trained RFC crew would never fly again:

> From the beginning of the engagement to the end, my adversary was never able to get out of the range of my gun.[186]
>
> Oberleutnant Manfred von Richthofen, Jasta 11, German Army Air Force

ON 29 April Major Hubert Harvey-Kelly, the first British pilot to reach France when the RFC crossed the Channel in distant August 1914, flew his final patrol. The accounts that have survived of the significant dogfight that ensued are littered with exaggeration and propaganda from both sides:

> While I was in the hangar attending to the guns, Harvey-Kelly came to me and said that the Wing Commander was 'hot-airing' about Richthofen's 'circus' having been seen over Douai and he wanted three Spads to go up and deal with them. Owing to the fact that the machines of the other flights were either away on patrol or not ready, I was ordered to send up three from C Flight. In the ordinary course of events, the other group should have taken the job as mine had already done one patrol that day, but, as the matter was urgent, I agreed to take up my pilots again. At the last moment, Harvey-Kelly insisted that he himself would go instead of me, but, as I declined to be left behind, I detailed one of my pilots, Harding, to remain behind, and to let Harvey-Kelly have his machine.[187]
>
> Lieutenant W. N. Hamilton, 19 Squadron, RFC

The third pilot was Second Lieutenant Richard Applin. The 19 Squadron response was optimistic in the extreme and certainly inadequate to meet the threat. Three Spads VIIs could hardly hope for much success if they were truly being sent to deal with Richthofen's 'circus' and the whole scenario seems altogether unlikely. As the men got into their aircraft, Applin encountered engine trouble and, as Harvey-Kelly and Hamilton felt they could not wait, they set off from Vert Galant without him. Shortly after their departure, Trenchard and Baring arrived at the airfield:

We went to Vert Galant to see Harvey-Kelly who commands 19
Squadron. When we got there we were told he had gone up by himself
and one other pilot for a short patrol. We stayed there all morning.[188]

Captain Maurice Baring, Headquarters, RFC

Meanwhile, to his credit, Applin had managed to get his aircraft aloft and
even managed to catch up to rejoin Harvey-Kelly and Hamilton:

He took up a position on my right rear as we always flew that way, in a
'V' formation, with No. 1 plane leading and No. 2 slightly higher than
No. 1, and No. 3 slightly higher than No. 2. In this formation it was the
duty of No. 3 to protect Nos. 1 and 2 from attack from behind. Soon
after Applin joined us, we sighted the 'circus' about a 1,000 feet below
us. There were eighteen planes flying more or less on a line ahead,
slightly echelon. As we were only 4,000 feet up, I did not expect
Harvey-Kelly would attack, but at the same moment we noticed six
Triplanes, Royal Naval Air Service, flying towards us. Harvey-Kelly
immediately gave the signal to attack the enemy, but the Triplanes
sheered off and left me to it. Harvey-Kelly had already turned and
dived at the tail Hun, and I was turning to attack the centre machine,
so as to break up the formation and prevent the leading machine
getting above us. Applin was following me.[189]

Lieutenant W. N. Hamilton, 19 Squadron, RFC

Numbers in the air war are a movable feast, but in this case they cannot
be easily reconciled. Someone was exaggerating or lying:

Our aggressors were three Spads, one-seater machines. Their occupants
thought themselves very superior to us because of the excellence of
their apparatus. Wolff, my brother and I, were flying together. We were
three against three. That was as it ought to be.[190]

Oberleutnant Manfred von Richthofen, Jasta 11, German Army Air Force

In just a few short weeks, Lothar von Richthofen had carved out his
own formidable reputation and by the end of the month of April he had
already claimed sixteen victories. With the Richthofen brothers was
Leutnant Kurt Wolff. Of all the Jasta 11 aces it was Kurt Wolff, born on 6
February 1895 in Pomerania, who had most enjoyed the 'shooting gallery'
that was the month of April over Arras. During the month he had claimed
an incredible twenty-three victories, one more even than Manfred himself

had managed. Yet Wolff's achievement can also be counted in any assessment of Richthofen's achievements in his role as Jasta leader. From the time when Wolff was posted to Jasta 11 in November 1916, to January 1917 when Richthofen arrived, he had failed to score a single victory. Richthofen seems to have galvanised him and after he had scored his first success on 6 March 1917 he certainly gained the knack and became virtually unstoppable.

The combination of the Richthofen brothers and Wolff that the three 19 Squadron scouts faced was certainly deadly. The difference in numbers can probably be explained by propaganda on one or both sides. However, Richthofen's suggestion that he preferred a fair fight – three against three – is faintly absurd. He would have been a fool not to prefer the odds in his favour – and he was no fool:

> Immediately at the beginning of the encounter the aggressive became a defensive. Our superiority became clear. I tackled my opponent and could see how my brother and Wolff handled each their own enemy. The usual waltzing began. We were circling around one another. A favourable wind came to our aid. It drove us fighting away from the front in the direction of Germany. My man was the first who fell. I suppose I had smashed up his engine. At any rate, he made up his mind to land. I no longer give pardon to anyone. Therefore, I attacked him a second time and the consequence was that his whole machine went to pieces. His planes dropped off like pieces of paper and the body of the machine fell like a stone, burning fiercely.[191]
>
> Oberleutnant Manfred von Richthofen, Jasta 11, German Army Air Force

Poor Second Lieutenant Applin had paid a terrible price for going out of his way to do his duty. As Lieutenant Hamilton subsequently described the fight, he and Major Harvey-Kelly were then each surrounded by a group of German scouts:

> I carried out my original plan of attacking the centre machine, noticing, as I did so, that Harvey-Kelly had apparently accounted for two Huns and was pretty busy with four or five more. I joined battle a second or two later, our position at that time being somewhere over Epincy. I didn't see Harvey-Kelly again, as I was fully occupied with my little bunch and carried on a running fight until, over Douai, my gun jammed. I made a rapid examination and found my cursed drum had

forced a double feed, so that there was nothing to be done except get away. I 'split-arsed' to get toward our lines, when they managed to hole my main tank, which, being under my feet, was force-fed into the engine. Of course, the moment the pressure was released, my engine stopped, and as it stopped on the turn, I stalled and spun. I got her out of the spin almost immediately, switched on to my gravity tank, and dived to pick up my engine, but in doing so I naturally lost a bit of height and cooled my engine to such an extent that she wouldn't give me full revolutions, so that I was now much slower than my opponents, in addition to being below them.

I held my bus down to keep up speed and steered for our lines, but very soon had four of the enemy on my tail – at least one was on my tail, one above, and one on each side behind. They made pretty good shooting and managed to shoot away all my instruments and most of my struts and flying wires, so that, before long, I was practically flying a monoplane, as my bottom plane was flapping. I was now down to about 300 feet off the ground, when they holed my gravity tank, and my engine stopped for good. I made a good landing just behind Oppy Wood about a kilometre short of the line, and while the Huns on the ground were running up to secure me, I endeavoured to fire my bus. During this time, however, the four Huns in the air (one of them was Richthofen's brother, flying a red-nosed Albatros) continued firing at me.[192]

Lieutenant W. N. Hamilton, 19 Squadron, RFC

There are no records of any German casualties for Jasta 11 on that day, so Hamilton's claims for various German scouts shot down by Harvey-Kelly look more than a little doubtful. Indeed, Hamilton's account of misfortune and understated heroism differs considerably from an equally suspect account left by Leutnant Lothar von Richthofen. In his version of events he pursues Hamilton alone as he dives away. Lothar fires burst after burst of machine-gun fire but is unable to hit the weaving Spad VII. Then his gun seems to jam:

Confound it! I had discharged all my shots, 1,000 cartridges. Never before had I used such a lot. 'You must not let him get off!' is my idea. I approached him nearer and nearer. I calculate: 10 metres, 5 metres, 3, now only 2 metres! Finally, I think of a rather desperate measure – shall I knock off his rudder with the help of my propeller? Then he is done for, but with me it would be the same. Another theory – if I turn off the engine the moment I touch him with my plane, what then? In this moment, my Englishman turns and looks in a horrified way at me. Then he stops his engine and goes down, landing somewhere near our third line.[193]

Leutnant Lothar von Richthofen, Jasta 11, German Army Air Force

The veracity of Lothar von Richthofen is thrown seriously into question when his account goes on to describe how he opened fire on Hamilton to prevent him setting fire to the Spad VII. Yet surely, by his own account, Lothar had run out of ammunition. It is tempting to regard both Lothar von Richthofen and Hamilton as fantasists, but the need for propaganda was muddying the shallow waters of truth. Meanwhile, the intrepid Major Harvey-Kelly had been shot down by Leutnant Kurt Wolff and ultimately succumbed to his head wounds three days later in hospital. Back at the airfield of 19 Squadron, Trenchard and Baring waited in vain as their hopes decayed into gloomy presentiment:

By luncheon time he had not come back. He was due and overdue. When we went away the General said, 'Tell Harvey-Kelly I was very sorry to miss him', but I knew quite well from the sound of his voice he did not expect this message would ever be delivered. Nor did I. Harvey-Kelly never came back. He was the gayest of gay pilots.[194]

Captain Maurice Baring, Headquarters, RFC

As for the Richthofen brothers, their father was waiting for them as they landed at Douai airfield. Manfred had not finished for the day – inspired by the presence of his father, he took off and soon struck again, this time shooting down an FE2b crewed by Sergeant George Stead and Corporal Alfred Beebee of 18 Squadron. This was Richthofen's fiftieth victory. Still he had not finished with the RFC on 29 April. The brothers took off again and soon encountered two BE2es of 12 Squadron:

Suddenly, I noticed two hostile artillery flyers approaching our front in the most impertinent and provocative manner, I waved to my brother and he understood my meaning. We flew side by side increasing our speed. Each of us felt certain that he was superior to the enemy. It was a great thing that we could absolutely rely on one another, and that was the principal thing. One has to know one's flying partner. My brother was the first to approach his enemy. He attacked the first and I took care of the second. At the last moment I quickly looked round in order to feel sure that there was no third aeroplane around. We were alone and could see eye to eye. Soon I had got on the favourable side of my opponent. A short spell of quick firing and the enemy machine went to pieces. I never had a more rapid success. While I was still looking where my enemy's fragments were falling, I noticed my brother. He was scarcely 500 yards away from me and was still fighting his opponent. I had time to study the struggle, and must say that I myself could not have done better than he did. He had rushed his man and both were turning around one another. Suddenly, the enemy machine reared. That is a certain indication of a hit. Probably the pilot was shot in the head. The machine fell and the planes of the enemy aircraft went to pieces. They fell quite close to my victim. I flew towards my brother and we congratulated one another by waving. It is a splendid thing when one can fly together with one's brother and do so well.[195]

Oberleutnant Manfred von Richthofen, Jasta 11, German Army Air Force

There were no survivors from the two British crews. It was Manfred's fourth victory of the day while Lothar had a highly creditable two. The Richthofen brothers had now been joined by other pilots from Jasta 11 and shortly afterwards they were attacked by a group of Sopwith Triplanes from 8 Squadron, RNAS and some Nieuports of 40 Squadron. One of the aircraft dived on Richthofen:

I greeted him at once with quick fire from my two machine guns. He tried to escape by dropping down. That was fatal to him. When he got beneath me I remained on top of him. Everything in the air that is beneath me, especially if it is a single-seater, a scout, is lost, for it cannot shoot to the rear. My opponent had a very good and fast machine. However, he did not succeed in reaching the English lines. I began to fire at him when we were above Lens. I started shooting when I was much too far away. That was merely a trick of mine. I did not mean so much to hit him as to frighten him, and I succeeded in catching him. He began flying curves and this enabled me to draw near. I tried the same manoeuvre a second and a third time. Every time my foolish friend started making his curves. So I had gradually edged quite close to him. I approached him almost to touching distance.

I aimed very carefully. I waited a moment, and when I was at most at a distance of 50 yards from him I started with both machine guns at the same time, I heard a slight hissing noise, a certain sign that the petrol tanks had been hit. Then I saw a bright flame and he disappeared below.[196]

Oberleutnant Manfred von Richthofen, Jasta 11, German Army Air Force

There is much confusion over the identity of the aircraft that Richthofen shot down in this dogfight. Originally it was thought to be Captain Frederick Barwell of 40 Squadron, but some experts now tend towards the belief that it was the Sopwith Triplane of Flight Sub-Lieutenant Albert Cuzner.

Meanwhile, Leutnant Hermann Göring had struck to claim a sixth victory. Several Albatros scouts, according to the British up to thirteen strong, struck at a patrol of Nieuports from 6 (Naval) Squadron, RNAS:

About 7.45 p.m. aerial fight over Ramicourt with a Nieuport single-seater. I shot it down. He tried to land south-west of Ramicourt. Turned over on landing. The pilot Second Lieutenant Fletcher was severely wounded with a ricochet shot to his lower calf. When I flew at 100 metres height to Bohain a second enemy single-seater came from above, chased by another Albatros. The British attacked me shortly and hit my lateral control. He himself was then pursued by an Albatros and forced to land. I could not observe any further developments since I had to fly without any lateral control which demanded my whole attention.[197]

Leutnant Hermann Göring, Jasta 26, German Army Air Force

It has been suggested[198] that it may have been Flight Sub-Lieutenant R. R. Winton who nearly put paid to Göring, as he made a claim for an Albatros DIII 'spinning out of control', which may well have been an exaggerated perspective of Göring's problems with his shattered controls. Leutnant Bruno Loerzer also claimed a Nieuport victory and he may well have been the Albatros pursuing Winton, who was indeed badly knocked about, although he too got back to safety. Here again we can see a pattern of optimistic claims emerging. However, Flight Sub-Lieutenant Albert Fletcher was indubitably shot down by Göring and thereby condemned to a period as a prisoner of war – he managed to recover sufficiently from his wounds to return to serve in the South African Air Force in the Second World War. Göring himself claimed one slightly more dubious victory before being posted to command Jasta 27. He finished the war with twenty-two victories in all. Ahead lay his personal apogee as a prominent Nazi when he became firstly Commander-in-Chief of the Luftwaffe and ultimately Reichsmarschall of Germany.

Sunday, 29 April was also the day that another unsung hero – Second Lieutenant George Bate – finally ran out of borrowed time after his narrow escape when he and Lieutenant Zink had been shot down by Leutnant Hermann Göring on 23 April. This time he was flying with Second Lieutenant Dinsmore, in an FE2b on a photographic reconnaissance mission. They were attacked over Pronville:

> My machine engaged three of the enemy. One circling in front, one coming from top and rear and one from beneath to the rear. My observer fired about thirty rounds at the front HA at about 25 yards range and it fell in flames. He motioned to me to pull up the nose of the machine and then engaged the top rear machine. This was evidently hit and dropped out of the fight. At the same time the bottom rear machine fired a heavy burst from below. My observer fell over and the rear gun, instruments, etc., were all hit. The left aileron control snapped at the control lever and I dived for our lines, side-slipping to avoid further shots. I crossed the Hindenburg Line at 500 feet and landed. I was followed down by the remaining HA to within 100 feet of the ground, but it was driven off by rifle and machine-gun fire from our lines. The machine was at once brought under enemy machine-gun and artillery fire, but a detachment of the Border Regiment secured the body of my observer who had been killed instantaneously.[199]
>
> Second Lieutenant G. H. S. Dinsmore, 18 Squadron, RFC

So died Second Lieutenant George Bate, hit by a bullet through the heart. He was the third victim that day of Leutnant Kurt Wolff, who was obviously not sated after his afternoon clash with 19 Squadron.

Yet in the midst of all this mayhem, the RFC corps aircraft still had their job to do and many of them managed to perform their duties. The German scouts simply could not be everywhere, and where they were not the British prospered. Second Lieutenant Charles Smart went up with Lieutenant Hendry as his observer:

> Went up to take photos of the new line at Oppy. Very sticky job and I did not like it at all. The sky was full of machines and fights were going on all round us. We had to retire halfway through the job on account of

a Hun which came much too near us. When he cleared off we went over again and finished. Photos were a great success and I managed to get all the prints I was told to take. 'Archie' was most annoying, we got two holes through the wings and one through the tail.[200]

Second Lieutenant Charles Smart, 5 Squadron, RFC

There was one other great boon that befell the RFC on 29 April. After his triumph in shooting down four aircraft in a day and achieving the incredible total of fifty-two accredited victories, Richthofen finally went off on six weeks' well-earned leave – leaving his brother, Leutnant Lothar von Richthofen, in command of Jasta 11. At the end of April 1917 Manfred von Richthofen was at his peak, not a wild force of nature like Captain Albert Ball, but a cool, calculating formation leader able to secure the maximum advantage from any situation with the moral strength to avoid engaging in battle if he felt the odds were stacked against him. This was not cowardice, but sheer common sense. War is not a game. And he was all the time, by the example of his words and deeds, training the new young pilots of Jasta 11, moulding callow young men into the group of deadly aces who would in turn prey on the British. From having achieved no victories at all before Richthofen joined them, within the next three months the pilots of Jasta 11 would collectively make over one hundred kills. By the time Richthofen returned from leave in June 1917, the focus of the war had moved to the battlefields of Flanders. But, for the moment at least, the RFC had seen the back of him.

ON 30 April, the day began early for Oberleutnant Adolf von Tutschek who had just taken over command of Jasta 12 based at Epinoy:

At 0500 my telephone rattled, 'English bombing machines on the way!' I shouted in the phone, 'Get the aircraft ready immediately!' Out of bed, no time for a shave etc. We dress quickly in our leather kits. Outside everyone is running to the shelters. Everyone was familiar with air attacks which in the last few weeks had been directed against my new Staffel almost every night. They were almost over us and very high. I race along the village road to my machine. The first planes are already airborne. A long drawn out whistling sound – I throw myself to the ground BOOM!! The bomb hits. I jump up again, to my aircraft with the prop already turning. In and off. The bombs are digging holes in the airstrip, but none of the planes are hit. The mechanics and other personnel are in the shelters. A bomb landed 20 to 30 metres from the big hangar.

My zeal to fight was awakened and upon light signals from me my men gather behind and we give chase to the lattice tails who are high above us. Cutting out all curves we are able to get closer and closer to the 'Tommies'. They, in turn, attempt to get quickly to their lines in the direction of Arras. Now we've caught up with them. My machine guns have just begun to hammer away when all at once the whole group banks and heads towards us. Threads of light from their tracers whistle past my ear. I shrink down behind my engine and press after the enemy squadron which is racing on a few metres above me. I turn immediately and am after them.

An FE lags slightly behind the group and I get close behind him and start shooting. The engine is hit and the enemy pilot puts the machine into a dive. The observer mans his machine gun standing up, but before he gets a shot off he keels over backwards, hit in the chest. Now the battle is simple. In the meantime my comrades are busy with the other lattice-tailed two-seaters and are unable to intervene. In steep spirals I follow my FE down. A short time later his wing goes into the ground as he comes to rest nose in the ground and tail high in the air, about 4 to 5 kilometres behind our front lines near a railroad embankment. The pilot removes his dead comrade from the plane and is taken prisoner by German personnel who rush to the scene.

I commit the crash site to memory and go back up because above me the shooting continues. Again a lattice tail goes down in uncontrolled spirals. Close behind a red Albatros – that's von Richthofen. This one hit the ground not quite 300 metres from mine, and then there is a third and fourth. In an area of 2 kilometres, four Englanders stand on their heads – their tails pointing heavenwards.[201]

Oberleutnant Adolf von Tutschek, Jasta 12, German Army Air Force

The red Albatros was flown by Leutnant Lothar von Richthofen. Although British records confirm the claims made by Richthofen and von Tutschek, they seem to indicate that the FE2ds of 57 Squadron had been on an early line patrol rather than a bombing raid. From the British perspective, the pilots considered they had been caught by a deadly combination of scouts from the 11, 12 and 33 Jastas.

This heralded the new German tactic of up to four Jasta cooperating in the air to form what the British would describe as the 'Flying Circus'. This combination of the four Jasta was an interim measure. In June 1917, Jagdstaffeln 4, 6, 10 and 11 were brought under the control of Manfred von Richthofen to form Jagdgeschwader Nr. 1. The presence of a force of about twenty German scouts marauding up and down the line and doing as much damage as it possibly could – this was to foreshadow the future of scout tactics. The day of the individualist was drawing to a close as formations increased exponentially in size and dogfights filled the sky with whirling aircraft.

AS the month ended the RFC could reflect that it had carried out its duty in the face of relentless casualties. These casualties were not heavy in numerical terms when compared to the losses suffered by infantry battalions when left exposed to German machine-gun fire and artillery in attacks across No Man's Land. But the cumulative losses could rapidly rip out the heart out of a squadron:

> In three days, ten out of eighteen pilots were lost, and had to be replaced from England by officers who had never flown this particular type of machine, because there were none in England. Our new machines were collected from Paris, and the chance of a trip to fly one back was eagerly looked forward to by every pilot. Some of these new machines were not well built, and began – to add to our troubles – to break up in the air.[202]

Major Jack Scott, 60 Squadron RFC

The RFC casualties were quite startling. Nearly 250 British aircraft were shot down and over 400 men killed or wounded during April 1917. The achievements of the German scouts were staggering. Of the eight Jasta deployed on the Arras front there would be, on average, only seven aircraft flying a day – a total operational strength of just under fifty aircraft. Four men in particular stand out for their astonishing achievements during the month of April: Kurt Wolff with twenty-three victories, Manfred von Richthofen with twenty-two, Karl-Emil Schäfer with twenty-one and Lothar von Richthofen with fifteen. Nevertheless, for all their success, it remains the case that day by day, through what became rather luridly known as 'Bloody April', the men of the RFC had succeeded in performing their core function of providing photographs and artillery observation for the army:

> During three days I have never once seen a German aeroplane behind the line of 'sausages' [German observation balloons] which mark the course of the British front. Many of our machines were seen going over and coming from the German lines, where they were speedily lost to view, but there were no fights in the air on our side of the front. The enterprise of our airmen knows no limits, but it is exacting its toll of machines, and this is where our American Allies can come in with immediate help.[203]
>
> Lieutenant-Colonel A. M. Murray, Royal Artillery

Certainly, the German infantry seemed to have had enough of the attentions bestowed upon them through the good offices of the RFC:

> The Germans posted a notice up in their trenches which read, 'For God's sake give your pilots a rest!' We sent three BEs along at once and machine-gunned the trench where the notice was – such is war. [204]
>
> Second Lieutenant Edward Mannock, 40 Squadron, RFC

The efforts of the RFC were also not unappreciated by their own High Command:

> The splendid work of the Royal Flying Corps under very adverse weather conditions, and in face of most determined opposition, has contributed largely to the success of the operations and calls for the highest praise.[205]
>
> Field Marshal Sir Douglas Haig, General Headquarters, BEF

Haig was determined to fight on to distract attention from the chaos that was engulfing the French Army. The tired men of the First, Third and Fifth Armies would have to battle on for at least two more weeks. Their gains must be consolidated and the ground prepared for possible further advances. But above all they must fight. For the men on the ground, the Battle of Arras was turning into a nightmare that mirrored the endless attritional fighting on the Somme the previous year. Conversely, from their different perspective, the rank and file of the RFC felt that the tide was turning. New machines had at last begun to arrive in substantial numbers and they had proved themselves to be effective weapons of war. The casualties were still numerous, but the whole mood began to mellow. And, of course, unbeknown to them, Manfred von Richthofen had finally gone on leave. Even cynical Second Lieutenant Marcus Kaizer began to feel that the ground offensives planned for 1917 might yet batter the Germans into submission:

> Since the war has begun, it has been conclusively proved month by month that the Germans were making their last effort, and month by month I have laughed at this; but this month I believe it. From what little I have seen of the battle, and from what I have heard about it, I should think that the Hun is really at the last gasp – though of course it may be a long gasp. I think it is only a question of time now, because the enemy must be very much weakened.[206]
>
> Second Lieutenant Marcus Kaizer, 18 Squadron, RFC

The men of the RFC stood ready to play their part in the next act of the Battle of Arras.

CHAPTER SIX

A LIFE LESS ORDINARY

As the fighting raged in the skies over Arras there was a constant stream of raw new British pilots making their way out to France. Many would go first to the Royal Flying Corps pilots' pool at St Omer, but some were posted directly to their squadrons. Major-General Hugh Trenchard had a long-standing policy of ensuring that 'there were no empty chairs at breakfast' so replacements for any casualties would arrive at the earliest possible moment. Officers were encouraged not to dwell on the memory of a dead comrade, whose possessions would be brusquely spirited away and a newcomer installed in his billet. Social niceties then ensured that the new man would be made welcome in the mess, drinks bought, old stories exchanged and soon it was as if the man who had died had never existed.

This policy was somewhat ruthless, but psychologically it suited the adolescent young men who made up the vast majority of the squadrons. After all, it was not as if these men had known each other for long; they were briefly thrown together only by the exigencies of the service. A true grieving process was simply not appropriate to their situation. Pilots and observers could not properly function in their appallingly dangerous vocation if they spent too much time contemplating the fate of those who had gone before them.

Infantrymen normally travelled out to the front in drafts, where at least they could gain confidence from the easy comradeship of their peers as they faced the unknown. Pilots and observers usually travelled alone, and for many of them the lonely journey exposed their total lack of experience in almost everything military:

> I travelled by the ordinary leave train from Victoria to Dover and
> thence by ship to Boulogne, where we arrived about dark. Everybody

else disembarking there seemed to know exactly what to do and where
to go, but I had no idea whatsoever and stood by my camp kit and
valise, feeling rather lost. Some kindly soul, who had perhaps had the
same experience himself at an earlier date, asked me where I was
going and, when I told him, advised me to report to the RTO (Railway
Transport Officer). He laughed when I naively asked him what an
RTO was! The RTO said, 'Oh yes, 22 Squadron, RFC. They'll pick
you up at Amiens railway station. You can catch a train early in the
morning. The squadron is at a place called Bertangles'.[1]

Second Lieutenant Geoffrey Hopkins, 22 Squadron, RFC

The naivety of these youngsters is almost impossible to overestimate.
They were painfully young and yet they were just days away from active
service in the most hostile of environments:

My dear old Mum,
Your last letter so sunk into my heart that it made me feel quite sad.
Your words, 'When will you get leave because I am living for it?' show
me how much you must love me and if a mother loves her son to that
extent, how much more must the son love the mother. It makes me feel
all the more how little I did for you when I was at home and how much
you all did for me, I am longing to see you all again and your smiling
faces. Darling I shall never forget in all my life how wonderfully you all
kept up when I left home to come out here. You can't think what a difference it made to me and I really think you must be extraordinarily
plucky. Well there is no need why I should go on moping about now and
make you feel miserable so I will try and turn to a brighter subject …
Your ever-loving little son, Leslie[2]

Second Lieutenant Leslie Mansbridge, I Squadron, RFC

There were a few older men amongst the flyers, and they suffered
similar feelings of loss at the thought of leaving their beloved wives and
sweethearts. Only the most ostrich-like of pilots could be unaware of the
casualty rates prevalent throughout the RFC in early 1917. It magnified
the simple power of normal emotions to an almost unbearable degree:

I can't think of anything I want you to send me except your letters and
your love. It is so much sweeter to be out here knowing that I have
someone who matters so enormously to me. I am very happy *ma bien*

Esmée. When I was in the train and leaving London, I thought for the first time of your precious tears. It thrilled me, darling, to think of them – to remember you lying in my arms making my face all wet. I realised that I couldn't realise how much I love you. Darling wife, I am glad you wept in my arms. I shall treasure the memory of it intensely.[3]

Captain William Bond, 40 Squadron, RFC

Almost before they knew it, they would be meeting their new comrades as they joined a squadron for the first time. Normally this was a low-key affair; after all, the arrival of replacement personnel was not a novelty to the men they were joining, no matter how strange it seemed to a newcomer:

Next day an RFC corporal met me on the platform at Amiens station, took my kit to a Crossley tender outside and drove me to a bar where, he said, I would find some other officers from the squadron. I found them there having a drink before returning to the aerodrome, I was introduced all round and we had a drink before setting off. We had a very crowded and noisy drive back. They belonged to C Flight and told me that I'd been posted to B Flight, where they dropped me at the mess, on a very cold night with thick snow on the ground. The first person I met on going into the mess was Gladstone, who had joined up with me from school. He introduced me to the others there, told me that the commanding officer and our flight commander were not there that night, and that I should report in the morning. After something to eat and drink, I was shown my billet. This was a farmhouse in the village, my room being a sort of cubby-hole off the main living room with a bunk bed containing a *palliasse*, filled with straw. I have no recollection of any bathing or sanitary arrangements – I don't suppose there were any – but have vivid memories of how cold it was.[4]

Second Lieutenant Geoffrey Hopkins, 22 Squadron, RFC

It was all too similar to the first day at boarding school and sure enough Second Lieutenant Leslie Mansbridge wrote home to his mother in the time-honoured public school fashion:

My dear Mum,
I have only just got here after a very long journey. I spent last night in a dirty old train. I hope you got my telegram alright. I have been greeted very cordially but I would rather have stayed with you. I did

enjoy myself and feel ever so much better. I am just going to tea now so I will stop for the present with best love to you, Dad and Rene,

    From Your ever-loving Son,

    Leslie[5]

Second Lieutenant Leslie Mansbridge, I Squadron, RFC

Meanwhile, concerned eyes were assessing the new arrivals. They were not yet ready to face the German scouts and before they were allowed over the lines it was imperative that they be given the chance to increase their flying hours. These green young pilots needed a chance to improve basic skills and to get the 'hang' of flying their new aircraft:

I am very bucked as I have got over the dull period I was passing through the week before. You know how you reach a stage in every game (billiards, golf, etc.) when you go hopelessly off for a bit – at least I always have that stage in everything. Before today my last half-dozen landings or so have been absolutely rotten, and I had lost all my judgement and confidence. However, I knew it was only my dull phase I was passing through, and that it wouldn't last long. Sure enough I have enjoyed flying no end today, and have felt completely at home in the air and landing just as before – which is very satisfactory, isn't it?[6]

Lieutenant Bob Kay, 46 Squadron, RFC

Even a pilot with previous experience as an observer could find his first mission over the lines a disorientating experience. Second Lieutenant Albert Godfrey of 40 Squadron made almost every mistake it was possible to make during his first flight as a scout pilot early in April 1917:

I had never flown a Nieuport, but the Flight Commander gave me some very good advice on the machine and engine, and in one flight I was quite familiar with it. On the evening of the first day with the squadron I carried out my first patrol with the Flight Commander and another pilot. This patrol was entirely a new adventure to me. It is necessary to mention that during all my previous experiences I had never been higher than 12,000 feet. We took off from the aerodrome in formation and climbed towards the lines. I had been accustomed to climbing for some time before crossing the lines, so this procedure seemed quite different to me. The machines climbed at such an angle that I expected them to stall, but knowing the danger in getting behind my formation, I stuck with them. On crossing the lines we received the usual welcome from the 'Archies', but it was so slight that I could not understand the reason, because when flying in France before we were seldom out of range of 'Archies'. All this time I had kept my eyes on the leader, but I became so curious that I peeped into the cockpit and to my astonishment saw we were at 19,000 feet, hence the reason for no 'Archie'.

In a few minutes the Flight Commander flapped his wings, a pre-arranged signal for Huns. I could not see anything, but suddenly the leader banked directly in front of me. This sudden movement certainly gave me shock. I immediately tried the same thing, but alas, it was too much for me. I had never been within 10,000 feet of this altitude before. In trying to turn the machine it went into a spin. Luckily I was many thousand feet up; it spun like a top, but pulling myself together, I applied the old formula and it came out as easily as it went in. I was still at 17,000 feet so felt safe. From this moment onward the experience gained while an observer was always the greatest help to me. I turned westward into the sun although I could not see anything of the ground in that direction, not even the sign of a trench. I decided to continue this course until I found my bearings, but fate played me a trick; I saw two machines on my left and thinking they were my formation I decided to join them; suddenly I saw a third machine, but still thinking it was my formation chasing a Hun I continued on my way – and to my astonishment found they were all Huns and after me like a pack of wolves.

It was then that I really learned to fly. I knew I must protect my tail, as under the circumstances to shoot at them was a secondary consideration. I had never fired a gun from a scout machine; I knew where the lever was to fire with, and that was all. When a Hun would get on my tail I tried a sharp turn and the machine would turn into a half roll or some other evolution. I do not know how long I did this, but it seemed hours. Suddenly a flight of Triplanes appeared; it would have been difficult for me to know they were our machines, but knowing the Huns did not have Triplanes at this time I was greatly relieved. The Triplanes did not shoot any of the Huns down but they certainly dispersed them. Arriving at the aerodrome I only had a few minutes petrol left. The other pilots had returned and were greatly relieved by my appearance. Thus ended my first flight in a scout without firing a single shot.[7]

Second Lieutenant Albert Godfrey, 40 Squadron, RFC

Godfrey had been incredibly lucky – many others only got the opportunity to make one mistake.

Since the corps squadrons flew two-seaters, someone eventually had to risk their life with a new pilot. When Second Lieutenant C. F. Horsley joined 18 Squadron he found that he was simply not trusted. This is perhaps not surprising, as he had only twenty-three hours of solo flying, had not flown for a month and had never flown the higher powered version of the FE2b:

> At that time the squadron was extremely fortunate in the possession of four or five exceptionally capable and experienced observers, and the Squadron Commander rigidly pursued the policy of thoroughly testing the flying and landing ability of new pilots before trusting them with the lives of others. Looking back in my logbook I find that I was sent up and did twenty-nine practice landings before I was allowed to take an observer. I can well remember, after the Squadron Leader signalled me to finish, taxiing slowly in and expecting, with fear and trembling, to be told that I should be sent back to England.[8]
>
> Second Lieutenant C. F. Horsley, 18 Squadron, RFC

The reasons that informed the caution of his commanding officer, Major G. R. M. Reid, were soon apparent when the veteran Second Lieutenant E. D. G. Galley was sent up as observer to accompany the newly arrived Captain W. E. Salter:

> As you became an experienced observer you had to go up with a green pilot and I was up one day with such a fellow. An enemy machine got onto us and the pilot flew dead straight. First of all I got a bullet through my arm, then he got one in the ankle, and we went, not completely out of control, we drifted, circling in a rather flat way, like a leaf sometimes comes down and crashed just behind the front line where the Australians were.[9]
>
> Second Lieutenant E. D. G. Galley, 22 Squadron, RFC

Many pilots had insufficient hours of solo flying and only minimal experience in the aircraft they would actually be flying in action. In life or death situations where split-second reactions were all important, such a lack of familiarity with the basic tools of the pilot's trade was a dangerous and often fatal handicap. Too often the raw pilots simply froze or lost control of their aircraft altogether:

When an officer reported to the squadron he had usually about twenty hours flying to his credit. With few exceptions he never failed to 'crash' at least one machine when landing at Avesnes; owing, no doubt, to the small size of the aerodrome. Having proved himself safe, an officer was then sent up to do a shoot on the 'puff target'. If this was successful, he was considered ready to fly to the line for the first time. A very senior, but thoroughly frightened, observer was sent with him in order that the Corps front should be carefully scrutinised and obvious landmarks pointed out.[10]

Lieutenant Donald Stevenson, 12 Squadron, RFC

When he first joined 22 Squadron, Lieutenant Geoffrey Hopkins found that his flying skills came under the usual scrutiny from concerned observers:

I was asked in some detail about my flying experience. When this was now, twenty hours in the air in all, I was ordered to take up an FE2b and do a series of circuits of the aerodrome and landings. Naturally, none of the observers was particularly keen to go up with me until he knew whether I could handle an aircraft or not. Our Flight Commander got over this difficulty by saying it was Second Lieutenant T. G. Fawcett's turn, and, in this way, he became my permanent observer. After a series of circuits and bumps had been safely negotiated, Fawcett guided me up to the lines to see what they looked like and showed me over the neighbourhood locality so that I could soon find my own way back to the aerodrome.[11]

Second Lieutenant Geoffrey Hopkins, 22 Squadron, RFC

When Lieutenant John Slessor joined 5 Squadron he flew over the lines the day after he arrived with the man who was to become his observer in a fruitful partnership over the next five months:

We went down to the Somme country, and flew right up the line from Beaumont Hamel to Loos. It is impossible adequately to describe the appalling wastage of that country. All of the same uniform colour, mud, mud and shell holes. The shell holes overlapping three and four on top of the other, woods looking like a stumpy collection of blackened toothpicks, villages just a charred and crumbled mass of mud and brick dust, and then the great row of mine craters and battered white chalk ditches where the old front lines were. The Vimy Ridge is the most extraordinary sight of all I think, simply a huge shoulder of hills running in a south-easterly direction, about 200 feet high, with a fairly steep slope off the east side, partly covered by what were once woods.[12]

Lieutenant John Slessor, 5 Squadron, RFC

For those flying over the front for the first time the state of the battle zone was quite simply fantastic. They had read about it, some of them had seen the *Battle of the Somme* film the previous year, but nothing could prepare them for the reality of total war:

There was not a house left standing; just as if a big steamroller had passed over them. As we went further east, the shell holes in the ground grew more numerous until we reached the zone where each shell hole literally touches four or five others. I cannot describe the appearance of this to you – there were billions and all full of water. The whole looked like a wet sponge; hardly a house or a tree visible; only desolation.[13]

Second Lieutenant Marcus Kaizer, 18 Squadron, RFC

Second Lieutenant Francis Penny had been originally in training as a pilot, when he volunteered to go out early as an observer. Observers were in dreadfully short supply after the excessive casualties. He joined 12 Squadron based at Avesnes le Comte. It was obvious that one of the pilots would have to go up with the completely inexperienced observer, leaving their back dangerously exposed:

I was taken by Captain Garrod on what was described as a familiarisation flight. He warned me to watch out for any enemy aircraft, especially into the sun, from which direction an enemy aircraft usually pounced on his unsuspecting victim. As this was my first close-up of the 'line' I was naturally interested in what was going on down below, when suddenly the tat-tat of a machine gun was quite clearly heard coming from an enemy aircraft. From our machine, a BE2c, I could see a few pieces of wing fabric fluttering in the wind, where enemy scout machine-gun bullets had gone through both fuselage and wing. Fortunately none had hit the cockpit. Between pilot and observer there was a communication tube, through which conversation could be carried out with some difficulty above the roar of the engine and exhaust noise. What the pilot said could not be repeated here – it was not complimentary![14]

Second Lieutenant Francis Penny, 12 Squadron, RFC

The familiarisation process applied as much to a new squadron as it did to an individual. When 66 Squadron arrived in France in March 1917 there was simply no point in throwing them into action without allowing them time to get to know their new surroundings:

> For the first few days the squadron concentrated on establishing itself in France. Each flight went out in formation to practise the flying we would do in the coming patrols. We memorised the pattern of the earth below us: roads, towns and villages, woods, and even the shapes, colours and contours of fields, so that we would be completely familiar with the view from the air and always know where we were.[15]
>
> Second Lieutenant Gordon Taylor, 66 Squadron, RFC

Gunnery was of vital importance if the airmen were to have any chance of shooting down a German aircraft. Assuming the pilot managed successfully to stalk his prey, he still only had the first burst before the enemy would inevitably take sharp evasive action. In the helter-skelter lunacy of a dogfight there was never any chance of more than a snapshot in the chaos that ensued. Real opportunities were rare and if they were missed through bad marksmanship then their opponents would live to fight again and more importantly fight back. The most common method of target practice used was a simple static ground target:

> We put out a target sheet, 6 feet square, on the ground, and then go up and dive on it, firing short bursts with the Lewis gun. It is rather trying, because you get so keen to sight properly on to the target, when you are coming down almost vertically, that you forget the ground is coming near.[16]
>
> Captain William Bond, 40 Squadron, RFC

This was a vital part of the training, and it also tested their flying skills to the limit. The slightest misjudgement could lead to a nasty and probably fatal accident:

> I was out before breakfast diving at a target on the ground, firing my gun. The target is in a small gully, and I dived to within a few feet of the ground and then flew along the gully – going up slightly over a rise and down a hollow, hopping trees, hedges, etc., in one's stride. The people from the aerodrome had seen me dive but not reappear, and

were quite surprised when I appeared suddenly from the other side. This contour chasing is the thing to give you an idea of the pace you are going.[17]

Lieutenant Bob Kay, 46 Squadron, RFC

This form of practice was obviously risky for green pilots but they had to improve their accuracy somehow if they were to stand a real chance over the front. Soon after 66 Squadron arrived in France one former cavalry officer found that a highly strung Sopwith Pup was not necessarily as responsive as a horse:

Pilots dived individually on a ground target near the aerodrome, firing their guns at the outline of a German aircraft laid out on the grass. I was watching a Pup dive on this target only a day or two after we arrived. He was coming down steeply with engine on, firing, but holding his dive beyond the time when he should have started to pull out. I was in agony, trying to will him out of the dive before it was too late. He must have realised his mistake, seen the ground coming up, and pulled back far too heavily on the stick. With a ridiculously harmless sound, like a child's balloon bursting, the aeroplane disintegrated. The fuselage dived straight into the ground with the crunching noise of somebody treading on a matchbox. Tattered fragments of wing followed it, fluttering slowly to earth. The silence which settled over the scene was appalling.[18]

Second Lieutenant Gordon Taylor, 66 Squadron, RFC

Target practice clearly exposed the poor standards of marksmanship that were endemic in the RFC. Many of the new pilots had had no experience of firing their machine guns before they arrived in France. They were distressed to find how often near pristine targets bore incontrovertible witness to their appalling inaccuracy:

I dived six times altogether and emptied one drum of ammunition – ninety-seven rounds. Then I asked on coming down if I had hit the target at all. 'Oh, yes!' the gunroom man said quite eagerly, 'There's one shot on the target'. 'One hit out of ninety-seven shots!' I gasped. 'Yes, Sir!' he replied, 'But you're the first to hit the target at all. It's been out five days too!' [19]

Captain William Bond, 40 Squadron, RFC

The more experienced pilots knew that there was more to hitting a target than pointing the aircraft in that general direction and letting loose with vigour and vim. Painstaking preparation was required. The machine guns had to be accurately aligned with both the aircraft and the sights, so that the bullets were actually going where the sights indicated. Furthermore, if they wanted to avoid the likelihood of the machine gun jamming at a vital moment, then it was wise to take personal responsibility for preparing and loading the guns:

> That meant hours at the butts with your machine trued up in flying position shifting your gun mountings about getting your sights synchronised on your gun burst at 200 yards. In addition to that there was the loading of the guns. The Vickers gun had a disintegrating belt made of little aluminium links and the bullets themselves were the pins between the links that held the whole thing together. In 56 Squadron we weren't allowed to have the armourers do any of the preparation of ammunition belts for fighting – we did it ourselves. We spent two or three hours every morning loading and making the belts that we should use on the afternoon patrol. By taking care with the way the belts were put together we got them so that they wouldn't jam in the breech.[20]
> Lieutenant Cecil Lewis, 56 Squadron, RFC

Yet pilots were still haunted by other less preventable jams caused by the vagaries of the Constantinesco synchronising gear. This was a plunger activated by a cam driven from the propeller shaft, which transmitted impulses to the breech-block mechanism through the medium of oil in a copper pipe. The gun could thus only be fired when the propeller blades were not in the line of fire. However, at high altitude the icy cold could freeze the oil and a jam was inevitable. This was only eventually resolved by the use of anti-freeze oil.

As soon as the newcomers were considered ready, they began flying the regular offensive patrols that punctuated the daily routine of the scout pilot. The dawn patrol has become a cliché, the be-all and end-all of aerial warfare. In truth these patrols *were* an important and eye-catching part of the air war over Arras in 1917, but it should never be forgotten that all patrols were there to protect the army cooperation corps aircraft and to destroy the German equivalents. The British scouts may have spent most of their time duelling with German scouts but their real role was to clear the way for the real death-dealing machines: the BE2s armed with their cameras and wirelesses.

Patrols took place at dawn, morning, afternoon and early evening. The pilots would emerge dressed for the extreme conditions to be found at altitude in open cockpits:

> We were, of course, muffled up to the eyes and wore fleece-lined thigh boots drawn up over a fleece- or fur-lined Sidcot suit, a fur-lined helmet complete with chin guard and goggles with a strip of fur all round them. Any parts of bare skin left open to the air were well coated with whale oil to prevent frostbite. For our hands we found that an ordinary pair of thin silk gloves, if put on warm and then covered with the ordinary leather gauntlet gloves, retained enough heat for the whole patrol.[21]
>
> Flight Lieutenant Robert Compston, 8 (Naval) Squadron, RNAS

Normally the patrol would be a flight of about four aircraft. The pilots would stumble out to their machines, brushing the sleep from their eyes:

> All pilots should be in their machines five minutes before the time of starting, the engines having been previously tested by the petty officer of the Flight. When all engines are ticking over and the petty officer signals to the leader that all the engines are running satisfactorily, the flight leader leaves the ground; the remaining four machines, if head to wind, should get off in thirty seconds, the order of getting off corresponding to each machine's position in the formation.[22]
>
> Flight Commander Colin Mackenzie, 8 (Naval) Squadron, RNAS

So the patrol would take off and head off towards the front line:

> Emerging from the mess we got into our machines, tested the engines, waved away the chocks and opened our engines out into the darkness. While gaining height we saw away on our starboard beam a dark mass, which we knew to be the town of Arras, while the silvery, twisting thread straggling eastward showed us the River Scarpe. An occasional bursting shell and some Very lights betrayed the whereabouts of the lines, while a star shell threw into clear relief the chalky contour of the Hindenburg Line. Rudely we disturbed that quiet hour before the dawn.[23]
>
> Flight Lieutenant Robert Compston, 8 (Naval) Squadron, RNAS

As they gained height they would be looking round to check their personal orientation as they flew over the lines. Some pilots, like Second Lieutenant Gordon Taylor, were naturally well organised and tried to maximise the efficiency of everything they did:

> For quick and easy reference I had pasted maps of the region for about 30 miles each side of the lines on pieces of plywood, and had made a holder for these which I fitted beside my seat. With the map on my knees I checked the country as we climbed out east for the lines. Here ahead of us, before Arras, the country below was green with spring, the small villages of the farming community lying in apparently undisturbed peace.[24]

> Second Lieutenant Gordon Taylor, 66 Squadron, RFC

Cloud conditions were a wonderful distraction and a pilot carrying out a solo patrol could easily be tempted to play: to explore the amazing peaks and valleys that abounded, although it was best to remember that these might also conceal a German ambush:

> These April clouds are perfectly clearly defined, and are like great mountains and castles of snow. You are sailing along in the sparkling sun under a clear blue sky and underneath is a fluffy white carpet. On the earth perhaps it is quite a dull day. You see one of these great fluffy columns ahead and buzz up to it, and it is so sharp that you can actually fly round it with one wing in it and yet be right out in the sun. A steep turn and a dive into its soft depths and all sun would be gone, and most idea of where you were, too. It is priceless finding a small and narrow gap through a pretty thick layer of cloud, say 3,000 feet, and then come winding down through it in a series of spirals, side-slips and dives.[25]

> Lieutenant George Kay, 46 Squadron, RFC

Gaining height was all important in aerial combat; it acted much as the possession of the weather gage did in the age of sail. It allowed a far greater freedom of manoeuvre and gave a flight commander the opportunity of seeking or evading battle, depending on the situation and the possibility of responding to events as they might transpire:

> We were about 20 miles behind the lines so we had time to climb up on our way over to get height this side of the lines. We usually got up to 15,000 or 16,000 feet before we actually crossed the lines into enemy

territory looking for trouble. Our eyes were continually focusing, looking; craning our heads round, moving all the time looking for those black specks which would mean enemy aircraft at a great distance. Between clouds we would not be able to see the ground or only parts of it which would sort of slide into view like a magic lantern screen far, far beneath. Clinging close together about 20 or 30 yards between each machine, swaying, looking at our neighbours; setting ourselves just right so that we were all in position.[26]

Lieutenant Cecil Lewis, 56 Squadron, RFC

If they flew too low they were liable to attract the attention of the German anti-aircraft guns. These were not too much of a threat, as individually the guns were fairly inaccurate and there were rarely enough of them to set up a barrage that would splay across the skies to make evasion a difficult proposition. Nevertheless the guns did occasionally hit their targets. It took on many of the characteristics of a game of cat and mouse as pilots tried to second guess the gunners by changing course and speed to try and put them off their aim during the period the aircraft were within range of the guns:

Suddenly the 'wuff-wuff' of anti-aircraft shells bursting in front of us disturbed our peace of mind, for we were now at a height of only 9,000 feet and a good target. As the bursts were in front of us we altered course to starboard and increased speed at the same time. The next bursts were on our port beam and not far away, so we altered course slightly to port and again increased our speed. The following bursts were well behind and to our right, so we were through with that battery.[27]

Flight Lieutenant Robert Compston, 8 (Naval) Squadron, RNAS

Occasionally the harmless 'puffs' of smoke showed their venom and aircraft were hit, as Captain William Bond found to his cost:

I headed over the lines and crossed at 10,000 feet. Then war broke out and for several minutes I couldn't see the two fellows who were following, for the black shell burst all around us. To put the anti-aircraft gunners off their range I side-slipped and stunted and then climbed above a cloud. The others did the same. It was only a small cloud, however, and soon came to an end. Promptly on reappearing we got another salvo and I felt a violent shock on the joystick. The whole machine shuddered, but before I had begun to wonder what had been hit I stuck my nose down hard and due west. Everything looked all right. Leaning out and peering round the engine cowling I found the undercarriage still there. I waggled the joystick. The tail controls were all right. Again I waggled the joystick. Wing controls all right. But no, nothing happened. I looked at the ailerons. The left one moved, but the right one did not move. Then I glanced at the aileron controls. Just against my screen the right aileron control had been shot away! I kept my nose down, heading for home, and found that I could still get a sufficient amount of wing controls to make slow turns. Landing became a problem, as the moment I switched off the engine the right wing dropped. I flew right on to the ground, though, without smashing anything.[28]

Captain William Bond, 40 Squadron, RFC

Bond had been remarkably lucky. The scout patrols, however, were not normally excessively troubled by the German anti-aircraft batteries. But the guns posed a real risk to the army cooperation aircraft:

Had to go a long way over again so went up with a strong team, six machines all told, three with cameras and three as escort. Saw no Huns but 'Archie' beat all records. Before we crossed the lines we were met with a perfect tornado of bursting shells which was kept up all the time we were in the vicinity. Tried a new game for dodging 'Archie' – just kicking the rudder from side to side which makes the machine slide about in the sky like a skimming plate. It was hardly a success today for you were just as likely to slide into one as out of the way of one. When I am being badly 'Archied' I often try and cast my mind down to the gunners below and imagine I can see the gentle Hun with his eyes cast glued to the sights of his gun, saying, 'Got him! No! Oooh! That was near, a bit more to the right!' Then uttering the German equivalent to a good English 'Damn!' when the machine gets back to our lines undamaged. It does seem strange that all the best mechanical brains in the world have been used to put an aeroplane in the sky and then another set of brains comes along to devise something to knock it out of the sky. It's all in the game, I suppose, but very, very silly.[29]

Second Lieutenant Charles Smart, 5 Squadron, RFC

The pilots' response to 'Archie' was a strange mutating phenomenon that betrayed a great deal about their overall state of mind. At first 'Archie' scared callow pilots; then they became blasé as they gained confidence;

then slowly and insidiously the guns wormed their way back into the pilots' consciousness as they became more and more stressed, until once again they feared the little puffs of smoke that would occasionally surround them and which they knew also acted as an effective indication of their presence to any German scouts lurking in the vicinity.

It was vital that a scout patrol maintained a strong formation, tightly focused and responsive to the every whim of their leader. Communication between aircraft was obviously non-verbal, but constant practice, as Flight Lieutenant Robert Compston found, could bring remarkably sophisticated results over a period of time:

> It was remarkable to what pitch efficiency in manoeuvring a flight could be brought by merely moving the aeroplane; for example, a turn to the right would be signalled by rocking the machine from side to side and then dropping a wing down to the right and commencing the turn. The pilots on the right of the leader would slow down their engines and pull their machines up, slowing them as much as possible, while the leader would fly round in a normal manner; those on the left who had to complete the outer and greater circle, would put their noses down and go as fast as possible to catch up; thus would a turn be made, and when all were on an even keel after the turn each pilot would close up to his original distance from his next man. Such a manoeuvre came easily after practice but, to an inexperienced pilot, it was extremely difficult.[30]
>
> Flight Lieutenant Robert Compston, 8 (Naval) Squadron, RNAS

New pilots found that clumsy flying made their aircraft seem slower than the rest. Every time a small change of course was indicated by the flight leader, they would lurch out of the formation and then have to chase hard to catch up. One of the points constantly hammered home by the old hands was that it was fatal to become a straggler:

> Pilots came out untrained in formation flying and had to be initiated almost in the presence of the enemy. The result was that when the strain came on the invisible cords which bound the formation frequently gave way, and cohesion was lost. Once committed to the fight the leader could hardly influence his formation except by personal example; his greatest difficulty was to rally his machines, which were liable to become so scattered that they could be attacked piecemeal.[31]
>
> Lieutenant Roderick Hill, 60 Squadron, RFC

Another skill that only seemed to come with practice was the ability to 'see' what was happening all around them in the air. Most new pilots seemed to have a kind of tunnel vision – only aware of what was immediately in front of them – oblivious to the larger and often more threatening picture. In effect they were distracted by the necessity of concentrating on actually flying their aircraft, of desperately clinging to their place in the flight formation. These were things that a veteran pilot like Flight Lieutenant Compston could do by instinct without deflecting any of his attention from his ceaseless scanning of the horizon:

> It does not follow that because a man can see a figure on the ground and be able to see whether it be man or woman, that he will be able to see things in the air, for I have known many men with first-class sight who, when they commenced aerial work, appeared to be quite blind at times; this was chiefly due to the fact that an inexperienced pilot had to give most of his attention to the leader, watching closely for signals; he therefore could not be expected to see as much as one whose eyes were attuned to distance and whose whole attention could be given to finding the enemy. I remember one of my pilots, seeing me fire at something (he did not see it was an enemy aeroplane, although we were very close to it), fired his guns – presumably in sympathy – hitting the middle plane of my Triplane about 12 inches from my right shoulder![32]
>
> Flight Lieutenant Robert Compston, 8 (Naval) Squadron, RNAS

The beginner was also not accustomed to the array of dreadful physical challenges that flying an open-cockpit aircraft at high altitudes entailed. The extreme cold he might have expected – although it led to agonising circulation problems and even to cases of mild frostbite – but the consequences of oxygen starvation were not fully appreciated at the time:

> In an attempt to entice the Albatros up to meet us in the thin air of the higher levels where the Germans did not have such a disastrous margin of performance over the lightly loaded Sopwith, we pushed up the height of our patrols to 17,000 feet, and sometimes higher. We must have been affected by lack of oxygen at this height, but we never noticed it, and at least our opponents were in the same situation since neither side used bottled oxygen. Actually, in the light of later knowledge, I now think the regular flights in air with a low oxygen content must have stimulated the body's mechanism for absorbing a

relatively higher oxygen intake. The only noticeable effect I remember having from these patrols was a tendency to fall into a deep and dreamless sleep as soon as I returned to earth and my bed.[33]

Second Lieutenant Gordon Taylor, 66 Squadron, RFC

As he soared up way above the clouds sudden movements could leave the unwary pilot gasping like a stranded fish. Steep dives from altitude resulted in sudden changes of air pressure that caused dreadful headaches, disconcerting nose bleeds and occasionally bleeding ears. Amidst all these problems was the underlying effect of the castor oil spray flung back all over them by a rotary engine spinning round just a few feet in front of them. Many pilots could vouch for its powerful laxative effects.

As the pilots pressed forward over the lines they were looking for trouble wherever they might find it. Individual German reconnaissance and artillery observation aircraft, German offensive patrols – anything moving that warranted investigation. German tactics were constantly evolving as their pilots sought ways to maximise the advantage of superior aircraft while minimising the disadvantage of inferior numbers. Ultimately this was achieved by combining flights and even squadrons together, thereby increasing the size of formations, often layered one above the other, sometimes with a tempting decoy flying well below them. Thus scarce resources were tightly concentrated, so that when the Germans did encounter British scouts they would usually have the advantage of superior numbers in that immediate locality:

Sooner or later we would spot the enemy. If we were lucky it would be below us, but we were always under the enemy. Our machines, good as they were, were still not up to the Huns who usually had a 1,000 to 2,000 feet ceiling clear above us. Even at 16,000 feet we were liable to be jumped from on top. That didn't have to worry us. We were usually outnumbered two or three to one. We used to engage irrespective if there was anybody above or not – just chance it. Usually the top flight of enemy aircraft who were above us would come down and jump us as we went down.[34]

Lieutenant Cecil Lewis, 56 Squadron, RFC

Aerial tactics were developing all the time. Certain basic principles had been established early on by the Germans inspired by the genius of Oswald Boelcke. It took the British a little longer but, by 1917, they too had more or less hammered out their basic principles:

We always tried to get to eastward so that we had the advantage of the sun; in the afternoon of course we had this advantage, as it was in the west, and our attack was usually a surprise. This was very necessary as the odds were two to one against us, for if one sailed in on a level with the enemy there was little hope of all pilots coming back; better to take a little longer over the job, pick off one or two of the enemy and live to fight again. You will see how very important it was in such fighting for each pilot to select a machine to dive at and withhold his fire until the last possible moment, for to fire at considerable range seldom damages the enemy but gives him excellent warning of the attack. Possibly over an hour has been spent getting into the right position for the attack and this would be entirely wasted by premature firing.[35]

Flight Lieutenant Robert Compston, 8 (Naval) Squadron, RNAS

Whenever possible British scouts would attack from above and behind, seeking a deadly surprise. One experienced formation leader, Flight Commander Colin MacKenzie, summed up his tenets of aerial fighting in January 1917:

The following 'Ten Commandments' in aerial fighting are considered of vital importance. They may appear cowardly. The man who gets most Huns in his lifetime is the man who observes these Commandments and fights with his head. The others either get killed or get nerves in a very short time and the country does not get the full benefit of having trained them:

1. Do not lose formation.
2. Do not press an attack on a two-seater who fires at you before you are in a perfect position. Break away and attack him or another HA later with a chance of surprise.
3. Do not stay to manoeuvre with a two-seater.
4. Do not dive to break off a combat. Huns can dive better than you but are as a rule worse climbers.
5. Do not necessarily attack a superior formation; you will get a better chance if you wait five minutes.
6. Do not attack without looking for the machine above you; he will almost certainly come on your tail unawares while you are attacking if you are not watching him. Look behind continually while on a dive.

7. Do not come down too low on the other side or you will have all the enemy on to you.

8. Don't go to sleep in the air for one instant of your patrol, watch your tail.

9. Don't deliver a surprise attack by firing too soon unless you want to scare the HA off a friendly machine's tail.

10. Don't deliver a surprise attack at over 100 yards range at the very most.[36]

Flight Commander Colin Mackenzie, 8 (Naval) Squadron, RNAS

Although clearly stretched slightly to deliver the requisite 'ten' commandments, this was fundamentally sensible advice. However, there were no certainties in aerial warfare and the cautious, pragmatic Flight Commander Colin Mackenzie was himself shot down just a few days later during an offensive patrol over Bapaume on 24 January 1917. What he was teaching was the art of hunting pure and simple, with no sentimentality and not a trace of fair play:

When the leader attacks, it is usual for 'two' and 'three' to accompany him down. 'Two' is supposed to attack the same machine as the leader, but in practice things arrange themselves. If two machines attack an enemy machine simultaneously it more than doubles the chance of success. 'Four' and 'five' remain aloft for a short period to guard the tails of 'one', 'two' and 'three', and then join up again.[37]

Flight Commander Colin Mackenzie, 8 (Naval) Squadron, RNAS

The idea was to give their victims no chance whatsoever to return fire to kill without warning:

The moment arrived and, each choosing a machine to dive at, away we went, gluing our eyes to the Aldis sights and keeping our fingers on the triggers. My adversary seemed to rush towards me and rapidly his head became larger in the centre ring of my sight – I was tempted to fire, but held on until I thought I should crash into him, then pressing the triggers for a few seconds only I was forced to pull over on to my back to avoid hitting him. Very few rounds of ammunition are necessary when fired at point-blank range, for the rate of fire from two synchronised guns firing through our propellers was 2,000 rounds per minute. Once more on an even keel, I surveyed what had, a few minutes before,

been a peaceful German patrol and I saw one going down in flames
while another was spinning down, apparently out of control, for the
pilot did not right the machine, even when he disappeared against the
earth's surface, thousands of feet below us. The remaining six machines
had dived away and were making for home as fast as they could.[38]

Flight Lieutenant Robert Compston, 8 (Naval) Squadron, RNAS

This represented a successful action. The carefully planned approach had
secured surprise, altitude had been used to dive down on the unsuspecting target, fire had been opened at an effective range and two victories
would be claimed.

There is no doubt that optimism was the watchword of scout pilots
when making their claims. The nature of the fighting meant that it was
usually impossible for pilots to follow the victim right down to destruction on
the ground, particularly as they were usually over the German lines; nothing
was more likely to guarantee the early demise of the triumphant victor:

In the morning I went on an offensive patrol and attacked an Albatros
scout over Douai. I got on his tail and fired at very close range when he
went down in a vertical dive. I thought I saw black smoke and flames
but I am not sure. I find it very difficult to watch a machine go right
down to the ground. I always seem to lose it in a conglomeration of
objects on the surface.[39]

Flight Sub-Lieutenant Edward Crundall, 8 (Naval) Squadron, RNAS

Sanguine presumptions were routinely made about the seriousness of
damage the scouts had caused to German aircraft, and any signs of leaking
petrol vapour would be automatically supposed to mean that their erstwhile
opponent had gone down in flames. Under the British system, claims were
allowed, and indeed in some units encouraged, for 'out of control' aircraft,
which thereafter counted as kills in a pilot's victory list. Yet the very same
pilots would often congratulate themselves for having got out of trouble
when necessary by spinning away or diving flat out as if out of control –
that, of course, was different – they knew they had survived! Furthermore,
in the mad confusion of a dogfight, multiple claims would also result as
pilots, quite unbeknown to each other, successively poured bullets into the
same doomed aircraft and each, in all good faith, afterwards put in a claim.
When reflected in their combat reports the same aircraft could be 'shot
down' and 'claimed' many times over.

It was only human nature for pilots to be optimistic as to the effects of their fire. Controversially, some pilots seem to have used the absence of any effective system of corroboration deliberately and persistently exaggerated their scores for their own aggrandisement. Such a mixture of confusion and embroidery at least partially explains the vast numbers of RFC claims that cannot now be matched with a known German victim. The Germans, who mainly fought on their own side of the lines, did not usually have these problems in corroborating claims. If pilots claimed to have shot an aircraft down then it would be there for all to see, crashed behind the German front line.

Occasionally, when scout formations encountered each other they would split up out of all control and go at each other hammer and tongs in what was known as a dogfight. Aircraft were swirling, whirling, diving in and out, having near head-on collisions, while all was punctuated with brief staccato bursts of machine-gun fire. Very few men could keep control in such an environment:

It's not really possible to describe the action of a fight like that. Having no communication with each other we simply had to go in and take our man and chance our arm – keep our eyes in the backs of our heads to see if anybody was trying to get us as we went down. But there was always the point where you had to go down anyway whether there was anybody on your tail or not. The fight would begin – engage and disengage with burst of thirty or forty rounds three in one tracer so there was always some idea of where you were firing because your sights were really no good in these dogfights – there wasn't time to focus – it was just snap shooting. The whole squadron would enter the fight in good formation but within half a minute the whole formation had gone to hell. Just chaps wheeling and zooming and diving. On each other's tails – perhaps four in a row even – a German going down, one of our chaps on his tail, another German on his tail, another Hun behind that – extraordinary glimpses. People approaching head on firing at each other as they came and then just at the last moment turning and slipping away.[40]

Lieutenant Cecil Lewis, 56 Squadron, RFC

Sometimes dogfights could expand beyond all reason as neighbouring patrols on both sides spotted what was going on and cheerfully hurled themselves into the fray, until it seemed as if the whole sky was filled with maniacally spinning aircraft. A dogfight would not normally last very long, perhaps fifteen to twenty minutes at most, before the aircraft had lost all their precious altitude or suffered damage, their guns had jammed or run out of ammunition, they had been damaged or pilots simply lost their nerve and disengaged. But, while it lasted, it was a truly desperate business. None of the aces scored many kills in dogfights. It was a mess, too uncontrolled and far too risky. Better to take their kills in the first dive from a position of tactical superiority, then to disengage by diving away before zooming back up to regain altitude for a possible further attack. That kind of fighting minimised the risks as far as was possible.

Yet the men of the RFC could not run away from a fight. Their job was to sweep their enemies from the Arras skies. Any unmolested formation of German scouts was a serious threat to the army cooperation aircraft plying their trade over the lines below. They would fall on the helpless BE2s like wolves on a flock of sheep. This meant that even if the British scouts were outnumbered, outclassed and at a serious tactical disadvantage they still had a duty to engage the German scouts regardless of risk.

Second Lieutenant Gordon Taylor, a relatively unproven young scout pilot, was in a formation of 66 Squadron led by the experienced Captain John Andrews when they encountered four Albatros scouts slightly above them. His account may raise eyebrows as to the detail of his recollections, but it certainly conveys the spirit of such scraps:

> They had the height and were coming in to attack. Andrews held on,
> flying straight for the enemy formation, the distance between us closing
> rapidly. They were four dark machines, the leader a little ahead of the
> others. I saw the tracer, thin, harmless-looking white streamers,
> streaking towards us from the noses of the Huns. I pressed on, keeping
> plenty of speed, and chose the machine on the end of the line. Then
> I realised I had no choice, as he was already firing at me. I couldn't pull
> up to meet him head on because my machine would have stalled, so
> I nosed down and turned across him to force him into a deflection shot.
> I could hear the crackle of his guns as he flashed by overhead. I pulled
> the Pup round in a climbing turn and saw the Hun again, a black
> machine with white outlined crosses. We closed again and he tried to
> get into position to attack me from behind, but I found that I could

easily turn inside him – as Andrews had said. He hadn't a chance to pin me down that way. Realising this, he broke off the close manoeuvring and sailed up in a long, sweeping climb. Suddenly this wasn't a football match. This could mean somebody's death. He was high overhead, turning to come back in. I forgot all about flying techniques. My one thought was to get him firmly in my sights, in the stream of bullets from my gun. The death must be his.

I pulled the Pup up on her tail, firing as I held full throttle and brought the Hun into my sights. The Vickers rattled out, the aircraft hung suspended. Then the Pup dropped from under me and I felt the seat belt tighten and pull me back into the cockpit. The machine was falling vertically after the stall, with the nose pointing at the earth. Instinctively I pulled off the throttle, let go the firing cord. Technique took over, easing the aircraft out of the dive. Where was the Hun? I looked around as I drew the stick back. I saw him then, hanging above me, waiting. I turned in a kind of corkscrew pull-out, remembering that I must never fly straight. He was on me again in seconds. But before he could line up his sights I had whipped round into a turn and was trying to entice him closer. He knew his stuff however, and again trying to exploit the Albatros advantage on the climb by hauling up, flying away high over, manoeuvring to set me up for another diving attack. I could see this coming and was able to avoid it by turning in under him and spoiling his dive. He flashed on over again and I pulled around for a chance to get a burst into him. He wasn't there.[41]

Second Lieutenant Gordon Taylor, 66 Squadron, RFC

The German pilot had very wisely disengaged. The Albatros was a superb weapon but the agile fast-turning Sopwith Pup could be a formidable opponent at close quarters. The tactics employed by the Albatros pilot on this occasion were typical: the dive on to the victim, the burst of fire and the fast repeat, before his disinclination to get overly involved in close manoeuvring took over and he deliberately retreated. For the German scout pilot, fighting in an overall defensive battle, there was simply no need to fight to the finish. His job was to take his kills with the minimum possible risk to himself and his precious Albatros. While one for one was no good to the outnumbered Germans, it was a more than acceptable rate of sacrifice for the numerically superior British.

When the British scouts encountered German reconnaissance or artillery observation aircraft they had the chance to really strike a blow directly in defence of the men below them, who would surely suffer if these aircraft were allowed to successfully carry out their missions. These were the equivalent of the British BE2s that Richthofen preyed upon with such success, but they were more modern and nowhere near as vulnerable as the British BE2cs. Here too some subtlety and skill was required:

> We used to meet a number of lone two-seaters. Attacking tactics had not been very carefully thought out, and the general rule was to go bald-headed at the Hun as soon as he was sighted. It was not long before we learnt the futility of this method, but in the meantime many opportunities were lost. Looking back now the most glaring fault of those days was that the experience gained by individuals and squadrons was not passed on to others. Squadrons and staffs seemed too full of their own little worries to bother about such things and the people at home seemed to be too far away even to be thought of. Too few people even now realise the importance of passing on their experience for the benefit of others.[42]

Flight Lieutenant Leonard Cockey, 1 (Naval) Squadron, RNAS

On one occasion, Lieutenant Gordon Taylor and Captain John Andrews engaged two German reconnaissance machines that they had sighted well below their patrol. In the fight that ensued Taylor made a series of elementary mistakes through a mixture of inexperience and sheer, brash overconfidence:

> As we closed, Andrews made for the leading aircraft and I slewed away for the other which was behind and to the right. My excitement was terrific. It was all I could do to hold my fire to effective range instead of shooting away my ammunition at a range of half a mile or more. Then I saw tracer coming up, and the rear gunner actually crouching in his seat and firing at me. Strangely, I had no fear that he would hit me, even though the pilot was holding the aircraft on a magnificently straight course. I pulled the gun ring as the Hun came in, filling the view over the nose of my Pup. He had to go down. I almost flew into his tail, pulled out, and swept over above his wing. At the top of my climbing turn I looked down to see what had happened. The Hun was diving vertically into some scattered cloud that hung over the land below.[43]

Second Lieutenant Gordon Taylor, 66 Squadron, RFC

Taylor was unable to gain confirmation of a kill because when he tried to follow his victim down he was immediately strafed by 'Archie' as he appeared below the cloud level. It was only in retrospect that he realised just how stupidly rash he had been in his bald-headed approach:

> I could see that I had been very foolish to come on in through the rear-gunner's fire, instead of attempting to approach on his blind spot behind and under the tail. I had acted under the terrific excitement of my first chase, not working out anything at all. The gunner may have looked harmless, almost pathetic in the face of my little fighter, but in fact he had been a courageous, level-headed man behind a gun. I had given him a perfect target, coming in straight from above and behind, I was very lucky still to be alive.[44]

> Second Lieutenant Gordon Taylor, 66 Squadron, RFC

Given the rawness of their subordinates, flight commanders like Captain John Andrews had a vital role to play. Andrews had almost unrivalled experience. He had flown the Vickers Fighter with 5 Squadron in 1915, DH2s with 24 Squadron in 1916 and even led the patrol during which Major Lanoe Hawker VC met his unfortunate end under the guns of Richthofen in November 1916. The formal role of a flight commander is neatly summed up here by Flight Lieutenant Robert Compston:

> First and foremost his duty was to bring down, drive down, or prevent from working all enemy aircraft in that sector of the front which his Commanding Officer had ordered him to patrol, and at the same time to preserve the lives of his pilots. How easily written this last sentence, but how difficult of attainment was the preservation of those lives.[45]

> Flight Lieutenant Robert Compston, 8 (Naval) Squadron, RNAS

Each flight commander had to take into consideration the nature of his aircraft in formulating tactics. Each of the scouts available to the British in April 1917 had both strengths and weaknesses and to be successful flight commanders had to maximise the advantages, while at the same time trying to evade situations that exposed any weak points:

> The poor speed, climb and inadequate armament of the Pup developed the formation flying of the Flight to the extent that it was able to withstand attacks by superior numbers of aircraft of better performance, without being scattered. The good manoeuvrability of

the Pup at altitude, due to its low wing loading, was a great asset. The importance of good formation flying and of mutual confidence and knowledge was emphasised by the experience of one Flight, which, owing to early casualties, first to its flight commander, and then to its flying officers, was never able to settle down and had more casualties than the other two Flights combined. The necessity for a rigid formation discipline when the enemy possesses an advantage in material cannot be over emphasised.[46]

Captain John Andrews, 66 Squadron, RFC

Captain Andrews' 'boys' fully appreciated what he was doing for them. Time and time again he saved their lives by means of his teaching, his example and above all his overriding insistence that teamwork was not an optional extra to be abandoned in times of stress; it was all important to the efficiency and safety of the Flight:

Andrews' leadership was wonderful. By his example he had inspired us all not only to make the best of our equipment, but almost to enjoy the challenge of becoming an effective fighting unit in spite of its limitations. The Flight was already fused into a team, in a united squadron. But within that team each of us retained his individuality – in fact circumstances encouraged us to develop this, since we inevitably had our different reactions to war in the air and had to work out for ourselves the best way of dealing with these.[47]

Second Lieutenant Gordon Taylor, 66 Squadron, RFC

When a patrol was finally over, the pilots would fly back to make their landings at the airfield. In the case of 66 Squadron they were based at Vert Galant:

Our squadron was located on the west side of the road, where a small area of grassland sloped gently down to a fold in the ground. It was very small, but anybody in doubt about getting into it could land on the big field across the road and taxi back. The snag was that 43, 56 and 19 Squadrons were all based in this big field, and it soon became known that there was some loss of face involved in having to land on the other side of the road.[48]

Second Lieutenant Gordon Taylor, 66 Squadron, RFC

Some pilots would risk catastrophe to avoid the humiliation before their peers of being seen to choose the easier option of landing in the bigger field. Strangely, Captain John Andrews was one such; perhaps he simply did not want to show any fallibility before his adoring young lads:

> Caught without engine on his final approach to land, and trying with considerable skill to retrieve the situation, he literally landed on top of the canvas hangar. There was a strong wind at the time and this, coupled with the very low landing speed of the Pup, allowed the aeroplane to subside gently into the folds of the hangar. In due course Andrews emerged from his machine and climbed unhurried to the billowing ground. He stood for a moment, taking off his gloves as if to remove any soiling effects of the incident. Then he turned to the somewhat shaken onlookers and raised his eyebrows slightly, 'Ah, Flight Sergeant Ramsay, there you are. You might have this mess cleared up, please'.[49]
>
> Second Lieutenant Gordon Taylor, 66 Squadron, RFC

His superb *sang froid* served to raise his reputation still higher amongst his men.

It was only when they got back that pilots often realised how close a brush with death they had just undergone. The brain-numbing noise of aerial combat, the rattle of the machine guns, the underpinning roar of their engine; all meant that, unless they actually saw the bullet holes stitching as if by magic across the fabric of their machine, if nothing vital was hit, then they would simply fly on in all ignorance:

> A great deal of an aeroplane could be holed without affecting its ability to fly. Wings and fuselage could be, and often were, pierced in fifty places, missing the occupants by inches (blissfully unaware of how close it had come until they returned to base). Then the sailmaker would carefully cover each hole with a square inch of Irish linen frayed at the edges and with a brushful of dope make our aircraft 'serviceable' again within an hour. I have had bullets through my engine, bullets through my tanks, bullets through my windscreen and up through the floor of the cockpit between my knees and out over my shoulder and even, on one occasion, had the control stick knocked out of my hand by a splinter of wood chipped off the floorboards by a chance shot – yet never, such is the mystery of destiny, that one bullet which would have been enough to settle my account.[50]
>
> Lieutenant Cecil Lewis, 56 Squadron, RFC

However, once back on the ground, a pilot was suddenly virtually out of harm's way. The transition between uttermost peril and an almost civilian detachment from the worst of the war was extremely marked and strangely this served as an added cause of nervous tension:

> When were on the ground all the strain was gone. The strain was only there for two and a half hours perhaps twice a day. The rest of your time was your own – once you were out of the air it was quiet. It was safe. You were 15 to 20 miles behind the lines, you had a comfortable bed, you had sheets, even an electric light. You didn't have this strain that could occur if you never could get out of gunfire and the possibility of being hit even when you were asleep. So we lived always in the stretch or sag of nerves. We were either in deadly danger or no danger at all. This conflict between something like being at home, and being in really a quite tight position, had a great effect on us all and produced a certain strain probably because of the change.[51]
>
> Lieutenant Cecil Lewis, 56 Squadron, RFC

Airmen's lives formed an amazing contradiction. Although many were only dimly aware of the ramifications, they all had to deal with it in their own way:

> By virtue of living on the surface, by turning away our faces and refusing to acknowledge death, by casting off that thin veneer of civilisation with the excuse that we were, after all, as it were, hired 'assassins' in the cause of patriotism, we were able to sit down and enjoy a good breakfast. How marvellously can the human mind adapt itself, how easily persuade itself that its course is right, from a nation to the individual; so that all experience, all knowledge, even religious beliefs can be laid on one side until the lust to kill is satisfied, leaving a charred and blackened earth and the sweet sickly smell of blood.[52]
>
> Flight Lieutenant Robert Compston, 8 (Naval) Squadron, RNAS

AS the pilots returned from patrol the work was only just beginning for the dedicated band of mechanics who made up their flight ground crew. The riggers would repair any bullet holes in the doped fabric covering, check all the manifold control and flying wires that operated the control surfaces and make sure that the aircraft was structurally sound and not liable to fall apart under the stresses of combat. The mechanics had the job of checking the engine from top to bottom. All moving parts were cleaned and oiled as appropriate. If problems were discerned in the smooth running of the engine, the fitters would have to work all night in dimly lit hangars, struggling to completely overhaul the engine so it was fit for action next day. It was painstaking and responsible work that had to be carried out to the highest possible standard. Without a doubt, the life of a pilot rested on the diligence and quality of their work. Mistakes that made themselves apparent in the hurly-burly of the dogfight could doom a pilot. The pilots had to place complete trust in their mechanics and largely that trust was well rewarded by the unstinting efforts of these dedicated men:

> One of the essentials in successful single-seater fighting is confidence in the aeroplane, and one might truly say the morale of the Squadron depends largely on this. In No. 8 we had, without exception, the finest lot of men the Royal Naval Air Service could produce, drawn from every branch of trade, many of them ex-naval ratings. They all worked unsparingly to keep our machines in good conditions. I say 'unsparingly' advisedly, for the conditions under which they sometimes had to work were deplorable. Imagine nine inches of snow on the ground, with icy wind blowing through many holes in a canvas Bessoneaux Hangar, the feel of the cold spanners and frozen oil, the making of delicate adjustments with hands numbed to the bone; thus would our men willingly work if any one of us had come back from patrol and complained that his engine appeared a little rough. Truly did these men deserve our praise. With confidence did we trust them implicitly, knowing they realised that – although not spectacular – their work was the foundation of all our hopes and victories, without them we could have achieved nothing.[53]
>
> Flight Lieutenant Robert Compston, 8 (Naval) Squadron, RNAS

No proper working relationship could expect to survive, however, without an occasional tiff in the stressed circumstances of the time. Second Lieutenant Charles Smart found on two days running he had an irritating mechanical problem in winding in the aerial used to transmit artillery observation corrections. Smart was not inclined to accept any nonsense from his flight sergeant on his return:

Had great trouble in winding in my aerial, the reel being very stiff. As I had complained about this yesterday I took the flight sergeant on one side when I came down and asked why it hadn't been put right. He was inclined to be cheeky and said he hadn't had time to attend to it, so I told him what I thought about him. He seemed rather hurt when I explained to him that the greatest risk he ran in this war was death from over-eating, but he quite saw the point when I asked how he would like to fly the machine in half a gale and wind in the aerial with the reel in its present state. I don't think that I shall have any further trouble, but if the reel isn't right tomorrow I will have this chap arrested.[54]

Second Lieutenant Charles Smart, 16 Squadron, RFC

A 'them and us' tinge could grow up to mark the relationship between a pilot and his ground crew, who would often roundly curse him behind his back for the state to which he wittingly or unwittingly reduced the aircraft by the time he returned it to its hangar. But the all too common sight of a group of mechanics waiting beyond any logical hope for their pilot to return from a mission showed that a bond of true affection could cross the social divide, as can be seen in a curious letter sent by Aircraftman Leslie Tupping to Captain Garland shortly after Garland had been posted away from 10 Squadron in March 1917:

Dear Mr Garland,

I trust that you will forgive me for writing to you but I feel that I really must. I am absolutely fed up now and I have been ever since you left the good old 10th Squadron.

I managed to get over to the concert last night thanks to the kindness of Sergeant Major Reeves. It bucked me up somewhat, especially when I saw you again. I would have liked to have a chat with you but my luck was out. Well, may I congratulate you on your well-earned promotion, perhaps I am not quite in order here as there is such a vast gap between an ordinary corporal and a captain, but in civilian life I believe we are not so far apart. I expect by now you are wondering why I am writing to you but it is simply because I feel the loss of you. I think that is only natural after so long a period of time with you, which by the way must be quite nine or ten months. I feel proud to have had your valuable life in my keeping so to speak for so long and I may add that my duty has also been one of my

282

chief pleasures. I hope that you have a reliable mechanic on your new bus and a 'silky' engine. God help the man who lets you down and thus injures you if I meet him! I am very glad in a way that you have left this front as I know what would have happened. Every time I saw you take wing my thoughts were far from happy until you returned, in fact they have always been the same but more so here. I have often wished to open my mind somewhat to you but you were always of a retiring nature with me much to my chagrin. I know you are not so with your brother officers. If you could spare time nothing would please me more than to hear from you. Well Captain Garland, I wish to thank you for all you have done for me as I fully realise that it is through you that I find myself a corporal and I still think that I did not deserve my promotion. You have been a sport and a gentleman to me since I first had the honour to be your mechanic on that glorious bus the BE with that *super*!! engine the 90 hp RAF. Well, I will now act as that engine does when it thinks fit – cut right out – as I am sure that you are bored to death by now. Again, asking you to overlook any statement in this letter which you may think too familiar. Jolly good luck,

I remain,

Your faithful mechanic,

Leslie Tupping [55]

Corporal Leslie Tupping, 10 Squadron, RFC

It is often forgotten that not all of the pilots and observers were commissioned officers. The sergeant pilots and observers had a strange ambivalent status. They would fly together as 'equals' in a two-man team in the aircraft, only to revert to a complete state of subservience when back safely on the ground:

We were all professional soldiers. I always said, 'Sir' and they always said, 'Sergeant' to me. We had our job to do and we did our job. I knew what time I was going up but I didn't even know what job I was on until the observer came out, always an officer – I said, 'Good morning, Sir' and we got on with our job. When we came down he got out and went off to make his report. He did all the reporting – what he'd found, what he'd seen, what he'd photographed. I went to the sergeants' mess or sat down on the aerodrome and took the sun – I had no further contact. I couldn't make friends. I had nothing in common – I didn't have access to the officers' mess, I didn't know what they thought. In the sergeants' mess they were all fitters and riggers – I wasn't in their world any more than they were in mine. Dreadfully lonely.[56]

Sergeant George Eddington, 6 Squadron, RFC

Many of the ground crew were bitter at their lack of status and the extra duties that sometimes came their way while the officers were relaxing in the mess. After all they shared the risks:

As the gun-layer you were the working party of the camp – you weren't thought anything of. We used to kid ourselves we were helping to win the war but when you got down below the Master of Arms used to say, 'Have you cleaned your guns and loaded up the machine with bombs?' We used to say, 'Yes!' 'Right, there's some roads wanting making and latrines to clean!' We were the dirty working party of the camp.[57]

Air Mechanic Charles Burne, 3 (Naval) Squadron, RNAS

In charge of forming a coherent team from all these miscellaneous elements that made up a Flight was the ubiquitous flight commander. There were usually three Flights, each with five or six officers and a further rigger and fitter for each aircraft. His duties were almost as onerous on the ground as in the air:

Each flight commander was responsible to the commanding officer for the condition of his aeroplanes, the fitness of his pilots, and the welfare and efficiency of his men. It will be seen, therefore, that a flight commander had plenty to keep him occupied when he was not in the air. For example, his aeroplanes had to be maintained in good condition, so that he could produce the maximum number at all times for duty. To do this necessitated close cooperation with the chief petty officer in charge of the Flight as to the best time to undertake repairs etc., whether to allow a certain machine to fly a few more hours before overhaul, or whether to work a night shift and have all ready for the morning. The fitness of his officers covers rather a lot. It was definitely a flight commander's job to become well acquainted with each one of his pilots, to make friends of them and to help them in every possible way to pick up the threads of aerial warfare and to carry on perfecting themselves in their piloting (many officers came to France immediately after passing out of flying schools in England). To this end it was

necessary to arrange gunnery practice and formation flying in addition
to the lighter but nevertheless important side of keeping the body
healthy by football matches, for a war pilot should be clear of eye and
have the blood pulsating healthily through his veins if he is to bring all
his energies and faculties to bear when facing the enemy in the air.
Much could be gathered about the methods of aerial fighting by
discussion, and it was part of a flight commander's duty to see that
his pilots gained all possible knowledge which could be imparted on
the ground. An aerial combat discussed afterwards in comfort on the
ground often revealed where a mistake had been made and by such
methods a Flight could be brought to a high pitch of efficiency and
developed into an invaluable fighting unit.[58]

Flight Lieutenant Robert Compston, 8 (Naval) Squadron, RNAS

A squadron normally would be under the command of a major. For
obvious reasons, promotion was often quick in the rapidly expanding RFC
and RNAS and few officers had had much relevant pre-war experience.
Nevertheless, each commanding officer had a large degree of autonomy
and was able to exercise considerable influence over the character of his
squadron:

The fact that the squadron was a good one, and remained so, was
entirely due to the commanding officer, whose methods, although
unorthodox, were original. He himself never flew; he was not a scout
pilot and he realised the fact. He therefore contented himself with
making a few standard rules as to the general conduct of operations,
and left the execution entirely in the hands of his flight commanders.
His rules were: 1) Always stick together. 2) When on escort duty, the
escorted machines are on no account whatsoever to be left until they
have recrossed the lines. 3) No enemy machine is to be claimed unless
there is no shadow of doubt that it has been destroyed. The first rule
enabled us to inflict maximum damage with the minimum loss; the
second gave the squadrons which we had to escort complete confidence
that we would look after them properly; and the last rule prevented the
squadron drifting into that ultra-optimism in the number of their
victories, which was favoured by so many squadrons, and which gave
them on paper a scintillating record. The general result of these rules
was that the squadron obtained an excellent reputation for reliability

in any work allotted to it; the pilots were amply satisfied with this reputation, and were prouder of it than if the squadron had been included in the number of 'ace' squadrons.[59]

Second Lieutenant Robert Foster, 54 Squadron, RFC

The army cooperation corps squadrons had a more complicated tactical role and many of their commanding officers felt almost swamped by the all-enveloping paperwork generated by the complex liaison elements that naturally dominated their work:

I came to the conclusion that an army cooperation squadron commander must be one of the busiest individuals in France. He had to keep in personal touch with Corps Headquarters, Corps Intelligence, Corps Heavy Artillery and the CB office, as well as the numerous artillery and divisional headquarters in the Corps. In addition he had to do his share of flying, administer the unit and look after the numerous branches of which it was composed. There was the training of the new arrivals to ensure and operations to look after. I soon came to the conclusion that twenty-four hours *per diem* were not enough, particularly when the squadron consisted of twenty-four or more aeroplanes. I became convinced that a second-in-command was essential to an army coopera-tion squadron, a conviction which I have never altered. A recording officer and equipment officer can do a lot of work for the commanding officer, but they cannot make those responsible decisions for him, which a senior officer, such as a second-in-command would be, can do. I now realise that I must have been fairly near the end of my tether. The last four months of high pressure, coming on the top of some eighteen months continual flying in France, was too much.[60]

Major Paul Maltby, 16 Squadron, RFC

As one might expect the squadron commanders varied greatly in quality and some neglected elements of their work to the detriment of their squadron. Corps Squadrons existed to serve the artillery and various infantry headquarters. Although it was hard work, even tedious, an effort had to be made to establish exactly what was wanted, and then com-manders had to strain every sinew to deliver it to their ultimate masters:

The squadron was, I think, not nearly making full use of its opportuni-ties. There was an absolute lack of liaison, as far as I could see, with the

infantry and artillery, and a general absence of energy and organisation all round. It was an awful pity, because the flying officers and
observers were the best and keenest lot I ever struck. This however did
not last. The Major went home shortly after I joined for a job at home,
accompanied by his senior flight commander, who was a rotter, and
Major E. J. Tyson came out from home to command No. 5. Tyson was
an ideal squadron commander. He pulled the squadron up before he
had been with it a week. He got into touch with the Corps and established a firm liaison with heavy artillery and counter-battery officer.
He was a mine of energy and absolutely fearless himself. He got an
absolute maximum of work out of the squadron with an absolute
minimum of what is best described as hot air. It should be sufficient to
say that by the end of the first month he was with us, No. 5 Squadron
was recognised as the best squadron in the Wing and continued to turn
out better results, particularly in the photography line, than one would
ever have believed possible when one considers the state it was in.[61]

Lieutenant John Slessor, 5 Squadron, RFC

If a squadron commander wanted his men to remain keen and efficient
then it was as well to ensure that their living conditions were as comfortable
as it was possible to make them. In the freezing weather extra efforts were
required to try and keep warm:

I embarked upon a programme of wangling and wire-pulling to try
and get additional supplies from the local units of the Army Service
Corps and the Royal Engineers. Requests for more supplies through
official channels produced some results, but eventually I had to take the
law into my own hands; and under the cover of darkness we conducted
– much to the delight of those who participated in it – a large-scale raid
upon the nearest dump of the Royal Engineers. From that we were
able to gather enough timber and building materials to improve upon
our meagre accommodation. But even then it was a constant struggle
to get enough fuel to burn in order to keep just barely warm.[62]

Major Sholto Douglas, 43 Squadron, RFC

Some squadron commanders really threw themselves into this side of their
duties and prided themselves on the superior conditions of service enjoyed
by their men:

The Commanding Officer devoted his time to making a life as pleasant as possible for his personnel. The men were the best fed and the best housed in the whole Flying Corps. At regular intervals there were lorries available to take the men to the Corps baths and the Corps cinema. The officers' mess was well known over a wide area for its comfort and hospitality. The mess had its own jazz band, and its own bards who produced topical songs, the more respectable of which have even been published. An artist was also unearthed, who adorned our walls with sketches of considerable merit. The cow, Marjorie, gave us new milk. I have heard unkind words spoken of her because on one occasion she occupied a lorry, which might have contained more warlike stores, but the squadron would have no more thought of leaving the cow behind than the Royal Welch would of omitting to take their goat with them. Beside the cow, we had fifty-four chickens and one cock. This cock was called Robert after a famous actor who was also in the Corps, though the imputation that the latter had fifty-four wives was a base libel. Lastly, but not least, we had four horses. These were obtained from the 16th Lancers in exchange for a tender to take the cavalry officers to Amiens once a week. They gave us a lot of exercise and one of them distinguished himself in the jumping class at the Cavalry Division show. The combination of all these comforts went to keep the personnel at the top of their form, and they certainly helped them to forget about the war when they were not actually engaged in fighting. The squadron commander held to the axiom, 'If we have to fight, let us fight in comfort when we can, for we fight better when we are comfortable!' [63]

Second Lieutenant Robert Foster, 54 Squadron, RFC

One further burden that might descend on any squadron commander at almost any time was an inspection visit from Major-General Hugh Trenchard, usually accompanied by Captain Maurice Baring:

We had been warned of the advent of Trenchard and 'Boom alert' had been ordered in the Second Wing so there was a feeling of considerable unrest all the morning. We got half-hourly telephone messages from the victims of his visits, reporting his progress and the sort of questions he was asking, of which we then proceeded to get up the answers. De Dombasle was in quite a panic. At about 12.30, the great man arrived.

I sat tight in the office, and all pilots and observers stood by their machines. Trenchard went booming round asking impertinent questions. He asked why we hadn't got double Lewis drums. De Dombasle said we had tried to get them but hadn't been able to. Webb-Bowen had refused to send on our indent, saying that Headquarters would not hear of any alteration being made in the armament. But 'Boom' turned on him and said, 'Why haven't they got their double drums yet?' Webb-Bowen murmured something about, 'It takes time …' 'Well it oughtn't to take time!' was the retort. 'Boom' asked several officers when they were last on leave. Unfortunately all that he asked in our squadron had had it very recently, but in 42 Squadron he hit on two who had not been for six months and I hear he was quite rude to Webb-Bowen. On the whole the thing went off quite satisfactorily. 'Boom' addressed the officers afterwards, told them of the importance of the part they were playing and were to play in the Great War.[64]

Lieutenant Thomas Hughes, I Squadron, RFC

It was undoubtedly the case that 'Boom' Trenchard could be a bullying commander when the mood took him. It is thus doubly ironic that this 'great man' should be utterly at the mercy of his assistant, the illustrious Captain Maurice Baring, who had a highly developed sense of humour which he deployed with zest whenever harassed or bullied squadron leaders, appealed for retribution after an unmerited roasting from Trenchard:

He instituted a series of punishments numbered from 'One' to 'Five X', and varying in that order in degree of severity. Punishment Number One consisted in taking away or hiding 'Boom's' pipe. Punishment Number Five consisted in breaking the window of 'Boom's' car so that he had to sit in a draught which he abhorred.[65]

Recording Officer Lieutenant Thomas Marson, 56 Squadron RFC

The redoubtable Baring acted as judge, jury and executioner and even reported back to the squadron that the 'sentence' had been carried out:

The aggrieved party was always rung up and informed, 'The General behaved very badly today. He had Punishment Number one all the way home. He almost cried for his pipe; but I was adamant. I had it in my pocket, but I said I could not think what he had done with it. At dinner he was very penitent, so he was allowed to find his pipe afterwards. I think he is really sorry and will be better now!'[66]

Recording Officer Lieutenant Thomas Marson, 56 Squadron RFC

It may have been a joke, but the combination of the committed energy and direct methods of the overly blunt Trenchard and the sophisticated wit of Baring did a great deal to maintain a good relationship between RFC Headquarters and their hard-pressed squadrons in the field.

THE squadron airfields were scattered behind the British lines. Some were close enough to villages to allow the officers to be billeted in houses and barns. As they were generally out of artillery range the French civilians were often still in occupation and much in evidence:

> Savy, a typical little French village with its church and sugar factory. Its endless *estaminets*, *épiceries* and *brasseries*; with children and fowls wandering about the streets, the damsels dallying lightly with *soldats Anglais* in *estaminet* doors; its incredibly aged *grandpères* and *grandmères* sitting on the doorsteps of rather grimy stone cottages. The Arras–St Pol main road with its trees along the sides and its endless streams of lorries, limbers and staff cars, runs along the southern edge of the village. The only signs of war in the village itself are the aforementioned soldiery with tin hats at picturesque angles, and, nailed up on some cottages and barns, little black boards bearing the legend, 'Billet: Officers 4, Other Ranks 80'.[67]
>
> Lieutenant John Sessor, 5 Squadron, RFC

More often, the airfields simply had wooden huts built alongside them to provide them with accommodation. As usual the men had a crowded communal existence while the officers had both more space and a modicum of privacy:

> I had a corner in the Nissen hut which housed the pilots of A Flight, and to this I gave some individuality by building a low partition virtually fencing me off in a small apartment of my own. This drew some acid comments from the other members of the Flight, as if I was being stand-offish. But it wasn't really that. I just liked to have my own quarters, and to keep on the ground something of the isolation I felt in the air.[68]
>
> Second Lieutenant Gordon Taylor, 66 Squadron, RFC

Many felt the same way. They tried to turn the few square feet they were allowed into a 'home' that reflected their personalities and interests:

> My little den is about four or five yards long and about three across at the bottom, and I have got the sunny side of the hut looking out on the aerodrome, with a quaint little suburban garden in front consisting of a circular bed with some bedraggled daisies and violets in and two outer beds with nothing in them at all except Mother Earth and some choice weeds. The man next door did it before I came in – appalling effort! I have got all my photos up round the room and a row of books on an excellent fold-up wood and wicker table I have bought in the town where I first landed in France.[69]
>
> Second Lieutenant Arthur Rhys Davids, 56 Squadron, RFC

Interests varied: some, like Rhys Davids, gathered family photos and improving books, in an echo of the university study which he would have occupied but for the advent of the war. Others, like Taylor, had more prosaic requirements:

> To equip our quarters for really comfortable living and with some measure of individuality, we sometimes went to Amiens on shopping expeditions, and brought such things as mats, chairs, small tables, pictures and bedside lamps. These small articles helped to make a temporary home of the bare huts. To them we added in many cases glamorous pictures of the current Kirchner girls and a well-chosen selection of illustrations from *La Vie Parisienne*.[70]
>
> Second Lieutenant Gordon Taylor, 66 Squadron, RFC

More seniority inevitably meant more space and Captain Bernard Rice made a 'home sweet home' in a shared hut, which he called Quirk Cottage in affectionate reference to the contemporary nickname for the BE2s:

> I am writing this on the veranda which we have fixed up outside the Cottage. Robby and I are fearfully busy fixing up the cottage. We have glass in the two windows. We've painted the walls green. Tacked white fabric over the ceiling. Erected a veranda about 12 feet square outside, with green canvas top and scalloped edging. It has a trench-board floor, a wooden rail all round with wire netting down to the ground and flower beds all round.[71]
>
> Captain Bernard Rice, 8 Squadron, RFC

Most were conscious of their relative good fortune compared to the infantry and artillery units living up to their knees in mud and blood just a few miles in front of them:

> I suppose it is one of the most deep rooted instincts of man to grumble, so we all have to do our share of it, but as a matter of fact I don't think anyone could wish for a more pleasant and peaceful life than we get. We are quartered right in the country, in an orchard. We lie around in the sun all day long, except for the few hours we are working. We have nothing to do or worry about, get the best of food and billets and if it wasn't for the *Daily Mail* which we get every morning, we would hardly know 'there was a war on'. And yet somehow the quiet freshness of Warwickshire seems far more fascinating than ever it did before, and the thought of perfectly white flannels and a perfectly flat cricket ground seem to be the things only to be found in heaven. I think I'm going to live in white flannels when I get home – does anyone play tennis this year – I do hope so! Altho' I'm afraid I shan't be able to put up any sort of performance against the Fillongley Knuts. I could probably go to sleep in a shorter space of time than most, but that is the only achievement I can claim any competence in at present.[72]

> Flight Sub-Lieutenant Bernard Ellis, I (Naval) Squadron, RNAS

The incredible stress of flying over the lines brought with it physical and mental exhaustion and symptomatically the desire to spend as much time as possible in bed. As both corps and scout pilots were usually woken at dawn, if not before, they naturally looked forward to the kind of bad weather that made flying impossible. This would give them absolute *carte blanche* to sleep without any qualms over dereliction of duty. They would not have been human had they not rejoiced as storm clouds raged above them:

> The greatest joy I know is to be wakened after an all-too-short sleep by, 'It's six o'clock, Sir, but I don't think there'll be any flying'. When a pilot starts his day thus, he manages to murmur, 'Is Captain Dash up?' The batman goes to ascertain and returns with, 'No, Sir, the patrol's a washout'. A still-tired head falls back on to a pillow and a pleased airman mutters something about, '9.30' and 'waking'.[73]

> Lieutenant Stanton Waltho, RFC

Three hours later they would begin to stir from their slumbers. Pilots had few real duties when flying was impossible:

> Everyone is late for breakfast and arrives in some futurist garb which consists usually of brilliant pyjamas, bright scarf, flying boots and a grease-ruined tunic. Most spend the morning sitting over the Mess fire. One or two discharge their duties as regards correspondence, and the rest, from their seats, remark at intervals, 'I must write some letters too'. Perhaps a card game starts or two, one or two are sufficiently energetic to complete their toilet and walk over to see their machines. The squadron gun expert, who is usually also the best fighting pilot, drags the gunnery officer over to the sheds to explain some new device he wishes to be fitted.[74]
>
> Lieutenant Stanton Waltho, RFC

One duty that remained was censoring the letters written by the other ranks. This could be a mundane and dreary task – but occasionally some gentle amusement was to be found in the complex love lives of their men:

> Thank God! Do you know what's happened? Gladys is engaged!! Hurrah! That is one less letter to censor. One sportsman of a fitter in my Flight is conducting a correspondence with no less than six 'flappers', and I see today, 'Well Flo, I am pleased to hear Gladys is fixed up with Tom Fowler'. Exit Miss Gladys from the gentlemen's list![75]
>
> Captain Bernard Rice, 8 Squadron, RFC

When free, they would normally gather together in the officers' mess. These bore little resemblance to the formal messes which typified the British Army in peacetime. The war brought a relaxation throughout the army and in the RFC there were very few senior officers to bring any sense of seriousness to the mess. Even the squadron commanding officers were only majors:

> Old simple, whitewashed rooms with terrible old furniture and the food good, but rough. Lamps hanging on strings from the ceiling, thick with dead flies and a general rudimentary primitive sort of life. Sometimes an old upright piano in the Mess with keys so yellow they looked as if the keyboard had been smoking for about fifty years! And we had one chap who played the piano and he'd sit down in the evenings and there were two or three notes missing, it was out of tune and it was a terrible piano

– but it didn't matter. He'd play the tunes of the time, the revues of the time, the things we knew by heart, we used to sing in chorus. Occasionally a bit of Chopin or something like that on the nights when we felt that that sort of thing was appropriate. All very easy and go as you please.[76]

Lieutenant Cecil Lewis, 56 Squadron, RFC

Naturally, every squadron tried to secure the use of a competent piano player to help while the evenings away. This was not always possible and the consequences could be painful to the musical ear. Lieutenant Oliver Stewart of 54 Squadron, and a former student of the Royal College of Music, remembered one pianist who was seemingly capable of inducing tinnitus without electrical amplification:

He was of immense size and he took all the front of the piano out, 'So as not to hinder the notes in coming out!' he explained. The result was that, when he was performing, one could watch all the hammers working, and a prodigious and awe-inspiring sight it was. Strictly speaking, I suppose, it was not so much piano playing as furniture removing. Incredible numbers of hammers worked at the same time, the strings became blurred with their frantic vibrations while this remarkable artist rocked on his seat and emitted a loud buzzing sound. This I will say, that although I have listened with interest to pianists from Paderewski and Pachmann to Schnabel and Cortot, not one of them – no, not one – has ever succeeded in producing the net volume of sound that this officer used to produce.[77]

Lieutenant Oliver Stewart, 54 Squadron, RFC

The atmosphere prevalent in the officers' mess would be familiar to those accustomed to the time-honoured habits of British men gathered together with nothing in particular to do:

The old hands of the RFC sit around over coffee and discuss old members in familiar terms – referring to generals by pet names and talking of machines of which the newer members of the squadron have never heard. A card game or two commences, the Canadian element usually forming a 'poker school'. We ground officers, having by length of years and experience, learnt the folly of the game, start bridge. Conversations round a Flying Corps Mess fire are really wonderful. Almost invariably these conversations start by the narration

of an incident of the day, which is 'beaten' by several others. A pilot
will say, 'Well, "A" rolled at 150 feet today and came out so near the
trees he almost brushed them with his undercarriage!' 'Why "B" will
roll right across an aerodrome at 100 feet!' another will declare, 'I've
seen him roll between two trees and finish lower than the top of them!'
At this, the first narrator becomes annoyed and, with a perfectly serious
face, tells of 'C' who 'Took off in a roll!!!' With a series of groans the
discussion closes.[78]

Lieutenant Stanton Waltho, RFC

Undoubtedly, some of the more sensitive souls such as Rhys Davids found
the relentless 'old chap' atmosphere a little disheartening:

There are only one or two people in the squadron I have the faintest
hope of making a real pal of, and it is next to impossible that I can do
even that. They are all just the 'ordinary good fellows' with nothing
remarkable about them; none of them have any real intellectual
ambitions.[79]

Second Lieutenant Arthur Rhys Davids, 56 Squadron, RFC

Mess food varied wildly depending on the occasion and the talents of
the cook. Living far behind the lines and in the country, there were opportunities to vary the diet from official rations:

We had an excellent dinner. Starting with a thick soup we went on to
tinned salmon hot with yellow sauce, followed by hot mutton, mashed
potatoes and cabbage. Lime juice and whisky helped wash down the
'dog' biscuit (bread once a week). A tinned fruit sweet followed by
dessert of nuts and oranges finished a record repast. I doubt if a
restaurant could do one better.[80]

Captain Bernard Rice, 8 Squadron, RFC

The officers' mess offered more than mere conversation and food – crucially
it also afforded easy access to alcohol:

The centre of the squadron seemed to be in the bar. When you think of
the tensions they lived through day to day – they would come in in the
evening and ask about their best friend, 'Where's old George?' 'Oh, he
bought it this afternoon!' 'Oh, heavens!' The gloom would come, the
morale would die and the reaction was immediate, 'Well, come on,

chaps, what are you going to have?' That was the sort of spirit that kept you going and although people are against alcohol I think that it played a magnificent part in keeping up morale.[81]

Lieutenant Frederick Powell, 40 Squadron, RFC

However, the prevailing idea that pilots spent their time getting leglessly drunk night after night is not true of most of the squadrons. They did drink, on occasion heavily, but in this they were little different from most gatherings of young men released for a few hours from almost unendurable pressure:

It was No. 32 RFC who at one of our parties at Bertangles taught us the game of 'Cardinal Puff'. When we played this game everyone was expected to take part in turn. The first in the queue had his glass filled up and raising it once said, 'Here's to Cardinal Puff'. He then carried out a series of movements with his hands, each movement being done once only. Again he raised his glass, but this time twice saying, 'Here's to Cardinal Puff Puff'. The hand movements were then repeated each time twice. Finally the glass was raised three times saying, 'Here's to Cardinal Puff Puff Puff', and after repeating the former movements three times he drank the contents of the glass. More often than not a mistake would be made in carrying out the correct procedure and in that case the contents of the glass had to be drunk by the offender, the glass was refilled and he had to start all over again. Very few people got through the ordeal successfully and the game usually broke up and turned into a roughhouse after only a few had had a turn.[82]

Flight Sub-Lieutenant Leonard Rochford, 3 (Naval) Squadron, RNAS

When all was said and done most of the officers were just young men letting off steam. With an average age in the 19–23 years bracket, there was very little harm in most of their pranks. There was much of the public school in the overall atmosphere:

Thank goodness for Tom Purdey who, every night, used to keep us cheerful by songs at the piano and alternatively, when we got bored with that, allowed us to hold him by his feet and shake him upside down in his kilt! It may sound childish these years past, but it was only such stupid and light-hearted behaviour as this that kept us going.[83]

Lieutenant Harold Balfour, 43 Squadron, RFC

The traditional British Army officers' mess games were popular. They were basically excuses for nothing more than a bit of 'rough and tumble'. One of the most dangerous was called 'Hi-cockalarum':

> The game started with the tossing of a coin to decide who should go 'down' first. Each side probably numbered between ten and fifteen. The side to go 'down' selects a position at one end of the room, preferably with a sofa or soft chair to be the head post. When all are down in the shape of a rugger scrum the captain, seeing that his scrum is well knit together, informs the opposing side that they may start. The object of the game is for the 'up' side to mount the backs of those 'down', without rolling off or touching the ground in any way, whilst the aim for those 'down' is to be so strong that no one succumbs under the weight or sinks to the floor thereby losing the round. There is quite a lot to the game. The captain of the 'up' side must make a careful reconnaissance of the enemy's dispositions, pick out the weakest point and direct his heavy stuff on to that point. This usually means sixteen stone hurling itself across the room at top speed, leaping as hard into the air as possible, and descending with no mean velocity on the back of some herring gutted young man of ten stone. On the other hand you might have a real enemy on whom you decided to pay off a score. This was a wonderful opportunity![84]
>
> Captain Eric Routh, 16 Squadron, RFC

The underdogs would give way and collapse to the ground in a scramble of crushed and badly bruised bodies. Compared to the mayhem caused by mess games a spot of boxing was a relative relief, enjoyed by Second Lieutenant de Burgh and Second Lieutenant Edward Mannock:

> Mannock was very keen on boxing, and as I had done a good deal, we often used to blow off steam by having a set to in the Mess. In fact, it used to be a stock event, if the evening was livening up, for Mannock and me to have a round or two – and he nearly always said, 'Let's hit out', and we used to have a good slog at one another. I think, on the whole, that I used to get more than I gave, as he had the height of me, and a slightly longer reach; but I had him at footwork.[85]
>
> Second Lieutenant de Burgh, 40 Squadron, RFC

Such bouts would be the centrepiece of mess celebrations that could be triggered by a variety of circumstances. Promotions, departures, successful missions, birthdays – almost anything would do if they were 'in the mood' to let loose:

> Another 'rag' in the mess. Boxed with de Burgh. Crocked my knee and arm. Old McKechnie's farewell night as he's proceeding home tomorrow morning. Great doings. Returned to bed at 2 a.m. and to be called at 5.30. Went to St Omer by side-car at 6 p.m. to fetch a new machine, feeling like a wet rag. Mouth felt like the bottom of a parrot cage. [86]
>
> Second Lieutenant Edward Mannock, 60 Squadron RFC

Mess celebrations would often feature the rowdy bawling of popular songs, usually bastardised by parody and rendered either obscene or topical to the concerns of the day. One rather clever parody of Edward Lear's *Jabberwocky*, written by Captain William Bond, was popular in the 40 Squadron mess. It was prompted by the success of a BE2c in shooting down an Albatros:

> 'Twas brillig and the Slithy Quirk
> Did drone and burble in the blue,
> All floppy were his wing controls
> (And his observer too).

Lewis Carroll

> 'Beware the wicked Albatros',
> The 'OC quirks' had told him flat;
> 'Beware the Hun-Hun bird and shun
> The frumious Halberstadt'.

> But while through uffish bumps he ploughed,
> The Albatros, with tail on high,
> Came diving out the tulgey cloud
> And let his bullets fly.

> One, two; one, two, and through and through,
> The Lewis gun went tick-a-tack,
> The Hun was floored, the Quirk had scored,
> And came galumpling back.

> 'Oh hast thou slain the Albatros?
> Split one, with me, my beamish boy,
> Our 'RAF'-ish scout has found them out',
> The CO wept for joy. [87]
>
> Captain William Bond, 40 Squadron RFC

Lieutenant Edward Mannock obviously must have appreciated this 'nonsense' because a copy of Bond's parody remains attached to his diary deep in the bowels of the RAF Museum to this very day.

Sometimes the officers' mess would organise special trips or jaunts as the whim took them. These affairs could be fairly lively but give a picture of the essential youth and innocence of the pilots:

> The squadron did a thrilling exploit last night. It went bathing at
> midnight. The Padre Keymer of course, was the leader. Some miles
> away there is a most topping valley occupied by a chateau and its
> grounds. A river runs through it and about a week ago the Command-
> ing Officer and Keymer got permission from the people at the chateau
> to dam the stream – or, as Keymer prefers to put it, 'To erect an artifi-
> cial barrier across the stream in order to form a swimming pool'. The
> Squadron did the work and it was finished yesterday. After dinner the
> CO suggested that we should all go and bathe in the pool. We had a
> tender and fifteen of us went – some of us armed with pocket lamps
> and all attired in pyjamas, towels and flying coats. The water was
> beautifully deep and clean; and it was eerie to see the naked bodies
> scrambling about the barrier of tree trunks amongst the shadows
> thrown by the huge monsters on the bank. Padre Keymer was the
> noisiest of the crowd. He did high dives into the black pool, shouting
> and splashing like a water baby. Today four of the fellows have
> developed colds, and even Keymer is a little off colour. I tell him that
> midnight revels with water nymphs do not suit him![88]
>
> Captain William Bond, 40 Squadron, RFC

The mess was the natural habitat of the eccentric officer. One such was Major Robert Lorraine who commanded 40 Squadron in early 1917. Lorraine had been a reasonably well-known actor on the London stage and had retained many of the affectations of his former incarnation to the unconcealed delight of his young officers, especially Lieutenant Frederick Powell:

> Lorraine had just been promoted major. But of course being an actor, the
> major on the stage always had an eyeglass, and who should acquire an
> eyeglass but of course Robert Lorraine. When I went on leave in London
> I bought from Harrods a whole box of plain glass eyeglasses with broad
> black ribbons. When I returned to the squadron I issued the ribbons and

eyeglasses to the officers. That night at dinner, everybody wore an eyeglass. I must say that Lorraine was quite good – he took it in good part, he didn't comment at all. He didn't even try to say that he had a defective eye![89]

Lieutenant Frederick Powell, 40 Squadron, RFC

Lorraine was an energetic commanding officer who tried to entertain and distract his young officers. Drawing on his own acting experiences he decided to 'put on a show'. This was to be no ordinary concert party affair but a full-blown theatrical production:

Lorraine found a Red Cross hut, which he saw and noted that no one seemed to own it. All the officers went off in their cars, we dismantled the hut and brought it back to our aerodrome and built it again. We then had a wonderful theatre, it had a stage and would hold about 250 and we used to do plays. We acted two unpublished plays by Bernard Shaw and, to our intense delight, who should arrive to stay with us for a week but Bernard Shaw himself. Lorraine at dinner excused himself. He said, 'We're doing a dress rehearsal for the men, *The Inca of Perusalem*, one of your plays, Shaw!' He said, 'Powell, will you bring Shaw down as soon as he's finished his meal?' So I took Bernard Shaw down to the theatre and sat on a seat just behind him. I was worried to see that all the way through this play he roared with laughter. He roared so much he actually cried and brought out a handkerchief to wipe his eyes. In those days he had a ginger beard and I remember this beard wobbling up and down. It struck me at the time that it was extremely bad form for a playwright to laugh until he cried at his own comedy. When it was finished, I leant forward and said, 'I am so glad, Sir, that you appreciate our poor efforts at your play'. He turned round, still wiping his eyes and he said, 'Do you know, if I had thought it was going to be anything like that, I wouldn't have written it!'[90]

Lieutenant Frederick Powell, 40 Squadron, RFC

Another notable RFC eccentric was the irrepressible Major Hubert Harvey-Kelly, who had been killed on 29 April 1917. Harvey-Kelly had been the first RFC pilot to land in France in August 1914, after which he was photographed nonchalantly smoking in a potentially lethal fashion next to his aircraft and an equally combustible haystack with the remarkable insouciance that clearly marked him out from his contemporaries:

He was a delightful personality; medium height, with sleek fair hair, which he wore brushed back and parted in the middle, and sleepy blue eyes. His manner and speech were unperturbed and imperturbable, and he had an inexhaustible fund of humour. He was a brave and skilled pilot, who gave one the impression that the air with its spaciousness was his rightful element. When in France he always took up with him in his machine a small bar of copper and a large potato. These, he said, in the event of his having a forced landing in enemy territory, would ensure him a great reception; in fact he would be the most popular person in Germany.[91]

Recording Officer Lieutenant Thomas Marson, 56 Squadron, RFC

He had earlier been briefly posted to 56 Squadron before he was sent out to France to take command of 19 Squadron. Before he left them, he bequeathed one outstanding mess jape that surely never faded from the minds of any of those lucky enough to be present:

Harvey-Kelly had seen the first tanks in action, and was very enthusiastic about their performances. On one occasion in the Mess, some Doubting Thomas expressed the opinion that they would not be much use against entrenched infantry as soon as their novelty had worn off. This proved too much for Harvey-Kelly, who proceeded to arrange a demonstration to prove his point of view. Protected with the coal-hod – a large iron one – he enacted the part of the tank, while the rest, armed with coal, were the infantry. The tank attacked from the end of the Mess and made excellent progress until it came into contact with the big stove, which, surmounted by a long length of piping, stood well out into the room. The tank, true to tradition, and despite a heavy and accurate fire of coals, boldly tackled the stove, which overturned, and the piping came down and scattered the infantry in all directions. There was no doubt the tank gained a great tactical and moral victory – though it and the infantry had together to make good the damage next day.[92]

Recording Officer Lieutenant Thomas Marson, 56 Squadron, RFC

The nearest big town to most of the airfields was Amiens. It slowly attained the status of a great metropolis in their minds, promising easy access to all the simple pleasures that life could offer a young lad in his prime. Their usual transport was the Crossley light tender:

The magic words, 'There's a tender into Amiens tonight!' were enough
to rouse an entire Mess to enthusiasm and to cause a panic for the list
of the ten officers officially allowed to travel by it. The last patrol
over-revving their engines unmercifully in order to get back in time
to change; of the comparative quiet on the way and the carefully
arranged plans for the evening – all foredoomed to failure. The
splitting up into pairs for shopping and the buying of absurd bargains
and novelties. The call in Charley's Bar or the Savoy for 'the odd one'
before we meet the others. Then the gathering for dinner and the con-
sumption of countless oysters – until dinner became unnecessary and,
indeed, undesirable.[93]

. Lieutenant Stanton Waltho, RFC

Food, wine, women and song: what more could a young man want?
Naturally, the order of events depended on their personal preferences and
the state of their finances:

We'd find some sort of an *estaminet* or restaurant, probably a girl or two
around the place. We'd begin to have a drink or two and start singing
songs and enjoying ourselves. Whooping it up to, say, midnight and
then get into the tender and come back to the airfield again.[94]

Lieutenant Cecil Lewis, 56 Squadron, RFC

Finally, on the journey home the copious quantities of alcohol cheerily
imbibed took its inevitable toll on the valiant warriors:

The fight for the front seats, the gathering of stragglers, the 'All-aboard!'
and the start for home. On the way some are morbidly silent, while
others are uproariously noisy. Those inclined for ordered conversation
tell how they, 'Met 'so-and-so' tonight – not seen him since the Central
Flying School – with No. 1 on Nieuports up North'. Others sing,
'Outside the hangar door' and similar RFC ditties; while others preserve
a heavy silence and brood on the evils of the world. The car pulls up
with a jar and its occupants trickle out. The silent ones walk deliberately
to their huts, the singers enter the mess and find one or two who are not
on the early show, sitting round the fire smoking and chatting.[95]

Lieutenant Stanton Waltho, RFC

For all these tales of jollity and drunkenness, this aspect of the pilots'
lives was usually kept firmly in check. Many of the myths of outright excess

originate with the highly publicised 'wild colonial boys' of 85 Squadron who ran riot for a brief period in 1918. In most RFC messes drinking was mostly done in moderation with the exception of the wilder guest nights and the occasional trip to Amiens. After all, the dawn patrol meant just that; a bad hangover could be a life-threatening complaint. This then was the dichotomy that underlay the men's daily lives: and with it the need to adjust from seeming normality to extremes of violent terror in a matter of minutes:

> Every day I am more staggered by this amazing life. It is the contrasts in it, the abrupt changes that make it so astounding. Before lunch I was sitting in a cosy Mess writing to my wife. At tea-time I was 15 miles over the lines, flying over Hunland, aiming my gun, and shooting to kill. And then, later, changed into clean clothes, I dined in comfort, unsurpassed even in England just now.[96]
>
> Captain William Bond, 40 Squadron, RFC

England was the fulcrum of most pilots' dreams. Their lives had shrunk in perspective so that a home posting seemed an event far beyond their horizons. Yet they could hope and dream of leave. A chance to live again without the imminent threat of death hanging over them. A chance to explore the new parameters of life they had tasted in France. But, strangely, news of long awaited leave brought its own additional pressures. As soon as pilots knew they were going home they began 'sweating on leave'. Every time they took off they were haunted by the idea that some disaster in the air might prevent them from taking their precious leave:

> Lieutenant Burlton with his leave warrant in his pocket was attacked by three Huns at the same time. He did a nose dive, the Huns diving behind him. They made a hole six inches in diameter in his tail plane and put six bullets through the undercarriage. He got home without a scratch.[97]
>
> Second Lieutenant W. J. Lidsey, 16 Squadron, RFC

As the longed for day approached, the tension mounted, as it did for 25 Squadron's Sergeant Harold Taylor:

> From the 1st of April onward I was in the unhappy position of knowing that my leave to England might be granted any day. As I survived every day and my leave got nearer, my life became tense –

would I survive to have this leave or would I be wounded, taken prisoner or be killed before that happy day arrived? But that wonderful day did arrive for me and Lieutenant B. King who at this time was my pilot. On April 20th, we had use of a tender to drive us to Boulogne where we shipped for Folkestone and then train to Victoria. We agreed to meet at Victoria on the 30th April on our return. When once more I arrived home, I could not help thinking that only a miracle had got me there. My parents, brother and sister were delighted to see me and there is no doubt that I had a wonderful homecoming.[98]

Sergeant Harold Taylor, 25 Squadron, RFC

For many officers, London was the magnet and focus of their leave. It offered nightlife in all its forms, a positive whirlpool of madcap variety that was designed to tempt the most jaded of palettes. Yet, by and large, in this as in so much else, they were young men with much to learn. There were certainly plenty of people willing to teach them:

Of the famous hotels, clubs and restaurants popular among officers on leave, many are still going strong – the Piccadilly, Murrays Club, the Berkeley, the Savoy, the Ritz, Browns, Claridges – others have fallen by the wayside – the Cecil, Oddininos, Ciros, the Langham, the Carlton, Romanos, the Monica. I might also mention that great monument to Venus – the Empire – the nearest approach to a Paris theatre tarts' promenade – all very correct and proper in those days. Generally speaking each distinct branch of the services had their favourite spots in the West End when on leave. The Royal Flying Corps used the Piccadilly as 'home from home'. I cannot speak for the others, but I think that each service remained very tribal. For instance it will be noted how I met the same colleagues at certain places almost every occasion I happened to be there. There were certain tramlines one stuck to when on short leave in London. The Leicester Lounge was another world famous rendezvous where boy met girl. In spite of such places, the streets swarmed with tarts who brazenly accosted officers in the West End in broad daylight.[99]

Lieutenant Ewart Garland, 10 Squadron, RFC

For sergeant pilots with their lower pay, lack of private means and restricted social status there was far less opportunity to 'run off the rails'. For them, for the rare married officers, and for the quieter sort of men, leave meant the longed for return to the arms of their cherished families:

> The war was hardly mentioned at home and I certainly did not speak of the mortal dangers that I was in every time I took to the air. All the family appeared to know what my life had been like out in France and I think they realised maybe I would be happier if the war was not mentioned.[100]
>
> Sergeant Harold Taylor, 25 Squadron, RFC

Perversely, the very tranquillity of home life was spoiled for Taylor by the realisation that, for him, reality lay over the English Channel. Leave was the dream; the Western Front the grim awakening that lay just a few days ahead:

> I had been home two days and then I began to doubt whether this leave was really so wonderful. In a few days I would have to return to France. I would have to say farewell to my parents, brother, sister and my friends – and I knew that this was going to be very hard. I knew all the terrible dangers ahead of me. When the day arrived for me to return to France I bid farewell to my parents at home, my sister came to see me off at Victoria and whilst bidding these farewells it was most difficult to restrain the tears. They were very emotional moments, unless I was exceptionally lucky this would be the last time that I would see them, as I was fully aware of what could be my fate.[101]
>
> Sergeant Harold Taylor, 25 Squadron, RFC

THE pilots and observers of the RFC were a brave crowd, but there is no doubt that the strain told on them as hour by hour, day by day, week by week and month after month they took off and flew their dangerous missions over and behind the German lines:

> I know of few things more terrifying than to be alone in a BE with an observer, and to meet seven or eight enemy scouts. One feels so utterly hopeless, as one has no field of fire – and anyway only one gun and a maximum speed of 65 mph; whereas your Albatros has two guns and a speed of 130 mph.[102]
>
> Lieutenant John Slessor, 5 Squadron, RFC

They were not stupid, they could work out the odds of survival for themselves. One casualty a day might not seem much to an infantry battalion of approximately 600 men; but for a squadron of around eighteen to twenty-four aircraft it was nothing more than a looming death sentence:

> We had some thirty-two officers in our squadron, pilots and officers. During February, March and April we suffered heavy casualties and in one of those months we had thirty-five casualties out of our establishment of thirty-two officers.[103]
>
> Lieutenant Harold Balfour, 43 Squadron, RFC

Close escapes from such seemingly hopeless circumstances could actually make things worse. Men were reduced to near gibbering wrecks as they contemplated the terrifyingly fine line that separated life and death:

> Went over Hun lines and got attacked by two Hun machines – Albatros destroyers. I stalled machines often but was into a spin. Observer got eleven shots into him. Aileron control got half shot away. Dived from 9,000 feet and levelled out at 500 feet on our side. My pipe in pocket shot through; a sleeve torn by three bullets. My observer died overnight. My nerves in a terrible state.[104]
>
> Second Lieutenant Gerald Jamieson, 16 Squadron, RFC

Flyers could see the luck of others run out in a rattle of machine-gun fire and the smoking trail of a burning aircraft, and each death brought their own demise statistically closer:

> I sometimes think that courage is a material, and expendable, thing of which men are given so much. At first, they use it splendidly, without thought. Then, as they sense the supply getting low, with greater and greater care, growing more and more nervous in the process. For only a fool could come back day after day with the evidence of enemy target practice all over his machine and not be affected by it.[105]
>
> Lieutenant Cecil Lewis, 56 Squadron, RFC

For a while they endured, often evading the realities that faced them by a variety of mental stratagems. Many feared being exposed as a coward to their comrades almost as much as they feared the German Albatros. Lieutenant Balfour had to learn to become detached to be able to keep going:

I first realised the full terror of aerial combat, but, at the same time, learnt in some way to cultivate a detachment of mind which enabled one, not to overcome fear but to separate oneself from it. Going into a fight, after some mental practice of attaining this state of mind, was something like going into a cold bath; but once in the fight one became impersonal: some secondary person did the right thing at the right moment; this secondary being took the initiative and would do some brave act or some clever manoeuvre; it was not oneself, for one's own real mind could watch this secondary being in operation. The trying and exhausting time was when at the end of the fight, one's personality displaced once more this secondary being and took charge of one's body; then would be realised the full terror, then would hands and feet shake and mouth go dry with fear and the full reaction set in. This secondary being detachment was the only means that one kept going. I have often wondered if any of my fellow pilots felt the same, but in those days such thoughts were too sacred and too intimate to bring to light. Each of us had such secrets closely guarded and treasured.[106]

Lieutenant Harold Balfour, 43 Squadron, RFC

The British pilots' attitude to their enemies was ambivalent. Many saw the German aircraft as the enemy and spared little thought for the human being tucked away inside:

As far as my squadron was concerned, our fighting was largely impersonal in respect of the individuality of our opponents, and this feeling was one that the majority of the other squadrons shared. Such admiration as we might have felt was for the technical skill displayed by some of their pilots. Of hatred there was none, of the chivalry of the air which is so fatuously and ignorantly written about, neither side could afford to indulge in it if it involved any risks, such as crossing the lines to drop messages, if this were not necessary in the ordinary course of daily duty. Our chief feeling towards the enemy Flying Corps was one of envy. Envy that our enemy could be equipped with better aeroplanes than those which we were forced to fly for the same corresponding duties. As to reflections on war guilt, who started the war and the objectives of war, these did not concern us outwardly or actively in any way. Rather was the point of view that we had a job of work, and if we did not fulfil what was required of the unit we should, in comparison to our other squadrons lose standing in their eyes and our own eyes. It was a case of collective self-respect. We, like the whole of the Expeditionary Force, were gathered up into the great machine of war and formed one cog of the vast mechanism. It was not for us to think as to the whys and wherefores, but only not to look very much further than the end of our noses whilst any daily task yet remained unfulfilled.[107]

Lieutenant Harold Balfour, 43 Squadron, RFC

For the scout pilots, such as Lieutenant Cecil Lewis, it was a particularly lonely ordeal. Once in the air they had no one to talk to and no communication was possible in the midst of desperate fighting:

People were being killed every day: my best friend was there one evening and he wasn't there next day at lunch. This was going on all the time. People reacted to that. You couldn't live that sort of a life and be entirely indifferent. You may have been cold-blooded in the air because you had to fight as if there was nothing but you and your guns. You had nobody at your side. Nobody who was cheering with you, nobody to look after if you were hit. You fought alone and died alone.[108]

Lieutenant Cecil Lewis, 56 Squadron, RFC

Some found that they struggled with nerves right from the start of their aerial career. Despite his outward confidence and generally brash behaviour, Edward Mannock was a highly strung individual who was badly afflicted by deep-seated fears that he could not always control:

Old Mackenzie goes away on leave today. Fourteen days. He is in need of it. If ever a lad was cracking up, Mac is. I wonder if ever I shall get like that? And what my friends will think of me if I do? Old 'Paddy' the 'devil may care' with nerves. I feel nervous about it already.[109]

Second Lieutenant Edward Mannock, 40 Squadron, RFC

Any degree of intelligence, sensitivity or vivid imagination, such as Mannock possessed, were by no means advantages in maintaining one's nerve in the face of the multifarious horrors of aerial fighting:

Business out here still very chock-full of excitement. I have an idea that my nerves won't stand very much of it. It's beyond a joke now. Plenty of scrapping and lots of 'Archie', although I am feeling perfectly fit and well. Really I haven't much to say under the circumstances. I always feel tired and sleepy, and I can lie down and sleep anywhere or at any time.[110]

Second Lieutenant Edward Mannock, 40 Squadron, RFC

Men under stress, and doubtless worried about their own performance, can be very cruel to those they think are not living up to the prevailing code of behaviour. Rumours would soon gain a currency whether justified or not:

Mannock was not actually called 'yellow', but many secret murmurings of an unsavoury nature reached my ears. I was told that he had been in the squadron two months, and that he had shot down one single Hun out of control, and that he showed signs of being over-careful during engagements. He was further accused of being continually in the air practising aerial gunnery, as a pretence of keenness. In other words, the innuendo was that he was suffering from 'cold feet'.[111]

Captain George Lloyd, 40 Squadron, RFC

Lloyd confronted Mannock, who was disarmingly frank about his fears, but insisted that he saw air fighting as a science demanding tactical study and relentless practice. It was not long before he did indeed prove his skill and demonstrate his ability to overcome the fears that held him back. A few sad cases took to drink, not socially to release their tensions, but more in an effort to bury their fears beneath a veritable Niagara of alcohol. Many more resorted to the primitive nostrums of superstition in an effort to evade their demons:

The variety of forms of 'ju-ju' believed in, and practised, were legion. There were those who would not drink unless a preliminary drop from the bottle had been spilt upon the floor; and the bottle, when passed, had to go round with the sun. One might not say anything with certainty without touching wood, else the contrary would occur or a run of good luck change to evil. In almost every Service Camp there was a certain ill-omened hut, tent or bed. Something always happened to the man who slept there. The older squadron members would not sleep in the fated spot for a King's ransom. It was unlucky to go up in a machine with another man's mascot on board. Numberless crashes were instanced as proof of this. They would not sit down thirteen at table. They were unwilling to take up a bus with a number like '3523', the units of which add up to thirteen. One man always turned round three times before getting into his bus.[112]

Second Lieutenant Norman Macmillan, 45 Squadron, RFC

Most airmen felt that they could not expose families and loved ones to the reality of their situation. Letters home reveal attempts to reassure their nearest and dearest that all was well; that the air war was little more than a picnic:

> I'm afraid you must feel this war at home a great deal more than we do. Anyhow you may be quite sure that I'm not running any unnecessary risks. Our game here is, as far as I can see, a case of the best man, or rather I should say, the man who knows how to look after himself and being able to do so, coming out all right. Well every casualty that I've personally known of has either been foolhardiness, or incompetence. I've given up the foolhardy touch – after seeing the results of it – and I don't think I'm incompetent now, not below the average anyhow. Beyond that the only thing to do is to become a fatalist, which I am now. The chances are one in a hundred in our favour and there we must leave it, having reduced it to that. Thank God I've got the safest job in this war. Don't worry about me, I'm having the time of my life, am enjoying myself hugely and the war can't last for ever.[113]

Flight Sub-Lieutenant Bernard Ellis, 1 (Naval) Squadron, RNAS

Others, knowing the reality was that they would probably be killed, justified their sacrifice by pointing out that it was their plain duty to soldier on. Men like Lieutenant Walter Porkess of 10 Squadron were willing if necessary, like so many that had gone before them, to lay down their lives for their country:

> I appreciate your loving interest for my safety. Please never worry on my behalf; only live a day at a time. I am thankful I can do it and never think of what the future holds. Please do likewise, and do not spend anxious moments about my safety. I have long given up worrying about what might happen to myself. I have given myself completely to my country, and whatever my lot is I accept it as from Providence and am quite willing to stand by it, so please never have an anxious moment on my behalf. If God wills it I shall return safe and sound after all is over, and I sincerely pray it may so be willed. When we realise that this is one

life out of hundreds sacrificed every day, it more than ever brings home the fact that the war is the most terrible that ever raged. It will be fought to the bitter end, until we secure that for which we stand, and I am proud to be able to do my share.[114]

Lieutenant Walter Porkess, 10 Squadron, RFC

On 10 February Lieutenant Porkess, accompanied by his observer Second Lieutenant Roberts, was shot down in action. It was his commanding officer's job to inform the unfortunate parents:

It is with the deepest regret that I have got to inform you of your son's death. He died instantaneously, serving his country in the stoutest manner imaginable. There have been considerable operations on our front during the last week, and to enable the infantry to reach their various objectives it has been necessary to get all the Boche gun batteries knocked out. Your son has been in the counter-battery flight, ranging our howitzers on to active German batteries. During the four days prior to the attack your boy has ranged on no less than six German batteries, doing invaluable work, having been thanked many times by the Colonel of the Wing. On the very day of the attack his machine was hit by anti-aircraft fire while ranging a 6-in howitzer on a battery which would have hung up our advance considerably. His machine fell in our lines and we are burying your son tomorrow with every rite of a dead hero. His observer has not been found, unfortunately, he may have fallen out of the machine. His name was Roberts. I have lost, in your son, a white man, a gallant and loyal officer, and he was a boy not easy to replace. You have my deepest sympathy.[115]

Major George Ward, 10 Squadron, RFC

Friends of the dead man also wrote to try and assure the bereaved parents of the popularity of their son and they provided a few more details of how he had lost his life, as he had predicted, in the service of his country:

He was doing some special observation work with his observer, Lieutenant Roberts, when by a singular piece of ill-fortune his machine received a direct hit from an anti-aircraft shell, which is a very rare occurrence. They fell from a height of 8,000 feet, but it is very probable that they were both killed instantly by the explosion.[116]

Lieutenant Walter James, 10 Squadron, RFC

As ever, such accounts were heavily edited for the sake of the parents' feelings. Lieutenant James may have hoped that his friends were killed instantly, but this was probably only an attempt at consolation, rather than a reflection of the grim truth; for the BE2g flown by their son had fallen wreathed in flames. It is not surprising that this detail was somehow omitted from the letters of condolence.

The losses seemed never-ending and on 12 March, Major William Read of 45 Squadron sat down to write to the parents of one of his young pilots, Second Lieutenant Horace Bawden:

> I am writing to tell you some very sad news. Your son was killed yesterday in an aerial combat. He, as pilot in one machine, and another machine with him was flying over our lines when two German machines attacked and both our machines were brought down. I am deeply grieved to have to tell you this sad news, I am sure it will be some consolation to you to know that your son died a very gallant airman's death. The pilot who was flying the other machine which accompanied him was Captain Hon. Lubbock, who together with his observer was also killed. Captain Lubbock was brought down first and your son put up a very brave fight against superior odds until he also was brought down. I can only say that his death is felt very much by the whole Squadron. He was loved by both officers and men and was one of the best pilots in my Squadron. His observer was Lieutenant Stevenson who was also killed. His death was quite instantaneous as I myself know who went to see him where his machine fell just on our side of the lines. We buried him this afternoon together with his brother officers and many of us attended his funeral. Please accept my deep sympathy and that of all the Squadron in your sad loss.[117]
>
> Major William Read, 45 Squadron, RFC

Bawden was shot down at approximately 11.15 on 11 March, 1917. Read's letter seems even more heart pulling when one considers the inarticulate emotion poor Bawden tried to express in a letter home just five days before his death:

> I frequently have the same trouble as Dad. There are dozens and dozens of things to say, but I can't think of them at the time.[118]
>
> Second Lieutenant Horace Bawden, 45 Squadron, RFC

As usual Bawden's friends wrote additional letters of sympathy destined to be lovingly preserved as a last memory of a beloved son:

> I write in a personal and not official capacity to extend my sincere sympathy to you. Bawden was liked by everyone, a jolly good pilot and fellow too. We all miss him awfully. I find that his wristwatch and fountain pen were both crushed in the fall but it might make the blow less severe for you to hear, if I tell you that he had been shot and was instantly killed before his machine started to fall. Everything we could find belonging to him, has been returned. Again expressing my most sincere sympathy. [119]
>
> Lieutenant Walter Bryant, 45 Squadron, RFC

 In truth, the reality was that Bawden's brief contribution with 45 Squadron was soon forgotten. He was quickly replaced and before long the replacement was replaced as the casualties inexorably mounted. At the squadron all they had lost was one casual acquaintance amongst many; his parents had lost their beloved son:

> It is the same story as it always was. Those at home have a harder time in bearing losses and anxiety than those out here. [120]
>
> Major William Read, 45 Squadron, RFC

CHAPTER SEVEN

MAY:THE EBBING STORM

On 1 May, Generals Sir Edmund Allenby, Sir Hubert Gough and Sir Henry Horne found themselves in a peculiarly invidious position. At a conference held at Third Army Headquarters they were ordered by Field Marshal Sir Douglas Haig to launch an immediate offensive starting on 3 May. This once again left them with a totally inadequate amount of time to prepare. It was ironic that Haig, who just a month ago had baulked at allowing Allenby to launch the original attack with just 48 hours of con-tinuous bombardment, should now find himself in the position of allowing just two days of far less concentrated gunfire before the infantry went over the top. Of course this was not what he wanted, but the cruel exigencies of war had left him no choice if the French Army was to survive as a mean-ingful force in the field. Just as the RFC had had to make sacrifices for the common cause in April, now, in May, the British Army must fight what would be known as the Third Battle of the Scarpe and Second Battle of Bullecourt for the overall greater good of the Allied Powers.

For the umpteenth time the reconnaissance aircraft and artillery obser-vation aircraft took to the skies. However, one thing had changed. At long last the much delayed RE8s were beginning to pour out in an ever-increas-ing stream to the army cooperation squadrons in France, though all the BE2s could not be replaced overnight. One old BE2e hand, Second Lieu-tenant Charles Smart, was sent back to St Omer for a conversion course to prepare him for the imminent advent of the RE8s in his squadron. Not unnaturally he was slightly nervous at the prospect, being fully aware of the rumours on the grapevine that even experienced pilots had killed them-selves in their first flight in an RE8:

> The course of instruction consisted of a three-minute lecture from a
> man who stuttered and a seven-minute flight as a passenger, then up

you go 'with best of luck' sort of style. This machine has got an adjustable tailplane for varying the speed and climbing powers; it can be moved in the air by means of a wheel and is a most fatal gadget if used at the wrong time. My first flight was not a success for the engine conked as I was taking off and we 'pitched in the rough' bending the axle. I then got another machine which went alright, I flew up to 1,000 feet before turning and climbed to 4,000 feet before monkeying about with the wheel. Things went fairly well and I got down again quite safely. I cannot say I like the machine, it is much too heavy and cumbersome more like a flying steamroller than an aeroplane. Still they do 105 mph which is quite an advantage over the old BE2e.[1]

Second Lieutenant Charles Smart, 5 Squadron, RFC

As an experienced pilot, Second Lieutenant Smart had got his assessment just about right. The RE8s were overly stable and lacked the manoeuvrability needed in the threatening Arras skies; they needed careful handling during the first few flights while a pilot got used to their eccentricities. But in the end, when the chips were down, the RE8s were faster and more powerful than any of the BE2 variants. Much of the criticism directed at the new machine was caused by the difficulty the pilots found in adjusting to a new aircraft, combined with the wrench at giving up an old friend whose faults may have been legion but at least were well known and understood.

The need for photographs was still the pressing concern each and every day. There could be no let up in sight as long as the offensive endured:

At about ten o'clock, the photography formation stands by. Two machines from each flight, making six in all, are lined up at the end of the aerodrome towards which the wind is blowing, so that when the time comes they can go straight off upwind at 15–20 second intervals, and pick up formation quickly. The corporal in charge of the Photographic Section goes round and sees that all cameras are in order. Mechanics are swinging the propellers preparatory to starting the engine; observers are attending to their Lewis guns, seeing that the drums slip on and off easily, and that the springs are the right weight. As a flight commander I used very often to lead the formation and carry streamers on tail and wing tips so that the other pilots could distinguish my machine. Orders have been received that photographs of such-and-such squares on the map are urgently wanted. Each man in the formation knows his place and exactly when he is to pass over, and the scout squadron covering your bit of the front has been warned. We are to meet the escort at 6,000 feet over Arras at 10.30. I start up my engine suddenly, nearly blowing out of his seat the excellent Tymms, who is leaning out of his seat indulging in mild repartee with the C Flight commander, who has already done his job for the day and therefore is amusing himself by ribald enquiries as to what sort of flowers we like and have we any messages we would like sent to parents or fiancées.[2]

Lieutenant John Slessor, 5 Squadron, RFC

The cameras being used were constantly improving as the technology adapted to reflect the urgency and increasing sophistication of the requirements placed upon it. The FE2bs of 22 Squadron were fitted with new cameras designed for a better standard of oblique photography:

Oblique photographs were now required of the whole of the line on our front to be taken from a fairly low altitude (about 1,000 feet) and about 1,000 yards back (into enemy territory). The camera hitherto used for this class of photography was one fitted with a long focus lens which pointed out through the front of the nacelle of the FE, consequently, after each exposure the machine had to turn, which was not very practical when a large area had to be photographed and also when stereoscopic photographs were required, which meant that two exposures had to be made on each subject. A new camera had been introduced called the P-type which was intended to be used in the hand for taking occasional obliques. A fitting was made in the squadron to take two of these cameras for the purpose of taking two photographs, almost simultaneously, and this was fitted inside the nacelle, but instead of the photographs being taken from the front, they were taken from the side.

Major Learmount made some tests with this fitting which were quite satisfactory and the same day started out with Lieutenant Ward to obtain the photos. The machine was flown at an average height of 600 feet and in places well to the rear of the enemy's front line. Despite heavy machine-gun fire from the ground, about fifty exposures were made and excellent results obtained, the machine returning safely to the aerodrome, bearing much evidence of the heavy fire experienced. A day or so later another flight was made by Major Learmount and

Lieutenant Ward to obtain further photographs. On this occasion they took some from the rear of the Hindenburg Line looking towards our lines, the machine again being flown at a height of 600 feet and some 2 or 3 miles over enemy territory. Intense machine gun fire was again experienced and when the machine returned to the aerodrome Major Learmount said he was afraid he had missed a few photographs in consequence, and intended to go up again to obtain them, despite the fact that a large number of successful ones had been obtained on this flight.

The machine left the aerodrome once more, and within an hour returned. Major Learmount had been wounded, but he had succeeded in completing his self-imposed task. Lieutenant Ward had not been with the Squadron long, but was very keen on taking these photographs. Learmount said that he was exceedingly cool and collected whilst the machine-gun fire was heavy and continued taking the photographs as if nothing was happening; which indeed must have been the case as it would have been perfectly easy to have made mistakes which would have ruined the photographs. I think, if I remember rightly, there were only two spoiled plates out of about a hundred which were exposed on these three flights.[3]

Lieutenant B. F. Crane, Photographic Section, 14 Wing, RFC

Major L. W. Learmount was wounded on 10 May while the seemingly imperturbable Lieutenant Ward was shot down in flames and killed a few days later on 19 May. Such men understood that failure was only a temporary option; a failure one day was merely tomorrow's assignment, and so on until the required photographs had been successfully taken.

Back in Oxford, young Sergeant Ernest Cook had lived up to his name and been far too shy to proposition a more than willing woman, but he proved himself more than capable of facing German scouts in action over the front in an effort to carry out an essential mission:

This has been a good day so far. The photos taken yesterday proved dud so today they had to be got at all costs. We started at 9.30, got height over St Omer and toddled to the line where we broke into two diamond formations. Captain McArthur led us over and we did good running. Three Huns followed and attacked; two we drove off but one daring bounder thought he could follow us over our side. I had old gunner Lambert up and we hung back for the Hun. Over Arras he plucked up courage to attack and I banked round so as I could get a good shot. Devil of a lot of firing but no hits. Suddenly Lambert pointed down and I nosedived to find him, but couldn't pick him again. Gunner had shot the Hun down. Corroborated by gunners.[4]

Sergeant Ernest Cook, 45 Squadron, RFC

Ordinary, quiet-natured men such as Sergeant Cook or Sergeant Harold Taylor found themselves capable of great endurance and heroism in the face of awful adversity. When Taylor returned from his home leave he found himself immediately flung back into the fray on rejoining 25 Squadron at Auchel on the afternoon of 1 May. It was not to be a happy return as he took off with his pilot, Lieutenant King, as part of a formation of FE2bs sent on a bombing mission:

I sent a field postcard to my parents to tell them that I had arrived back safely. A number of my friends had been killed or taken prisoner during my leave and there were new faces around. Knowing the shortage of crews I went to the hangar and found that I was briefed for a bombing raid at 5 p.m. Lieutenant King had arrived back and I was paired with him for this raid. There were six FEs briefed for the operation and we were to bomb a camp at Inzel-lés-Sperchin. We had dropped our bombs and we were returning to our lines – my machine had become detached from the main formation. I saw a formation of nine Albatros scouts and two other enemy aircraft. Our formation was attacked, three Albatros immediately attacked me on the tail. Within seconds, I felt bullets hit my thigh which blew it to pieces, at the same time a bullet hit me in the right arm going straight through the muscle. This paralysed my arm. Bullets were spraying everywhere, I felt them pass my head, my rear gun was hit many times, the petrol tank had been pierced and petrol was flowing all over the machine. I slumped on to the floor of the nacelle bleeding profusely from my leg and arm. And then there was oblivion.[5]

Sergeant Harold Taylor, 25 Squadron, RFC

The out-of-control FE2b crash-landed onto Arras racecourse. The juddering impact brought Taylor back to vague consciousness but broke his collar bone at the same time. The successful German pilot was adjudged to have been Leutnant Lothar von Richthofen:

I was brought back to life by the machine hitting the ground. It ran a few yards, then turned up on its nose and then settled down again over on to its right-hand wing tip. Had the machine gone right over I doubt whether I would be writing this account as the engine would most likely have buried both Lieutenant King and me underneath. I remember Lieutenant King getting out of the plane, luckily not having been hit. A number of infantrymen came along and with great difficulty got me out of the plane. Then must have been another period of unconsciousness, but the next time I awoke I was lying on a stretcher on the floor of Arras cathedral, which was being used as a casualty clearing station. The floor was massed with wounded men and I realised that if I did not get attention quickly that I would very likely bleed to death. I was very lucky; it was always assumed by ground troops that only officers flew in the RFC and with my flying clothes on, I must have been given preferential treatment, because shortly I was taken from the floor to receive first aid treatment. I will never know how many days I was unconscious – the next time I awoke I was on a hospital train.[6]

Sergeant Harold Taylor, 25 Squadron, RFC

Once injured, Taylor was in the hands of the Royal Army Medical Corps who had had plenty of opportunities to practise the best methods of treating and evacuating the wounded from the battlefields of France and Flanders. Soon he was once again back home in England:

I will never forget my homecoming at Charing Cross. It had become the habit of many hundreds of men and women to meet the hospital trains so that they could welcome the wounded. We were transferred to the ambulance, it had an open back and as it went out of the narrow exit, flowers and cigarettes were handed to the medical orderly to give to us. These people were trying to convey to us their appreciation of our service.[7]

Sergeant Harold Taylor, 25 Squadron, RFC

Harold Taylor suffered for the rest of his life from the after-effects of those wounds received in that burst of mayhem above Arras. His leg was initially saved, but then slowly deteriorated, until eventually Taylor gave up the struggle and chose an amputation in 1960 – some forty-three years after the German bullets had ripped it apart. His 'lucky' pilot, Lieutenant Berry King, was killed when his FE2b caught fire just two days after his escape of 1 May.

However brave the air crews were it was impossible to remain calm when a damaged aircraft started to fall out of the sky. There were no parachutes so the crew would almost invariably share the fate of their machine. If it burnt, so did they; if it was smashed up, so were they. Even if they retained the use of the flying controls a crash-landing in the shell-scarred wasteland near the front lines was a horrendous ordeal that many did not survive:

> I floated, losing height, and hoped to crash-land on our side of the lines. This I succeeded in doing, but the terrain was so pock-marked with shell craters that it was impossible to make a safe landing. We had been followed by two Huns, which were driven off by accurate fire by my observer. I hit the edge of a large crater and the aircraft whipped over on to its back and broke off the front part of the machine, with me pinned down by a spar across my chest. I thought that the engine was on top of me and shouted to Stanbrook, 'For God's sake lift the bloody engine off me!' He, being suspended in his harness, had difficulty getting free; by the time he came to my aid, I had passed out. I was told later by Stanbrook that blood was oozing from my mouth. A few peasants appeared on the scene and one was sent to find an ambulance.[8]
>
> Second Lieutenant C. C. Knight, 55 Squadron, RFC

MEANWHILE, new plans were under development to try and increase the effectiveness of scout attacks on the German kite balloons that still provided the enemy with observation over much of the Arras battlefield. As ever the balloons were defended by an interlinked combination of anti-aircraft batteries, machine guns, flaming onions and lurking German scouts. With a new phase in the offensive looming, it was once again vital to put out these unblinking German eyes that peered down on the British preparations. Major Leonard Tilney commanding 40 Squadron came up with a plan to subvert these defences by making a concerted low-level attack. His squadron immediately began a period of intensive training, although they were initially unaware of its purpose:

> A new game is being evolved. It comprises the act of rushing 'all out' (and by 'all out' is meant opening the engine throttle to its fullest power)

around houses, chimneys, barracks, tents, hills and valleys, trees and telegraph poles, at a height from the ground of anything less than 10 feet. Nothing more exciting could be imagined, and when one considers the speed of these machines, just guess what it means.[9]

Second Lieutenant Edward Mannock, 40 Squadron, RFC

The attack went in on 2 May, timed for maximum effect just before the new offensive planned next day. Amongst those on the mission was Captain William Bond. They flew across the lines at an altitude of just 50 feet:

Padre Keymer was down there to watch us start for the balloon strafe. He was fearfully grave and just walked round the machines – hardly saying a word. I don't think he expected any of us to return. Six of us attacked six balloons and we destroyed five. One fellow failed because his gun jammed. I had eleven bullet holes in my machine and some of the others were nearly as bad. I was the second to get back. The first was the one whose gun had jammed. I lost my engine on landing and stopped on the far side. Keymer sprinted out, beating the 'ack-emmas' (mechanics) by yards. 'Any luck?' he shouted. He was fearfully excited. 'Yes, it's all right', I said. 'Oh, damn good!' he exclaimed. 'Damn good! Absolutely topping!' The others came in at intervals, and he beat the CO and everyone in welcoming them. He ran about from pilot to pilot saying, 'Damn good! How completely splendid!' The CO joined him in a duet of jubilation and supplemented his 'damn good' by extracts from the 'new' vocabulary.[10]

Captain William Bond, 40 Squadron, RFC

Such a notable success made a repeat mission almost inevitable and a few days later they tried again. This time the raiders attacked the balloons at the even lower height of just 20 feet above the blurring ground, while the rest of the squadron sat above them to try to distract the attention of the German scouts. It was a nerve-racking experience:

Went over the line from north of Arras to 5 miles behind the German trenches at a height of less than 15 feet, attacking Hun balloons. Six of us: Captain Nixon, Hall, Scudamore, Redler, Parry and myself. All except the captain returned safely but with machines almost shot to pieces. Hall crashed on home aerodrome, as did Scudamore, Parry crashed just our side of the lines at Canadian headquarters. Redler crashed at Savy, but returned here later and damaged his machine on landing. I was the only one to return properly to the aerodrome, and made a perfect landing. We got all our objectives. My fuselage had bullet holes in it, one very near my head, and the wings were more or less riddled. I don't want to go through such an experience again.[11]

Second Lieutenant Edward Mannock, 40 Squadron, RFC

Watching from high above in the covering force was Captain William Bond:

From miles away I watched three balloons start burning and collapse. Tootling round I spotted three more balloons a good deal south of the ones we had to attack, and went over to investigate. Three machines were flying behind them – Hun two-seaters. I spiralled down above them to have a nearer view and when at about 1,200 yards' range, I heard one of them firing. So I changed my spiral into a dive on to the nearest one and heard the gun going again. Then they dived too and eastward. Next moment I knew the reason, for five of our new scouts came tearing past taking up the chase. Soon the whole eight were out of sight. I turned round, and being now only a couple of thousand feet above the balloons I thought I'd have a go at one. I didn't get far. They had been watching me too long from the ground and immediately I was greeted with machine guns. The tracer bullets came up in silver streaks and the next minute there was a nasty cough behind as their anti-aircraft fired its ranging shot. I didn't wait, but tootled home.[12]

Captain William Bond, 40 Squadron, RFC

Seven balloons were claimed in all, but the British machines were badly damaged and Captain W. E. Nixon was shot down and killed. The natural dangers and costs of attacking kite balloons had clearly begun to reassert themselves. The Germans could not be caught out twice by the same *ruse de guerre*.

THE last major offensive of the Battle of Arras began on 3 May. The First, Third and Fifth Armies all went over the top on a 16-mile front that spread from Vimy to Bullecourt at 0345 before dawn had broken. The lack of time in making the preparations proved a fatal handicap: the British artillery bombardment was frankly inadequate, the counter-battery arrangements skimped, most of the assaulting troops were not fresh, those that were had had no chance to practise or assimilate their orders. Worst of all the German defensive positions and wire were mostly intact and garrisoned by largely fresh divisions of equal numbers. To put it simply, the scene was set for disaster. It could not have been more different from the precision planning, careful preparation and annihilating bombardment that had brought such a dramatic success on 9 April:

> Our orders didn't get through until the last minute and then they were all garbled. No one, including our officers, seemed to know what we were supposed to be doing, or where we were going. Officers were supposed to have synchronised their watches in so far as it was possible at that time of day. At a certain time, our barrage was supposed to lift and we were to climb out of the trenches and go forward. Well we did – but it wasn't all at the same time! We were given false information and told the artillery had smashed the enemy defences and we would get through the wire – did we hell![13]
>
> Sergeant Jack Cousins, 7th Battalion, Bedfordshire and Hertfordshire Regt, 54th Brigade, 18th Division

Unsurprisingly, the attack towards the village of Cherisy was not a success. For the most part this confused scenario was repeated all along the British line. In front of Guémappe, the 1/5th London Rifle Brigade were ordered to attack towards the St Rohart factory:

> We had fix bayonets, we were all keyed up. It was still dark or semi-darkness when suddenly all the guns flash out, an enormous barrage goes up. A mass of smoke in front. The first wave went on and they must have reached the German lines. Five minutes or so later, we were told to start off, so off we started, wondering what we were going to find. Whether we would bayonet anybody or what we would do. We felt elated more than fear. The first part was quite easy. As we got nearer, three Germans came out with their hands up, without their helmets on – they were young chaps about our own age perhaps 19 or 20. They were prisoners and one of our older ones, one of the 40-year-olds, he came along and said, 'Oooohh, I'll take these prisoners back!' That was a very good way of getting out the fight! We carried on, over this bashed up trench, then we got down the other side of the

Ridge. The last thing I saw in front of us was a factory of some sort. Then we found bullets were flying all round us from the Germans and everybody in front had dropped into shell holes. I dropped into one with my pal with me – they were tiny little shell holes – not big enough for one really! We squashed down as hard as we could and each of us had a shovel tied to our back. His shovel was showing and the Germans were firing at his shovel and every now and then there would be a hit on it – a wonder we didn't get a ricochet! Then our own artillery started dropping shells amongst us. That worried us no end of course. Either they hadn't got the range or they didn't know where we were. They got nearer and nearer. Then finally one went just in front of us and we heard one of our chaps – a Devonshire man – cry out. Then one of our planes came over and we lit a flare hoping that he'd be able to report where we were. Anyway the guns stopped firing after that.[14]

Private Victor Polhill, 1/5th Battalion, London Rifle Brigade, 169th Brigade, 56th Division

They sat stuck in the shell holes all day until dusk fell, when they fell back. The men got nowhere fast; their lives thrown away in the cause of maintaining the spirit of Anglo-French cooperation.

One exception was on the northern flank where the Canadians managed a small advance at terrible cost to take the village of Fresnoy, while alongside them the 31st Division pushed towards Oppy Wood. Above them Second Lieutenant Charles Smart was once again in the hot seat, accompanied by his observer Lieutenant Hendry. This time he was on a contact patrol hovering just above the infantry objectives:

We had to go up and fly amongst the shell barrage and spot our infantry flares to see where they had got to. The shell fire was simply terrible and an awful war was going on underneath us. There was a heavy ground mist and a lot of smoke from the bursting shells, we had to fly at about 900 feet in order to see. A lot of machine-gun fire was put up at us. I was expecting to get one any moment, shells were whipping through the air in thousands bumping us about all over the place. We managed to spot the position of one of our flares and returned to Divisional Headquarters and dropped our message. Then back to the lines again, just as we got over Oppy we got an awful bump and a crack, one of our own shells carried away the right lower wing tip leaving it hanging in shreds of canvas and wood. I thought all was up, but found I could still fly the machine by keeping the stick right over on the left-hand side. I handled her very gently and managed to crawl back to the aerodrome and landed safely. Both of us heaved a great sigh of relief when we got down alright. This is the worst trip I have had up to now and I feel more than a bit shaken.[15]

Second Lieutenant Charles Smart, 5 Squadron, RFC

It had been a very lucky escape. As the battle rose to a crescendo in the northern sector, the Sopwith 1½ Strutters found that they were expected to try something new to assist the struggling infantry:

Only two days before we had received orders that were specially designed for such an event, and which, new in conception, were known as counter-attack patrols. We were instructed to fly these patrols from dawn to darkness low down behind the captured positions, and we were to concentrate on reporting immediately on the enemy preparations for counter-attacks.[16]

Major Sholto Douglas, 43 Squadron, RFC

Later that morning, threatening enemy troop movements were observed. Before the exhausted British troops could consolidate their gains, it looked like they would be counter-attacked by fresh German troops. It was a desperate situation and Major Douglas and the Sopwith 1½ Strutters were sent in to do their utmost to hold them back:

I was given instructions that my squadron should make very low-level machine-gun and bomb attacks on the enemy positions. We flew at heights varying from 50 to 300 feet, shooting up and bombing scattered parties of the enemy troops, trench positions and transport. On one occasion I came down very low and started shooting at a row of German heads that had appeared along the top of a parapet. They shook me a little by answering back, and I could distinctly hear the popping sound of small arms fire flashing past my ears. Our success appeared to be mainly due to the enemy's being so startled by the audacity of our attack and bombardment that they could not bring themselves to throw at us any very heavy fire. The Sopwith 1½ Strutter came into its own in this work, its performance and manoeuvrability near the ground being good; and the chief danger that we had to face was from our own artillery barrage. When we shut off our engines for a moment we could clearly hear our own shells rumbling past our ears with a noise that sounded like a succession of trains passing through a tunnel.[17]

Major Sholto Douglas, 43 Squadron, RFC

At last they had found something at which the Sopwith 1½ Strutter could still excel. Yet the experienced flight commander Lieutenant Alan Dore still found himself threatened by nagging engine problems:

We are ordered out to try to stop a counter-attack on Oppy and Arleux which we have just taken. Our big guns being unable to get over Vimy Ridge. At eleven o'clock we learn that the Huns are massing at Mauville Farm. Flying low I crossed at 1,500 feet with a missing engine. At Neuvireuil I dive to 600 feet and fire with front gun at Huns. I can see in the trenches and village. Dare not go lower. Engine hardly takes me over the Ridge. My other four machines do finely.[18]

Lieutenant Alan Dore, 43 Squadron, RFC

The only other pyrrhic success achieved was made by the Australians of Gough's Fifth Army who had managed to get a small lodgement of troops through the German lines. The Australians had been preparing for weeks after their bloody nose on 11 April, but the challenge of breaching the Hindenburg Line still tested them to the utmost. The Germans threw in numerous counter-attacks and this tactically insignificant gain that provoked so much suffering was not finally secured for another two weeks of murderous attrritional fighting that became formally known as the Second Battle of Bullecourt.

WHILE the vicious fighting continued there remained a near insatiable need for photographs and artillery observation. The crippling losses of the RFC continued throughout May and eventually almost every RFC and RNAS mess was hit hard. Sometimes it seemed that almost every day brought bad news:

About our casualties. I haven't said much in this direction have I? But we have had some and pretty heavy too. Somebody comes down an hour before dark, and reports a good shoot, a couple of Huns driven off etc; he also reports seeing a machine of our squadron attacked and sent down in flames. Off I rush to the 'drome. 'How many have you got out Jack?' 'Mine are all in, old man, but C Flight has one out still'. I have one out myself so I wait. Presently the droning of an engine and a machine goes by. 'One of 51's!' says somebody. 'Get the flares out!' howls the 'orderly dog' and I keep myself quiet by firing Very lights and rockets, to help one of these two home – the lucky one. At last when everything is becoming blotted out, the drone of an engine, and somebody swoops down and lands – blue wheels – mine are red – so poor old Bill and Mike are gone this time. I order the empty waiting hangar to be closed down, and go in to a sad little Mess with two vacant places. Somebody says he saw the scrap, 'Old Bill and Mike they put up a damn fine fight but the Huns were too numerous and fast for them'. A message on the phone and we despatch a party to bring them in. And next morning we go and salute at the graveside led by the CO himself.[19]

Captain Bernard Rice, 8 Squadron, RFC

The losses occasionally swelled to a volume that threatened to undermine an entire squadron. However, most of the survivors held firm, their diary entries merely recording the melancholy strings of losses:

Poor old Lorimer and his observer were brought down by 'Archie' this morning – both killed – crashed our side of the lines. We buried Lorimer and Osborne – machines were taking off and landing at our aerodrome. It seems fitting to see and hear machines when burying an airman. Poor little Weekes crashed into trees on edge of aerodrome when coming in to land on practice night flying. Burst into flames – *finis*. Watson got lost night flying – crashed miles away but not hurt. We buried Weekes today – I was a pall bearer as yesterday and our machines were flying above as if looking at the scene. Directly we got back from the funeral Bulmer and I went up and were three hours doing a shoot for 6-in howitzers.[20]

Captain Ewart Garland, 10 Squadron, RFC

These men would not have been human if they had not nurtured some antipathy towards the staff officers they knew were ultimately responsible for sending them up time after time to photograph seemingly minute changes in the German defences. Second Lieutenant Charles Smart was given a very rare opportunity to let the staff see what it was like far above the trenches:

> We have had a lot of photographs to take and got a bit sick of it, someone suggested that the Corps Intelligence Department ought to come up and see the job done, after a lot of talk and chaff we managed to rush them in for the job. Two machines were to take photographs and me (myself) to act as escort. Off we went with an intelligence officer in each machine – my passenger Staff Captain Mcleod complete with his DSO, MC and red tabs. Mcleod knew nothing about aerial gunnery and had never seen a Hun machine in his life, in fact he had only been up in the air once before so I couldn't expect very much from him. We no sooner got well over the lines when six Huns swooped down on us from nowhere and a rare mix up followed. The Huns were of course two to one so we at once turned west and made a running fight of it. A Hun settled himself on my tail and started shooting. I just threw my old floating fort about as though it was a scout, finishing up with a dive at about 130 mph.
>
> McLeod is a very stout fellow but an awful fool. When I got in the dive the Huns was still sticking to us and shooting; I looked over my shoulder and McLeod was sitting there with a 'what do I do next' expression on his face. I jerked the throttle back so that he could hear and yelled, 'Shoot you darned fool!' He then got busy with the gun and fired straight through our own rudder post. Fortunately for us five of our Triplanes turned up just in the nick of time and we got away. It was a close call and I am afraid we should have been dead meat if the scouts hadn't turned up and saved us. Our two other machines were both fired upon, luckily without anyone being hurt. One of McLeod's shots just missed the rudder hinge, if it had been half an inch higher it would have carried the rudder away and no one could say what would have happened. Went to dinner at Corps Headquarters at night. McLeod related the details of the fight with great gusto saying nothing about the rudder incident, of course I did not let him down, but no more amateur observers for me if I can help it.[21]

Second Lieutenant Charles Smart, 5 Squadron, RFC

Throughout the battle the men of the remaining FE2b squadrons tried to get the best they could from their elderly 'warhorses', but the writing was clearly on the wall. As a daylight, multi-purpose aircraft the FE2b was finished. Only courage kept them in the sky:

> My flight commander was an ex-cavalry officer, Captain C. E. Bryant, and even on our slow FEs he retained a large quota of the cavalry spirit. No amount of enemy aircraft seemed to disturb him. His custom was to dash with practically full throttle straight for his objective, bomb it or photograph it as required, turn round and dash for the lines nose down. Meanwhile his formation followed as best it could. After one or two trips we became used to his method and could follow reasonably well. He held the theory that the FE afforded no margin for finesse and that 'quick in' and 'quick out' gave the greatest chance of doing our job with the least casualties. He was probably right.[22]
>
> Second Lieutenant C. F. Horsley, 18 Squadron, RFC

When they were caught, the sheer drama of an FE2b's cockpit in close combat situations can hardly be overexaggerated:

> Our experienced gunners became expert with the rear Lewis gun, firing over the top plane and sometimes taking chances and firing between the planes. I have never been able to understand why some of the observers were not lost overboard. Standing high on the strengthened sides of the nacelle, clinging to the gun on the high extended mounting, straining into all sorts of positions in order to fire a burst at an enemy behind, how they stayed with the aircraft has always been a puzzle.[23]
>
> Second Lieutenant C. F. Horsley, 18 Squadron, RFC

With the extended gun mounting bending under pressure like a reed and with the observer's heavy leather coat flapping out into the onrushing power of the slipstream, it seemed as though the FE2b gunners were deliberately defying the force of gravity. Still the men crewing the FE2bs and FE2ds had to fight on. There were simply not enough of the new aircraft to allow them to be scrapped or diverted on to the 'safer' night bombing duties.

THE British scouts helped when they could, but the overarching demands of the RFC offensive doctrine meant that they simply could not be every-where. They continued to fly offensive patrols deep behind the German lines seeking out the German scouts and army cooperation aircraft before they could get to the vital areas above the lines. But in the three-dimensional world of the air war it was difficult if not impossible to 'police' a battlefield of not just breadth and depth but also height. Cloaking clouds and mists further complicated the issue allowing the German scouts to fre-quently break through to prey on the vulnerable British reconnaissance aircraft. Yet, whenever the scouts saw one of their more vulnerable brethren in trouble, they did not hesitate:

> We crossed the lines at 12,000 feet and saw two 'Quirks' trying to crawl away from a large formation of Hun scouts – all red ones. We cut in between and stood over the Huns, who turned east again. We counted nine. They went out of sight, climbing, and reappeared to the south obviously trying to get between us and the sun. We defeated them in that and outclimbed them too and then went straight at them – three of us. They promptly turned east again and we never got within range. They are faster than us on the level. This business went on for nearly an hour. The nine red Huns came back four times, heading for us very bravely, but every time we got into the sun and then went for them. They never stayed, and ultimately went away for good.[24]
>
> Captain William Bond, 40 Squadron, RFC

The superior numbers deployed by the British did allow them a little leeway to compromise and spare at least some of their scouts for escort missions when it was almost certain suicide to send in photography machines unprotected. Thus it was that Captain Keen and C Flight of 40 Squadron were sent to escort four Sopwith 1½ Strutters in a mission that would take them directly over the lair of Jasta 11 at Douai. With them was Lieutenant Edward Mannock who was still a relatively inexperienced pilot. Sure enough they were attacked by a group of German scouts diving down on them and Mannock found himself in a dreadful quandary:

> I tried my gun before going over the German lines, only to find that it was jammed, so I went over with a revolver only. A Hun in a beautiful yellow and green bus attacked me from behind. I could hear his machine gun cracking away. I wheeled round on him and howled like a

dervish (although of course he couldn't hear me) whereat he made off towards old Parry and attacked him, with me following, for the moral effect! Another one (a brown speckled one) attacked a Sopwith, and Keen blew the pilot to pieces and the Hun went spinning down from 12,000 feet to earth. Unfortunately the Sopwith had been hit, and went down too, and there was I, a passenger, absolutely helpless, not having a gun, an easy prey to any of them, and they hadn't the grit to close. Eventually they broke away, and then their 'Archie' gunners got on the job and we had a hell of a time. At times, I wondered if I had a tailplane or not, they were so near. We came back over Arras with the three remaining Sopwiths, and excellent photos, and two vacant chairs at the Sopwith squadron Mess! What is the good of it all?[25]

Second Lieutenant Edward Mannock, 40 Squadron RFC

Mannock was wracked by his own emotions and was in no fit state to appreciate that as an operation of war the mission had been relatively economical in lives in comparison to the significant military results that had been achieved. The 'good of it all' lay in their excellent photographs. The Sopwith 1½ Strutter shot down was flown by Lieutenant C. R. O'Brien and Second Lieutenant E. L. Edwards. Both survived the crash to become prisoners of war.

AFTER 4 May, the attention of the High Command switched to Flanders where a new major offensive was planned. In essence the Arras operations in the Bullecourt sector became once again a diversionary operation to conceal the true nature of the Allied plans. Now, at last, Haig would have his way and launch a great offensive bursting out of the Ypres Salient as he had always craved. Here his real strategic objectives, the German submarine bases that plagued the Admiralty and the great rail junction of Roulers, were not far behind the German lines. In addition the new German tactics of defence in depth and tactically motivated retreats could only be taken so far before they ran out of ground: eventually the German Army would have no choice but to stand and fight. And of course a hammer blow at Ypres would comprehensively distract German attention far away from the frailties of the French front. So the Battle of Messines which began on 7 June became the curtain raiser for the Third Battle of Ypres that commenced on 31 August 1917.

It would have been far too obvious to move 56 Squadron and the rest of Ninth Wing straight away to this new area of concentration. Had this been done it would have acted as a 'moving finger' to conveniently direct the Germans' attention to the target of the next offensive. Instead they were kept on the Arras front in an effort to fool the enemy that it remained the focus of British plans. As a result, Arras became the last arena of battle for the valiant Captain Albert Ball. As well as acting as flight commander he continued his earlier habit of squeezing in as many extra lone offensive patrols as was physically possible. This culminated, in the first week of May, in a series of actions together forming a spiral of violence to which there could be only one logical end:

> At about 7.30 p.m., I sighted four red Albatros scouts between Douai and the lines going south. I dived on the nearest red HA scout, but four or five HA scouts were coming down on my tail, so I turned steeply and pulled down Lewis gun. Nearest HA fired at and overshot me, and I put in a good burst of 50 Vickers gun into HA. I then fastened on to the tail of HA and followed it down to 2,000 feet riddling HA meanwhile. HA dived into earth in the rough ground between Halte and Vitry. I then turned and climbed and joined the scrimmage which was now taking place between a number of double-seater HA and HA scouts, and Sopwith Scouts, Bristol Fighters and FEs. I was circling and manoeuvring for position and got on to the tail of a white HA scout with a pointed nose, and put in a good burst of Vickers. HA dived steeply and cleared. The mêlée gradually made towards Douai, HA being outmanoeuvred and yielding ground. I went south to Cambrai and over Sailly viewed a white two-seater Albatros. I dived down on HA and put in good bursts of Vickers and a drum of Lewis from 100 to 25 yards range. HA hurtled down, but owing to the dusk (the time now being 8.10 p.m.) his ultimate end could not be observed. I climbed, picked up SE5a. 4854 and returned home.[26]
>
> Captain Albert Ball, 56 Squadron, RFC

Ball had relied heavily on his luck to keep him alive thus far, but even he must have realised that his good fortune was not inexhaustible. His fellow pilots eyed him with a mixture of respect and amazement. One young 19-year-old, Second Lieutenant Roger Chaworth-Musters, was awestruck to find himself posted to the same squadron as his hero:

Captain Ball is surpassing his previous efforts and has already accounted for about six Huns off his own bat. He came back the other day with a huge hole right through the tail of the machine. The shell had carried away all his elevator controls except one strand of wire with which he managed to get the machine down. He got out and immediately got into another machine and was off again. He really is a marvel. He always comes back with his machine absolutely riddled with bullets.[27]

Second Lieutenant Roger Chaworth-Musters, 56 Squadron, RFC

Most found Ball an unassuming lad despite the fame and the honours that had been showered upon him during the last year:

He was the quietest young kid you ever saw, the most inoffensive youngster – you'd think he wouldn't punch anybody on the nose if he could duck him. But when he got into the air he was all hair-and-teeth! He was an excellent shot! He spent a great deal of time on the ground test-firing his guns in the pits.[28]

Second Lieutenant Reginald Hoidge, 56 Squadron, RFC

On 5 May, Ball crossed the lines with his patrol but soon found himself once again, by accident or design, separated from his comrades:

Crossing the line I travelled north-east at 8,000 feet and viewed two HA coming from the direction of Douai towards Carvin at 9,000 feet. I made towards Carvin in order to climb, HA following. I climbed to 11,000 feet, and by this time the nearest HA had got on my tail at a distance of 200 yards. I did a quick turn and got underneath HA, the other HA being then about a quarter of a mile away. I pulled the Lewis gun down and fired two drums at a very short range; HA made no attempt to get away. I fired another drum but HA by this time had got away. I followed and got on HA's tail and fired quick bursts from Vickers and Lewis guns at very short range, and HA went down out of control. By this time the other HA had started firing. I climbed again keeping away from HA and manoeuvred for a chance to get on HA's tail. This chance never came for HA came nose on at me firing two guns. I opened fire with Vickers gun and kept the trigger pressed, using one in one tracers, which could easily be seen going right into HA, until the machines came almost into each other. My SE5 was hit in the engine and I was covered in oil. I climbed and engine kept up revolutions but lost all oil pressure. No other HA came along and I went down to about 3,000 feet. Both HAs were lying on the ground, within 400 yards of each other, completely wrecked. I then went back towards the lines and met two other HA near Lens. Having only very few rounds of Vickers left and not being able to see through sights for oil, I put my nose well down and made for home. Although the engine got very little oil under no pressure, it ran for three quarters of an hour and got home OK.[29]

   Captain Albert Ball, 56 Squadron, RFC

The relatively cool words of this report belie the dreadful mental state to which Ball was reduced by the time he landed. There is no doubt that Ball was severely shaken by this traumatic near-death experience:

On his return to the aerodrome, his engine was found to have been shot through, and there were several bullets through the back of the pilot's seat. Flushed in face, his eyes brilliant, his hair blown and dishevelled, he came to the squadron office to make his report, but for a long time was in so over-wrought a state that dictation was an impossibility to him. 'God is very good to me.' 'God must have me in His keeping.' 'I was certain that he meant to ram me.' The possibility that his opponent, finding himself mortally hit, had determined to have a life for a life occurred to him. In that event his nerve failed him at the last – Ball did not flinch. But in nervous exhaustion he paid the price.[30]

   Recording Officer Thomas Marson, 56 Squadron, RFC

Ball betrayed many of the classic signs of severe combat fatigue; in truth he had not yet recovered from the damage inflicted on his nervous system in consequence of his heroic efforts on the Somme. That same night he wrote home to his girlfriend:

When I am happy I dig in the garden and sing. I don't get much time off but what I get is enjoyed. Oh won't it be nice when all this beastly killing is over and we can just enjoy ourselves and not hurt anyone. I hate this game, but it is the only thing one must do just now.[31]

   Captain Albert Ball, 56 Squadron, RFC

But there could be no rest at Arras. Next day Ball was back up in the hostile skies, flying his Nieuport Scout because the SE5 was undergoing much needed and extensive repairs. On 6 May, once again he was separated from the rest of the patrol. The Nieuport was simply not able to keep up with the faster SE5s:

> I went on towards Douai and viewed four red Albatros scouts, new type, going towards Cambrai at 10,000 feet, my Nieuport being at 11,000 feet. I got above HA and dived on the nearest one, getting in the centre of the formation of HAs, which broke up. I got underneath the nearest HA and at close range fired two and a half drums of one in one tracer which were seen to enter HA. The HA went down and was seen to crash on the ground near the crossroads and railway south of Sancourt. The remainder of the HA kept well away and did not attack me until on my way home. I easily outclimbed HA and also could easily outmanoeuvre them, HA being very slow on turns. I could not fight again owing to having no ammunition. HA only got three hits on my Nieuport.[32]
>
> Captain Albert Ball, 56 Squadron, RFC

Perhaps Ball should have been sent home at this point, but he was an experienced scout pilot and his task was to fly and fight. He was certainly more than willing, trapped as he was on the treadmill of competing victory scores, and there is little doubt that he would have resented being sent home before he had a chance to beat his French competitor, Captain George Guynemer, and rule the roost once more:

> I have got ten more Huns, and my total is now forty – two in front of my French rival. Oh, I'm having a topping time. Today or tomorrow I'm being presented to Sir Douglas Haig. Am very pleased. I just want to get a few more Huns if I can.[33]
>
> Captain Albert Ball, 56 Squadron, RFC

On the night of the 6 May he sent a last letter home. Again he referred to his French competitor:

> I made my forty-second Hun yesterday, so am now four in front of the French.[34]
>
> Captain Albert Ball, 56 Squadron, RFC

Ball, however, was a product of the skies of August 1916. The increasingly sophisticated scout tactics of 1917 had largely passed him by. His technique was still largely dependent on an amazing personal skill in close combat. In a sense, Albert Ball was the antithesis of Richthofen. His lone-wolf method of fighting could not really be passed on to a new genera-tion of pilots. Like a well-executed cover drive it looked easy, but few could even begin to emulate his methods. They suited Ball and Ball alone. Furthermore, as the size of the scout formations steadily increased, and as the skills and tactical acumen of the opposing German pilots developed, so the perils of coming under the concentrated fire of multiple pairs of Spandaus rendered the risks Ball was taking insupportable. Nobody could be that lucky all the time.

On the fateful evening of Monday 7 May, a call came through from the headquarters of Ninth Wing ordering a strong patrol to engage the new Jasta 'circus' tactic head-on. Ten SE5s of 56 Squadron would combine with the six Spads of 19 Squadron to sweep over Douai and Cambrai. Captain Albert Ball led A Flight (Lieutenant G. Maxwell and Lieutenant K. J. Knaggs) across the lines ascending to a height of some 7,000 feet; Captain Henry Meintjes led C Flight (Lieutenant Reginald Hoidge and Lieutenant Cecil Lewis) in a layer above them at 9,000 feet; Captain Cyril Crowe took B Flight (Lieutenant Roger Chaworth-Musters, Lieutenant Arthur Rhys Davids and Lieutenant John Leach) still higher at 10,000 feet. In the cloudy conditions the pilots almost immediately lost cohesion as a single tactical force:

> Three flights led by Ball, Meintjes and myself, left the ground at about
> 5.45 p.m. with the express purpose of engaging the Richthofen 'circus'
> if they were in the air. The weather was very bad. Layers of thick banks
> of clouds hid the sky, and they ranged from 2,000 feet to 10,000 feet
> with varying sized gaps. We crossed the lines south of Arras between
> the layers of clouds at 4,000 feet, and Ball, who was leading, shortly
> after led the formation into a large bank of clouds which resulted in
> the various members of the formation losing contact with one another.
> I found myself alone when I got into clear space again, but some
> distance on my right I could see a number of SE5s flying in very loose
> formation. I made for them, but a cloud bank enveloped me on the
> way and I lost them.[35]
>
> Captain Cyril Crowe, 56 Squadron, RFC

The German response was not long in arriving. No mass formation took to the air but different flights took off and roamed the skies searching for the British intruders. Amongst them was Leutnant Wilhelm Allmenröder – the brother of the rising German ace, Leutnant Karl Allmenröder:

> Suddenly, there came an alert – some enemy planes had crossed the lines. Four of us took off immediately. Lothar von Richthofen led our little formation, I flew to his left and a little to the rear, Mohnicke flew to his right and to the rear, and either Esser or Simon was last. We were flying patrol from south to north over the trenches at an altitude of about 2,000 metres, and I was searching for enemy fighters to the west, looking up and down.[36]

> Leutnant Wilhelm Allmenröder, Jasta 11, German Army Air Force

The scattered British flights encountered the various isolated German formations and all over the sky there were clashes between the two sides. The situation was by no means clear, then or now, and contemporary accounts are generously laced with inconsistencies. Captain Crowe and B Flight had soon lost touch with young Second Lieutenant Roger Chaworth-Musters who seems to have sighted a German aircraft though a chink in the clouds and darted away after him. In the process he encountered Leutnant Werner Voss who succeeded in shooting him down in the vicinity of Etaing. Voss had only just returned from his long leave on 5 May, so this was somewhat unfortunate for Chaworth-Musters. This young boy, who had been so impressed with his hero Albert Ball, went to his unmarked grave just over a month after his 19th birthday. Crowe continued on his way with Leach and Rhys Davids:

> Three of us, my Flight Commander, Leach, and myself got separated from the others in the clouds and after cruising around a bit we saw a Hun, a bright red beggar below us; this was about 5–10 miles over the lines. Down went the Flight Commander and down went I after him, but thank goodness that somehow I managed to remember to look behind me first, and saw another bright red and green beggar coming down on to my tail. So I came up again and we began turning round and round, he diving and firing at me, and then climbing up again, while I had all my work cut out to get out of the light and to climb up to him gradually. Meanwhile I had heard one bullet go into my under-carriage with the deuce of a wonk, one or two others were making

337

themselves unpleasant by spoiling the appearance of my immaculate planes, and the tiresome young man in the red bus finally was unkind enough to plonk one into my engine, which we found out afterwards made a hole six inches square in the water jacket. Then for some curious reason he completely sheered off, or in other words, cleared off towards Hunland i.e. the east. And I, knowing very well my engine was wounded, proceeded to turn west, and after about five minutes, during which time I must have covered about 10–12 miles (aided by a strong east wind) the engine stopped altogether. So, after gliding as far as I could – from 7,000 feet – I perched neatly in a field not far from another aerodrome. I'm jolly lucky to have got off so light, the man up against me was obviously a far better pilot and fighter than I was – one of the few Hun 'pros' I expect. I can't think why he left me when he had me 'stony' as if I had had to go on turning much longer I should not have been able to get so far over the lines with my glide. [37]

Second Lieutenant Arthur Rhys Davids, 56 Squadron, RFC

It has been suggested that the red and green Albatros was flown by the ace Leutnant Kurt Wolff, and indeed this would fit with his adopted colour scheme at Jasta 11, but, confusingly, the day before, 6 May, he was promoted to take over command of Jasta 29 after his recent award of the *Pour le Mérite*. Whoever it was, he had presumably either run out of ammunition or suffered some kind of engine failure. Whatever the case there does not seem to have been a victory claim as a result of the skirmish. In the affray below them, Crowe and Leach attacked the lone Albatros and after a quick skirmish Leach claimed to have shot it down. Retribution quickly followed, for Leach was separated from Crowe and encountered another German scout. This time the luck went the other way. Spandau bullets stitched their way through his petrol tank and leg forcing a difficult crash landing in the lunar landscape of Vimy Ridge. Leach was rescued by Canadian troops but his badly wounded leg was later amputated. Crowe was now alone in the darkening skies.

Elsewhere, Captain Meintjes and C Flight had collectively ambushed a lone white German scout, which they claimed to have shot down. Meintjes then led Lewis and Hoidge into action with another group of German scouts:

I'd say there might have been a dozen Huns. Whether they were all
from von Richthofen's squadron, I won't say, but I do know that some
of them were red planes. Two of them chased me to the lines and I was
damned lucky to escape. They were red planes, Albatros V-strutters.[38]

Second Lieutenant Reginald Hoidge, 56 Squadron, RFC

However many German scouts there were, the three SE5s were
separated in the general hurly-burly and Meintjes was unremittingly tracked
by a skilful opponent who forced him into a desperate spin to try and
escape. On emerging much lower down, he came across another red
Albatros flown by Leutnant Wolfgang von Pluschow of Jasta 11, which he
apparently managed to shoot down. Fresh from this triumph he too met
his match in a skirmish with yet another unknown Albatros. This time
Meintjes was totally outflown and caught by a burst of fire which smashed
his wrist and wrecked his controls. He was lucky not to succumb to unconsciousness until he had managed a reasonable forced landing.

Lieutenant Cecil Lewis was left fighting two Albatros scouts, but was
rescued by the timely arrival of Captain Albert Ball and Second Lieutenant Knaggs of A Flight. The Germans wisely disengaged, which was
relatively easy in the prevailing cloud conditions. Throughout the engagements the SE5 flight formations had fragmented, come together in varying
combinations for a few moments and then quickly lost contact with each
other again. In this confused picture of quick encounter battles and
dogfights, the four Albatros scouts from Jasta 11 undoubtedly played their
full part:

Suddenly, in a north-easterly direction, about 100 metres above us,
I spotted four enemy biplanes, which, turning left, tried to come in
behind us. They were led by a fighter plane with long pennants
attached to the wings. I don't remember if this attack surprised my
comrades as much as it did me. Naturally, I wanted to improve my
position by gaining altitude and clearing my tail. I began a flat, slowly
climbing turn to the left, always looking behind me, but when I had
flown a complete circle, I found that I could not see any other plane in
the sky, friend or foe.[39]

Leutnant Wilhelm Allmenröder, Jasta 11, German Army Air Force

Meanwhile, Captain Crowe had encountered the equally lonely Lieutenant Cecil Lewis of B Flight:

From now until the end of the patrol, which lasted until dusk, I flew about accompanied by Lieutenant Lewis whom I had found wandering about like myself looking for a mate. We were soon engaged at frequent intervals in short sharp combats with Albatros of variegated colours, including red, which was the hallmark of the members of the Richthofen 'circus'.[40]

Captain Cyril Crowe, 56 Squadron, RFC

In one of these vicious scraps Crowe had the unpleasant experience of having his goggles shot off his face – a close shave that could hardly have been closer. Then, a little ahead of them, Crowe sighted Albert Ball:

As it got darker and darker, I decided to return to our lines, and on the way I saw a solitary SE5 flying due north a few miles over the lines and firing Very lights. I immediately proceeded in its direction in an endeavour to join it, and getting close, I saw it was Ball. He did not appear to see me, for he flew straight into a cloud bank in a north-easterly direction. I followed him. When I got out of the clouds again I saw Ball diving after an enemy aeroplane which disappeared into a cloud and which was hotly pursued by Ball. I followed through the same cloud, which was a big one, and when I got through to the opening on the other side I could neither see Ball nor his opponent, and I did not see him again. The height was then 4,000 feet.[41]

Captain Cyril Crowe, 56 Squadron, RFC

Ball was in combat with the Albatros D III of Lothar von Richthofen. Allmenröder was also in the immediate vicinity, doubtless concealed from Crowe and Lewis by the heavy cloud cover:

I looked around and then saw, about 20 metres below me, Lothar in a wild circling dogfight with a British fighter. Both opponents circled around below me, but neither had a chance to shoot. As I was higher, I would have had a chance to fire, but I had a feeling that I had better not interfere. Besides this, I could not understand where the other aircraft had gone, and I was afraid that they might return.[42]

Leutnant Wilhelm Allmenröder, Jasta 11, German Army Air Force

Crowe tried his best to catch Ball, but another pressing consideration was beginning to make itself felt. The SE5s had been in the air for nearly three hours and they were all running short of fuel:

As I knew that my petrol must be running low, I reluctantly made for our lines, unaccompanied, as Lewis and I had lost one another in the clouds. On the way back I met a two-seater going home and had a quick crack at it without any apparent luck. I eventually had to land owing to the darkness at No. 8 (Naval) Squadron, Auchel at 8.15. When my petrol tank was examined, it was found to be almost dry.[43]

Captain Cyril Crowe, 56 Squadron, RFC

Captain Albert Ball must have been in the same position and if he had gone any further east would have been at severe risk of running out of petrol. Allmenröder claimed to be 'holding the ring' and still watching the contest between the two great aces:

Each tried to better his position by wide left turns; however, no one gained an advantage and not a shot was fired. Meanwhile it became darker and darker. Off to the north-east, Douai was barely visible. The sun had just gone down. Suddenly, as if both had received an order, the two left the circle and flew straight away, Lothar to the south, his opponent to the north. I had believed that they wanted to stop the fight because of the darkness, but then both turned and rushed at each other as if they intended to ram. Lothar dipped under the other and then both turned and rushed again at each other, only a few shots being fired. At the third frontal attack, Lothar came from the south, and his opponent from the north – I waited. The machine guns peppered again. This time, Lothar's opponent did not give way sideways but dived down to the ground. I had wanted to see where the plane crashed, but I became anxious because Lothar also went down in a rather steep turn and disappeared in the mist. I flew back to our airfield to order that a search be made for Lothar. As I jumped out of the plane, it was almost night. I was immediately informed that Lothar had made an emergency landing because his engine was hit. He himself was not injured.[44]

Leutnant Wilhelm Alimenröder, Jasta 11, German Army Air Force

In truth, there are probably no totally reliable accounts of this last combat between Albert Ball and Lothar von Richthofen, although it is known that someone's bullets caused sufficient engine damage to Richthofen's Albatros to oblige him to make a forced landing that evening. Whatever happened, shortly afterwards, Ball himself crash-landed near a farmhouse on the outskirts of the little village of Annoeullin. Fatally injured, he expired after a few minutes whilst cradled in the comforting arms of the young French woman who was the first to find him. The British hero, the idol of the RFC was dead at just 20 years old.

The official German version of his death insisted that he had been shot down by Lothar von Richthofen who had put in a claim for shooting down a triplane at about the correct time. Yet this makes very little sense, and the fact that the confirming witnesses also claimed it was a triplane only adds to the suspicion that this claim was opportunistic, if not actually disingenuous. The SE5 flown by Ball was clearly a biplane not a triplane, and as an experienced pilot Lothar von Richthofen would have seen the difference at a glance. Nevertheless propaganda and prestige meant that the Germans had no hesitation in proclaiming Ball the twentieth victory of Lothar von Richthofen.

The British had no idea what happened – indeed there were rumours at the time that Ball had survived and was taken prisoner. They decreed that Ball must have been shot down by anti-aircraft fire, probably directed from the local church tower. The evidence for such a claim is equally shallow. However, one eye-witness to the crash left an account of what he saw. Leutnant Franz Hailer was with a group of other German officers when he saw an SE5 emerge upside down from a large cloud, its engine apparently stopped and trailing a thin plume of smoke. Still upside down the SE5 crash-landed near the Fashoda farmhouse a mile from Annoeullin. He rushed over to find that Ball had been removed from the wreckage and was being cradled in the arms of a local French woman:

> The aircraft was upside down with the wheels 'sticking up'. It was leaving a cloud of black smoke and this I considered was caused by oil leaking into the cylinders. We examined the wreckage and we all came to the conclusion that the aircraft had not been either shot down in an air fight or anti-aircraft fire as the dead pilot had no marks or scratches and had not been wounded. I looked through his papers and found it was Captain Ball. We called him the English Richthofen. We were very disturbed by it all. I took his dead body to the field hospital. The doctor couldn't find any bullet wounds on the body, although the back and one leg were broken.[45]
>
> Leutnant Franz Hailer, German Army

The death of a great ace such as Captain Albert Ball often became enshrouded in as much mystery as the demise of a medieval saint. The fact that Ball was last seen flying into an ominous thundercloud only added to the slightly Arthurian nature of the reports of his death. The propaganda requirements of the time demanded that one of the new paladins of the air could not simply be defeated in combat – since he had come to embody the whole spirit of their nation's manhood that could not be allowed. Equally, it was natural that the opposing side would forgo no chance to gloat about the triumph over an enemy ace. The endless claims and counter-claims were often deliberately intended to obfuscate the prosaic truth and propagate the image desired. As time has passed the truth about Ball's death has become wreathed in legend and is almost impossible to determine. Lieutenant Franz Hailer, who had seen the crash and inspected both aircraft and body, had a fairly commonsensical approach:

> My own opinion, and you will appreciate I was not in the air at the time, covers just two possibilities: 1) The odd chance that Lothar von Richthofen, in exchanging shots with Captain Ball's SE5, hit the aircraft with a stray shot – the breech of the Vickers gun carried a bullet hole. 2) I have thought that Captain Ball, flying into a cloud, turned the aircraft over and was unaware of this until he broke cloud, then so low that he could do nothing and the aircraft flew into the ground. Again, when the SE5 crashed, it did not fire, and he must have been very low on fuel.[46]
>
> Leutnant Franz Hailer, German Army

It is certainly true that Ball's SE5 would not have taken kindly to being flown for any period of time inverted. The carburettor fitted to the early production model engines would undoubtedly flood the air intake, which would cause it to choke and stop the engine. If this happened when still upside down and at a very low altitude, then Ball would assuredly have had no chance of preventing the SE5 ploughing into the ground. Whatever the exact cause, and it cannot now be determined for sure, Ball's sad demise was a severe blow to the RFC as his sheer élan had inspired most of his contemporaries, including Captain Baring:

> We got news that Ball is missing. This has cast a gloom through the whole Flying Corps. He was not only perhaps the most inspired pilot

we have ever had, but the most modest and engaging character. His squadron, and indeed all the squadrons, will feel this terribly.[47]

Captain Maurice Baring, Headquarters, RFC

A month after his death, on 3 June, Albert Ball was awarded a posthumous Victoria Cross. The final score which had mattered so much to him and in effect lured him to his death was in the region of forty victories. He was buried by the Germans with full military honours as a respected opponent at Annoeullin.

CAPTAIN Albert Ball may have been dead but the RFC had little or no time to grieve. For the army cooperation squadrons the same old priorities and requirements endured; there could be no let up in their ceaseless campaign. Lieutenant Charles Smart took off with Air Mechanic Smith in his RE8 on 8 May:

> We had to go quite a long way over so we made up a strong party and flew in formation, three machines taking photos and two acting as escort. We had just got as far over as we were going when twelve Hun scout machines came right through us, a real ding-dong scrap followed. A Hun dived at the machine I was guarding and I had to do something so I pushed my nose down with the engine full on and dived at him firing my gun like hell, at the same time a Hun dived at me and my observer engaged him with the rear gun. My airspeed indicator only registers up to 140 mph and when I looked at it the needle was stuck right up against the side, so we must have been going some. Down we swirled for about 2,000 feet, both guns firing and making no end of a noise out of both ends, anyhow my machine made it so hot for both Huns that they broke off the flight and cleared east. Our other machines were all engaged, one by four Huns at a time and there was no end of shooting going on. The Huns got more than they expected, one went down in a spinning nosedive but managed to pull out after falling a good 3,000 feet. Right in the middle of the show one of the Huns fired a white light and off they all cleared into the east, leaving us cock of the walk, we then completed our job and came home. It was a glorious fight. I have never been through anything quite so exciting, machines were whizzing about all over the place like mad swallows, the air resounded with the, 'Pop! Pop!

Pop!!' of machine guns and tracer bullets could be seen flying in all
directions. No one in our crowd was hit, but the machines were pretty
well shot about. I only got two bullets through my planes. We now call
ourselves 'The Circus' and rightly so, for have not five RE8s engaged
twelve Huns on their own patch and licked them hollow? Aircraftman
Smith behaved splendidly right through the show, he just sat on his seat
like a block of wood and fired his gun like steam as long as there was
anything to fire at. It is strange how little fear enters into one during a
fight, I never thought of being hurt, my only desire was to kill a German
and I feel sure I would have rammed a Hun machine if I could have got
near enough to do it. As for handling a machine one can do *simply
anything* when there is a scrap on. You cannot compare fighting on the
ground with fighting in the air, the two are in about the same ratio as
tiddlywinks and big game shooting for excitement; perhaps I should
not say this if I had been at a bayonet charge![48]

Second Lieutenant Charles Smart, 5 Squadron, RFC

The RE8s were indeed a very different proposition to the BE2es that
5 Squadron had been flying for so long. They certainly had defects, but at
least they offered some realistic hope of survival if correctly handled. Yet
some of the army cooperation squadrons had still not been re-equipped.
Second Lieutenant Frank Thompson and his observer Lieutenant Arthur
Rawlins of 13 Squadron were still flying a BE2e on 13 May when they
had the misfortune to encounter Leutnant Lothar von Richthofen. They
themselves were an unusual crew, for while the pilot was considerably
under age at just 17 years old, the observer was a grizzled old man of 40.
They were quickly shot down but managed to land behind the British front
lines and both escaped to fight again.

Lothar, however, had come down low to track the crash site of his
victims and in doing so exposed himself to a considerable amount of British
anti-aircraft fire. One of the guns scored a hit and he was badly wounded
in the left hip. Struggling with nausea and a fast-fading consciousness
Lothar managed to make it back over the German lines before landing
and passing out. The wound kept him away from the front until late
September 1917 and thus froze his victory score at twenty-four for five
months, although the receipt of the *Pour le Mérite* on 14 May must have
acted as some small compensation. Lothar von Richthofen may have been
a rash tactician, and indeed he was frequently wounded in action, but it

has been estimated that he scored his eventual total of forty victories in just seventy-seven days of combat during his career as a scout pilot. The temporary removal of such a deadly opponent was of significant material assistance to the RFC in May 1917.

For the British scout squadrons the situation in the air was definitely beginning to offer a more hopeful countenance as if somehow the tide had turned. A combination of the arrival of the new types of aircraft, the departure on leave of the dread Manfred von Richthofen, the inevitable sprinkling of casualties and perhaps the accumulated fatigue that was now spreading through the seriously outnumbered German Air Force meant that at last things were slowly getting better:

> We are having things a good deal easier just now for some unknown reason. I really think that the period during which the Huns very seriously were threatening to be top dog in the air is at an end.[49]
> Captain William Bond, 40 Squadron, RFC

Of course, as things got easier, more and more of the RFC and RNAS pilots like Bond were able to accumulate the flying time and vital combat experience, which they slowly began to convert into concrete victories:

> I was with Gregory and when we were at 16,500 feet, about 5 miles over the lines, he dived on two Hun two-seaters at about 14,000 feet. I saw him go down and pass right underneath and then I went for the other. It was a big bus with polished yellow wooden body and green wings. At about 100 yards I started firing, and the Hun, who was going across me, turned and climbed round as if to get on my tail. Then came my Immelmann turn! With engine full on, I pulled the machine up hard and nearly vertical. When she was almost stalling I kicked her left-hand rudder hard and the machine whipped over on one wing, turned her nose down, and came out exactly in the opposite direction. The Hun was now dead in front of my gun about 200 feet below me. I opened on him again and almost immediately he started diving and slowly spinning. To keep my gun on him I had to go down absolutely vertical, and eventually went beyond the vertical and found myself on my back with the engine stopped through choking. When at length I fell into a normal attitude again, the Hun had disappeared. One of our patrols which had come over in time to see the scrap says he went down spinning and crashed.[50]
> Captain William Bond, 40 Squadron, RFC

As the pilots gained in experience, their 'air vision' improved and they began to see aircraft that previously had been missed. The skies were no longer perceived to be 'empty' and numerous fresh opportunities offered themselves for the interception of German aircraft now they could be seen. Even when he ran into trouble, Bond now had the experience to 'do the right thing' when seconds mattered:

> When a good way over, saw a Hun two-seater. Gregory gave chase and it headed north-east. I don't know for how long we followed, but we gained slowly, and at last Gregory dived. As he did so the Hun fired three rockets, evidently a signal. Gregory fired at close range and sheered off. The Hun observer fired back at him as the pilot dived. I then went down vertically after him firing dead on and did not stop until my drum was empty. The Hun was still going down – falling. He had not fired at me and we believe both pilot and observer had been hit. I started climbing while changing my empty drum for a full one, and, looking around, saw two scout machines above me. 'Gregory and Godfrey', I thought; and proceeded leisurely, climbing up to them. One of the pilots put his nose down and came towards me, and next moment I heard the familiar and horrid, 'Pop-pop-pop!' They were firing at me. It certainly was not Gregory nor Godfrey. As I had feared all through the chase the Hun two-seater had been a lure and now I was in a trap. They had 1,000 feet of height on me, so I put my nose westward and downward, and, glancing round, saw that they were doing the same. By losing height steadily I was able to keep up speed, but I hadn't realised how far east we had come. It seemed hours before I saw the trenches in the distance – actually it was fifteen minutes before I reached them. All the time the Huns were firing short bursts, but I was never going straight for three seconds together. I kicked the rudder and slid flat from one side to another, and at last as I crossed the reserve Hun trenches – now at less than 3,000 feet – I saw the Hun machines turn away. It wasn't all over though, for, first, tracer bullets came up from the ground and, after I had dived and side-slipped to avoid them, the anti-aircraft guns put up a barrage in front of me. For five minutes I turned and twisted to throw them off and finally got over our trenches at 1,000 feet.[51]

Captain William Bond, 40 Squadron, RFC

On landing Bond found that Gregory had also been attacked by a couple of German scouts, while Godfrey had sighted the threatening scouts but then got lost in the clouds.

In contrast, future ace Lieutenant Edward Mannock had still not managed to conquer either his fears or the technical problems that dogged his performance in combat. His deflection shooting was still poor, perhaps hampered by eyesight problems, and in May 1917 he simply lacked the 'knack' of shooting down his enemies:

> Captain Keen, Rastus and myself on second patrol – 9 to 10.30 a.m. Rastus left us early owing to engine trouble so we went on without him. We engaged a Hun over Henin Lietard and chased him over towards Courcelles. I turned east and Keen turned west. I was inevitably attacked by three Huns. My gun jammed – Keen was almost out of sight. 'Aldous' sight oiled up, and the engine failed at the crucial moment. I thought all was up. We were 16,000 feet up at the time. I turned almost vertically on my tail – nose-dived and spun down towards our own lines, zig-zagging for all I was worth with machine guns cracking away behind me like mad. The engine picked up when I was about 3,000 feet over Arras and the Huns for some reason or other had left me. I immediately ran into another Hun (after I had climbed up to 12,000 feet again) but hadn't the pluck to face him. I turned away and landed here with my knees shaking and my nerves all torn to bits. I feel a bit better now, but all my courage seems to have gone after that experience this morning. The CO was very good and didn't put me on any more line jobs for the rest of the day.[52]
>
> Lieutenant Edward Mannock, 40 Squadron, RFC

At the end of the war Mannock was rated officially as the highest scoring British ace and acclaimed as the finest patrol commander of his generation, so it is ironic that on this occasion his slow learning curve coupled with his highly strung temperament meant he came within a whisker of disgrace and consignment to home service.

There was now a seemingly endless supply of new British pilots, stepping brightly into the shoes of the dead, the exhausted and the mentally shot. One such young 'press on' pilot was Flight Sub-Lieutenant Bernard Ellis:

> At last I can claim a Hun. Last night I drove two down and with the help of another man crashed a third. It was a glorious scrap, but one

doesn't often get such a chance. I fought one down 5,000 feet and eventually saw him off, not crashed but 'driven down'. Then I found six on my tail, so the only thing to do was to fight them until something happened. Luckily the something was another of my lot and while he was there I drove another Hun down, then my partner had a gun jam and I had four to keep going till another of my lot turned up at which three of the four Huns thought fit to go. This other man dived on the remaining Hun and pumped quite a lot into him, and drove him below me so, as my partner had drawn off, I attacked and finished off the unfortunate Hun, who crashed. Then we were at 5,000 feet, ten miles the wrong side of the lines and had 'Archies' the whole way home. I found I had one strut nearly shot through and two hits from 'Archies', one within half an inch of my petrol tank – it's a great war isn't it?[53]

Flight Sub-Lieutenant Bernard Ellis, I (Naval) Squadron, RNAS

For such young men war was a game. They had not lived enough to fear the finality of death; they were filled with the unquenchable optimism of youth. Death and maiming were something that happened to other people – extras in the grand adventure of their personal life story:

We had great fun on patrol this morning, there were lots of lumps of cloud – about 3,000 feet high and perhaps 6,000 feet across – floating about with ripping great jagged edges and so when we got fed up patrolling we played hide and seek round these. It's a lovely game as long as you don't run into anyone or meet half a dozen Huns round the next corner when the rest of your crowd is out of sight, but that sort of thing doesn't really happen.[54]

Flight Sub-Lieutenant Bernard Ellis, I (Naval) Squadron, RNAS

It was this feeling of invincibility that led many pilots into more trouble than, in the end, they could handle. The 19-year-old Ellis who had so exultantly claimed his first kill just a week before, soon found that there was a bleak reverse image to the coin of aerial success. On 19 May he was caught up in a vicious dogfight and was last seen falling through the clouds, perhaps only realising the game was finally up when he jumped or fell from his doomed aircraft. The victory was claimed by Leutnant G. W. Groos of Jasta 4. Flight Lieutenant Roderic Dallas wrote in reply to a query from his grieving father:

349

I am afraid I was not actually leading the patrol on May 19th. I was leading one patrol, and was joined by another in which your son was. We became engaged in a big fight, and your son gave a very fine account of himself indeed. He had already shot down one of his opponents when I saw him attacked by another. Your son was very tenacious and fought it out, and went down out of control through the clouds.[55]

Flight Lieutenant Roderic Dallas, 1 (Naval) Squadron, RNAS

Tenacious Ellis may have been; dead he most certainly was. Just another tragedy; another victim in the tragic story of the Battle of Arras.

At least the scout pilots had some element of choice in their actions; the army cooperation pilots had no option but to sit and take it. For them there was only their routine duty, no glorious feats recounted in bold newspaper headlines. Captain Bernard Rice was in awe of the sheer guts and determination required by his brother Lieutenant Eddie Rice serving with the FE2bs of 55 Squadron on long-range reconnaissance and bombing missions deep behind the German lines. He even wrote home to their parents in a manner that can hardly have reassured them:

You are being shelled all the way and chivvied by fast scouts who belt lead at you all the time. Every now and then your pals on either side of you burst into sheets of flame and pitching forward dive to earth at frightful speed attaining perhaps 500 miles per hour before striking the earth some 5 miles below. What sort of nerve has the fellow got to stick this sort of thing, and he is so devilish cheery too? It hasn't taken any effect on him at all. You bred a man when you brought that old lad up let me tell you.[56]

Captain Bernard Rice, 8 Squadron, RFC

Yet the BE2cs and RE8s were suffering almost the same level of risks as they hovered above the front lines:

This morning I was up and watching some machines dodging 'Archie'. Suddenly a flare and something like a comet rushed earthwards. I looked the other way and tried to draw my observer's attention to an imaginary machine in the other direction. I won't say any more on that subject. I only broached it because it seems people at home are getting low spirited about things in general. Chiefly, I suspect, because they are getting their little luxuries cut off. But if we can keep cheerful out here amidst the above happenings can't those at home do the same? If

350

spirits drop at home now, after all these months of sacrifice and work, and they want to fix up a peace now that we have the end almost in sight, or perhaps I should say that the beginning of the last stage has arrived, of what avail the huge loss of life in the past three years?[57]

Captain Bernard Rice, 8 Squadron, RFC

INEVITABLY the Germans caught on to the British change of emphasis away from the Arras front as the offensive preparations in Flanders became more and more obvious. Slowly the skies above Arras emptied of the predatory German Albatros scouts as they began to transfer their Jasta to the north. One to leave the 'happy hunting grounds' was Leutnant Werner Voss who departed from the immediate area after promotion on 20 May to take command of Jasta 5. By this time he had shot down some twenty-eight aircraft.

As the skies got easier for the British it seems somehow typical that the scouts should spend their increasing freedom trying to scare their army cooperation colleagues into an early grave. Certainly the personal fears of Second Lieutenant Edward Mannock did not seem to have given him any insight into the sufferings of others who might also be afflicted by nerves:

The 'Uns seem to have been transferred to the Eastern Front. We roam all over Hunland without seeing an iron cross, although their 'Archie' devils are just as accurate as ever. Went out with Thompson this evening looking for scalps, but nothing doing. Amused ourselves by dodging about the low clouds and frightening the engine out of sundry crawling 'quirks' doing artillery work. Great sport. You come down vertically at approx 160 mph on a poor unsuspecting observer and bank away to the right or left when almost cutting off his tail. You can almost hear him gasp. They're always pleased to see us about though, and they forgive a little 'skylarking' occasionally.[58]

Second Lieutenant Edward Mannock, 40 Squadron, RFC

It is hard to imagine that the likes of Major Alan Dore, Captain Bernard Rice, Captain Ewart Garland, Captain Eric Routh and Lieutenant Charles Smart – in so many ways the real heroes of this grim story – would have been terribly amused by Mannock's antics. But he would earn their forgiveness for any passing annoyance during his inspirational career over the next year.

CHAPTER EIGHT

EPILOGUE

This Count Richthofen you mention, Dad, is nothing to worry about.
He will soon be brought down. Believe me, every machine of ours he
has brought down has been a slow old artillery observation machine,
practically incapable of defending itself.[1]

Second Lieutenant Walter Wood, 29 Squadron, RFC

The misconceptions and self-delusions contained within these few
words are quite startling. After the war there was undoubtedly a self-
congratulatory perception amongst the British public that the men of the
Royal Flying Corps had a great admiration for Richthofen; that he was
as much a hero to them as to the German Air Service. But an immersion
in the memoirs and accounts of the pilots and observers he was fighting
makes it more than apparent that for many their dominating emotions
were a mixture of fear and hatred. After the war many could not resist the
temptation to denigrate his record. Mean-spirited attempts abound sug-
gesting that his victory record was packed with fraudulent claims and there
were endless accusations that he was little more than a murderer preying on
defenceless victims in a thoroughly caddish fashion, or even that his victories
were spoon-fed to him by his 'henchmen'. As ever it is the hatred of a
man's enemies that best reflect his successes in life.

It is a remarkable fact that despite all the clouded confusions of aerial
fighting, for only a couple of Manfred von Richthofen's victories is there any
real doubt as to the identity of his victims. For all the mud thrown so
liberally at Richthofen, his victory list has now been pretty well confirmed
by modern researchers, with names and aircraft assigned for almost every
one of his claimed 'kills'. This stands in stark contrast to the lists of victories
claimed by some of the British and Canadian aces, although it should be

borne in mind that the Germans naturally found it easier to corroborate their claims as most of the fighting was on the German side of the lines. Of course some German pilots undoubtedly exaggerated their achievements, but this fades into insignificance compared to the endemic culture of optimistic claims prevalent amongst many of the RFC and RNAS scout pilots. In some cases innocent wishful thinking seems to have drifted into deliberate embellishment and even routine lying. Post-war investigations based on known German casualties have now severely undermined the status of many pilots' victory lists.

Yet after all the analysis, Manfred von Richthofen still stands acclaimed as a scout pilot and formation leader *par excellence*; it was his job to sweep the Allied observation aircraft from the skies and this he did to the very best of his ability. He *knew* that the photographs, clock-code corrections and zone calls guided unprecedented concentrations of British shell. The army cooperation airmen may not have killed directly, but their hands were metaphorically steeped in the blood of hundreds, if not thousands, of German soldiers. This was why Richthofen sought them out. Not, as is often implied, because they represented another easy 'kill', the chance of a gruesome souvenir, or a specially struck silver 'hunting' cup. Richthofen hunted them down because they were the real enemy and the *raison d'être* of the whole air war. He and the other leading German scout pilots were supreme practitioners of the defensive pattern of aerial fighting forced on Germany by the strategic situation and the sheer numbers of aircraft that flooded over the German lines in the relentless aerial offensive waged by the RFC. They were not cold-hearted murderers, but men fighting to the very best of their considerable abilities in the cause of their country.

Most paid the inevitable penalty for fighting against the odds in skies increasingly full of British aircraft: Hans Lübbert caught his final bullet on 30 March, 1917; Karl-Emil Schäfer died in action on 5 June 1917, Karl Allmenröder was shot down and killed on 27 June, 1917; Kurt Wolff died aged 22 on 15 September 1917; Werner Voss was killed aged 20 as he took on single-handed a Flight full of aces from 56 Squadron on 23 September 1917; Erwin Böhme died in combat on 29 November 1917; Adolf von Tutschek was shot down and killed on 15 March 1918; and the greatest of them all, Manfred von Richthofen, broke all his own rules and duly perished on 21 April 1918. Otto Bernert, who had been badly wounded as an infantry officer in 1914, was wounded again and rendered unfit for further flying on 18 August 1917, only to succumb in the deadly influenza pandemic of 1918. Ironically, the wild Lothar von Richthofen, unlike his cautious brother, survived the war, only to die in a peacetime flying accident in 1922. They were great heroes by any standards and it is difficult not to admire and applaud their very real achievements in the cause of their country. Of Hermann Göring perhaps the least said the better ....

Richthofen may have been a logical and thoughtful scout leader but he still killed his victims in the hot blood of aerial combat. The British army cooperation pilots and observers not only killed in cold blood, but in indubitably far greater numbers as they cruised up and down above the German lines. Most of them fully understood their vital role in building up the cumulative grinding pressure that typified the Allied war effort in 1917:

> If you read your newspapers, and hear about a lot of fights up and down the line, when casualties are big, or when a village capture is reported you say, 'We've won a big battle' or 'We've broken through'. Then nothing further happens for some days, or maybe weeks, and you grow first impatient and then dispirited, and say 'We can't win, it's no good, we'll never break through!' All the time everyone is working at fever heat out here and each of those seemingly isolated fights is a very important part of one large plan which takes months to materialise. You want to take a position with the idea of breaking through, there is another to the north perhaps, commanding that position, so that must be taken too, and so on. All the ground has to be photographed by us, batteries knocked out, communication trenches registered on by certain batteries told off to block them on the appointed day. When it is taken that position must be held, then off go the guns and are massed somewhere else for the next bit. Perhaps the enemy persist in counter-attacks, consequently delay – we have to keep troops and guns there. And again come the rumours of impatience from home. It is all very like a game of chess. Continued checkmating and counter-moves. We are now superior in 'heavy pieces'.[2]
>
> Captain Bernard Rice, 8 Squadron, RFC

These men who took off day after day in their clearly obsolescent army cooperation aircraft were the real British heroes of the aerial campaign that formed the backdrop to the Battle of Arras. They knew what they were doing and why; they understood the appalling risks they were running; they were more than aware of the grisly nature of the near-inevitable death that awaited them in the skies. Yet they kept on taking off, time after time. Many speedily suffered the deaths that haunted their worst nightmares; others lasted months until their luck finally ran out, their nerves gave way, or at last they were sent home exhausted. The numbers killed were not large *per se* but the percentages were terrifying.

According to figures collated by Trevor Henshaw in his book *The Sky Their Battlefield*[3], for 1917 the RFC suffered a total of 47 casualties (24 killed in action) during January; 96 casualties (52 KIA) in February; 188 casualties (92 KIA) in March; a devastating 421 casualties (207 KIA) during April and 262 casualties (98 KIA) in May. For March; this represented just 101 hours of flying time for every death, which fell even further to 92 hours in April at the height of the air battle. Not all of these men were involved in operations directly related to the Battle of Arras, but a good proportion most certainly were. Overall, between January and the end of May the RFC lost some 708 aircraft of which an incredible 275 fell in April. As one would expect the obsolescent models were particularly well represented in aircraft losses. In the period January to May the RFC suffered the loss of 151 assorted BE2s, 168 FE2bs and FE2ds and 64 Sopwith 1½ Strutters. Of the RE8s that would take on the mantle of the BE2s some 37 aircraft were lost. Total RFC casualties for the five months were 1,014, of which 473 were dead, 317 wounded and 224 prisoners of war. Even with the further massive expansion of air fighting in 1918 it was only in the last three months of the war that this scale of loss was exceeded.

The fate of individual scout pilots is often well known, but the army cooperation pilots and their valiant observers tended to die anonymous deaths, covered only as a brief entry in the ever-lengthening casualty lists. Early in the Arras campaign, the shy young Sergeant Ernest Cook had considered his prospects with a cold realism that belied his callow youth:

> Heard great rumours of things to be. Don't care. Time is flitting –
> I have lived now longer than I expected.[4]
>
> Sergeant Ernest Cook, 45 Squadron, RFC

In the end, against all the odds, he survived the Battle of Arras. But a new battle loomed before him in support of the offensive in Flanders, where he was still condemned to fly the sadly obsolescent Sopwith 1½ Strutter.

Like so many survivors of Arras, his ultimate destiny was little more than postponed. On 5 June 1917, Sergeant Cook was shot down and killed with his observer, Air Mechanic H. V. Shaw, whilst carrying out a photographic reconnaissance of the Menin sector.

But what of the total British Army casualties at Arras? This after all was the point of it all. The statistics of killed, wounded and prisoners for April and May make for grim reading: the First Army under General Sir Henry Horne lost 46,828; the Third Army under General Sir Edmund Allenby lost 87,226 and the Fifth Army under General Sir Hubert Gough lost 24,608 – a staggering total of 158,660 of which some 150,000 casualties were directly attributable to the Arras offensive. The casualties suffered by the RFC simply pale away into insignificance against this backdrop of wholesale slaughter, which would without any doubt have been far worse if the airmen had not carried out their duty in the skies above them.

The men who fought and died both on the ground and in the air at Arras have been done a considerable disservice by suggestions that they were mere pawns, sacrificed by stupid and insensitive generals, engaged in yet another futile offensive. Such perceptions are well wide of the mark. The Battle of Arras was fought for perfectly cogent military reasons; it was part of the Allied strategy in a global war to the death against a strong modern industrial nation state blessed with reservoirs of men to mobilise; a war against a Germany that had by no means reached the end of her rope in 1917. Such a battle could never be postponed indefinitely merely to await the arrival of the latest aircraft. The RFC may not have been ready in material terms, but it rose to the challenge. The pilots and observers carried out their duty and suffered the inevitable casualties in the service of the guns, which would one day bring victory to the Allies on the Western Front. They, and the young German aces that tried their best to hold them back, deserve our unstinting admiration.

NOTES

CHAPTER ONE **The Reason Why**

1 J. Charteris, *At G.H.Q* (London: Cassell & Co, 1931), pp. 178–9

2 E. Ludendorff, *My War Memories* (London: Hutchinson & Co, 1919), Vol. I, p. 267

3 Ibid. p. 307

4 National Archive: AIR 1/2392/228/11/186

5 IWM Docs: F. C. Penny, Typescript account, 'Memories of Flying, 1915–1918', pp. 13–14

6 von Below quoted in A. Morris, *Bloody April* (London: Jarrolds, 1967), p. 122

7 IWM Sound Archive: C. Lewis, AC 4162

8 H. Trenchard quoted in A. Boyle, *Trenchard: Man of Vision* (London: Collins, 1962), pp. 186–7

9 IWM Library: Anon, 'Extracts from German Documents and Correspondence' (SS 473), p. 3

10 H. Trenchard quoted in N. Macmillan, *Sir Sefton Brancker* (London: William Heinemann, 1935), p. 133

11 D. Haig quoted in H. A. Jones, *Official History of the War: The War in the Air* (Oxford: Clarendon Press, 1922–1937), Vol. II, pp. 296–7

12 S. Brancker quoted in N. Macmillan, *Sir Sefton Brancker* , p. 136

13 E. Böhme quoted in D. V. Fant, 'Many Battles and Many a Bold Venture, the letters of Oberleutnant Erwin Böhme', *Over the Front*, Vol. 5, No. 1, p. 49

14 D. Haig, *Sir Douglas Haig's Despatches: December 1915–April 1919* London: J. M. Dent & Sons, 1979, p. 54

15 RAF Museum: W. J. Lidsey, Typescript dairy, 25/12/1916

CHAPTER TWO **Winter's Freezing**

1 RAF Museum: O. B. Rice, Manuscript letter, 18/5/1917–21/5/1917

2 National Archive: AIR 1/2387/228/11/37 R. M. Hill

3 H. Trenchard quoted in A. Boyle, *Trenchard: Man of Vision* (London: Collins, 1962), p. 209

4 H. Trenchard quoted in N. Macmillan, *Sir Sefton Brancker*, p. 146

5 C. M. Clements quoted in W. F. J. Harvey, *Pi in the Sky: A History of No 22 Squadron RFC/RAF in the War of 1914–1918* (Privately published: Canterbury, 1969), pp. 25–6

6 IWM Sound Archive: H. G. Taylor, AC 307, Reel 1

7 G. M. Hopkins quoted in B. J. Gray, 'Pusher Pilot with 22', *Cross & Cockade*, Vol. 3 No. 2, p. 48

8 T. H. Gladstone, 'Another Pusher Pilot with 22', *Cross & Cockade*, Vol. 10, No. 3, pp.127–8

9 IWM Docs: H. G. Taylor, Typescript account, p. 14

10 G. M. Hopkins quoted in B.J. Gray, 'Pusher Pilot with 22', p. 48

11 B. F. Crane quoted in W. F. J. Harvey, *Pi in the Sky*, p. 27

12 M. von Richthofen quoted in F. Gibbons, *The Red Knight of Germany* (New York: Garden City Publishing Co. Inc, 1927), pp.111–12

13 O. Greig quoted in N. Franks, H. Giblin & N. McCrery, *Under the Guns of the Red Baron* (London: Caxton Publishing Group, 2000), p. 56

14 J. MacLennan quoted in N. Franks, H. Giblin & N. McCrery, *Under the Guns of the Red Baron*, pp. 55–6

15 IWM Docs: T. Hughes, Typescript diary, 1/2/1917

16 O. Greig quoted in N. Franks, H. Giblin & N. McCrery, *Under the Guns of the Red Baron*, p. 56

17 Ibid.

18 J. MacLennan quoted in N. Franks, H. Giblin & N. McCrery, *Under the Guns of the Red Baron*, p. 56

19 O. Greig, op. cit., pp. 56–7

20 J. MacLennan, op. cit., p. 56

21 O. Greig, op. cit., p. 57

22 M. von Richthofen, *The Red Air Fighter* (London: Greenhill Books, 1990), p. 104

23 RAF Museum: W. J. Lidsey, Typescript dairy, 11/1/1917

24 H. H. Balfour, *An Airman Marches* (London: Hutchinson & Co, 1933), pp. 71–2

25 RAF Museum: A. S. W. Dore, Transcript diary, 28/1/1917

26 S. Douglas, *Years of Combat* (London: Collins, 1963), p. 168

27 F. T. Courtney, *Flight Path: My Fifty Years of Aviation* (London: William Kimber, 1973) p. 89

28 H. H. Balfour, *An Airman Marches*, pp. 73–4

29 M. von Richthofen quoted in F. Gibbons, *The Red Knight of Germany*, p. 127

30 H. H. Balfour, *An Airman Marches*, pp. 73–4

31 RAF Museum: A. S. W. Dore, Transcript diary, 10/2/1917

32 S. Douglas, *Years of Combat*, p. 170

33 H. H. Balfour, *An Airman Marches*, p. 80

34 E. Böhme quoted in D. V. Fant, 'Many Battles and Many a Bold Venture, the letters of Oberleutnant Erwin Böhme', *Over the Front*, Vol. 5, No. 1, p. 49

35 RAF Museum: C. D. Smart, Manuscript diary, 3/2/1917

36 IWM Docs: E. J. D. Routh, Typescript notes

37 National Archive: AIR 1/2389/228/11/98 P. C. Maltby

38 RAF Museum: O. B. Rice, Manuscript letter 9/3/1917

39 RAF Museum: C. D. Smart, Manuscript diary, 4/2/1917

40 IWM Docs: F. Cave, Manuscript diary, 3/2/1917

41 Ibid., 4/2/1917

42 Ibid., 5/2/1917

43 Ibid., 6/2/1917

44 RAF Museum: C. D. Smart, Manuscript diary, 27/2/1917

45 Ibid., 1/3/1917

46 National Archive: AIR 1/2386/228/11/21 D. F. Stevenson

47 National Archive: AIR 1/2389/228/11/98 P. C. Maltby

48 National Archive: AIR 1/2386/228/11/21 D. F. Stevenson

49 National Archive: AIR 1/2391/228/11/149 W. R. Cox

50 IWM Docs: T. Hughes, Typescript dairy, 26/1/1917

51 B. F. Crane quoted in W. F. J. Harvey, *Pi in the Sky*, p. 27

52 J. Charteris, *At G.H.Q.* p. 200

CHAPTER THREE **March Squalls**

1 IWM Docs: L. Horridge, Manuscript letter, 3/3/1917

2 RAF Museum: C. D. Smart, Manuscript diary, 4/3/1917

3 RAF Museum: W. J. Lidsey, Typescript diary, 4/3/1917

4 RAF Museum: A. S. W. Dore, Transcript diary, 4/3/1917

5 K. E. Schäfer quoted in P. Kilduff, *The Illustrated Red Baron* (London: Cassell & Co, 1999), p. 35

6 H. H. Balfour, *An Airman Marches*, p. 72

7 RAF Museum: A. S. W. Dore, Transcript diary, 4/3/1917

8 M. von Richthofen quoted in F. Gibbons, *The Red Knight of Germany*, p. 127

9 National Archive: AIR 1/2392/228/11/187 H. E. P. Wigglesworth

10 RAF Museum: A. S. W. Dore, Transcript diary, 6/3/1917

11 M. von Richthofen, *The Red Air Fighter*, p. 106

12 Ibid., p. 107

13 RAF Museum: A. S. W. Dore, Transcript diary, 6/3/1917

14 Ibid.

15 M. von Richthofen, *The Red Air Fighter*, pp. 107–8

16 Ibid., pp. 108–9

17 L. von Richthofen quoted in P. Kilduff, *The Illustrated Red Baron*, p. 37

18 G. M. Hopkins quoted in B. J. Gray, 'Pusher Pilot with 22', *Cross & Cockade*, Vol. 3, No. 2, p. 50

19 National Archive: AIR 1/2389/228/11/108 J. L. Vachell

20 IWM Docs: L. Horridge, Manuscript letter, 7/3/1917

21 RAF Museum: H. Bawden, Manuscript Copy of Letter, 6/3/1917 (DC 75/15/3-7)

22 Ibid.

23 G.M. Hopkins quoted in B. J. Gray, 'Pusher Pilot with 22', p. 49

24 Ibid.

25 Ibid., pp. 49–50

26 Ibid.

27 E. Jünger, *Storm of Steel* (New York: Zimmermann & Zimmermann, 1985), p. 125–6

28 H. Gough, *The Fifth Army* (London: Hodder & Stoughton, 1931), p. 178

29 IWM Sound Archive: AC 9151, J. Fell

30 IWM Sound Archive: AC 7397, R. Cook

31 National Archive: AIR 1/2389/228/11/108 J. L. Vachell

32 IWM Docs: L. Horridge, Manuscript letter, 20/3/1917

33 RAF Museum: C. D. Smart, Manuscript diary, 21/3/1917

34 IWM Docs: L. Horridge, Manuscript letter, 17/3/1917

35 RAF Museum: O. B. Rice, Manuscript letter, 9/3/1917

36 RAF Museum: A. S. W. Dore, Transcript diary, 17/3/1917

37 M. von Richthofen quoted in F. Gibbons, *The Red Knight of Germany*, p. 142

38 IWM Sound Archive: M. Greener, AC 8945

39 T. Bowyer-Bower quoted in N. Franks, 'A Father's Love', *Over the Front*, Vol. 10, No. 2, p. 163

40 A. von Tutschek in 'The War Letters of Hauptmann Adolf Ritter von Tutschek', *Over the Front*: Vol. 3 No. 4, p. 293

41 Ibid., pp. 294–5

42 J. Charteris, *At G.H.Q.,* p. 205

43 RAF Museum: E. B. Rice, Manuscript letter, 18/4/1917

44 W. Bishop, *Winged Warfare: Hunting the Huns in the Air* (London: Hodder & Stoughton, 1918), pp. 43–5

45 Ibid., pp.63–4

46 A. von Tutschek in 'The War Letters of Hauptmann Adolf Ritter von Tutschek', p. 295

47 RAF Museum: C. D. Smart, Manuscript diary, 22/3/1917

CHAPTER FOUR **Fledglings Rising**

1 G. G. Preston quoted in K. M. Golden, 'The Reminiscences of an Aerial Observer in the Royal Flying Corps', *Cross & Cockade*, Vol. XV, No. 4, pp. 360–1

2 RAF Museum: D. McKergow, Manuscript letter, 12/4/1917 (X002–5594/002)

3 IWM Docs: F. C. Penny, Typescript account, 'Memories of Flying, 1915–1918'

4 RAF Museum: Manuscript diary, 11/3/1917 & 14/3/1917 Ortweiler (AC 88/7)

5 R. J. Brownell, *From Khaki to Blue: The Autobiography of Air Commodore R. J. Brownell* (Canberra: Military Historical Society of Australia 1978), p.134

6 Ibid., pp. 133–4

7 RAF Museum: Manuscript diary, 12/4/1917 Ortweiler (AC 88/7)

8 Ibid. 9/3/1917

9 IWM Docs: Macmillan Collection: F. A. Cook, Introduction to Diary, 4/1917

10 RAF Museum: Manuscript diary, 13/4/1917 Ortweiler (AC 88/7)

11 R. J. Brownell, *From Khaki to Blue, p.* 137

12 RAF Museum Manuscript diary, 11/5/1917 Ortweiler (AC 88/7)

13 Ibid., 13/5/1917

14 RAF Museum: D. McKergow, Manuscript letter, 22/4/1917 (X002–5594/002)

15 R. J. Brownell, *From Khaki to Blue*, pp. 137–8

16 RAF Museum: Manuscript diary, 14/5/1917 Ortweiler (AC 88/7)

17 Ibid., 15/5/1917

18 Ibid., 19/5/1917

19 Ibid., 19/5/1917

20 IWM Docs Macmillan Collection: S. Waltho, 'The Camel – in Memoriam', pp. 1–2

21 S. K. Jopp, 'Gosport', *Popular Flying*, 8/1936, p. 251

22 IWM Sound Archive: R. Fuljames, AC 14, Reel 2

23 IWM Docs: Macmillan Collection: E. A. Cook, Diary, 8/4/1917

CHAPTER FIVE **Bloody April**

1 IWM Docs: E. J. D. Routh, Manuscript diary, 6/4/1917

2 IWM Sound Archive: K. Page, AC 717, Reels 2 & 3

3 J. Charteris, *At G.H.Q.,* p. 200

4 IWM Docs: M. I. Hood, Typescript memoir

5 S. Douglas, *Years of Combat*, p. 182

6 National Archives: AIR 1/2389/228/11/98 P. C. Maltby

7 RAF Museum: C. D. Smart, Manuscript diary, 1/4/1917

8 Ibid., 2/4/1917

9 IWM Docs: E. Garland, Typescript diary, 2/4/1917

10 A. von Tutschek quoted in 'The War Letters of Hauptmann Adolf Ritter von Tutschek', *Over the Front*, Vol. 3, No. 4, pp. 296–7

11 Ibid., p. 297

12 RAF Museum: A. S. W. Dore, Transcript diary, 2/4/1917

13 P. Warren quoted in F. Gibbons, *The Red Knight of Germany*, p. 170

14 Ibid.

15 Ibid., pp. 170–71

16 M. von Richthofen quoted in N. Franks, H Giblin & N. McCrery, *Under the Guns of the Red Baron*, p. 91

17 IWM Docs: E. Garland, Typescript diary, 3/4/1917

18 D. P. McDonald quoted in F. Gibbons, *The Red Knight of Germany*, pp.176–7

19 Ibid., p. 177

20 M. von Richthofen quoted in F. Gibbons, *The Red Knight of Germany*, p. 175

21 G. M. Hopkins quoted in B. J. Gray, 'Pusher Pilot with 22', *Cross & Cockade*, Vol. 3, No. 2, pp. 48–9

22 H. Trenchard order, 26/3/1917, quoted in S. F. Wise, *Canadian Airmen and the First World War: The Official History of the Royal Canadian Air Force* (Toronto: University of Toronto Press, 1980), Vol I, p. 398

23 IWM Sound Archive: G. Hiscox, AC 4129

24 G. M. Hopkins quoted in B.J Gray, 'Pusher Pilot with 22', p. 48

25 M. von Richthofen quoted in F. Gibbons, *The Red Knight of Germany*, p. 180

26 National Archives: AIR 1/2390/228/11/136 J. MacDonald

27 RAF Museum: A. S. W. Dore, Transcript diary, 5/4/1917

28 G. Taylor, *Sopwith Scout 7309*, (London: Cassell, 1968), pp. 71–2

29 Peter Liddle Archive, Brotherton Library, Leeds University: N. A. Birks, Typescript account, pp. 5–6

30 IWM Docs: E. Garland, Typescript diary, 5/4/1917

31 M. von Richthofen, *The Red Air Fighter*, pp. 122–3

32 Ibid., p. 123

33 Ibid.

34 E. Böhme quoted in D. V. Fant, 'Many Battles and Many a Bold Venture, the Letters of Oberleutnant Erwin Böhme', *Over the Front*, Vol. 5, No. 1, p. 50

35 M. von Richthofen, *The Red Air Fighter*, pp. 124–5

36 F. T. Courtney, *Flight Path: My Fifty Years of Aviation*, p. 104

37 Geoffrey Cock quoted in C. G. Jefford, *The Flying Camels: The History of No. 45 Squadron, RAF* (UK: Privately Published, 1995), p. 21

38 F. T. Courtney, *Flight Path: My Fifty Years of Aviation*, p. 101

39 Ibid., pp. 101–2

40 IWM Docs: W. Read, Manuscript copy of diary, 17/3/1917

41 Ibid., 4/4/1917

42 F. T. Courtney, *Flight Path: My Fifty Years of Aviation*, pp. 102–3

43 Ibid., p. 103

44 Ibid., p. 104

45 IWM Docs: Wing Commander N. Macmillan, extensive papers concerning First World War aviation, including transcribed notes of Frank Courtney

46 C. G. Jefford, *The Flying Camels: The History of No. 45 Squadron, RAF*, p. 21

47 IWM Docs: Wing Commander N. Macmillan, extensive papers concerning First World War aviation, including transcribed notes of Frank Courtney

48 Ibid.

49 N. Macmillan, *Into the Blue* (London: Duckworth, 1929), p. 46

50 F. T. Courtney, *Flight Path: My Fifty Years of Aviation*, p. 105

51 N. Macmillan, *Into the Blue*, p. 47

52 RAF Museum: C. D. Smart, Manuscript diary, 6/4/1917

53 IWM Docs: E. Garland, Typescript diary, 6/4/1917

54 IWM Docs: T. Hughes. Typescript diary, 7/4/1917

55 G. Devenish, *A Subalterns Share in the War* (London: Constable & Co, 1917), p. 155

56 W. A. Bishop, *Winged Warfare*, p. 76

57 Ibid., pp. 77–8

58 Ibid., pp. 78–9

59 RAF Museum: A. S. W. Dore, Transcript diary, 7/4/1917

60 C. Darly-Pine quoted in C. Waugh, 'A Short History of

16 Squadron RFC/RAF, 1915–1918', *Cross & Cockade*, Vol. 18, No. 4, p. 307

61 RAF Museum: C. D. Smart, Manuscript diary, 7/4/1917

62 M. von Richthofen quoted in F. Gibbons, *The Red Knight of Germany*, p. 196

63 T. Hervey quoted in Peter F.G. Wright, 'Rigger to Pilot', *Cross & Cockade*, Vol. 14, No. 4, p. 156

64 M. Baring, *Flying Corps Headquarters, 1914–18* (Edinburgh & London: William Blackwood & Sons, 1963), p. 212

65 Anon quoted in *Naval Eight: A History of No. 8 Squadron, RNAS* (London: Signal Press Ltd, 1931), p. 27

66 R. J. O. Compston quoted in *Naval Eight: A History of No. 8 Squadron, RNAS*, pp. 77–8

67 A. Ball quoted in W. A. Briscoe & H. R. Stannard, *Captain Ball VC of the Royal Flying Corps* (Herbert Jenkins Ltd: London, 1918), p. 239

68 C. A. Lewis, *Farewell to Wings* (London: Temple Press Books, 1964), p. 48

69 IWM Sound Archive: H. N. Charles, SR 4060, Reel 1

70 R. T. C. Hoidge quoted in H. D. Hastings & L. Raidor, 'Captain Reginald T. C. Hoidge: 56 Squadron', *Cross & Cockade*, Vol. 7, No. 4, pp. 382–4

71 A. Ball quoted in W. A. Briscoe & H. R. Stannard, *Captain Ball VC*, pp. 240–41

72 M. Baring, *Flying Corps Headquarters, 1914–18*, p. 213

73 RAF Museum: C. D. Smart, Manuscript diary, 8/4/1917

74 National Archives: AIR 1/2390/228/11/136 J. MacDonald

75 J. Heagerty quoted in F. Gibbons, *The Red Knight of Germany*, pp. 200-201

76 IWM Docs: E. J. D. Routh, Manuscript diary, 16/4/1917

77 E. Böhme quoted in D. V. Fant, 'Many Battles and Many a Bold Venture, the Letters of Oberleutnant Erwin Böhme', p. 50

78 IWM Docs: A. Worman, Typescript memoir

79 IWM Docs: M. I. Hood, Typescript memoir

80 G. R. Alliston quoted in A. McKee, *Vimy Ridge* (London: Souvenir Press, 1966), p. 100

81 IWM Docs: M. I. Hood, Typescript memoir

82 Ibid.

83 J. G. MacArthur quoted in A. McKee, *Vimy Ridge*, p. 101

84 H. Kraft quoted in J. Nicholls, *Cheerful Sacrifice: The Battle of Arras, 1917* (Leo Cooper, 1993), p. 83

85 IWM Docs: S. Bradbury, Typescript account

86 W. Hay quoted in J. Nicholls, *Cheerful Sacrifice*, p. 92

87 IWM Sound Archive: K. Page, AC 717

88 IWM Docs: A. Worman, Typescript memoir

89 A. Richards quoted in J. Nicholls, *Cheerful Sacrifice*, p. 119

90 IWM Docs: E. J. D. Routh, Typescript account & Manuscript diary, 9/4/1917

91 RAF Museum: C. D. Smart, Manuscript diary, 9/4/1917

92 IWM Docs: E. J. D. Routh, Typescript account

93 National Archives: AIR 1/2389/228/11/98 P. C. Maltby

94 IWM Docs: C. E. L. Lyne, Typescript letter, 20/7/1916

95 H. H. Balfour, *An Airman Marches*, p. 89

96 RAF Museum: A. S. W. Dore, Transcript diary, 9/4/1917

97 C. M. Down, 'My Most Thrilling Flight', *Popular Flying*, 4/1935, p. 17

98 Ibid., p. 18

99 Ibid., pp. 18–19

100 Ibid., p.19

101 Ibid.

102 R. dA. G. Monypenny quoted in J. Nicholls, *Cheerful Sacrifice*, p. 125

103 Ibid.

104 Ibid., p. 126

105 M. Baring, *Flying Corps Headquarters, 1914–18*, p. 213

106 RAF Museum: C. D. Smart, Manuscript diary, 10/4/1917

107 A. B. Fanstone quoted in R. Bateman & L. A. Quinlan, 'A. B. Fanstone, No. 12 Corps', *Cross & Cockade*, Vol. 13, No. 4, pp. 65–67

108 National Archives: AIR 1/2386/228/11/21 D. F. Stevenson

109 RAF Museum: O. B. Rice, Manuscript letter, 11/4/1917

110 Ibid.

111 IWM Docs: E. J. D. Routh, Manuscript diary, 12/4/1917

112 National Archives: AIR 1/2386/228/11/21 D. F. Stevenson

113 Ibid.

114 National Archives: AIR 1/2386/228/11/23 A. A. Walser

115 G. R. Bromet quoted in *Naval Eight: A History of No. 8 Squadron, RNAS*, p. 30

116 Ibid., p. 28

117 H. Gough, *The Fifth Army*, p. 182

118 Ibid., p. 184

119 RAF Museum: O. B. Rice, Manuscript letter, 11/4/1917

120 J. S. T. Fall quoted in H. A. Jones, *The War in the Air*, Vol. III, pp. 347–8

121 RAF Museum: C. D. Smart, Manuscript diary, 12/4/1917

122 M. von Richthofen, *The Red Air Fighter*, pp. 119–20

123 RAF Museum: C. D. Smart, Manuscript diary, 13/4/1917

124 RAF Museum: E. Mannock, Manuscript diary, 13/4/1917

125 W. A. Bond quoted in E. Bond, *An Airman's Wife* (London: Herbert Jenkins, 1918), pp. 21–2

126 RAF Museum: E. Mannock, Manuscript diary, 13/4/1917

127 W. O. Russell quoted in F. Gibbons, *The Red Knight of Germany*, pp. 220–21

128 A. Binnie quoted in N. Franks & H. Giblin, *Under the Guns of the German Aces* (London: Grub Street, 1997), pp. 141–2

129 RAF Museum: R. Smith, Typescript memoir

130 Ibid.

130 Ibid.

132 Ibid.

133 Ibid.

134 E. D. Crundall, *Fighter Pilot on the Western Front* (London: William Kimber, 1975), pp. 57–62

135 W. A. Bond quoted in E. Bond, *An Airman's Wife*, edited from pp. 25–9

136 RAF Museum: E. Mannock, Manuscript diary, 14/4/1917

137 RAF Museum: O. B. Rice, Manuscript letter, 14/4/1917

138 National Archives: AIR 1/2391/228/11/149 W. R. Cox

139 RAF Museum: A. S. W. Dore, Transcript diary, 15/4/1917

140 Peter Liddle Archive, Brotherton Library, Leeds University: M. M. Kaizer, Typescript letter, 16/4/1917

141 W. Green quoted in F. Gibbons, *The Red Knight of Germany*, p. 223

142 Ibid., pp. 223–4

143 de Burgh quoted by I. Jones, *King of the Air Fighters* (London: Greenhill Books, 1989), pp. 100–101

144 W. A. Bond quoted in E. Bond, *An Airman's Wife*, pp. 33–4

145 RAF Museum: E. Mannock, Manuscript diary, 20/4/1917

146 W. Bovett quoted in I. Jones, *King of the Air Fighters*, p. 82

147 RAF Museum: E. Mannock, Manuscript diary, 20/4/1917

148 IWM Docs: E. J. D. Routh, Typescript account & Manuscript diary, 21/4/1917

149 A. B. Fanstone quoted in R. Bateman & L. A. Quinlan, 'A. B. Fanstone, No 12 Corps', *Cross & Cockade*, Vol. 13, No. 4, pp. 67–8

150 W. A. Bond quoted by E. Bond, *An Airman's Wife*, pp. 45–9

151 IWM Sound Archive: J. Murray, SR 8201

152 Ibid.

153 H. Lutmer quoted in J. Nicholls, *Cheerful Sacrifice*, p. 185

154 IWM Sound Archive: J. Murray, SR 8201

155 IWM Sound Archive: J. Yarwood, SR 12231

156 IWM Docs: T. Macmillan, Typescript account, pp. 194–5

157 Ibid., pp.195–6

158 A. Ball quoted in W. A. Briscoe & H. R. Stannard, *Captain Ball VC*, p. 240

159 Ibid., p. 244

160 Ibid., pp. 244–5

161 W. A. Bond quoted in E. Bond, *An Airman's Wife*, pp. 49–50

162 Ibid., p. 51

163 H. Göring, quoted by Frank Olynyk, "The Combat Records of Herman Göring", *Over The Front*, Vol. 10, No.3, p. 206–7

164 IWM Sound Archive: R. Haine, AC 33, Reel 4

165 RAF Museum: O. B. Rice, Manuscript letter, 29/4/1917

166 Peter Liddle Archive, Brotherton Library, Leeds University: M. M. Kaizer, Typescript letter, 25/4/1917

167 W. A. Molesworth quoted in J. Scott, *Sixty Squadron, RAF, 1916–19* (London: Greenhill Books, 1990), pp. 50–3

168 RAF Museum: R. Fletcher, Manuscript diary, 24/4/1917

169 J. Malone quoted in L. H. Rochford, *I Chose the Sky* (London: William Kimber, 1977), pp.77–8

170 G. R. Bromet quoted in *Naval Eight: A History of No. 8 Squadron, RNAS*, pp. 31–2

171 G. M. Hopkins quoted in B. J. Gray in 'Pusher Pilot with 22', p. 50

172 H. R. Hawkins quoted in B. J. Gray in 'Pusher Pilot with 22', p. 53

173 G. M. Hopkins, op. cit., p. 51

174 Ibid.

175 H. R. Hawkins, op. cit., p. 53

176 G.M. Hopkins, op. cit., pp. 51–2

177 H. R. Hawkins, op. cit., p. 53

178 C. Furlonger quoted in W. F. J. Harvey, *Pi in the Sky*, p. 29

179 H. H. Balfour, *An Airman Marches*, pp. 90–93

180 Ibid., p.93

181 RAF Museum: A. S. W. Dore, Transcript diary, 1/5/1917

182 A. Ball quoted in W. A. Briscoe & H. R. Stannard, *Captain Ball VC*, pp. 246–8

183 T. B. Marson, *Scarlet and Khaki* (London: Jonathan Cape, 1930), p. 144

184 A. Ball, op. cit., p. 251

185 F. Kirkham quoted in F. Gibbons, *The Red Knight of Germany*, pp. 230–32

186 M. v Richthofen quoted in F. Gibbons, *The Red Knight of Germany*, p. 234

187 W. N. Hamilton quoted in F. Gibbons, *The Red Knight of Germany*, pp. 241–2

188 M. Baring, *Flying Corps Headquarters, 1914–18*, p. 219

189 W. N. Hamilton, op. cit., p. 242

190 M. von Richthofen, *The Red Air Fighter*, p. 130

191 Ibid.

192 W. N. Hamilton, op. cit., pp. 243–4

193 L. v Richthofen quoted in F. Gibbons, *The Red Knight of Germany*, pp. 237–8

194 M. Baring, *Flying Corps Headquarters, 1914–18*, pp. 219–20

195 M. von Richthofen, *The Red Air Fighter*, pp. 132–3

196 Ibid., p. 130

197 H. Göring, quoted by Frank Olynyk, "The Combat Records of Herman Göring", *Over The Front*, Vol. 10, No.3, p. 207

198 N. Franks & H. Gilbin, *Under the Guns of the German Aces*, pp. 46–7

199 National Archives: AIR 1/1219/204/5/2634 G. H. S. Dinsmore, Combat Report, 29/4/1917

200 RAF Museum: C. D. Smart, Manuscript diary, 29/4/1917

201 A. von Tutschek in 'The War Letters of Hauptmann Adolf Ritter von Tutschek', *Over the Front*, Vol. 3, No. 4, pp. 299–300

202 J. Scott, *Sixty Squadron, RAF*, p. 45

203 A. M. Murray quoted in A. Morris, *Bloody April*, pp. 124–5

204 RAF Museum: E. Mannock, Manuscript diary, 3/5/1917

205 D. Haig, Special Order of the Day, 12/4/1917 quoted in *Naval Eight: A History of No. 8 Squadron, RNAS*, p. 29

206 Peter Liddle Archive, Brotherton Library, Leeds University: M. M. Kaizer, Typescript letter, 28/4/1917

CHAPTER SIX **A Life Less Ordinary**

1 G. M. Hopkins quoted in B. J. Gray, 'Pusher Pilot with 22', *Cross & Cockade*, Vol. 3, No. 2, pp. 46–7

2 RAF Museum: L. M. Mansbridge, Manuscript letter, 21/3/1917

3 W. A. Bond quoted in E. Bond, *An Airman's Wife*, pp. 16–17

4 G. M. Hopkins quoted in B. J. Gray, 'Pusher Pilot with 22', p. 47

5 RAF Museum: L. M. Mansbridge, Manuscript letter, ca 3/1917

6 G. P. Kay, *Letters from Bob* (Melbourne: Melville & Mullen PTY Ltd, 1917), p. 100

7 National Archives: AIR 1/2388/228/11/73 A. E. Godfrey

8 National Archives: AIR 1/2392/228/11/163 C. F. Horsley

9 Peter Liddle Archive, Brotherton Library, Leeds University: E. D. G. Galley, Typescript of interview tape 461

10 National Archives: AIR 1/2386/228/11/21 D. F. Stevenson

11 G. M. Hopkins quoted in B. J. Gray, 'Pusher Pilot with 22', p. 47

12 RAF Museum: J. C. Slessor, Manuscript account

13 Peter Liddle Archive, Brotherton Library, Leeds University: M. M. Kaizer, Typescript letter, 13/4/1917

14 IWM Docs: F. C. Penny, Typescript account, 'Memories of Flying, 1915–18', pp. 11–12

15 G. Taylor, *Sopwith Scout 7309*, p. 51

16 W. A. Bond quoted in E. Bond, *An Airman's Wife*, p. 63

17 G. P. Kay, *Letters from Bob*, p. 127

18 G. Taylor, *Sopwith Scout 7309*, p. 51

19 W. A. Bond quoted in E. Bond, *An Airman's Wife*, pp. 63–4

20 IWM Sound Archive: Cecil Lewis, SR 4162, Reel 1

21 R. J. O. Compston quoted in *Naval Eight: A History of No. 8 (Naval) Squadron, RNAS*, pp.89–90

22 National Archives: AIR 1/686/21/13/2249 C. R. Mackenzie, Note on Aerial Fighting, AIR 1/686

23 R. J. O. Compston quoted in *Naval Eight*, p. 90

24 G. Taylor, *Sopwith Scout 7309*, p. 59

25 G. P. Kay, *Letters from Bob*, pp. 122–3

26 IWM Sound Archive: Cecil Lewis, SR 4162, Reel 1

27 R. J. O. Compston quoted in *Naval Eight*, pp. 94–5

28 W. A. Bond quoted in E. Bond, *An Airman's Wife*, pp. 85–6

29 RAF Museum: C. D. Smart, Manuscript diary, 18/5/1917

30 R. J. O. Compston quoted in *Naval Eight*, p. 85

31 National Archives: AIR 1/2387/228/11/37 R. M. Hill

32 R. J. O. Compston quoted in *Naval Eight*, pp. 87–8

33 G. Taylor, *Sopwith Scout 7309*, pp. 84–5

34 IWM Sound Archive: Cecil Lewis, SR 4162, Reel 1

35 R. J. O. Compston quoted in *Naval Eight*, pp. 97–8

36 National Archives: AIR 1/686/21/13/2249 C. R. Mackenzie, Note on Aerial Fighting, AIR 1/686

37 Ibid.

38 R. J. O. Compston quoted in *Naval Eight*, pp. 93–4

39 E. D. Crundall, *Fighter Pilot on the Western Front*, p. 70

40 IWM Sound Archive: Cecil Lewis, SR 4162, Reel 1

41 G. Taylor, *Sopwith Scout 7309*, pp. 63–4

42 National Archives: AIR 1/2387/228/11/33 L. H. Cockey

43 G. Taylor, *Sopwith Scout 7309*, pp. 65–6

44 Ibid., p. 67

45 R. J. O. Compston quoted in *Naval Eight*, p. 84

46 National Archives: AIR 1/2388/228/11/91 J. O. Andrews

47 G. Taylor, *Sopwith Scout 7309*, pp. 67–8

48 Ibid., p. 50

49 Ibid., pp. 50–51

50 C. A. Lewis, *Farewell to Wings*, p. ix

51 IWM Sound Archive: Cecil Lewis, SR 4162, Reel 1

52 R. J. O. Compston quoted in *Naval Eight*, p. 96

53 Ibid., pp. 83–4

54 RAF Museum: C. D. Smart, Manuscript diary, 31/3/1917

55 IWM Docs: E. Tupping, Typescript letter, 16/4/1916 in papers of E. Garland

56 IWM Sound Archive: G. Eddington, AC 13, Reel 5

57 IWM Sound Archive: C. Burne, AC 6, Reel 4

58 R. J. O. Compston quoted in *Naval Eight*, pp. 81–2

59 National Archives: AIR 1/2388/228/11/83 R. M. Foster

60 National Archives: AIR 1/2389/228/11/98 P. C. Maltby

61 RAF Museum: J. C. Slessor, Manuscript account

62 S. Douglas, *Years of Combat*, p. 169

63 National Archives: AIR 1/2388/228/11/83 R. M. Foster

64 IWM Docs: T. Hughes, Typescript diary, 15/1/1917

65 T. B. Marson, *Scarlet and Khaki*, pp. 160–61

66 Ibid., p. 162

67 RAF Museum: J. C. Slessor, Manuscript account

68 G. Taylor, *Sopwith Scout 7309*, p. 82

69 A. Rhys Davids quoted in A. Revell, *Brief Glory: The Life of Arthur Rhys Davids* (London: William Kimber, 1984), p. 102

70 G. Taylor, op. cit

71 RAF Museum: O. B. Rice, Manuscript letter, 10/5/1917

72 RAF Museum: O. B. Ellis, Typescript letters, 3/5/1917

73 IWM Docs: S. Waltho, N. Macmillan Collection, 'A Dud Day'

74 Ibid.

75 RAF Museum: O. B. Rice, Manuscript letter, 1/1/1917

76 IWM Sound Archive: Cecil Lewis, SR 4162, Reel 1

77 O. Stewart, 'Memorable Mess Nights', *Popular Flying*, 4/1939, p. 35

78 IWM Docs: S. Waltho, N. Macmillan Collection, 'A Dud Day'

79 A. Rhys Davids quoted in A. Revell, *Brief Glory: The Life of Arthur Rhys Davids*, p. 91

80 RAF Museum: O. B. Rice, Manuscript letter, 10/5/1917

81 IWM Sound Archive: F. Powell, SR 87, Reel 6

82 L. H. Rochford, *I Chose the Sky*, p. 68

83 H. H. Balfour, *An Airman Marches*, p. 80

84 IWM Docs: E. J. D. Routh, Typescript account

85 de Burgh quoted in F. Oughton, *The Personal Diary of Mick Mannock* (London: Neville Spearman, 1966), p. 153

86 RAF Museum: E. Mannock, Manuscript diary, 20/4/1917

87 W. A. Bond quoted in E. Bond, *An Airman's Wife*, pp. 34–5

88 Ibid. pp. 96–7

89 IWM Sound Archive: F. Powell, AC 87, Reel 4

90 Ibid., Reel 5 & 6

91 T. B. Marson, *Scarlet and Khaki*, pp. 132–3

92 Ibid., pp. 134–5

93 IWM Docs: S. Waltho, N. Macmillan Collection, 'The Amiens Tender'

94 IWM Sound Archive: Cecil Lewis, AC 4162, Reel 1

95 IWM Docs: S. Waltho, N. Macmillan Collection, 'The Amiens Tender'

96 W. A. Bond quoted in E. Bond, *An Airman's Wife*, p. 87

97 RAF Museum: W. J. Lidsey, Typescript diary, 5/2/1917

98 IWM Docs: H. G. Taylor, Typescript account

99 IWM Docs: E. Garland, Typescript diary, 1/12/1916

100 IWM Docs: H. G. Taylor, Typescript account

101 Ibid.

102 RAF Museum: J. C. Slessor, Manuscript account

103 H. H. Balfour, *An Airman Marches*, p. 74

104 RAF Museum: G. P. Jamieson, Typescript diary, 14/3/1917–15/3/1917

105 C. A. Lewis, *Farewell to Wings*, pp. ix–x

106 H. H. Balfour, *An Airman Marches*, pp. 76–7

107 Ibid., pp. 95–6

108 IWM Sound Archive: Cecil Lewis, SR 4162, Reel 1

109 RAF Museum: E. Mannock, Manuscript diary, 14/5/1917

110 E. Mannock quoted by I. Jones, *King of the Air Fighters*, p. 116

111 G. L. Lloyd quoted in F. Oughton, *The Personal Diary of Mick Mannock*, p. 156

112 N. Macmillan, *Into the Blue*, pp. 27–28/9. 113 RAF Museum: O. B. Ellis, Typescript letters, 3/5/1917

114 RAF Museum: W. A. Porkess papers

115 Ibid.

116 Ibid.

117 RAF Museum: W. R. Read, Manuscript Copy of Letter, 12/3/1917 (DC 75/15/3-7)

118 RAF Museum: H. Bawden, Manuscript Copy of Letter, 6/3/1917 (DC 75/15/3-7)

119 RAF Museum: W. E. G. Bryant, Manuscript Letter, 23/3/1917 (DC 75/15/3-7)

120 RAF Museum: W. R. Read, Manuscript Letter, 27/3/1917 (DC 75/15/3-7)

CHAPTER SEVEN **The Ebbing Storm**

1 RAF Museum: C. D. Smart, Manuscript diary, 1/5/1917

2 RAF Museum: J. C. Slessor, Manuscript account

3 B. F. Crane quoted in W. F. J. Harvey, *Pi in the Sky*, p. 31

4 IWM Docs: Macmillan Collection: E. A. Cook, Diary, 1/5/1917

5 IWM Docs: H. G. Taylor, Typescript account

6 Ibid.

7 Ibid.

8 Peter Liddle Archive, Brotherton Library, Leeds University: C. C. Knight, Typescript account, 'On Active Service in France'

9 E. Mannock quoted in I. Jones, *King of the Air Fighters*, pp. 88–89

10 W. A. Bond quoted in E. Bond, *An Airman's Wife*, pp. 67–8 & pp. 72–3

11 RAF Museum: E. Mannock, Manuscript diary, 9/5/1917

12 W. A. Bond quoted by E. Bond, *An Airman's Wife*, pp. 80–1

13 J. Cousins quoted in J. Nicholls, *Cheerful Sacrifice*, p. 197

14 IWM Sound Archive: V. Polhill, AC 9254

15 RAF Museum: C. D. Smart, Manuscript diary, 3/5/1917

16 S. Douglas, *Years of Combat*, p. 193

17 Ibid., pp. 193–4

18 RAF Museum: A. S. W. Dore, Transcript diary, 3/5/1917

19 RAF Museum: O. B. Rice, Manuscript letter, 18/5/1917–21/5/1917

20 IWM Docs: E. Garland, Typescript diary, 5/5/1917–7/5/1917

21 RAF Museum: C. D. Smart, Manuscript diary, 6/5/1917

22 National Archives: AIR 1/2392/228/11/163 C. F. Horsley

23 Ibid.

24 W. A. Bond quoted in E. Bond, *An Airman's Wife*, p. 68

25 RAF Museum: E. Mannock, Manuscript diary, 3/5/1917

26 National Archives: A. Ball, Combat Report, 2/5/1917 (N.B.: In the quote 'SE5 4855' has been replaced with 'I' for readability)

27 R. M. Chaworth-Musters quoted in D. Whetton, 'And not for Glory', *Cross & Cockade*, Vol. 10, No. 3, p. 224

28 R. T. C. Hoidge quoted in H. D. Hastings & L. Raidor, 'Captain Reginald T. C. Hoidge: 56 Squadron', *Cross & Cockade*, Vol. 7, No. 4, p. 385

29 National Archives: A. Ball, Combat Report, 5/5/1917 (N.B.: 'SE5 A8898' replaced with 'I' for readability)

30 T. B. Marson, *Scarlet and Khaki*, pp. 143–4

31 A. Ball, quoted in R. H. Kiernan, *Captain Albert Ball* (London: Aviation Book Club, 1939), p. 178

32 National Archives: A. Ball, Combat Report, 6/5/1917 (N.B.: 'Nieuport' replaced with 'I' for readability)

33 A. Ball quoted in W. Briscoe & H. R. Stannard, *Captain Ball VC*, p. 266

34 Ibid., p. 268

35 C. M. Crowe quoted in I. Jones, *King of the Air Fighters*, pp. 109–10

36 W. Allmenroeder quoted in H. J. Nowarra, 'Captain Ball's Last Flight', *Cross & Cockade*, Vol. 4, No. 3, p. 243

37 A. Rhys Davids quoted in A. Revell, *Brief Glory: The Life of Arthur Rhys Davids*, p.99–100

38 R. T. C. Hoidge quoted in H. D. Hastings & L. Raidor in 'Captain Reginald T. C. Hoidge: 56 Squadron', pp. 384–5

39 W. Allmenroeder quoted in H. J. Nowarra, 'Captain Ball's Last Flight', pp. 243–4

40 C. M. Crowe quoted in I. Jones, *King of the Air Fighters*, p. 110

41 Ibid.

42 W. Allmenroeder quoted in H. J. Nowarra, 'Captain Ball's Last Flight', pp. 243–4

43 C. M. Crowe quoted in I. Jones, *King of the Air Fighters*, pp. 110–11

44 W. Allmenroeder quoted in H. J. Nowarra, 'Captain Ball's Last Flight', pp.243–4

45 F. Hailer quoted in D. Whetton, 'And not for Glory', p. 228

46 Ibid.

47 M. Baring, *Flying Corps Headquarters, 1914–18*, p. 221

48 RAF Museum: C. D. Smart, Manuscript diary, 8/5/1917

49 W. A. Bond quoted in E. Bond, *An Airman's Wife*, pp. 70–71

50 Ibid., pp. 84–5

51 Ibid., pp. 92–4

52 RAF Museum: E. Mannock, Manuscript diary, 9/5/1917

53 RAF Museum: O. B. Ellis, Typescript letters, 12/5/1917 & 15/5/1917

54 RAF Museum: O. B. Ellis, Typescript letters, 14/5/1917

55 R. S. Dallas quoted in D. Whetton, 'Roderic Stanley Dallas: Forgotten Ace', *Cross & Cockade*, Vol. 2, No. 1, p. 4

56 RAF Museum: O. B. Rice, Manuscript letter, 18/5/1917–21/5/1917

57 Ibid.

58 RAF Museum: E. Mannock, Manuscript diary, 21/5/1917

Epilogue

1 W. B. Wood quoted in Jack Wales, 'Ace from 29: Lieutenant W. B. Wood MC', *Cross & Cockade*, Vol. 2, No. 1, p. 11

2 RAF Museum: O. B. Rice, Manuscript letter, 18/5/1917–21/5/1917

3 T. Henshaw, *The Sky Their Battlefield* (London: Grub Street, 1995), p. 576

4 IWM Docs: Macmillan Collection: E. A. Cook, Diary, 18/5/1917

ACKNOWLEDGEMENTS

As always, I hope that this book will encourage more people to delve into the original archives and literary sources that are the mainspring of this text. My grateful thanks are due to Margaret Brooks and her staff at the IWM Sound Archive: Richard Hughes, Richard McDonough and John Stopford-Pickering who collectively have a placid tranquillity in the face of adversity that is quite remarkable. I would also particularly like to thank Rod Suddaby, Tony Richards, Stephen Walton and Mandy Mason of the IWM Department of Documents. Thanks are due to the staff of the IWM Photographic Archive for their permission to use the photographs included in this book and the redoubtable Rose Gerrard, Glyn Biesty, Damon Cleary, Greg Smith and Gordon McLeod who were also spectacularly helpful. My grateful thanks also go to Peter Elliott, Simon Moody and Katherine Boyce – all present or past members of the Department of Library and Information Services at the RAF Museum, Hendon. In addition, Richard Davies and the staff of the Special Collections at the Brotherton Library, Leeds University were also extremely helpful. Finally, The Public Records Office at Kew is an amazing public institution that we must all cherish, even if its name has now been randomly changed in accordance with transient fashion. These institutions together house the raw material of our collective national history and I thank them all for permission to quote from their fantastic collections.

'Real' aerial historians of the First World War are a strange bunch. Their work is conducted with an intensity and to a level of detail bordering on a surreal masochism. Having ploughed their lonely furrow, they then benevolently present their research in published form in an altruistic effort to keep lesser historians on the 'straight and narrow'. Their sheer generosity of spirit is quite staggering. For me, Trevor Henshaw is usually the first port of call when checking facts, utilising his masterwork *The Sky Their Battlefield: Air Fighting and the Complete List of Allied Air Casualties from Enemy Action in the First War*, published by Grub Street in 1995. The indomitable Barrington Gray has written for years in Cross and Cockade and, furthermore, has arranged for the IWM Sound Archive to preserve his collection of tape recordings of veterans made back in the 1970s. I am most grateful for his lifetime of hard graft.

Norman Franks and his team of diligent co-authors deserve particular acclaim. Together they have produced an incredible and invaluable stream of books detailing the casualties and victories and, where possible, marrying the two. In particular I would mention: *Under the Guns of the Red Baron* by Norman Franks, Hal Giblin and Nigel McCrery; *Under the Guns of the German Aces* by Norman Franks and Hal Giblin; *Casualties of the German Air Service, 1914–1920* and *The Jasta War Chronology* both by Norman Franks, Frank Bailey and Rick Duiven; *Above the Lines, Above the Trenches* and *Bloody April … Black September* all by Norman Franks, Russell Guest and Frank Bailey.

There are several works of particular brilliance that for me stand out. Alex Revell has produced a true object lesson in historical research in *High in the Empty Blue: A History of 56 Squadron, 1916–1920*. Long ago, in the 1930s, the American journalist Floyd Gibbons performed an invaluable service by contacting and interviewing as many surviving victims of Richthofen as was humanly possible. The accounts collated and printed in his book, *The Red Knight of Germany* are priceless. In trying to ensure a proper link to the ground fighting I am greatly indebted to Jonathan Nicholls who has written the best account of this battle in *Cheerful Sacrifice*, which I urge you to buy. He has made arrangements to allow others to benefit from all his research by depositing his valuable collection of veterans' interviews with the IWM Sound Archive. Chris McCarthy was also enormously helpful in kindly making available a first draft of the eagerly awaited book, *Arras: The Day-by-Day Account*. Often imitated by lesser mortals, his original formula has truly stood the test of time. On a personal note, I have treasured both the cheery advice and good-natured banter from one of the only successful writers that I have ever met – the irrepressible Max Arthur. When everything is taken into account, any mistakes in this book are truly all my own work.

On a gloomy note, I have to confess that this book is tragically not, as was originally intended, entitled *Up the Arras: the RFC and the Battle of Arras*. Sadly, my editors and publishers conceived of an unspeakably vulgar double meaning for this fine original title that, quite honestly, still astounds me. Clearly they have a wealth of experience of the seamier side of life denied to the average author! Nevertheless, I would like to thank the handsome, charming, brilliant and above all, modest Keith Lowe who has been far more of a friend to me than perhaps is entirely natural in an editor. Thanks also to his team of designers and indeed all of the production staff. Finally, I dedicate this book to the very wonderful Polly Napper, who proofread – without a murmur of complaint – this text. Without her I would very probably have been in the pub.

I apologise profusely to any copyright owners that I have been unable to locate prior to the publication of this book. I hope they will forgive me – I have of course clearly acknowledged the source of all quotes in the footnotes. I would thank them all for their kindness. Any omissions will be corrected in future editions.

INDEX

BLOODY APRIL